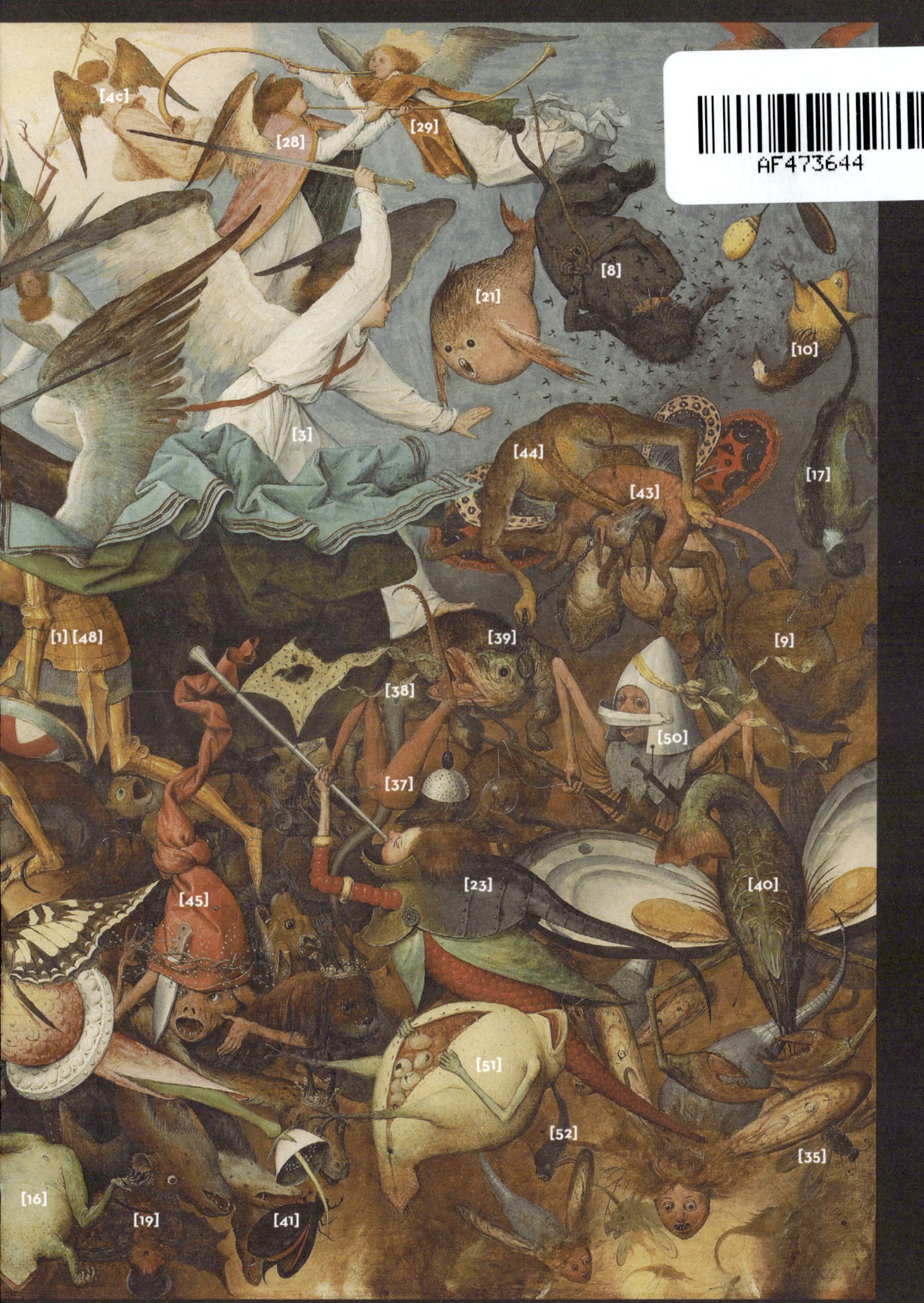
[4c]
[28]
[29]
[21]
[8]
[10]
[3]
[44]
[43]
[17]
[1] [48]
[39]
[9]
[38]
[50]
[37]
[23]
[40]
[45]
[51]
[52]
[35]
[16]
[19]
[41]

TINE LUK MEGANCK

# PIETER BRUEGEL THE ELDER

## *Fall of the Rebel Angels*

Art, Knowledge and Politics
on the Eve of the Dutch Revolt

SilvanaEditoriale

To Gloria, August and Violetta
Darkness is only the absence of light.

Tine Luk Meganck has been researcher at the Royal Museums of Fine Arts of Belgium in Brussels, funded by the Inter University Attraction Pool 'City and Society', program sponsored by the Belgian Federal Science Policy, until 2018. She obtained a PhD in Art History from Princeton University, and published numerous studies about Bruegel and his era.

Published with the support of

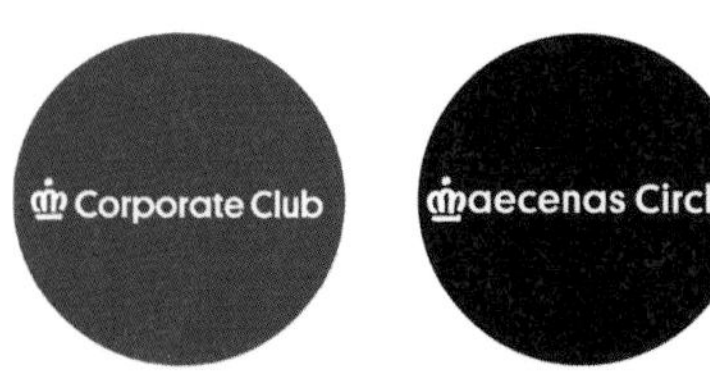

# Contents

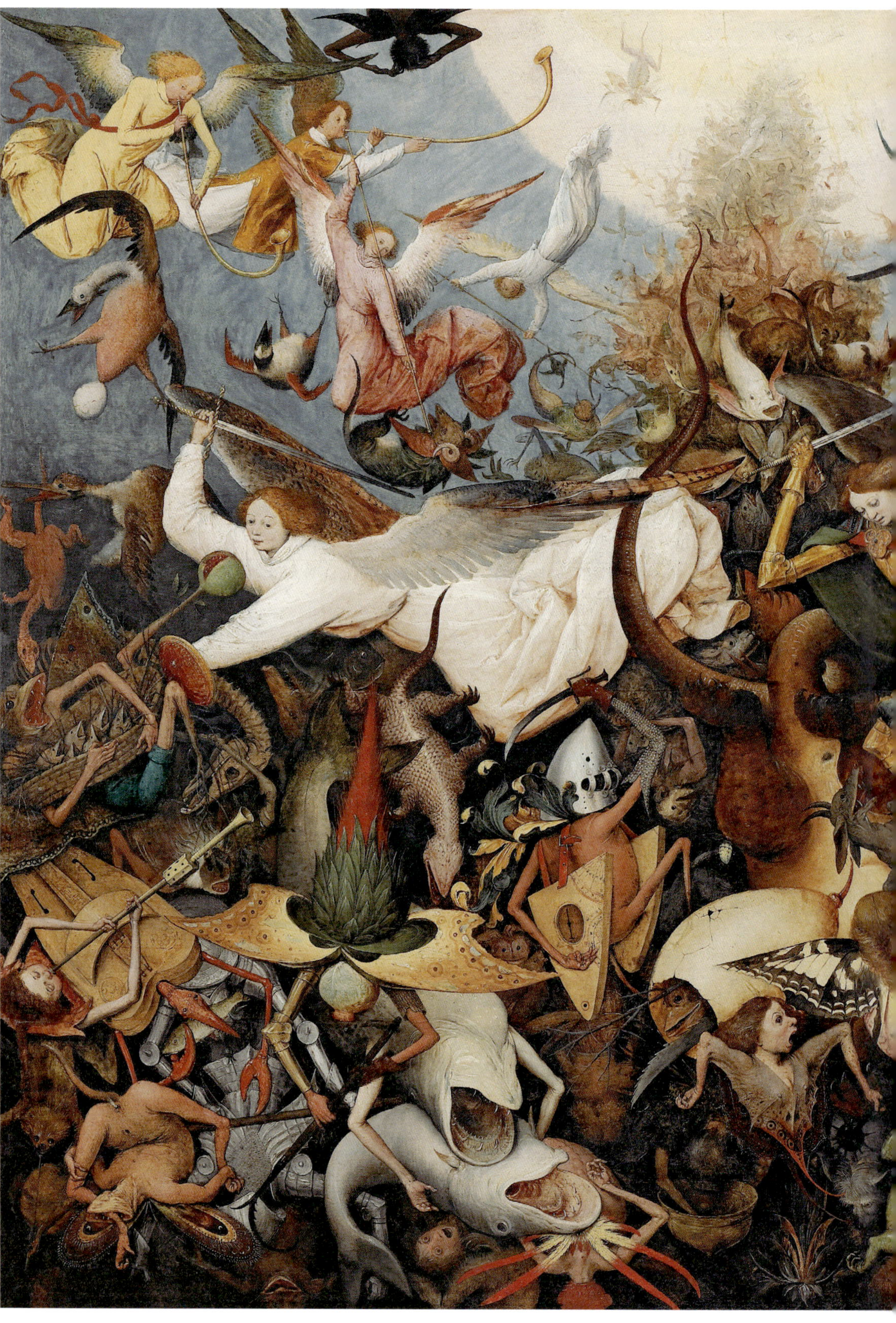

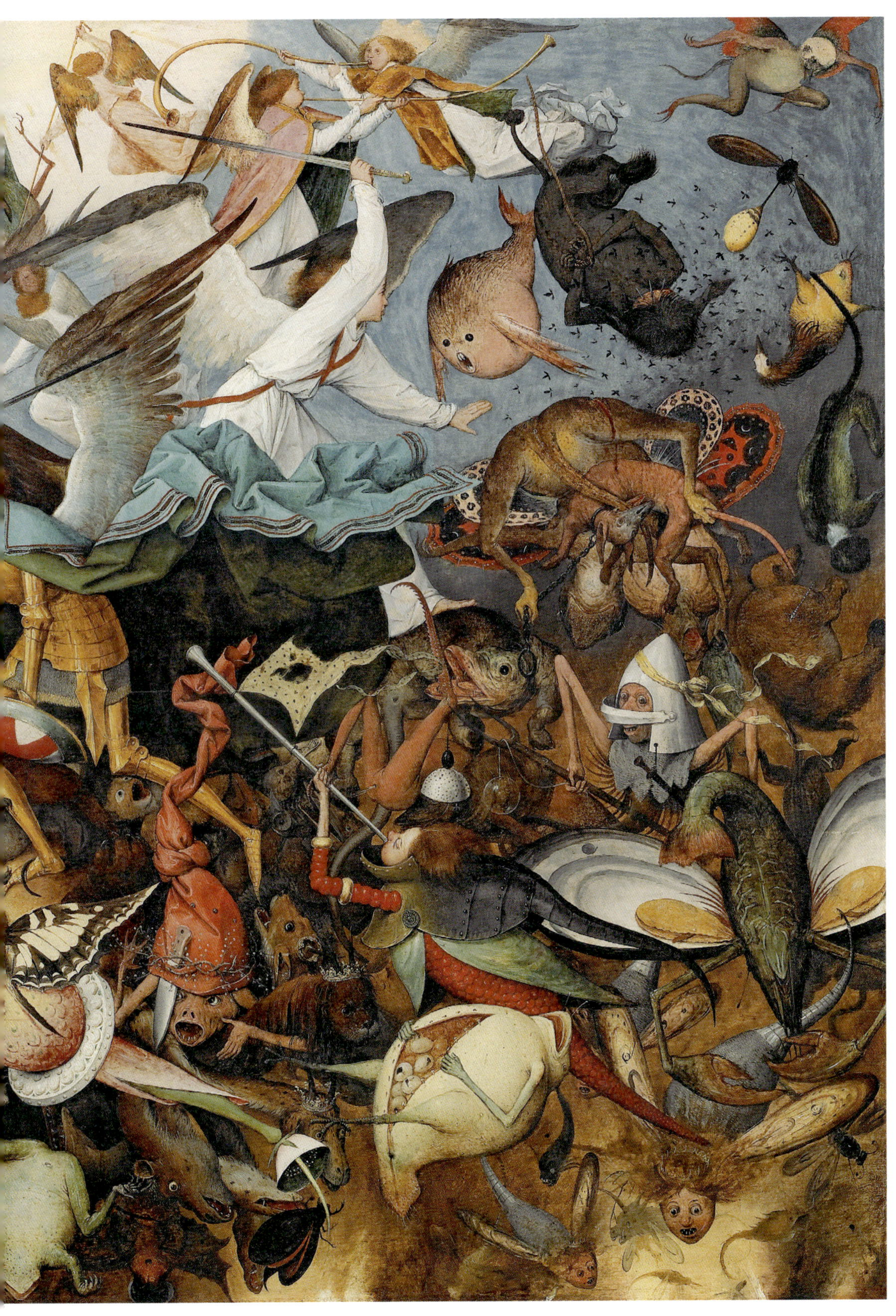

# Foreword to the second edition

*Pieter Bruegel the Elder. Fall of the Rebel Angels. Art, Knowledge and Politics on the Eve of the Dutch Revolt* appeared in 2014, solely in English, as the 16th *Cahier des Musées royaux des Beaux-Arts de Belgique.* The host of commemorative events held in 2019 in connection with the 450th anniversary of Bruegel's death (in Brussels in 1569) bear witness to the great esteem in which his art is still held at both the national and the international level after four and a half centuries. I am therefore delighted at the publication of this second edition not only in English but also in Dutch and French. While the work has been slightly updated in line with new ideas, it was decided to leave the bibliography unchanged, apart from a few corrections, and not to include any of the works that have appeared since 2014. This would indeed have involved countless additions, as the book not only addresses Bruegel's masterpiece with reference to a vast cultural and historical context but is also aimed at specialists and general art lovers alike.

The studies on the artist have never ceased to multiply since 2014.[1] The largest ever Bruegel exhibition has taken place at the Kunsthistorisches Museum in Vienna and many new publications have appeared.[2] While this short preface would hardly suffice to mention all the developments, it should be noted that this anniversary year has primarily raised new questions and clearly reminds us that there is still a great deal to discover and examine in the master's work. As the unique and outstanding exhibition organized by the Kunsthistorisches clearly shows, Bruegel is a painter to whom an entire lifetime can be devoted. Susceptible of interpretation at a whole variety of levels, his inexhaustible masterpieces demand slow and repeated observation. Examining just one of his paintings already offers ways of exploring them all. The master's works are now once again scattered all over the world, but each masterpiece is well worth a pilgrimage.

Bruegel's paintings can indeed be seen as a visual pilgrimage, as the viewer's eye is required to unravel very complex compositions in order to grasp of all their aspects and dimensions. Like a pilgrim on the march, he or she must travel every inch of the painting and examine its unexpected elements. Bruegel constructed this process of visualization in order to interact with the viewers of his time but also with those of the present. He also included elements referring to the new developments and upheavals of his day. In observing this world in transition, he did not take a stance but posed questions. This is why his paintings have also been described as works of dialogue: they prompt contemplation and reflection but also discussion among viewers, a priceless quality in the polarized society in which Bruegel lived and worked, and one that is still highly relevant today. In-depth analysis of *The Fall of the Rebel Angels* shows that Bruegel's references are not only to the religious and artistic traditions but also to the culture of knowledge and art collections around 1562. Taking this idea as my cornerstone and encompassing a broader vision of the history and culture of the time, I formulated the hypothesis that the client for whom the work was painted was Cardinal Granvelle, a great collector of *artificialia* and *naturalia*, elements that are indeed incorporated in *The Fall.* In 1562, the year of its creation, Granvelle was also involved in a struggle for power with William of Orange, the owner of Hieronymus Bosch's *The Garden of Earthly Delights*, a masterpiece that still hangs in Brussels, which Bruegel endeavoured to surpass.

Prompted by the potential of this visual pilgrimage through Bruegel's work, I then turned to another large-scale painting in the Royal Museums of Fine Arts, namely *The Census at Bethlehem.* Once again, I believed that undertaking a long, slow examination of this work and dissecting it all its constituent elements, thus reversing Bruegel's creative process in a sense, would provide insight into the original visual experience and the dialogue established with the client. This research led in 2018 to a joint publication with Sabine van Sprang entitled *Bruegel's Winter Scenes. Historians and Art Historians in Dialogue.*[3] Among other things, examination of *The Census at Bethlehem* reveals the importance of a topographic reference to Wijnegem, a hamlet near Antwerp. In 1566, the year when Bruegel painted the work, rights of lordship over Wijnegem were conferred on Jan Vleminck, a merchant banker from Antwerp closely connected with the law courts in Brussel. Vleminck had lent money to Margaret of Parma, Governor of the Netherlands, and to Nicolas Jonghelinck, whose possessions included Bruegel's Seasons.[4] These discoveries corroborated that hypothesis that *The Fall of the Rebel Angels* was painted for Cardinal Granvelle, who knew Vleminck and sent condolences on his death to his brother Aert. Granvelle, Jonghelinck and Vleminck were all members of the *nouveau riche* and owed their power not to noble lineage but to personal merit and success in trade. In-depth cultural and historical research on Bruegel's two major paintings in the Royal Museums thus opened up new horizons for examination of the rest of his work in relation to his network of patrons.[5]

While Bruegel responded to the desires of his rich clients with his monumental paintings, he also posed subtle questions in every case about human aspirations for wealth, power and knowledge. He did not paint works of propaganda but visual quests open to a range of interpretations. Bruegel worked during the transitional period of 1557–58, when the golden age of the Burgundian and Habsburg Netherlands was threatened by social, religious, (geo)political and even climatic upheavals. In response to all this, he produced works of dialogue and reflection that prompted not only the client but all viewers to look more closely, to think and to discuss the consequences of both individual and collective choices and conduct.

1 Two major studies preceded the Bruegel commemorations but appeared after the first edition of this book: Stephanie Porras, *Pieter Bruegel's Historical Imagination*, University Park (PA), The Pennsylvania State University Press, 2016; Joseph Leo Koerner, *Bosch and Bruegel. From Enemy Painting to Everyday Life*, Princeton-Oxford, Princeton University Press, 2016. Koerner was apparently unaware on my book on Bruegel's *Fall of the Rebel Angels*. In the meantime, I have also published *Erudite Eyes. Friendship, Art and Erudition* (Leyde-Boston, Brill, 2017), which focuses in particular on the master's *Death of the Virgin*.

2 Elke Oberthaler, Sabine Pénot, Manfred Sellink, Ron Leap and Alice Hoppe-Harnoncourt, *Bruegel : la main du maître*, exh. cat. (Vienna, Kunsthistorisches Museum, 2018), Furnes, Hannibal, 2018; Reindert Falkenburg and Michel Weemans, *Bruegel*, Paris, Hazan, 2018; Thomas Schauerte and Jürgen Müller, *Bruegel. L'œuvre complète*, Cologne, Taschen, 2019; Nils Büttner, *Bruegel. De schilder van boeren en heiligen*, Amsterdam, Meulenhoff, 2019.

3 T.L. Meganck, 'The Census at Bethlehem. Winter of a Golden Age', in Tine L. Meganck and Sabine van Sprang, *Bruegel's Winter Scenes. Historians and Art Historians in Dialogue* (Brussels: Mercatorfonds / New Haven-London: Yale University Press, 2018), pp. 85–127.

4 My recent study on the spatial construction of these works demonstrates that they do in fact constitute a series depicting the four seasons. See T.L. Meganck, 'Between Brussels and Antwerp. New perspectives on Bruegel's Cycle of the Seasons', in E. Oberthaler, S. Pénot, M. Sellink, R. Sprong and A. Hoppe-Harnoncourt (eds.), *The Hand of the Master. Materials and Techniques of Pieter Bruegel the Elder* [provisional title], Furnes, Kannibaal/Hannibal, 2019. The series is referred to as the Seasons in the catalogue of the Vienna exhibition (2018, p. 214–41).

5 See T.L. Meganck, 'Bruegel's Patrons. How "close viewing" may reveal original ownership', in *The Bruegel Success Story. Papers presented at Symposium XXI for the Study of Underdrawing and Technology in Painting, Brussels, 12-14 September 2018*, Brussels, [to be published in 2019].

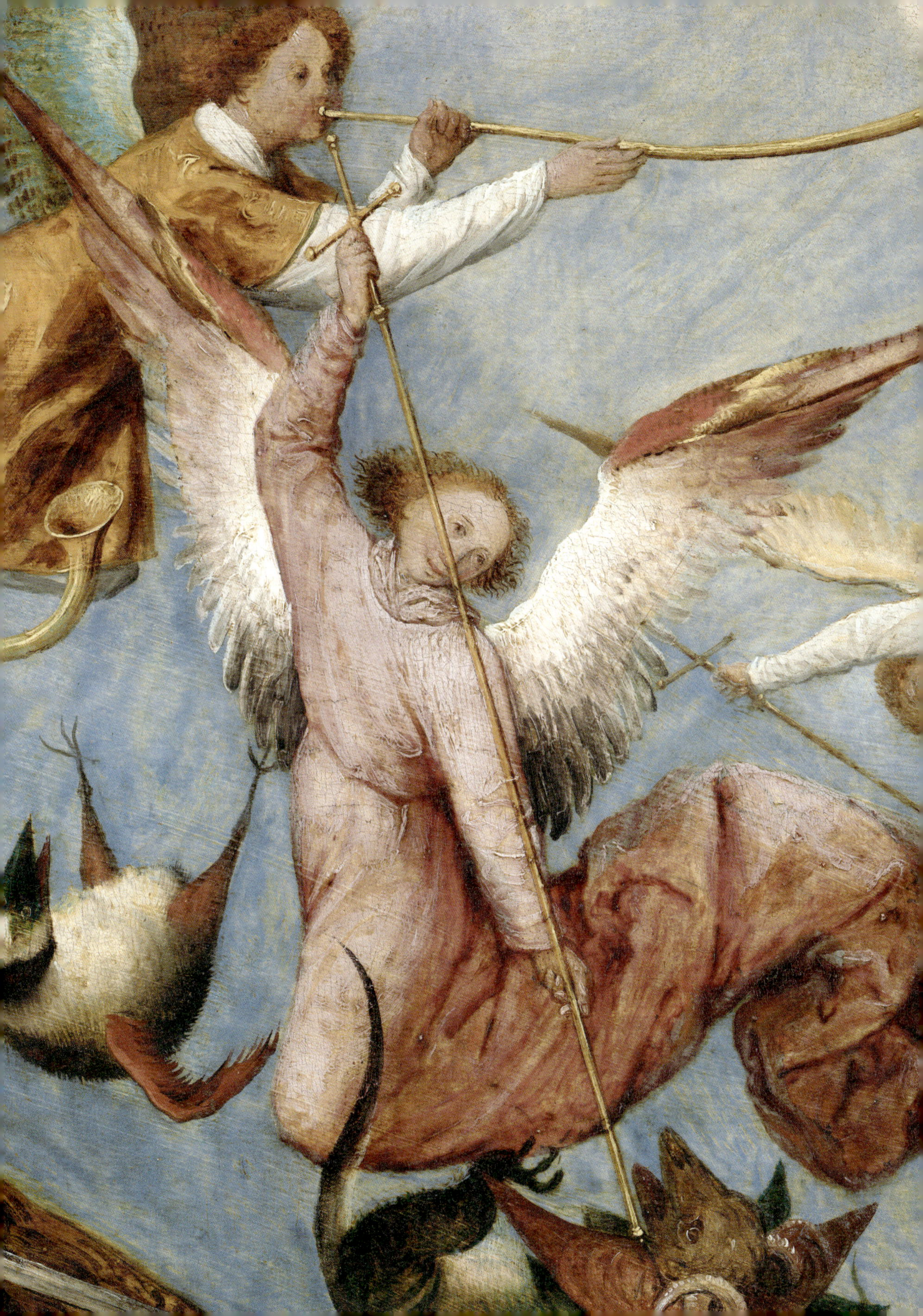

# Acknowledgements

A book that has been several years in the making owes debts to many people. I should like to express my gratitude above all to Sabine van Sprang who initiated the museum's participation in the Interuniversity Attraction Pole program 'City and Society' of Belgian Science Policy (Belspo) and ensured me a research position in the first place. Her pointed comments and friendship are very dear. I am grateful to other colleagues in the Old Masters Department of the Royal Museums of Fine Arts of Belgium, especially Joost vander Auwera, who likewise read early versions of the manuscript, as well as Véronique Bücken, Liesbeth De Belie, Stefaan Hautekeete, Alexandre Galand, Hilde Cuvelier, and also to the museum library staff, Anne-Marie De Moor, Freya Maes, and Brigitte de Patoul. My former colleague at the museum, Irene Schaudies, thoughtfully translated the text into English. I acknowledge my colleagues at the Interuniversity Attraction Pole 'City and Society,' in particular Marc Boone, director of the program, and Anne-Laure van Bruaene, who generously shared her insights into Brussels rhetorician culture. Thomas DaCosta Kaufmann's advice on the history of collecting proved invaluable as ever. Nadja Aksamija helped me to identify some key contacts of Bruegel at the University of Bologna. I benefited from lively conversations in front of Bruegel's painting with Yoko Mori, Jürgen Müller, and Tanja Michalsky. Questions from Christine Göttler and Sven Dupré pressed me to deeper reflection on the intricate connections between art and knowledge. I am most grateful to all of them. A special word of thanks goes to Michel Draguet, director general of the Royal Museums of Fine Arts of Belgium, for giving me the opportunity to publish academic research within the museum's Cahier series. The greatest debt I owe to Carl. His unwavering support makes it possible to blend life and art. I fondly remember our summer visits to Bologna, Innsbruck, and Bomarzo together with our beloved children. I dedicate this book to them.

# Preface

Pieter Bruegel the Elder is one of the most famous Northern Renaissance painters. It is perhaps little known that the Royal Museums of Fine Arts of Belgium houses the second largest ensemble of Bruegel the Elder paintings, after the Kunsthistorisches Museum in Vienna. The museum owns no less than three Bruegel the Elder paintings, *The Fall of the Rebel Angels* (1562), the *Winter Landscape with a Bird Trap* (1565), and the *Census at Bethlehem* (1566), as well as a preparatory drawing for *Prudence* (1558), from the print series of the *Seven Virtues*. In addition, it possesses three works that are closely associated with Pieter Bruegel the Elder, but of which the attribution is disputed, among them the much cherished *Fall of Icarus*.

Bruegel the Elder's *Fall of the Rebel Angels* is an absolute masterpiece, but it is certainly not the painter's best-known work; indeed most visitors may not readily recognize it as a Bruegel, and at first glance attribute it to Bosch. To trick the beholder in this way was probably a deliberate strategy of Bruegel's. A young and unknown draftsman, Bruegel entered the art marked by designing preparatory drawings for prints in imitation of Bosch, the enigmatic artist who was still very much in demand half a century after his death. By 1562, the year he painted the *Fall*, Bruegel had gained enough fame of his own: he increasingly shifted to painting, and a year later, in 1563, he moved to Brussels. In the present book, Tine Meganck demonstrates convincingly that the Brussels Fall of the Rebel Angels is a pivotal piece in Bruegel's career.

Most importantly, she argues that Bruegel, in a most ingenious attempt to surpass Bosch, transforms the traditional moralizing story about the sin of pride into man's latest theater of knowledge, the early modern world of collecting. Many of the hybrid falling angels are carefully composed of closely observed *naturalia* and *artificialia*. Bruegel's preference for rare and wondrous elements as well as the overall composition recalls the orderly chaos of early modern cabinets of curiosity that originated precisely around that time. That Bruegel, known to be an alert witness of his times, chronicled the burgeoning culture of collecting may seem evident, but had thus far gone unnoticed.

The focus on the courtly city of Brussels further offers fascinating insights in the role of art in local politics on the eve of the Dutch revolt. The author argues that Bruegel's references to Bosch's *Garden of Earthly Delights* - that was kept in Brussels, in possession of William of Orange, when Bruegel was painting his masterpiece - is a key to understand who commissioned the *Fall of the Rebel Angels*. She also suggests new connections of Bruegel with the Brussels chambers of rhetoric and with the Brussels tapestry industry, avenues of investigation with much potential for future research.

It is particularly fitting to publish these new findings on Bruegel and the history of collecting in a museum series, as our present museums are heir to early modern collections and cabinets of curiosities. This innovative study illustrates moreover that museums not only preserve and present artworks, but also foster art historical research. I here would like to render special thanks to Sabine van Sprang, who heads the Interuniversity Attraction Pole program (Belspo) within the museum. This program has generously funded the research of Tine Meganck. The museum Cahier series is beautifully illustrated, greatly benefiting Tine Meganck's cultural historical argument, which is also very much a visual demonstration: one has to see the details of Bruegel's densely packed painting to believe. The high definition photographs made by Freya Maes in the context of the material-technical Bruegel project directed by Veronique Bücken make this book a true theater of art.

I sincerely hope that this book will inspire art lovers to visit and revisit the museum and view Bruegel's masterpiece with new eyes.

**Michel Draguet**
*Director General*

# Preface

It is with pride that I welcome Tine L. Meganck's long awaited study on Pieter Bruegel the Elder's masterpiece the *Fall of the Rebel Angels*. The scientific team of the Royal Museums of Fine Arts of Belgium in which Tine Meganck takes part under the direction of Sabine van Sprang has been embedded in successive Interuniversity Attraction Pole programs (phases VI and VII) of the Belgian Science Policy Office (Belspo). One focus of this network of universities and federal research institutions is the study of urban societies in the former Low Countries during the late medieval and early modern period. Within this framework, Tine Meganck's research contributes to the program's second work package, "Urban Memories and Counter-memories."

The historical Low Countries constitute an important case study, since from the Middle Ages onwards this part of Europe was among the most densely populated areas of the old continent. Urban history offers a field of study that allows for a multi-disciplinary approach since cities past and present are the crucibles in which answers to society's most pressing issues are formed. The sixteenth century was one of the historical periods in which several acute problems came together, profoundly influencing contemporaries' vision of the world they were living in. One can point out three fields of far-reaching change and evolution. First, and most obvious to the contemporary observer, there was a drive towards an unprecedented political unity within Europe thanks to the unification of several extensive regions under the control of a single dynasty, the house of Habsburg, whose holdings brought together the old Burgundian Netherlands, the German Empire, the Spanish crown and its overseas territories, and important parts of the Italian peninsula. Like all such consolidating movements it also provoked a counter-reaction by nations that felt threatened, leading to an almost uncontrollable drive towards war and military innovation. At the same time, the presumed unity of Christianity was being questioned as never before. The criticism now launched at the Roman Catholic Church by Lutheran, Calvinist, and other Protestant sympathizers was not as easily controlled as the waves of dissent that had swept through the church in the Middle Ages. The invention and spread of new print media made it impossible to control the hearts and minds of the flock; moreover, the Catholic Church and its clergy had lost the cultural monopoly they had enjoyed for centuries. While all this was happening, the Ottoman threat at the southeastern border of Europe was stronger than ever before, upending the relationship between Christianity and Islam that had persisted since the days of the Crusades.

Finally, the discovery of the "New World" not only brought unexpected wealth to Europe, since the gold and silver of the Americas led to an unprecedented input of monetary means, they also brought an upsurge of inflation and the gradual spread of the feeling that the economy was evolving on a much larger scale, beyond the range of the urban corporations that had until then largely controlled production and commerce. Henceforth, the world economy would undergo an unprecedented process of globalization. On all these fronts, men and women living around the middle of the sixteenth century must have felt uncertain, threatened, forced to question the vision of the world that had been theirs until then. Not surprisingly, an extremely gifted painter like Pieter Bruegel the Elder - and with him many painters, writers, musicians, and artists of all persuasions - engaged in reflecting on the fundamental questions faced by society, dancing as it was on the volcano that urban societies of the Low Countries had become. In 1563, one year after painting the Fall, Bruegel moved from Antwerp, a thriving economic metropolis and one of the places in the world where the new commercial capitalist economy and its effects were most visible, to Brussels, a court city where the Spanish Habsburg power was now firmly entrenched and ready to act as gatekeeper of traditional political, religious, and societal values.

In this book, Tine Meganck explores the way Bruegel succeeded in reflecting these ongoing debates. She also formulates a seductive hypothesis when she points to the patronage of Cardinal Antoine Perrenot de Granvelle, a key figure in the struggle for power, and his competition "in artes" with William of Orange, who was gradually emerging as one of the leading figures in the opposition to Habsburg power. In the context of the Dutch revolt against the king of Spain, who posed as God's own vicar on earth, the reference to Lucifer, who led his fellow angels into rebellion against God and thus to their fall, may have had special resonance. With subtle visual references to contemporary actors and their interests, Bruegel's work of art transforms into a tool that operated in the complex processes of disseminating political meaning. At the other end of the Eighty Years War, in 1654, the Dutch playwright Joost van den Vondel staged a much more sympathetic Lucifer, torn between reason and faith, revolt and order. Bruegel's Fall of the Rebel Angels is an important milestone in this sequence of shifting images, allowing observers to reflect on the meaning of orthodoxy, rebellion against the powers that be, and changing alliances.

This study can, in the best art-historical tradition linked with history tout court, be considered a very fine example of "micro storia," starting with one fact or object - here Bruegel's painting - and treating it in such a way that it becomes a diaphragm through which we may view society and its many internal struggles as a whole. This study is bound to become a major contribution to the way we look at urban society in one of Europe's most developed urban belts and how that society dealt with fundamental shifts in its economic, religious, and political organization. It did so during the turbulent sixteenth century, but the well-informed reader of today will doubtless recognize many contemporary problems reflected with uncanny precision.

**Marc Boone**
Dean of the faculty of Arts and Philosophy at the Rijksuniversiteit Gent and director of the Interuniversity Attraction Pole program "City and Society in the Low Countries (ca. 1200-ca.1850). The 'condition urbaine' between resilience and vulnerability."

# Prologue

That is the reason why you must open this book, and carefully weigh up its contents. You will discover then that the drug within is far more valuable than the box promised; that is to say, that the subjects here treated are not so foolish as the title on the cover suggested.

François Rabelais, *Gargantua*, 1534*

A single glance at a single image often contributes more to the memory than the lengthy perusal of many pages.

Samuel Quiccheberg, *Inscriptiones*, 1565**

The *Fall of the Rebel Angels* by Pieter Bruegel the Elder is one of the masterpieces of the Royal Museums of Fine Arts of Belgium in Brussels. It is painted in oil on oak wood and measures 117 × 162 cm. The Royal Museums purchased the painting in 1846 as a work by Bruegel's son Pieter II, to whom the hell scenes and underworld landscapes that were actually painted by Bruegel's other son, Jan, were wrongly attributed.[1] Later, the piece was attributed to Hieronymus Bosch (1450-1516) until 1898, when the signature "M.D.LXII/BRVEGEL" was found hidden behind the frame in the lower left-hand corner and the painting was finally reattributed to its rightful maker.[2]
The earlier attributions may have been incorrect, but they immediately suggest a number of key questions concerning the painting's meaning as well as the history of its creation and reception. Mistaking Bruegel for Bosch would undoubtedly have pleased and honored the former, because even during his lifetime he was already acclaimed as the "new Bosch"[3] (fig. 3). The incorrect attribution to Pieter II Brueghel, once dispensed with, leads directly to the opposite question: why then, since Pieter II was known for his exact copies after his father's inventions, did he *not* paint a *Fall of the Rebel Angels*? Had he never seen this masterpiece, or even a preparatory drawing left behind in his father's workshop? Does not the preponderance of infernal scenes by Jan, who was known as "hell" Brueghel, bear witness to his knowledge and appreciation of this particular invention of his father's?
This book will not answer all of these questions unequivocally; after all, straightforward simplicity is the antithesis of Bruegel's multilayered and often deliberately ambiguous works of art. It does, however, try to lay bare the various registers of this artwork and to sketch the broad context of its creation. Questions about the masterpiece abound, even though the frequency with which they are posed is astonishingly seldom.[4] We do not know for whom Bruegel's *Fall* was painted, or who its original owner might have been. As to the painting's subject few scholars agree. Since its purchase by the Royal Museums, it has simply been known as the *Fall of the Rebel Angels*.[5] Karel Van Mander (1546-1606) does not mention the painting in his biography of Pieter Bruegel in the famous *Schilder-boeck* (1604), which sets out the principles of painting and gives account of the lives of artists.[6]
The Antwerp collector Peter Stevens (1590-1668), however, noted in the margins of his exemplar of the *Schilder-boeck* that he had seen Bruegel's "Fall of Lucifer."[7] In his recent catalogue raisonné, Manfred Sellink refers to the work as *The Archangel Michael Defeating the Dragon of the Apocalypse*.[8] In the midst of swarming angels and devils, animals and things, Bruegel has

indeed depicted the seven-headed dragon of the Apocalypse [2], so cleverly concealed that not all viewers, critics, and historians have registered its presence. We shall see that Bruegel probably intended the ambiguity that has divided specialists to this day, and even made it into his trademark.

We do not know exactly when Bruegel was born. He probably entered into apprenticeship with Pieter Coecke van Aelst (1502-1550) in Antwerp sometime around 1545-50; he may also have been trained as a book illuminator by Coecke's wife, Mayken Verhulst. In 1551 he is listed as an independent master in the registry of the Antwerp Guild of Saint Luke. During his Antwerp period, Bruegel was primarily active as a designer of prints for the publishing company of Hieronymus Cock, Aux Quatre Vents / In de Vier Winden (At the Four Winds). From 1552 to 1554 he traveled in Italy. During his travels he drew mostly landscapes, views of mountains and harbors, several of which Cock published as prints after his return.[9]

From 1562, the year in which he painted the *Fall,* Bruegel began to produce paintings in increasing numbers. This shift in production more or less coincides with an important change in Bruegel's personal life. In 1563 Bruegel moved to Brussels, where his marriage to Mayken Coecke is recorded in the parochial archives of the Kapellekerk. His young wife was the daughter of his master Pieter Coecke van Aelst, the successful *artiste de l'empereur* of Charles V, and it seems likely that his marriage was also meant to serve his professional advancement. The court in Brussels undoubtedly exerted its considerable powers of attraction on the ambitious artist. Bruegel died in Brussels in 1569, where his tomb in the Kapellekerk still draws art-lovers in search of the few remaining material traces of this enigmatic artist.

The first chapter presents the most recognizable and most widely discussed level of looking at the painting: the Christian reading of its central iconography and its other most striking characteristic, Bruegel's reference to the art of Hieronymus Bosch. The fall of the rebel angels narrates the first punishment of evil, even before the creation of man. However, Bruegel allows the seven-headed monster of the Apocalypse to mingle with his falling angels, thereby showing that evil exists from the beginning to the end of time. Most studies analyze Bruegel's painting primarily as an artistic comparison to Bosch.[10] In only two paintings does Bruegel really show himself to be a "new Bosch": in *Dulle Griet,* now in the Museum Mayer Van den Bergh in Antwerp (fig. 28), and the *Fall of the Rebel Angels.*[11] A detour through the work of Bosch is thus indispensable, but it also reveals essential differences in the work of the two painters. We believe that the key to the *Fall* lies precisely in Bruegel's notable differentiation from Bosch.

A thorough visual study of the *Fall of the Rebel Angels* - the looking that must precede any art-historical analysis - shows that Bruegel painted elements that recall the art of Bosch, but that he allows them to mingle with animals and things that Bosch never depicted. Bruegel assembles his falling angels from *artificialia* ("things made by man") and *naturalia* ("things made by nature"), among which we find a feather headdress and animals from America, the New Continent. The second chapter examines all these components systematically, as they were collected in the art and curiosity cabinets of the time.

The image of Bruegel the peasant painter, launched by Van Mander, sometimes causes us to lose sight of the fact that Bruegel lived in an age characterized by the unprecedented explosion of knowledge. Antwerp was a clearinghouse for all manner of products, raw materials, and animals from all corners of the old and "new" world. The discovery of strange fauna and cultures encouraged the closer study of culture, traditions, and customs at home. Collecting was perhaps one of the most prevalent ways of ordering this new knowledge. Antwerp merchants such as Abraham Ortelius (1527-1598) amassed a renowned collection of *naturalia* and *artificialia.* Courtiers in Brussels, too, among whom Cardinal Antoine Perrenot de Granvelle (1517-1586), collected costly works of art and wonders of nature, and functioned as a channel of distribution for artistic products, natural specimens, and scientific knowledge from the Netherlands to the central court in Madrid. In 1562, the presence in Brussels of the collection of Charles V (1500-1559), particularly renowned for its American treasures, was still a vivid memory. Recent studies have explained Bruegel's paintings of *Proverbs* (fig. 1) and

**Fig. 1**
Pieter Bruegel the Elder, *Proverbs*, 1559
Berlin, Staatliche Museen zu Berlin, Gemäldegalerie

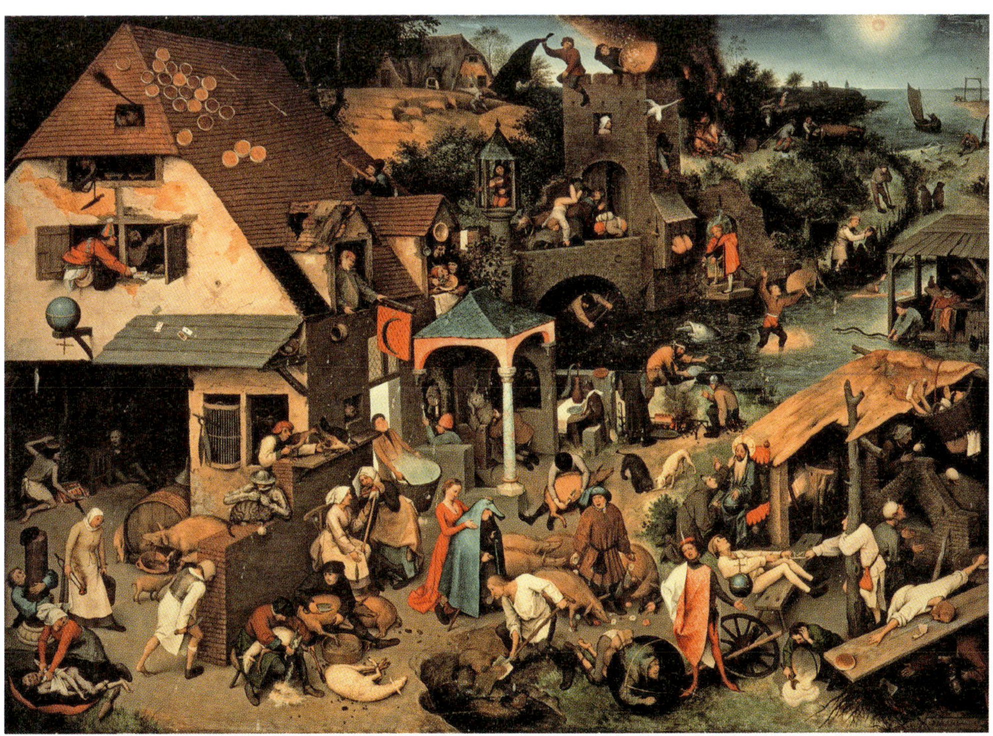

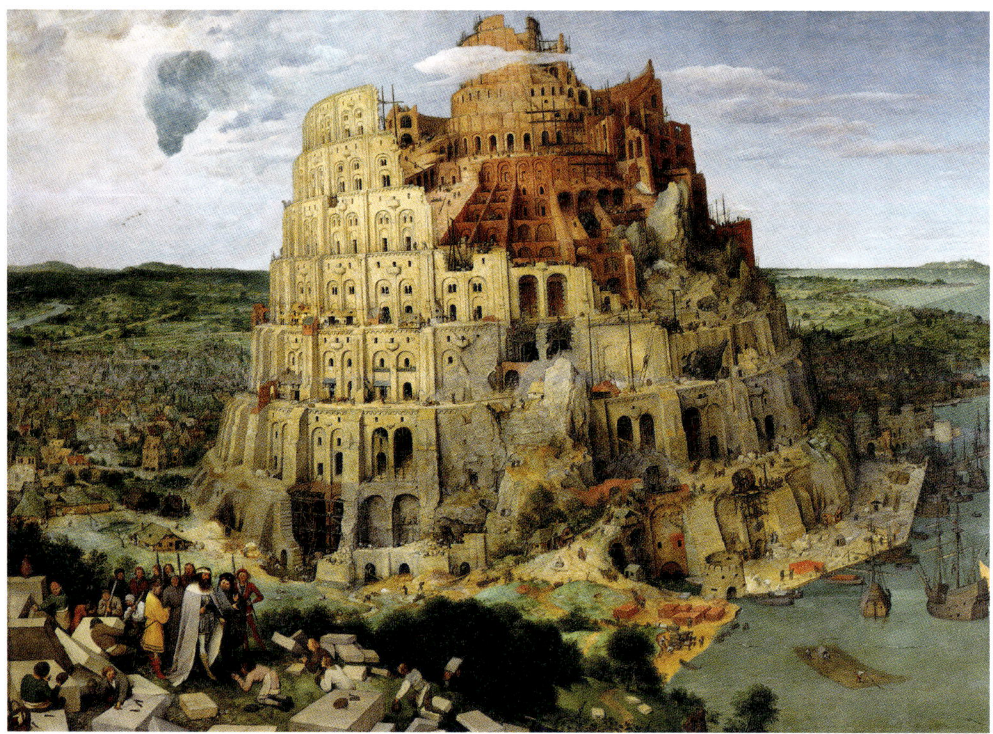

**Fig. 2**
Pieter Bruegel the Elder, *Tower of Babel*, 1563
Vienna, Kunsthistorisches Museum

*Children's Games* (Vienna) from the perspective of this culture of collecting.[12] It has never been remarked, however, that in the *Fall,* a heaping up of *artificialia* and *naturalia,* Bruegel offers a unique artistic commentary on the more erudite aspects of this culture of collecting at the very moment that it was manifesting itself in cabinets of art and curiosities. Both the composition and the components of the *Fall* recall these spaces, cupboards, or entire rooms filled to overflowing with the most curious objects of art and nature.

The third chapter shows how the culture of knowledge and collecting encouraged Bruegel to formulate a self-conscious commentary on his own artistic practice. Just as the art and curiosity cabinets displayed the contest between art and nature, Bruegel measured his artistic creations against the creative power of Nature. The earliest art-theoretical reception of his work – the well-known epitaph by Abraham Ortelius – presents Bruegel as an artist who had no other masters, but had only followed Nature, and had therefore become Nature among artists.[13] Although Ortelius presents Bruegel as an autodidact, Bruegel knew the work of his artistic predecessors quite well. In the *Fall* he refers not only to the art of Bosch, but also very subtly and ingeniously to that of Jan van Eyck, Rogier van der Weyden, Albrecht Dürer, and Frans Floris, painters who themselves excelled in the imitation of nature and whose work was therefore frequently displayed in art and curiosity cabinets. In this way he transformed nature and art into a fantastic work of art with which he sought to surpass not only his predecessors, but also Nature herself.

Bruegel shows himself to be a master observer of minute details in art and nature, which he nevertheless manages to transform into imaginary creatures. His works appear to be direct depictions of nature, but are instead artificial compositions, things in transition, in the process of becoming. We see this clearly in the devils of the *Fall of the Rebel Angels,* but also in his representation of landscapes as compilations of villages, townhouses, and princely palaces in the *Proverbs* (1559), or in his *Tower of Babel* (1563) (fig. 2), the doomed tower that he depicts as growing out of a cliff like some kind of fossil built up of a myriad of architectural styles.

The first commentaries by contemporaries such as Ortelius and Domenicus Lampsonius (1532-1599) praise Bruegel's imitation of nature, but also his spirited inventions (fig. 3). Several of Bruegel's falling angels are funny. Like the devil himself, Bruegel seduces the viewer with funny creations and supernatural beauty. Nevertheless, José de Sigüenza (1544-1606) writes of Bosch around 1600 - when Bruegel was unanimously praised as the "new Bosch" - that "his paintings are not at all comical, but like books of great wisdom and art, and if there are foolish activities, then they are ours, not his."[14] Behind Bruegel's jocular design is concealed a serious consideration: like the monsters in early modern curiosity cabinets - which were seen as nature's jokes, but also as omens - Bruegel's falling angels inspire reflection: on order and chaos in the cosmos, on the hubris of knowledge, and of art.

In the last chapter we propose a hypothesis as to the patron who may have commissioned the *Fall of the Rebel Angels.* Taking the year 1562 as a point of departure, and building on Bruegel's visual references to Bosch (chapter I) and to the sixteenth-century culture of knowledge and collecting (chapter II), we direct the spotlight at the political and artistic patronage of courtiers in Brussels, particularly the archrivals Cardinal Antoine Perrenot de Granvelle and William of Orange (1533-1584), proud owner of one of the most well-known paintings by Bosch, the *Garden of Earthly Delights* (fig. 21). The Brussels court functioned in a system of dynamic exchange with the city, so we will also reexamine the urban symbolism of Saint Michael, patron saint of Brussels. Saint Michael and the rebel angels were referred to frequently in a rhetoricians' competition organized in Brussels in 1562, which played on the idea of political unrest. Since Granvelle had been appointed archbishop the previous year, the climate in Brussels had been tense. Recent studies have shown, however, that Granvelle initially tried to persuade his sovereign to respect local customs and privileges. He was moreover one of the most refined collectors of art and nature of his time.

Bruegel created the *Fall of the Rebel Angels* at the intersection of all of these

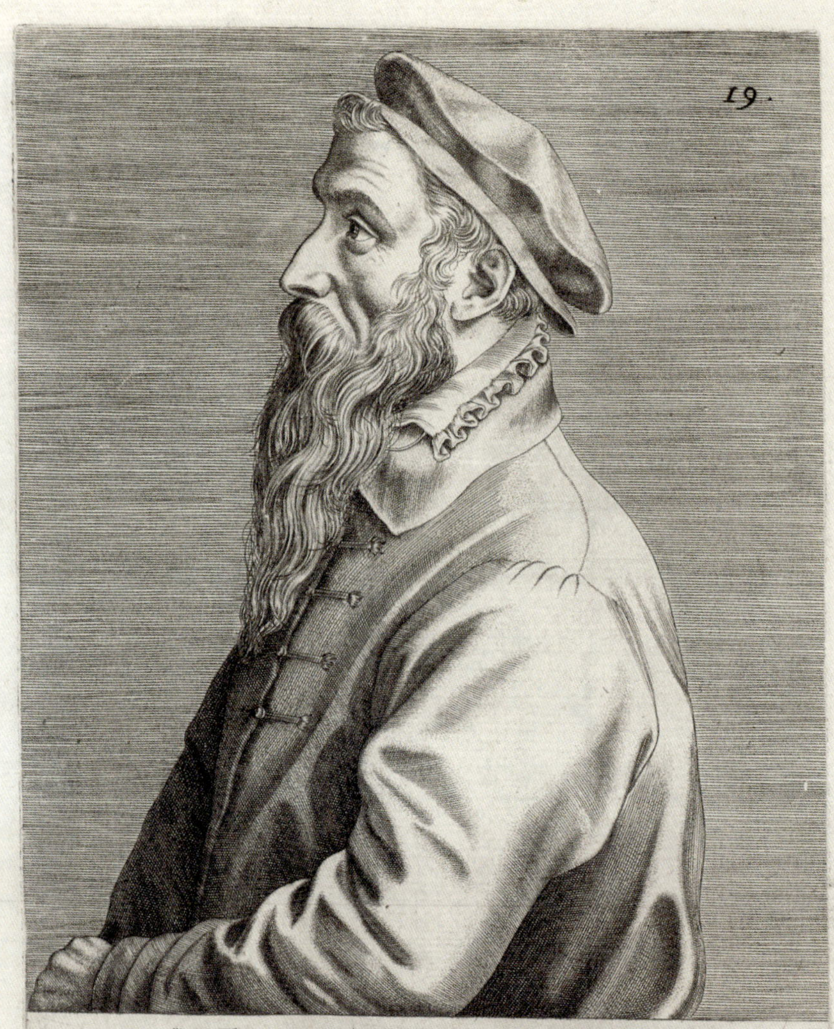


PETRO BRVEGEL, PICTORI.

*Quis nouus hic Hieronymus Orbi*
*Boschius? ingeniosa magistri*
*Somnia peniculóque, styloque*
*Tanta imitarier arte peritus,*
*Vt superet tamen interim & illum?*
*Macte animo, Petre, mactus vt arte.*
*Namque tuo, veterisque magistri*
*Ridiculo, salibusque referto*
*In graphices genere inclyta laudum*
*Præmia vbique, & ab omnibus vllo*
*Artifice haud leuiora mereris.*

19 Dj

**Fig. 3**
Attributed to Johannes Wierix, *Portrait of Bruegel*, from *Pictorum aliquot Celebrium Germaniae Inferioris Effigies* (Antwerp, 1572)
Brussels, Royal Library of Belgium, Print Cabinet

reflections, ideas, people, institutions, guidelines, and interests.[15] With his inimitable visual language he was able to weave a web of interpretations around a central narrative. Pride and hubris, whether in politics, the quest for art and knowledge - in any human aspiration whatsoever - inevitably lead to decline and decay. With his specific imitation of the world circa 1562, the art, nature, courtly and urban culture that determined the agenda at the time, he created a unique testament to a precise historical moment.

Bruegel paints a world in the awareness that faith, behavior, and customs are particular to a person, place, and time.[16] It is a world at war over freedom and religion, in which man revises his vision of his central place in the cosmos, and studies monsters from the *terrae incognitae* as *naturalia* from recently "discovered" parts of the world. Bruegel shows this world in transformation, between tradition and innovation, labor and contemplation, city and countryside, animals and objects, nature and culture. In a unique way Bruegel, like Leonardo, Arcimboldo, or Rabelais, visualizes the fascination for metamorphosis and change that were so characteristic of the sixteenth century - but at the same time so timeless.[17] With its brilliant colors, heavenly spheres, perfect angels, and monstrous devils, the *Fall of the Rebel Angels* continues to charm many a visitor right up to the present day.

Like Rabelais's book, Bruegel's painting is like a box, which does not always contain the medicine promised by the title. For those who would excavate the many layers of meaning in this masterly painting, this book hopes to serve as a guide: one book about one painting that opens like a box filled with unexpected things.[18] To assist the reader in this treasure hunt, a numbered legend that can serve as as a map of Bruegel's composition is printed on the inside front and back cover of the book. Throughout the text, numbers between brackets refer to this legend. Illustrations of details follow the same numbering.

# Chapter I

Lucifer set himself against his creator, the eternal God, and in an instant was thrust from the height of heaven into hell, and on this account God decided to create the human race, through which he could repair the fall of Lucifer and his cohorts.

*Speculum Humanae Salvationis*, 15th century

# Angels and devils of the new Bosch

## Saint Michael at the beginning and end of time

With raised sword and spread wings, Saint Michael [1] stands in the center of the panel. His azure cloak still flutters after the rapid descent from the empyrean realm, the highest of heavenly spheres. His golden armor glimmers in the light of eternity and his face is serene. In his left hand he holds a shield with a red Latin cross on a white background, a symbol of the Resurrection. The archangel's right foot rests on a gigantic monster [2], its seven heads and four claws scarcely visible in the midst of a diabolical tangle of animals and things. The underbelly of the beast gives Saint Michael a moment of relative stability, because in fact it is in torsion, with its belly turned upward and seven heads facing downward in free fall. Behind Saint Michael there follows an endless maelstrom of beings, which have turned into hybrid devils during their fall. We see helmets, hands, teeth, butterfly wings, feathers, fish, birds, pigs, bears, apes, twigs, pikes, instruments of measurement and music. Soft garments and bird feathers become claws, tails, thick skins. Several good angels help the archangel in his battle against evil. To his left and right [3 and 54] are angels in albs with sword and helmet to assist him; higher up three angels [4a, 4b, 4c] thrust at the damned with their cross-staffs, while four others [5, 6, 28, 29] already blast the triumph on their horns. The scene is heavenly white and blue above, gradually becoming earthy brown and glowing, hellish yellow at the lower right.

**Fig. 4**
*The Fall of the Rebel Angels*, in: Jacques Legrand, *Livre des bonnes moeurs*, 15th century
Paris, Bibliothèque nationale de France, Mss Smith-Lesouëf 73, fol. 1v°

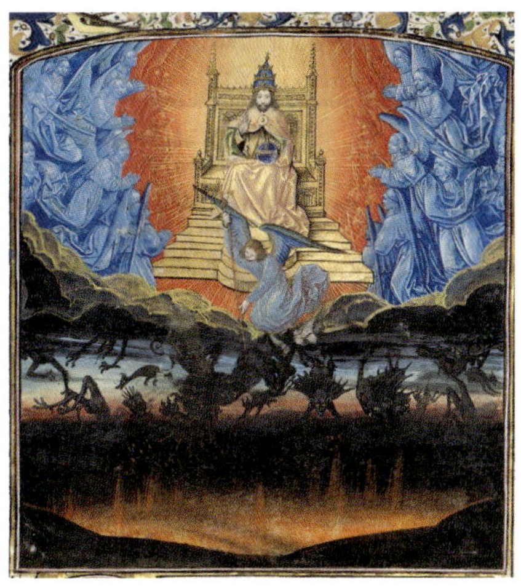

The panel, which Pieter Bruegel the Elder dated and signed "M.D.LXII/BRVEGEL" in the lower left corner, has long been known as the *Fall of the Rebel Angels.* This apocryphal story tells of the first confrontation between good and evil, even before the fall of man, when the highest-ranking angel, Lucifer, or "bearer of light," began to think himself higher than God himself and was therefore cast out of heaven at God's orders. It was the church father Augustine in particular (*De Civitate Dei,* XI), who interpreted Lucifer, as described by Isaiah (14:12), as the devil, which according to him explained how God had not created evil, but that evil manifested itself early on.[1] Angels are beings of light, created to live in wisdom and happiness, but some turned against divine illumination and became dark devils. Augustine moreover situates this dramatic

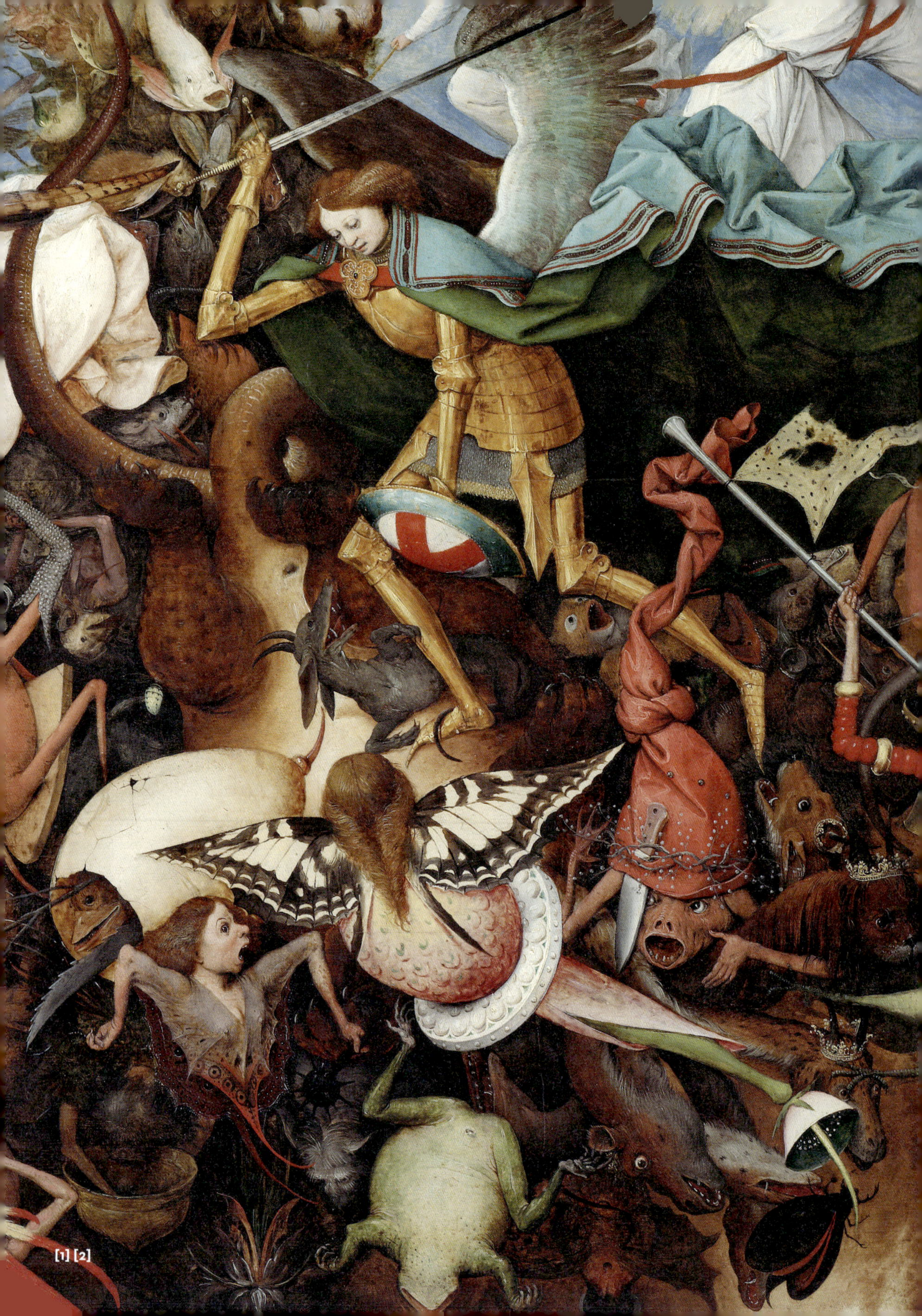

[1] [2]

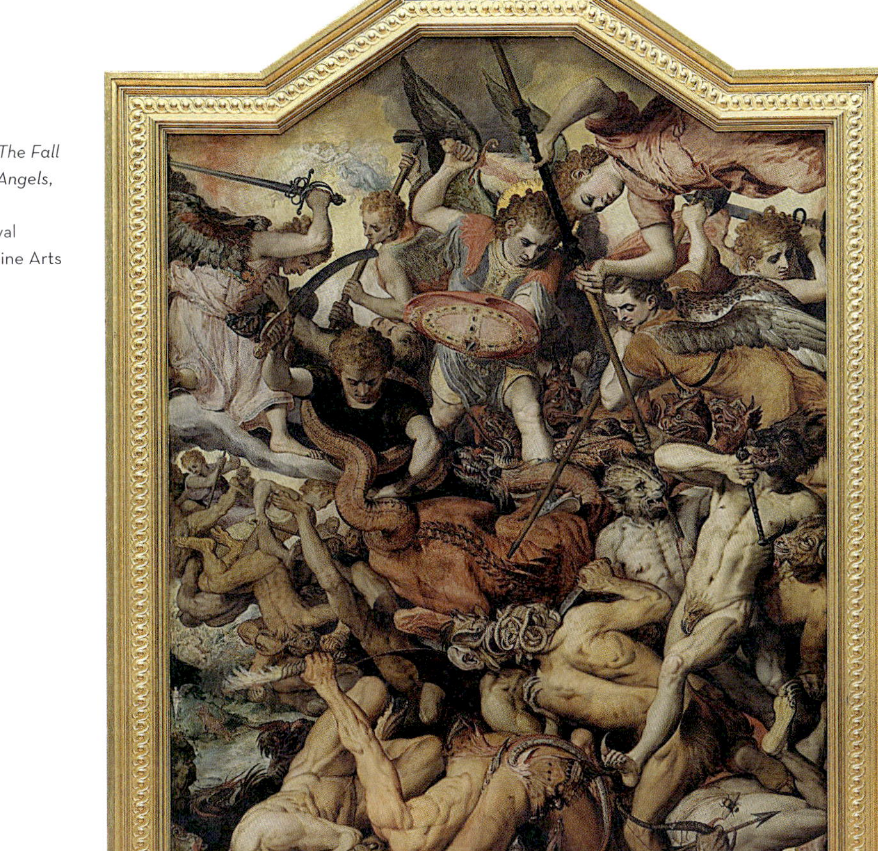

**Fig. 5**
Frans Floris, *The Fall of the Rebel Angels*, 1554
Antwerp, Royal Museum of Fine Arts

moment on the first day of Creation, at the moment when light is separated from darkness (Genesis 1:3-5), which Bruegel has skillfully depicted with the contrast between the light above and dark zone below.[2]

Familiar from devotional treatises such as the fourteenth-century *Speculum Humanae Salvationis*, an illustrated work of popular devotion in which Old Testament narratives are explained as prefigurations of the New Testament, the *Fall of the Rebel Angels* was particularly popular in illuminated book manuscripts. Illuminators usually painted devils as naked black or dark-skinned creatures with horns (fig. 4). In monumental paintings, however, the theme was rather unusual. Barend van Orley (1487/91-1541) may have painted a *Fall of the Rebel Angels* as the central panel of a lost triptych for the Church of St Michael and St Gudule in Brussels.[3] Another well-known example is the altarpiece for the Antwerp Fencers' Guild painted in 1555 by Frans Floris (1520-1570), one of the most prominent painters of the Antwerp art world at the time (fig. 5).[4] This masterpiece must have been familiar to

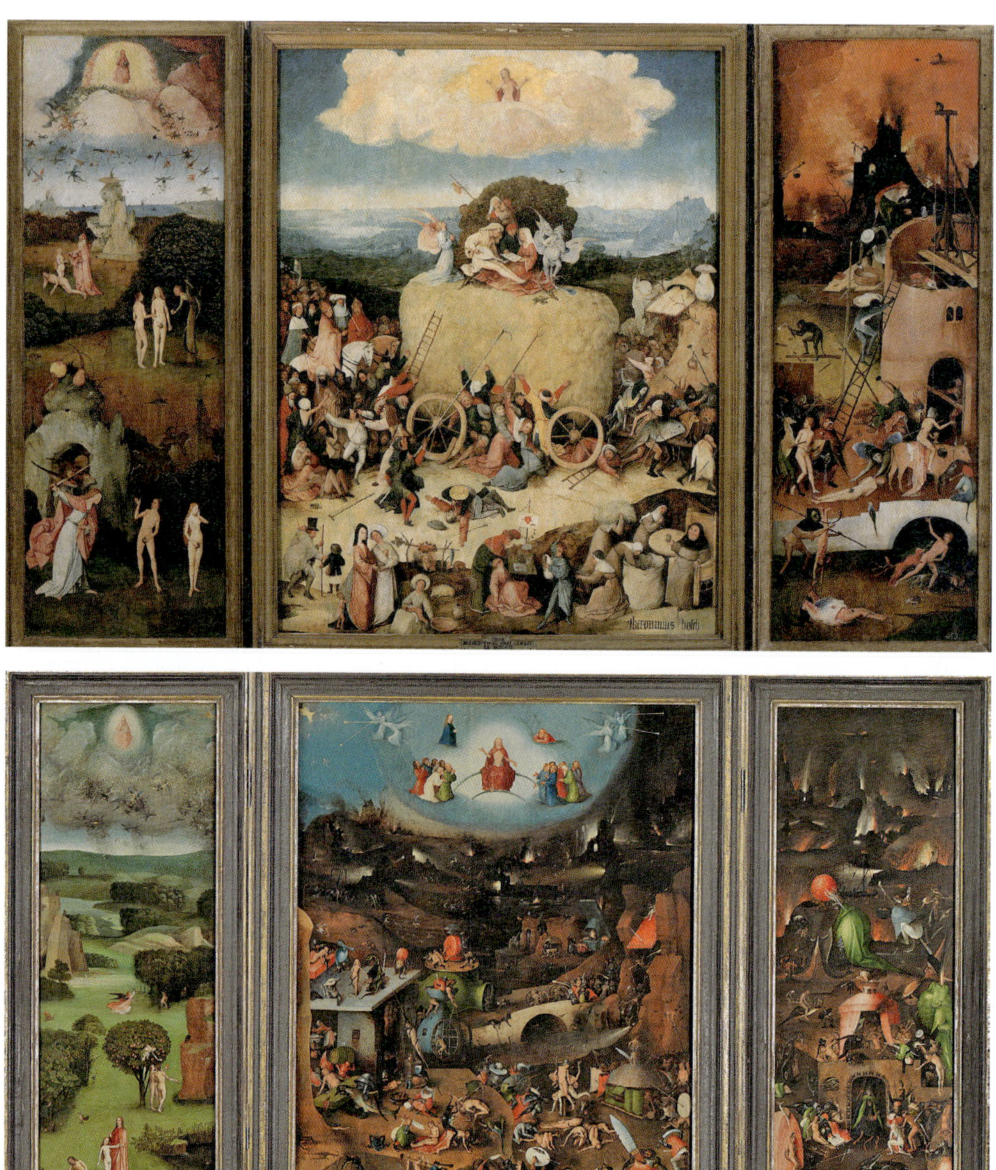

**Fig. 6**
Hieronymus Bosch,
*Paradise, Haywain,*
1500-1516
Madrid, Museo
Nacional del Prado

**Fig. 7**
Hieronymus Bosch and
his studio, *Paradise,*
*Last Judgment,*
1500-1505
Vienna,
Gemäldegalerie
der Akademie der
bildenden Künste

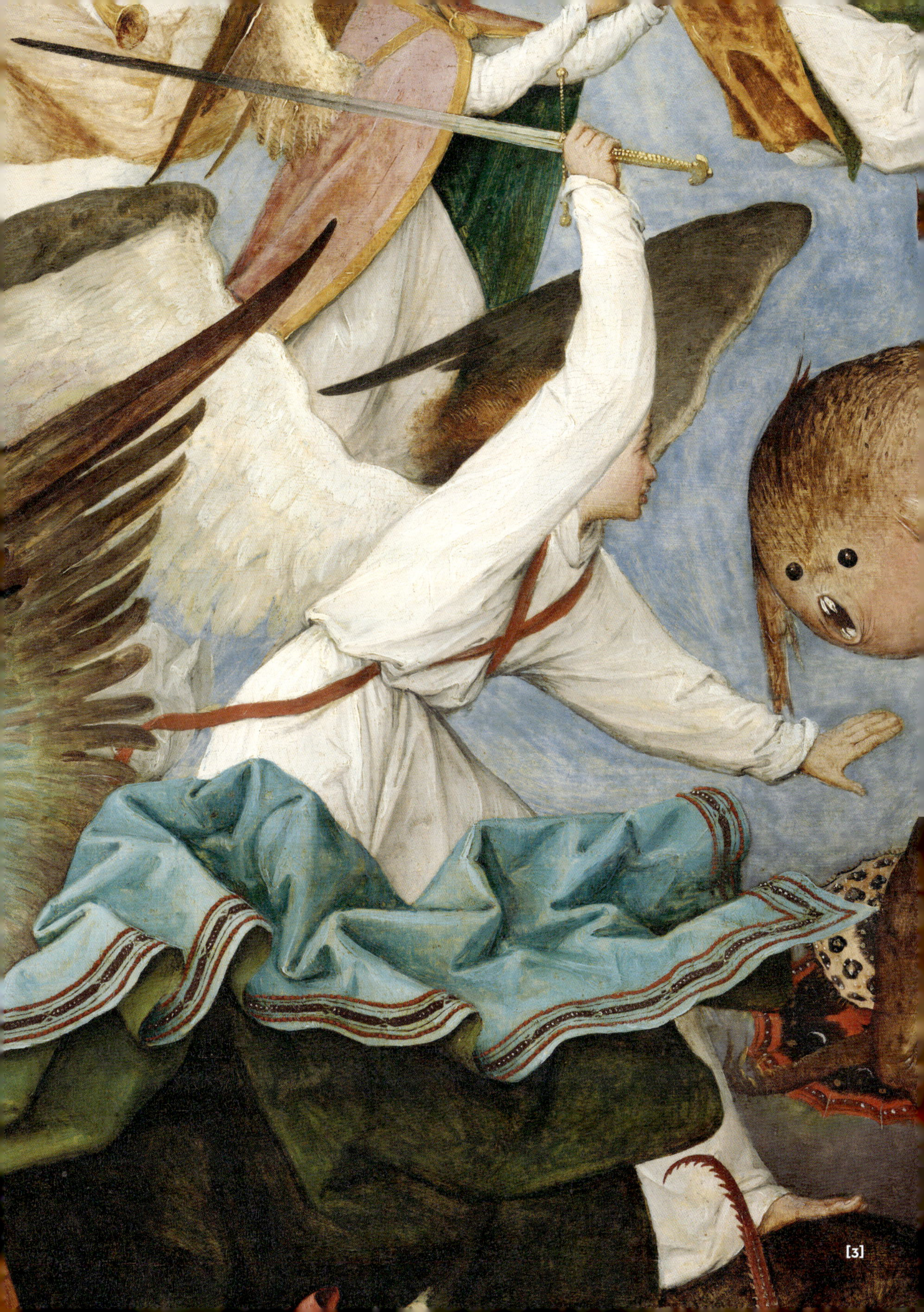

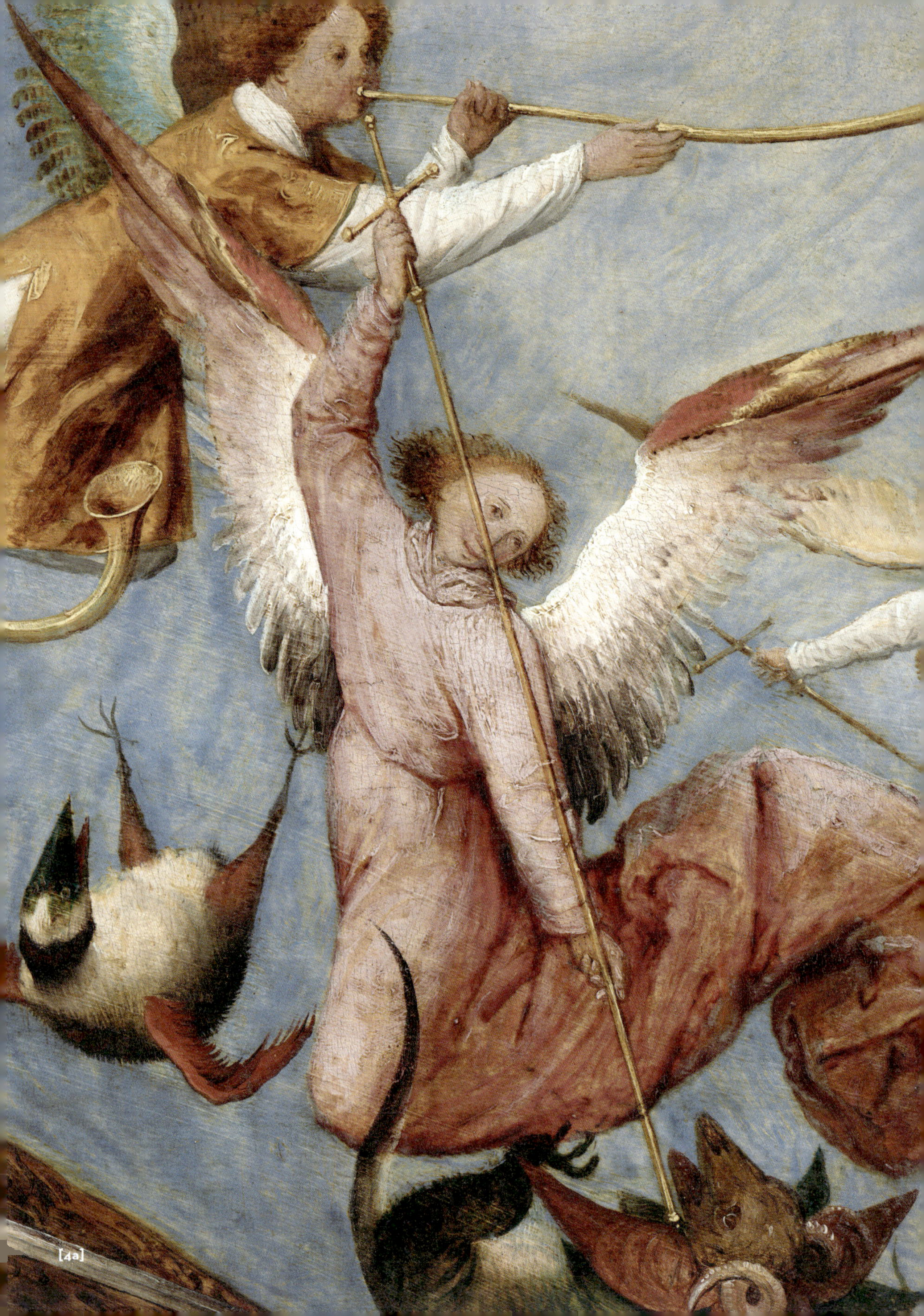

[4a]

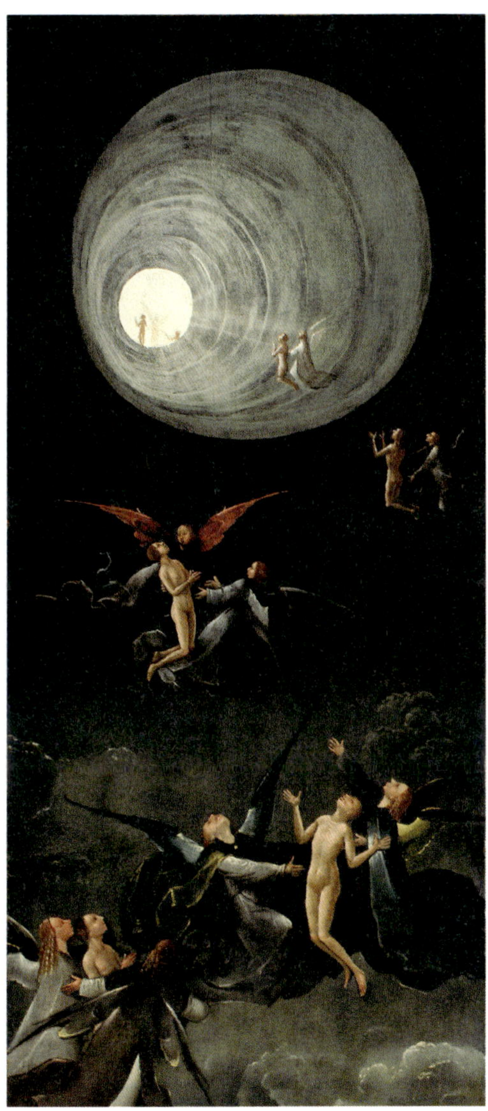

Bruegel, who still lived in Antwerp in 1562, and likewise shows falling angels in a state of transformation, from perfect angelic bodies to diabolical chimeras. Floris broke with the tradition of book illumination and gave the falling angels monstrous animal heads on muscular human bodies modeled after figures in the *Last Judgment* by Michelangelo (1475-1564). Bruegel distanced himself from this Italianizing interpretation and looked to the formal language of one of the most original local masters of the previous generation, Hieronymus Bosch.

Bosch himself only painted the rebel angels as a sort of marginal note in three triptychs. In two of these, the *Haywain* (fig. 6) and the *Last Judgment* (fig. 7), we see on the inner left panel, in the heavenly air above the Garden of Eden, Saint Michael, who drives the rebel angels - who have mutated into insect-like creatures - out of the heavens. In particular, the figure of Saint Michael in the *Last Judgment* triptych, with his golden armor, outspread wings, raised sword, and firm stance, seems to have been a direct model for Bruegel. In Bosch's triptychs, this scene is a prelude to what takes place in the earthly paradise below, where the archangel uses the same weapon to drive Adam and Eve from the garden. In the third triptych, the famed *Garden of Earthly Delights* (fig. 20), the fall of the rebel angels is more implicit. According to Yona Pinson, the monstrous creatures in the left panel, which depicts paradise on earth, suggests that for Bosch the world was already corrupt before the fall of man and that Lucifer, out of revenge for his own exile, disguised himself as a snake and seduced Eve into disobeying God. In the *Speculum Humanae Salvationis*, the fall of the rebel angels is similarly linked, conceptually and typologically, to the Creation and the Fall of man.[5]

**Fig. 8**
Hieronymus Bosch, *Ascent of the Blessed into Heaven*, 1505-1510
Venice, Palazzo Grimani

Bruegel seems to have taken the depiction of concentric heavenly spheres with angels in liturgical garments from miniature painting and enlarged it. Bosch, too, depicted the passage from the earthly to the heavenly sphere as a graduated tunnel in his *Ascent of the Blessed into Heaven* (fig. 8). Bruegel

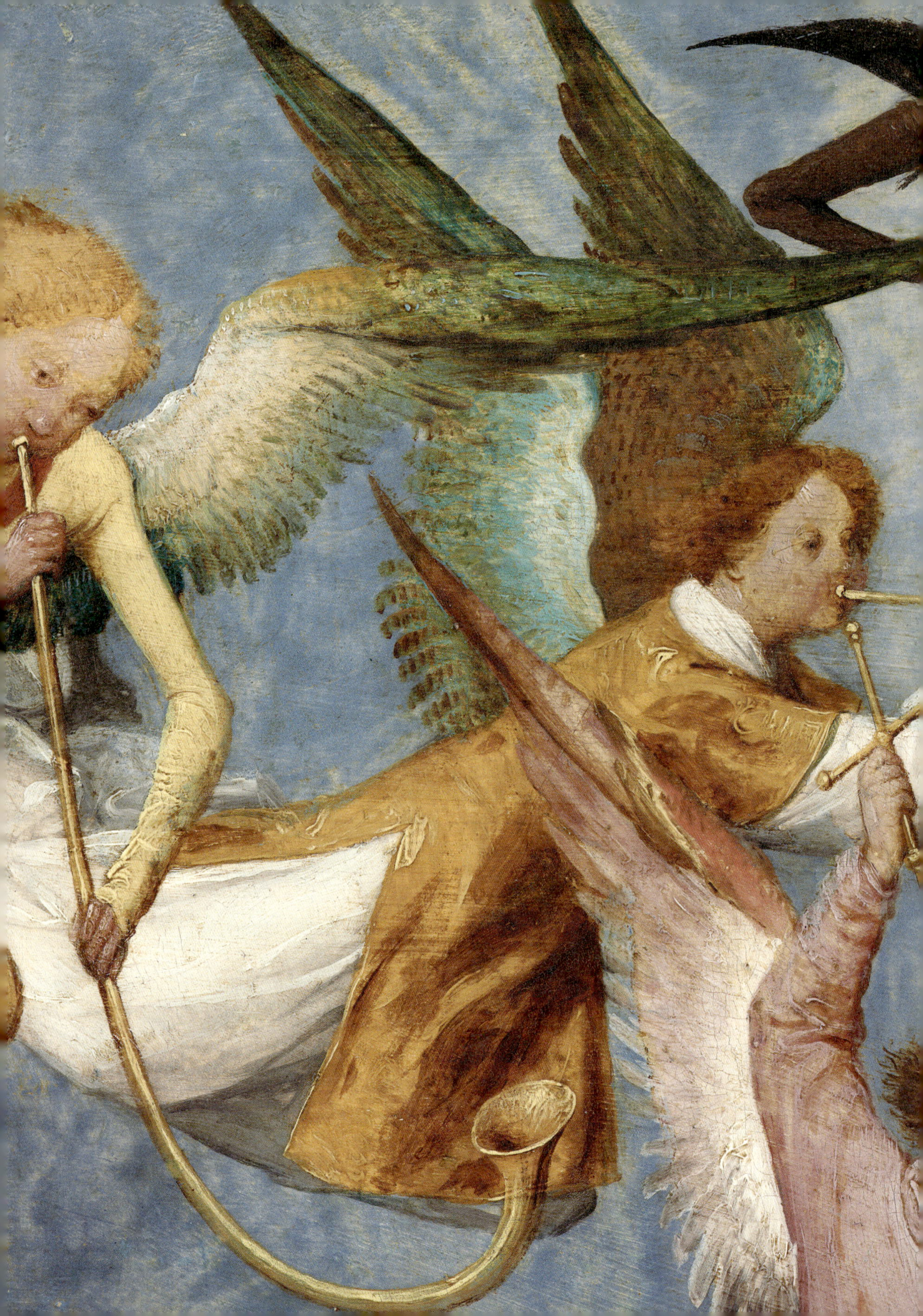

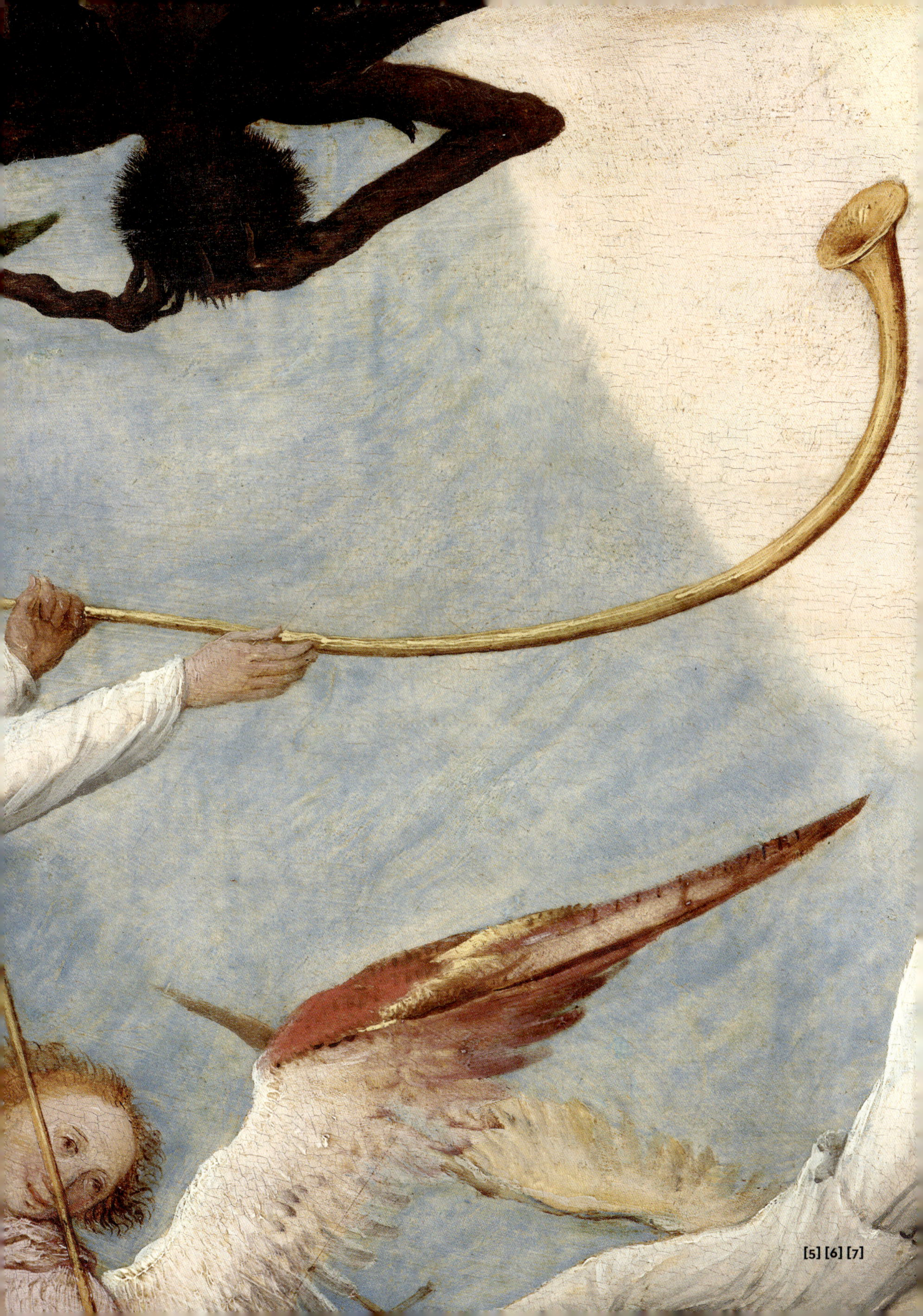

[5] [6] [7]

did not paint this tunnel as Bosch did - that is, as an entryway through which the good souls ascend into the divine empyrean realm - but rather as a maelstrom from which the bad angels come tumbling out of heaven. He cuts across the divine disc of light and its concentric spheres, thereby placing the viewer in the midst of a downward spiral.

It has recently been proposed that the presence of the seven-headed monster does not refer to the *Fall of the Rebel Angels*, but rather to the actions of the archangel Michael during the Apocalypse.[6] In the book of Revelation we read of the appearance of a seven-headed dragon at the end of time:

> XII, 7 And war broke out in heaven; Michael and his angels fought against the dragon. The dragon and his angels fought back, [8] but they were defeated, and there was no longer any place for them in heaven. [9] The great dragon was thrown down, that ancient serpent, who is called the Devil and Satan, the deceiver of the whole world - he was thrown down to the earth, and his angels were thrown down with him.
>
> XIII, 1 And I saw a beast rising out of the sea, having ten horns and seven heads; and on its horns were ten diadems, and on its heads were blasphemous names.

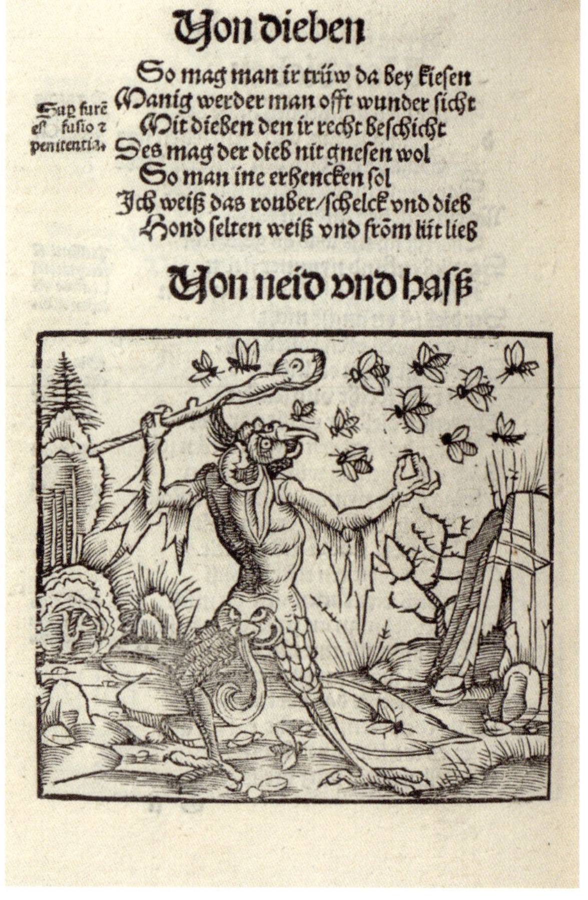

Von dieben

Sup furẽ eſt fuſio ꝛ penitentia.

So mag man ir trüw da bey kieſen
Manig werder man offt wunder ſicht
Mit dieben den ir recht beſchicht
Des mag der dieb nit gneſen wol
So man ine erhencken ſol
Jch weiß das rouber/ſchelck vnd dieb
Vond ſelten weiß vnd frõm lüt lieb

Von neid vnd haſß

**Fig. 9**
Belzebub, *Lord of the Flies*, in: Johannes Grüninger, *Freidanck*, Straβburg, 1508
Nürnberg, Germanisches Nationalmuseum

The beast of the Apocalypse is so well hidden in the diabolical host [2] that it has not always been noticed, or at least not perceived as the most important iconographic component in the picture. The seventeenth-century art collector Peter Stevens, one of the earliest visual witnesses, called the work a "Fall of Lucifer."[7] Bruegel zooms in on the falling multitude: most of the devils fall, literally, with their heads pointing downward. The strange devil at the upper right with a swarm of flies around his hairy, donkey-eared head seems to be Belzebub [8], the most important minion of Lucifer. Belzebub, translated from Hebrew as "Lord of the Flies," appears in this guise sporadically in prints (fig. 9).[8] Bruegel

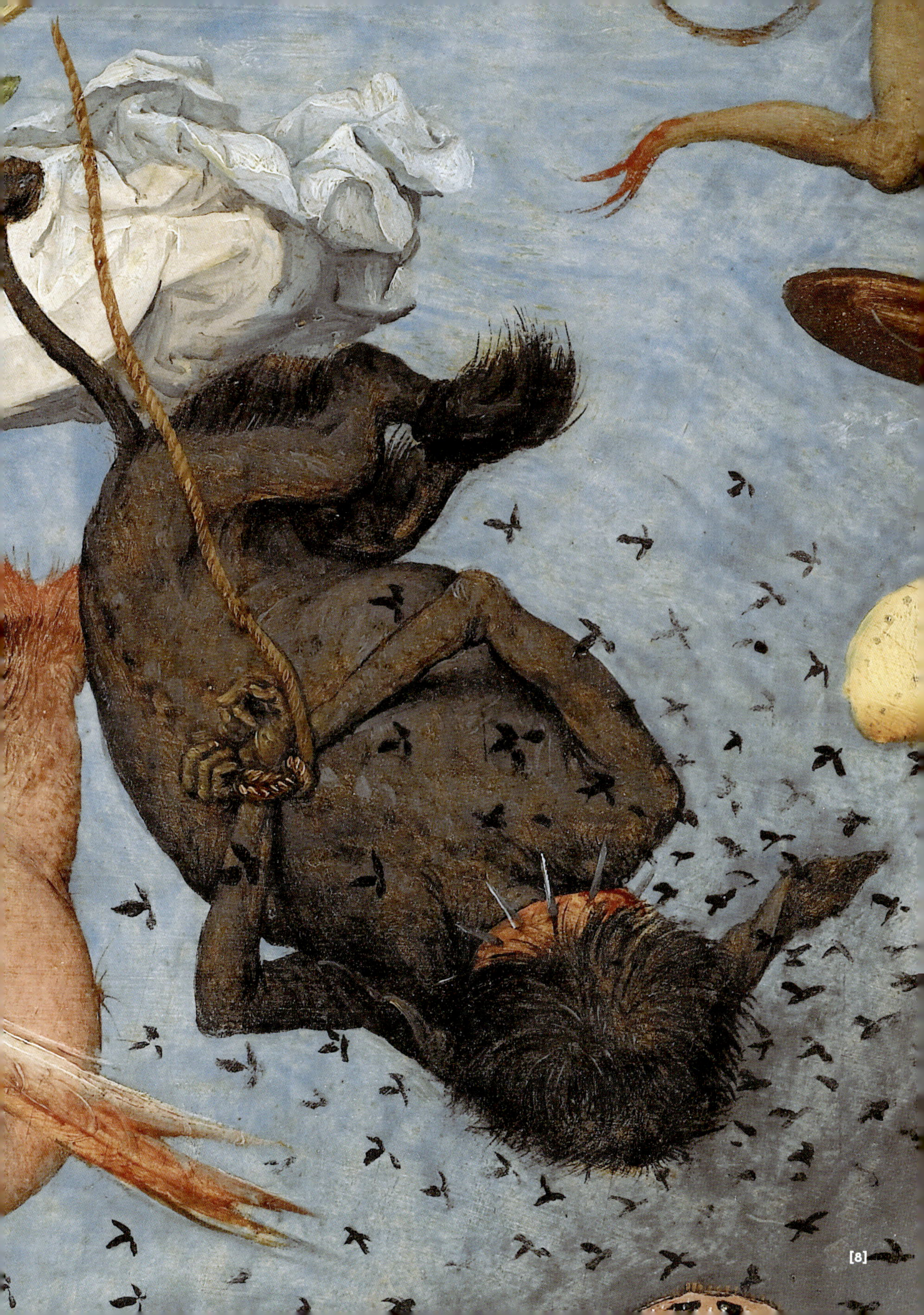

[8]

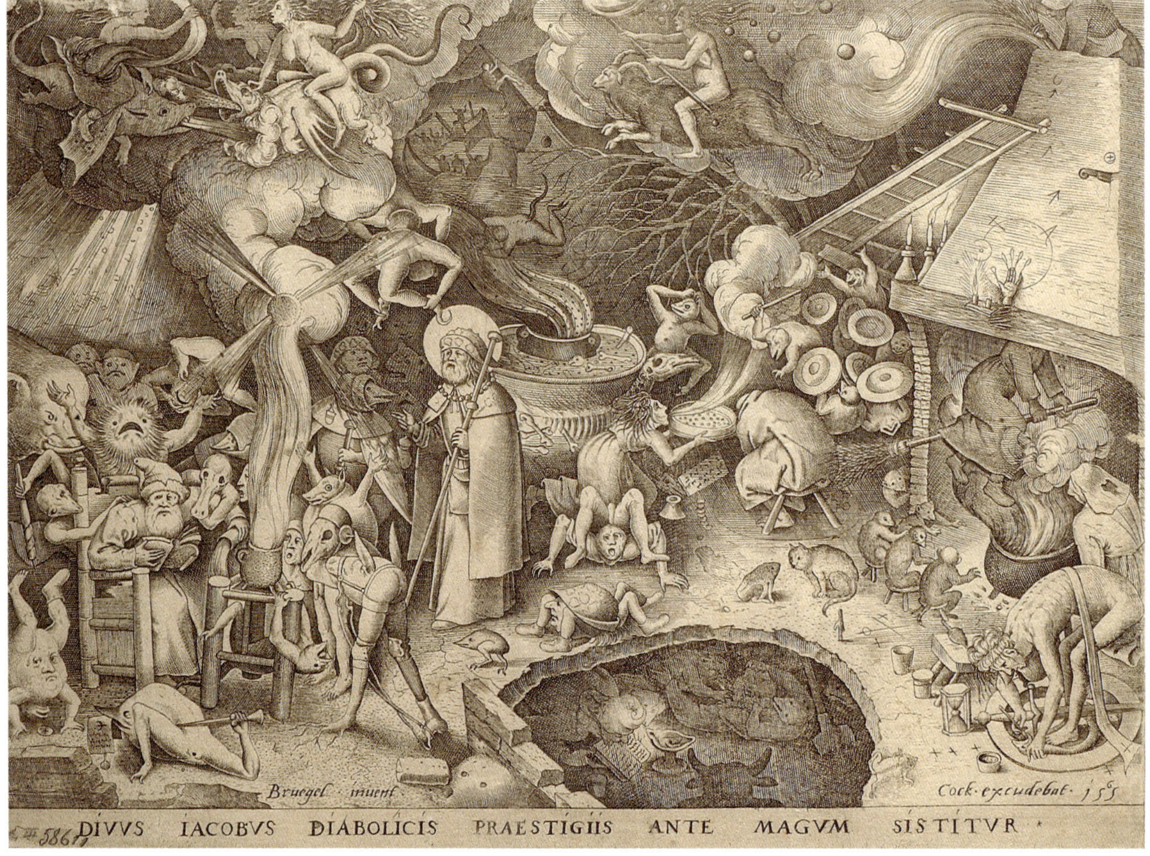


**Fig. 10**
Pieter Bruegel the Elder, *Saint James and the Magician*, 1565
Brussels, Royal Library of Belgium, Print Cabinet

gives him a spiked collar, a donkey-like body and ears, and bound hands. The "binding of the devil" was a popular saying that Bruegel also depicted in the *Proverbs* (fig. 1) and *Dulle Griet* (fig. 27).[9] The backlit half-figure that hangs upside down from the painted surface at the upper left [7] emphasizes the endless depth of the divine light: perhaps it is Lucifer himself, a figure in the margin, like the devil in the hole in the ground in Bruegel's print depicting *Saint James and the Magician* (fig. 10).[10]

Over time, the stories of Lucifer and the monster of the Apocalypse fused together.[11] Bruegel, a master of confusion and surprise, seems deliberately to have striven for this iconographic ambiguity. By referring to the fall of Lucifer before there were humans on earth and to Archangel Michael's struggle with the dragon at the end of time, he shows the permanence of the fight between good and evil, and its most important cause: pride. While Bosch spreads his "all-encompassing gaze at world history from prehistory to the end of time" spatially across the three wings of his triptychs, Bruegel condenses time and space into a single all-encompassing image.[12]

Fig. 11
Anonymous, *Saint Antonius triptych*, after Bosch' s original in Lisbon, ca. 1520-1530
Brussels, Royal Museums of Fine Arts of Belgium

## Bruegel and Bosch

Bruegel was fascinated by the devils of Bosch, and he was not alone. Indeed, Bosch's popularity never waned. Bosch was already copied immediately after his death, as in the case of the *Saint Anthony Triptych* (fig. 11) now in Brussels, painted after the original in Lisbon. The middle of the sixteenth century in particular saw a veritable "Boschiana" industry in the Antwerp art market.[13] One such example is the *Last Judgment* (fig. 12) by Peter Huys (ca. 1515-ca. 1581) from 1554, which clearly recalls Bosch's *Last Judgment* and which was itself copied in turn.[14] Don Felipe de Guevara, a Spanish nobleman in the entourage of Philip II, noted in his *Commentarios de la Pintura* (ca. 1560) that this copying mania did not always produce works of the highest quality. "What Bosch did with wisdom and decorum," he writes, "others did and still do with neither insight nor judgment," simply because they have seen how this sort of painting is in demand.[15]

### *Bruegel as Bosch in prints*

One person who took advantage of the demand for Boschiana and further fanned the flames of fashion was the Antwerp print dealer and publisher Hieronymus Cock (1507-1570).[16] Cock was a cosmopolitan publisher, who after the obligatory trip to Italy around 1550 opened a business in Antwerp with the ambitious name *In de Vier Winden* (At the Four Winds.) He initially specialized in landscapes and Italian or Italianate masters, but from around 1557 designs inspired by Bosch begin to turn up in his portfolio. Many of these designs are signed "Hieronymus Bosch inventor," even when these works were

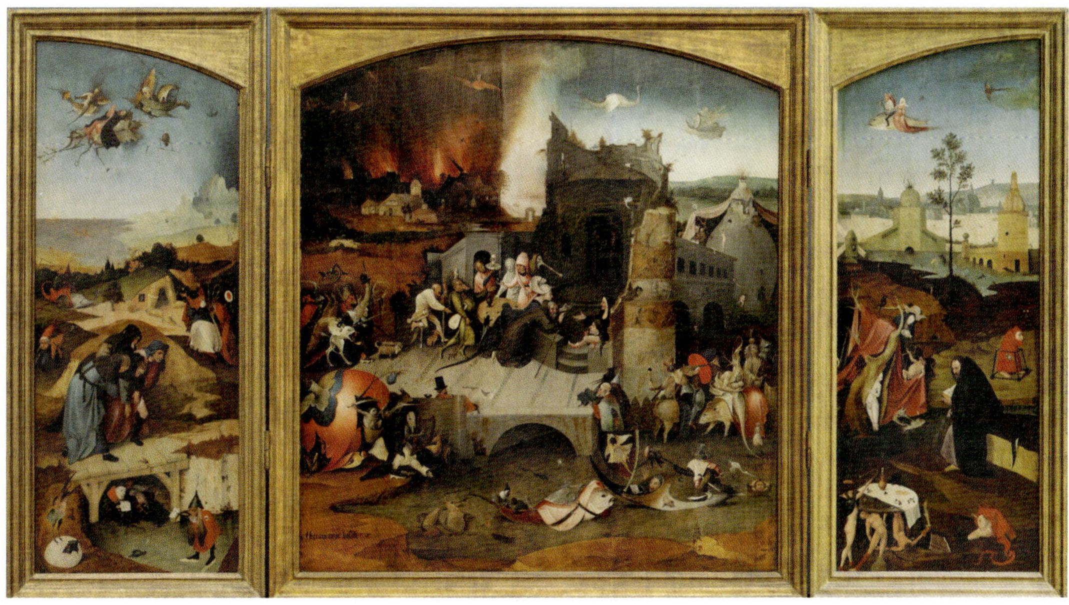

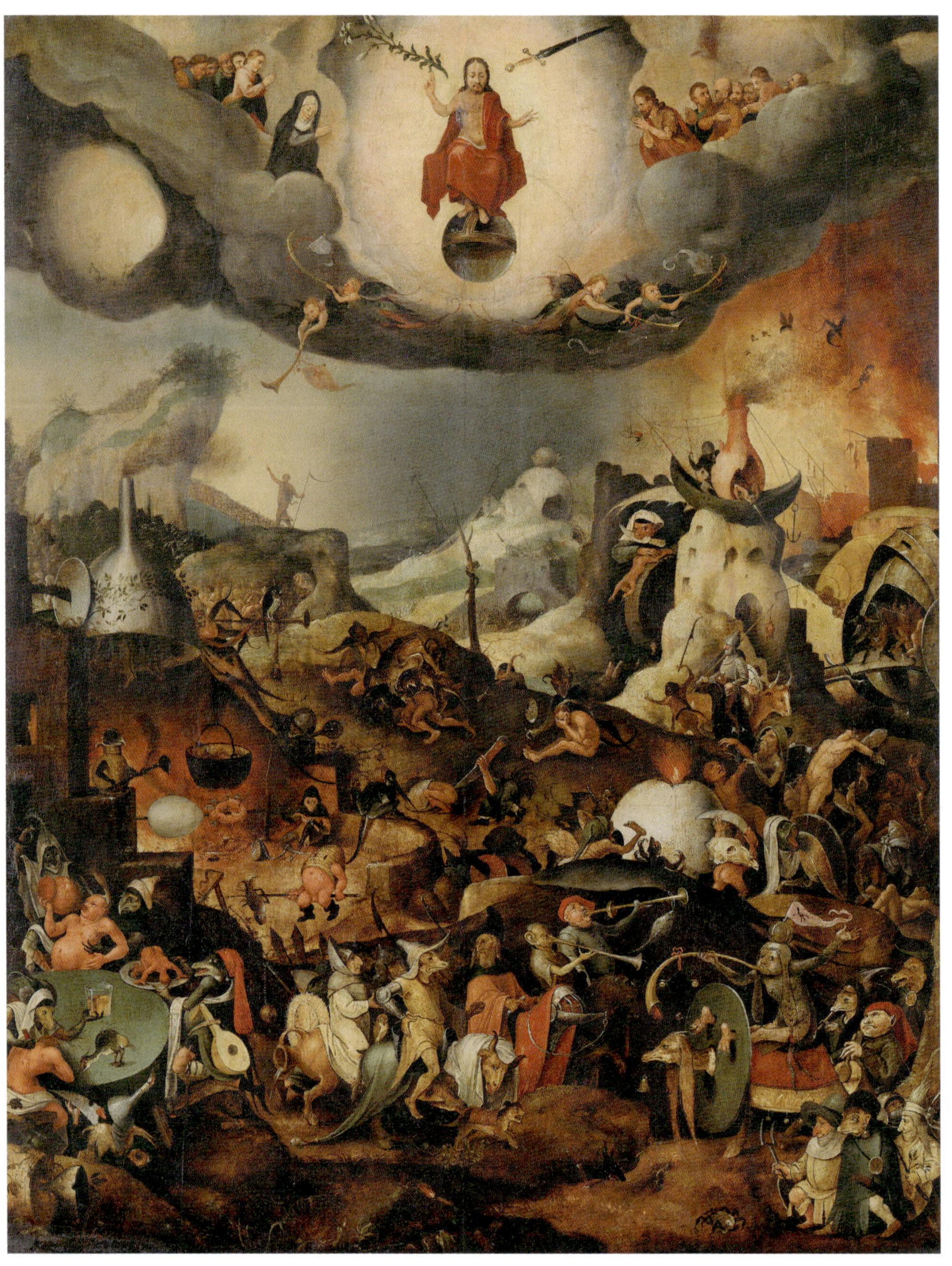

**Fig. 12**
Peter Huys, *Last Judgement*, 1554
Brussels, Royal Museums of Fine Arts of Belgium

**Fig. 13**
Pieter Bruegel the Elder, *Big Fish Eat Little Fish, (Hieronymus Bosch inventor)*, 1557
Brussels, Royal Library of Belgium, Print Cabinet

not actually based on original drawings by Bosch, but rather inventions in the master's style. In fact, one of the earliest prints signed in this manner, *Big Fish Eat Little Fish* (fig. 13), can be securely attributed to Pieter Bruegel: the preparatory drawing is signed by Bruegel.[17] Cock must have thought that the print would sell better under the name of Bosch than that of its actual draftsman, the still little-known Bruegel, who until then had provided Cock primarily with landscapes. Bruegel's designs in the style of Bosch proved very successful and Bruegel was soon recognized as their true inventor: between 1556 and 1558 he signed the series of the *Seven Deadly Sins* or *Vices* with his own name.[18]

The series announces the *Fall of the Rebel Angels,* not only because of its Boschian inventions, but also because Bruegel "catalogues" the sins, as it were, in seven separate plates. Bruegel depicts each of the seven sins as a female allegorical figure accompanied by a naturalistic animal: Wrath (fig. 14) is accompanied by a bear, Sloth sleeps on a donkey, Pride stands next to a peacock, a frog or toad creeps alongside Avarice, Gluttony sits on a boar, Envy points to a turkey, and a cock perches on the seat of Lust.[19]

Bruegel incorporated these same animals again in his design for *Fortitudo* (Fortitude) (fig. 15) from the series of the *Seven Virtues*, the pendant to the

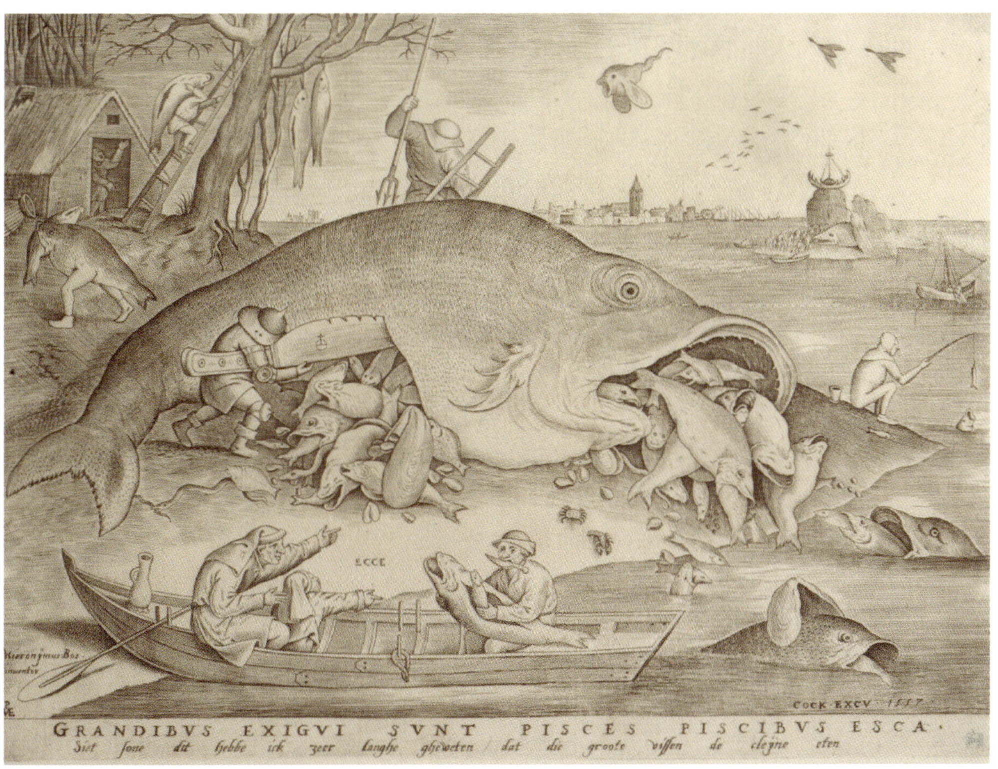

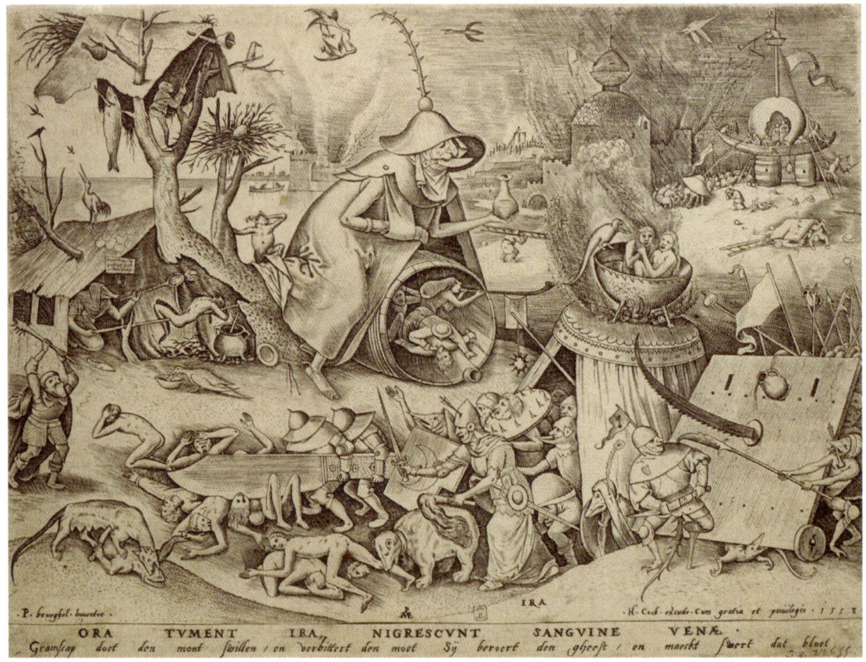


**Fig. 14**
Pieter Bruegel the Elder, *Ira/Wreath*, 1558. From the series of the *Seven Vices*. Brussels, Royal Library of Belgium, Print Cabinet

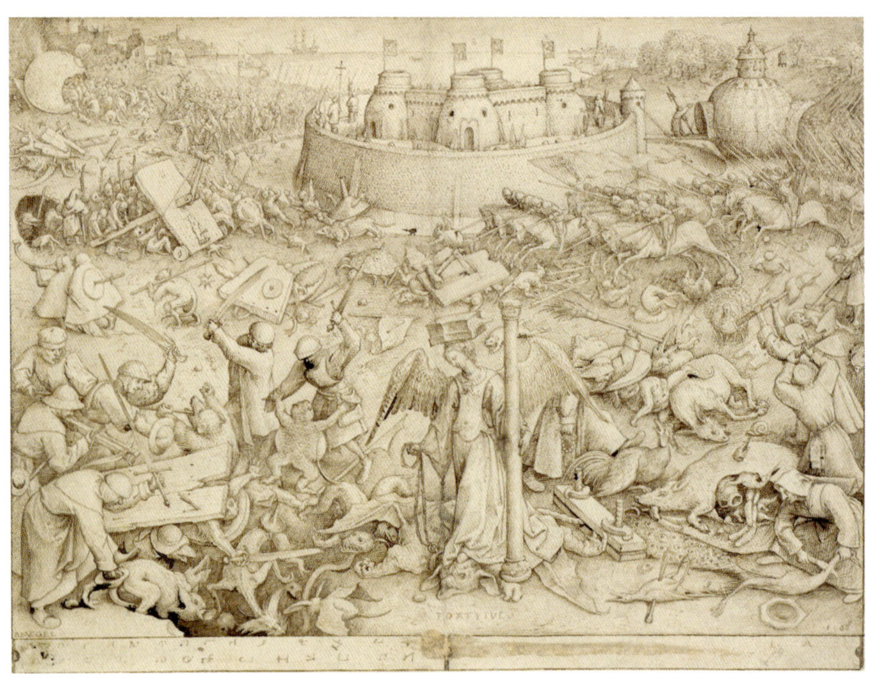

**Fig. 15**
Pieter Bruegel the Elder, *Fortitudo/ Fortitude*, 1560. From the series of the *Seven Virtues*; Rotterdam, Museum Boijmans Van Beuningen

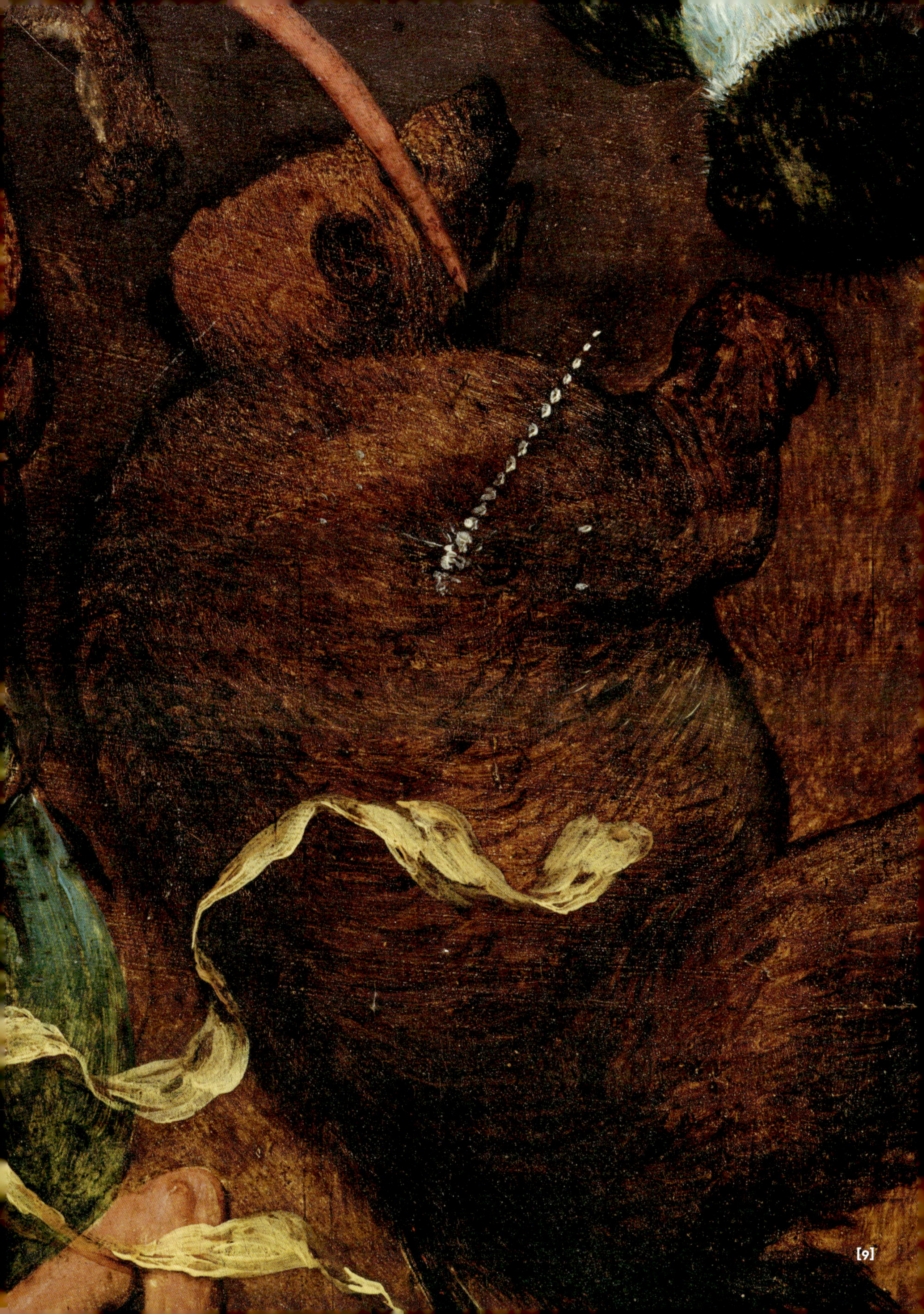

[9]

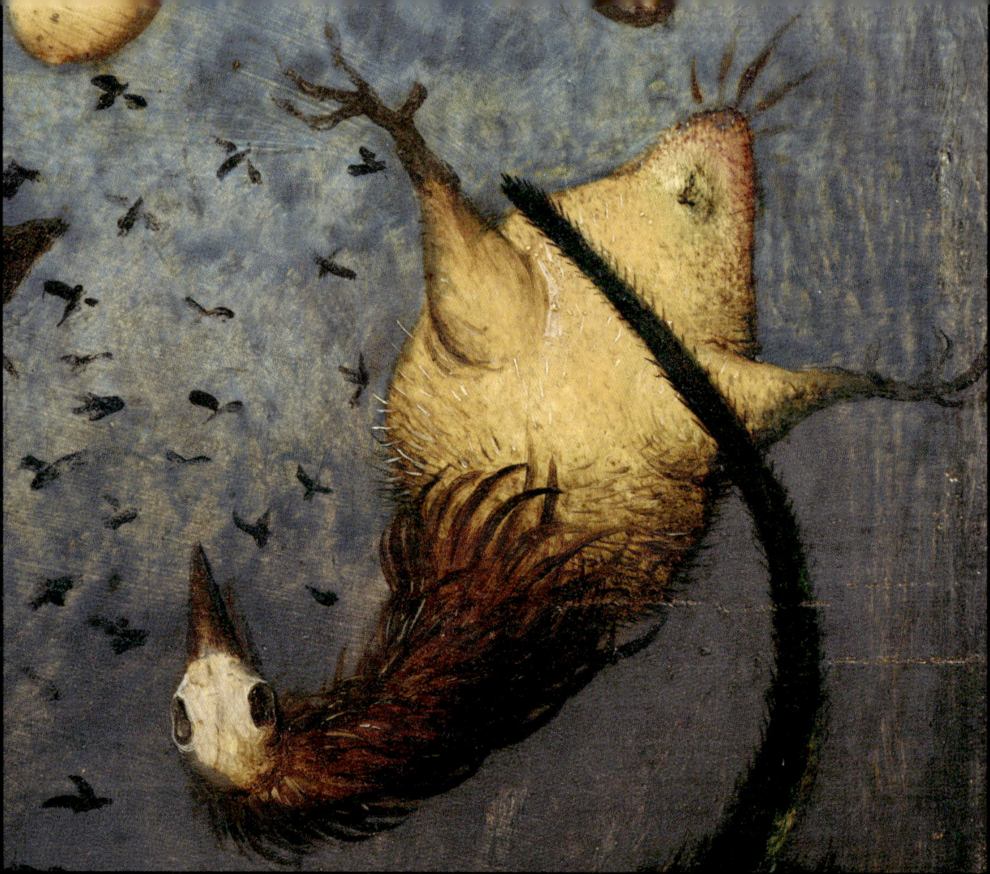

[10]

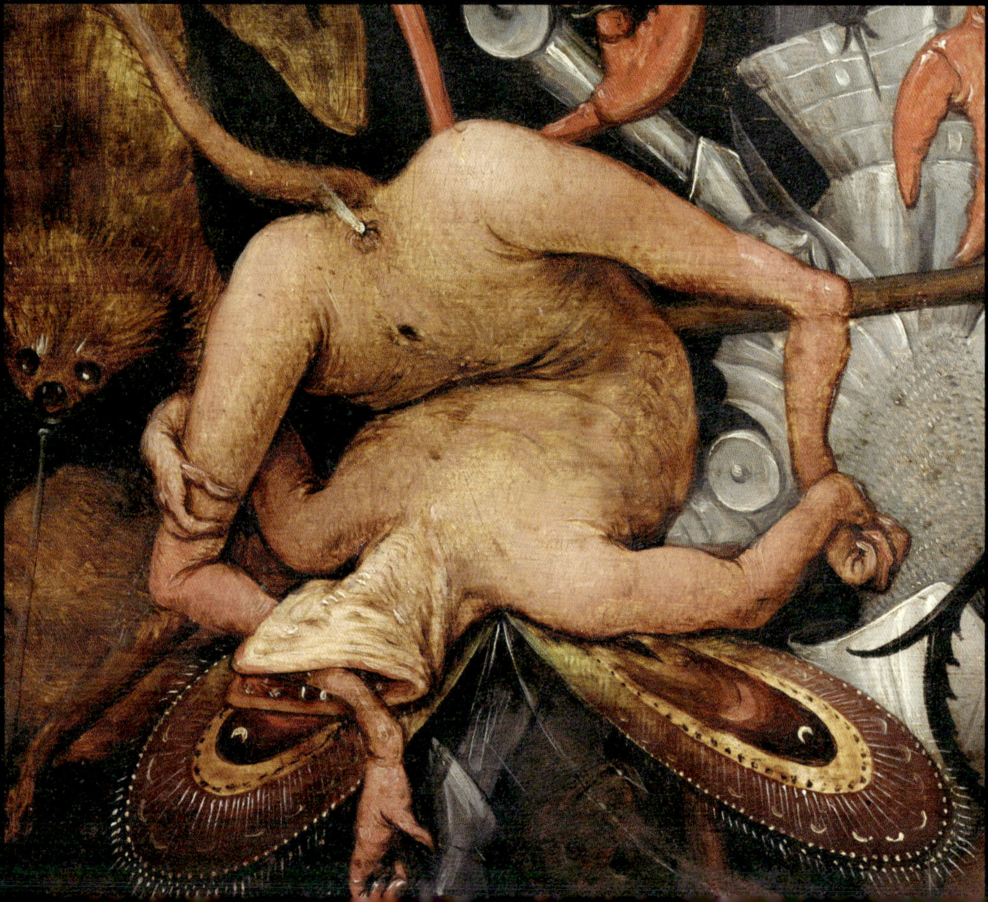

[11]

*Seven Vices* that Cock published in 1559-60.[20] Together with the men and women who follow her example - soldiers, housewives, people of all walks of life - Fortitude engages in fighting hybrid demons, and combats the seven sinful animals: bear, donkey, peacock, toad, boar, turkey, and cock.[21] The composition, with the principal winged figure in the middle, the helpers with raised swords, and the inscription added by Cock ("To conquer one's impulses, to restrain anger and the other vices and emotions: this is true fortitude") make the *Fortitudo* print a forerunner of the *Fall of the Rebel Angels.* Just as calm and collected as Saint Michael, *Fortitudo* - with her traditional column, but here exceptionally depicted as an angel with wings and a breastplate - tramples a chained monster.[22]

The falling angels in Bruegel's painting of 1562 are also guilty of sin, and a number of them take on the form of the same animals, among them the brown bear at the far right [9] and the boar [18] just under the arm of the good angel at the left. The black monster at the upper right, who may be Belzebub [8], seems to have a donkey's ears, and the bird next to him may be a plucked peacock [10].[23] Diagonally beneath them is a dog [43] fighting with a winged lizard [44], gravely injured by the blow of the sword of the good angel to the left. Near the bottom we see a toad [16].

In the *Fall,* Bruegel's devils, like those of Bosch, are composites of different sorts, mingling angel, animal, and thing. What makes Bosch's monsters particularly uncanny is their quasi-human character, whether in terms of anatomy, behavior, or clothing. In Bruegel's painting of the heavenly battle between good and evil there are no human beings present, but the human characteristics of the fallen angels leaves no doubt as to their relevance for humanity, its nature and experience. Let us therefore examine in more detail how Bruegel transforms his angelic inventions into devils by taking inspiration from Bosch.

### *Falling angels in the style of Bosch*

In the lower left-hand corner, just above Bruegel's signature, we see a devil with a human body and a lizard's head that bites his own arm while upside down, his anus turned towards the viewer, shitting [11]. Everything associated with the anus and its excretions was associated with the devil in the time of Bosch and Bruegel: Bosch's falling angels (figs. 6 and 7) also break wind.[24] Bruegel paints another fallen angel that breaks wind, a beast with lobster claws, the rest of its body obscured from sight [37].

Immediately above his shitting companion, a devil with soft pink angel's cheeks blows a windinstrument that resembles a shawm [12]. What has become of his body and legs is hidden behind the next monster with a lobster's head and claws and a hurdy-gurdy for a body [13]. The hurdy-gurdy was the musical instrument of the blind and beggars, as depicted by Bruegel in *The Parable of the Blind* (fig. 16).[25] Its music signals those who cannot see with their eyes, or their hearts. Bosch transformed it into an instrument of torture on the right panel of the *Garden of Earthly Delights* (fig. 17).

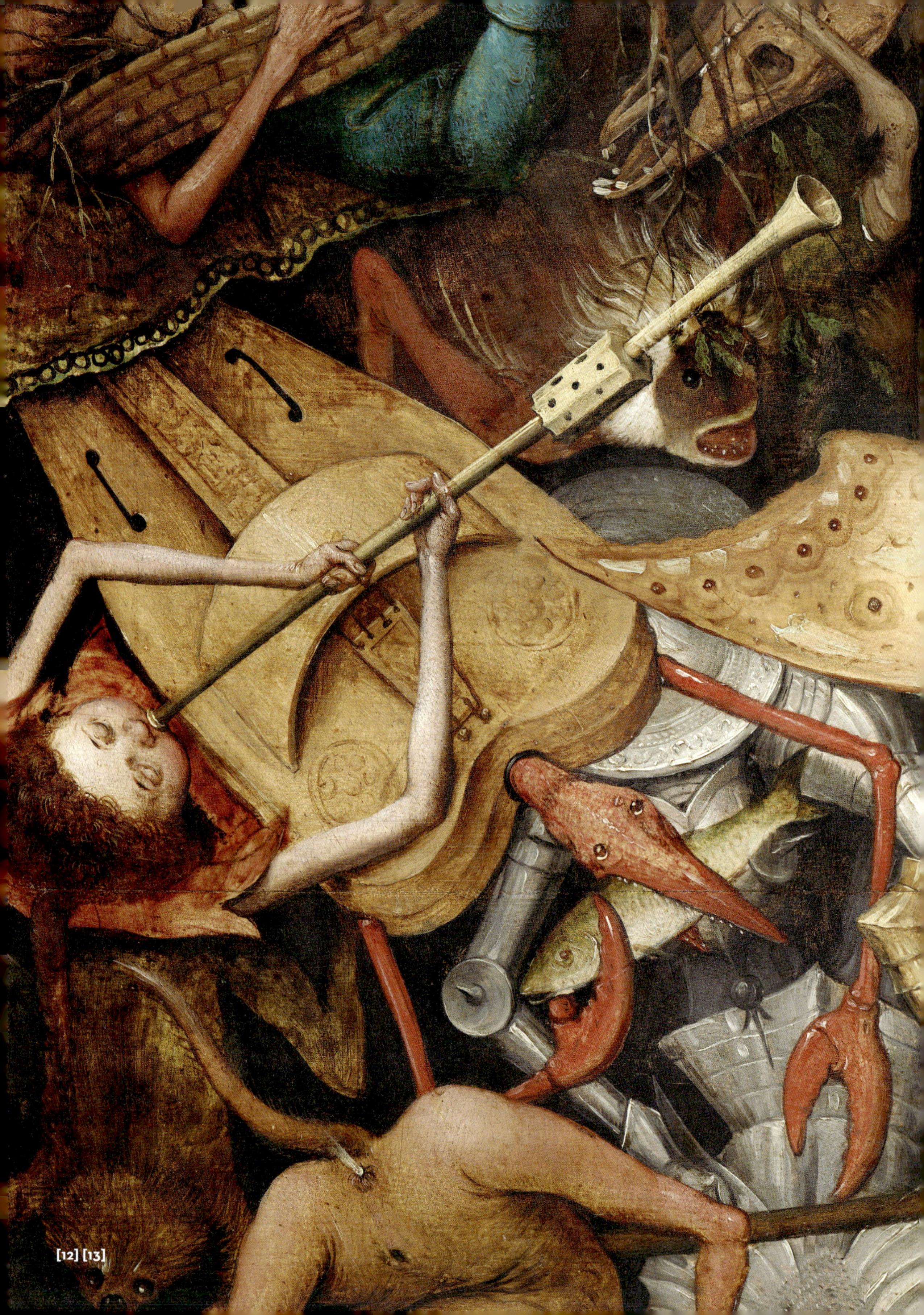

[12] [13]

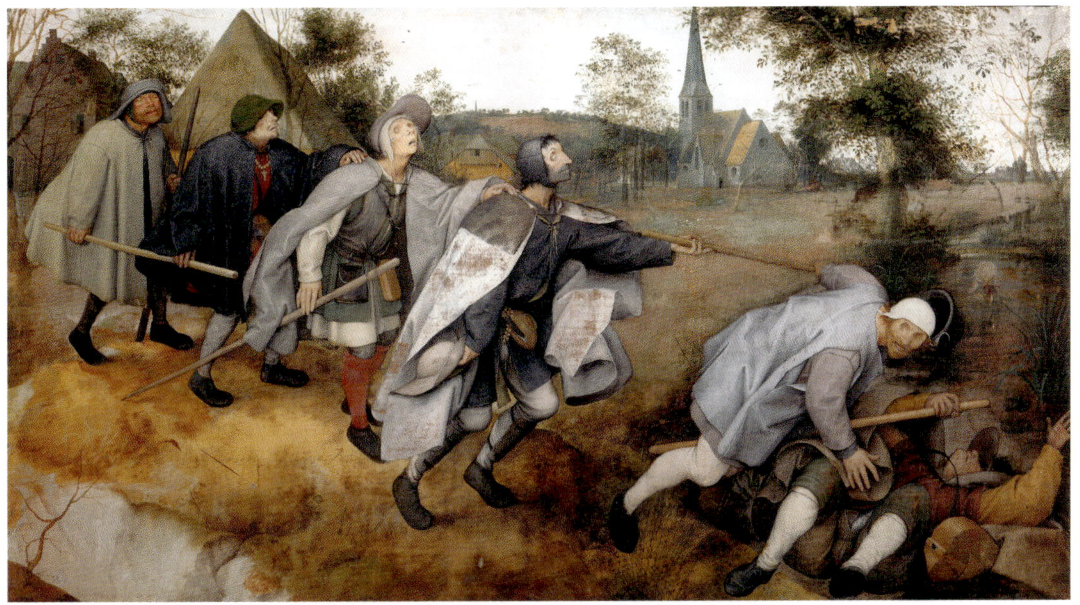

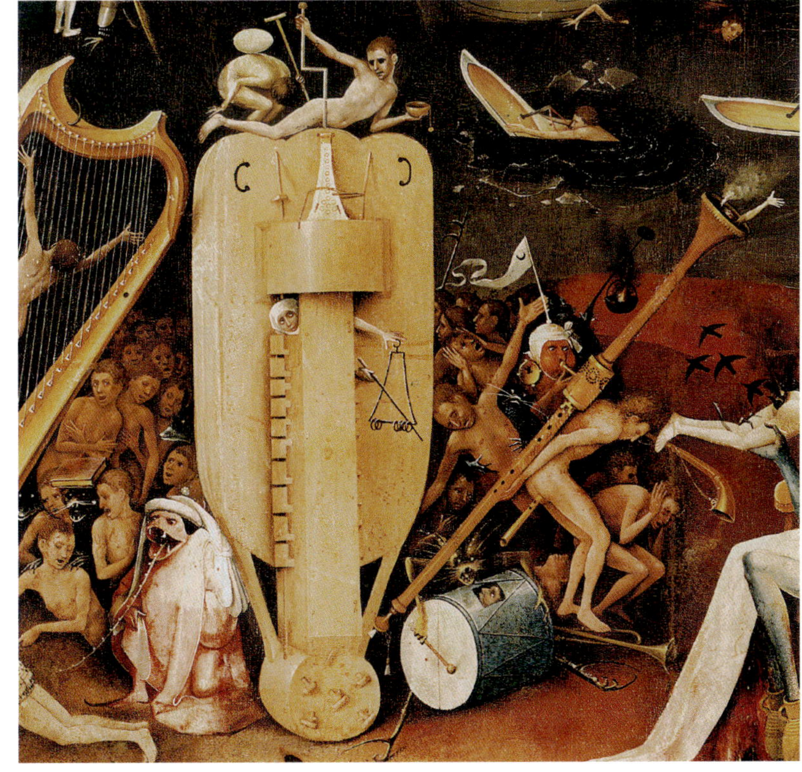

**Fig. 16**
Pieter Bruegel the Elder, *Parable of the Blind*, 1568
Naples, Museo Nazionale di Capodimonte

**Fig. 17**
Hurdy-gurdy, detail of figure 20 (Hieronymus Bosch, *Garden of Earthly Delights*)
Madrid, Museo Nacional del Prado

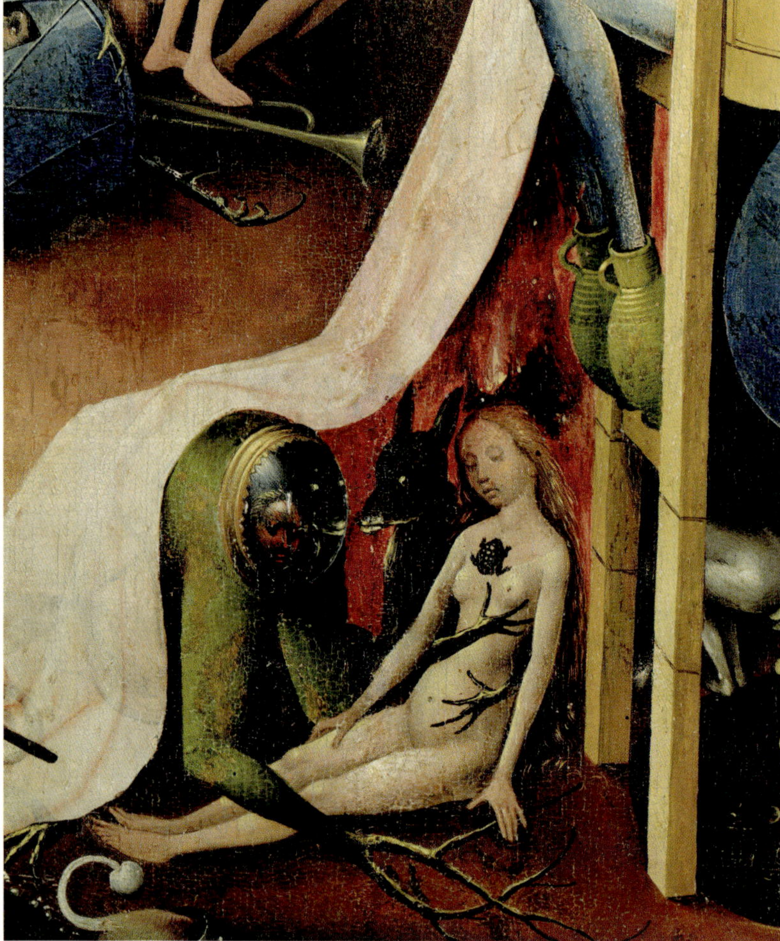

**Fig. 18**
Twig-monster, detail of figure 20 (Hieronymus Bosch, *Garden of Earthly Delights*) Madrid, Museo Nacional del Prado

Above the hurdy-gurdy flies a monster made of twigs [14], which strains to protect her infernal brood from the arc of a good angel's sword. Its arms and legs betray its angelic origins, but its muzzled snout is cruel and fish-like. Dry twigs sprout from several of Bosch's creatures (fig. 18), evoking a party-goer's attribute with diabolical connotations, or perhaps a symbol of worthlessness.[26] A few green leaves and the burst pomegranate that serves as its left foot reveal its vain hopes of fertility, particularly here, in the presence of the angel. Bosch, too, placed the pomegranate, the *malum punicum,* on the threshold between good and evil - literally, on the gates of paradise on the left panel of the *Haywain* (fig. 6). On the one hand, the pomegranate is the fruit that springs forth from the Enclosed Garden, as described in the Song of Songs (4:12-13); on the other, it is associated with the forbidden fruit of the Tree of Knowledge (Genesis 2:9), the origin of all evil.[27]

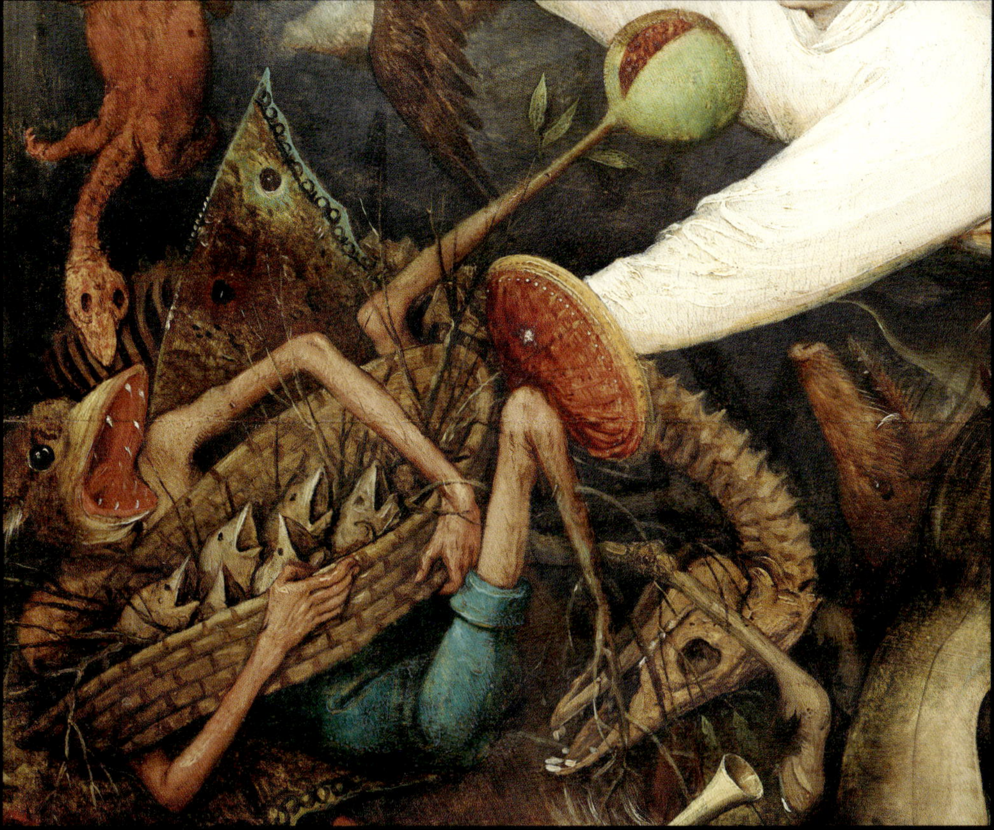

[14]

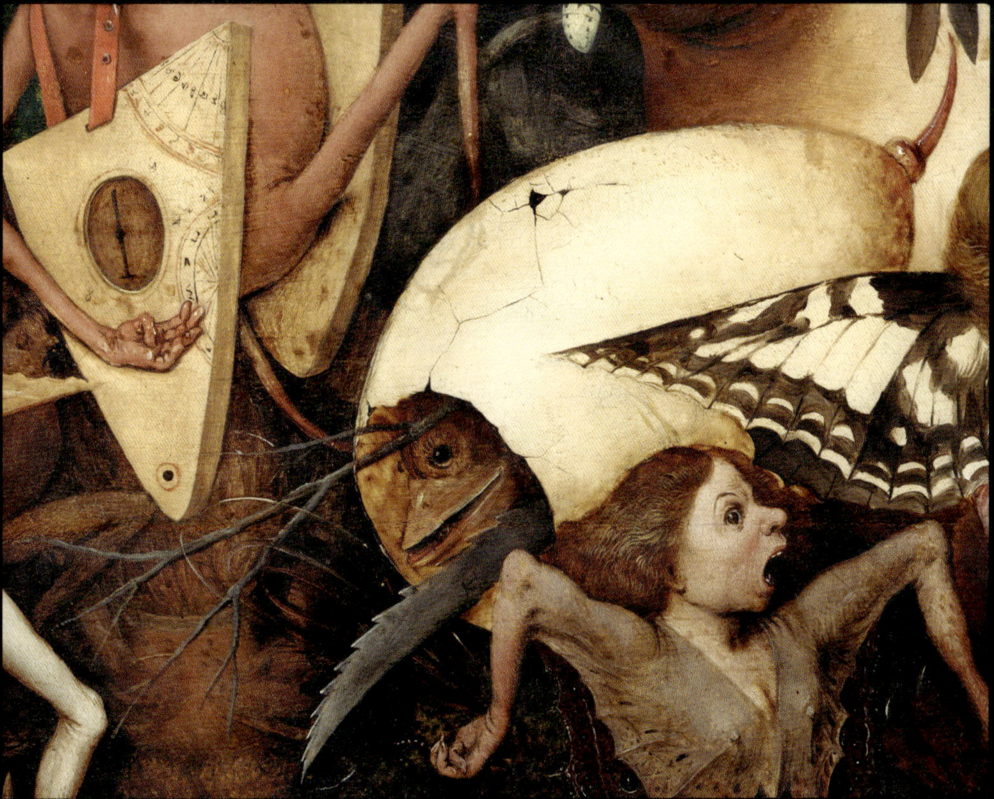

[15]

The fruitless propagation of the fallen between heaven and hell is further suggested by various other Boschian monsters, such as the puffed-up bird-fish [51] that unbuttons its own pregnant belly, even before its eggs are fully formed; the broken egg of the twig-chick [15] that risks injuring itself with its own saw-arm, or with the sting on its shell; or birds that lay eggs while in the midst of flight [42]. In Middle Dutch, "door" means both egg yolk and fool, and it is in this sense that both Bosch and Bruegel depict broken eggs - sometimes filled with fools.[28] The eggs of the infertile monsters in the *Fall of the Rebel Angels* seem to foreshadow disaster, like the freshly broken egg out of which emerges a chick that will soon be eaten by its mother in Bosch's *Saint Anthony Triptych* (fig. 11).

Like Bosch, Bruegel depicts the world upside down, a world of falling birds and flying fish. In the *Saint Anthony Triptych* (fig. 11) Bosch paints fish in the heavenly zones above the hallucinating hermit; in the *Fall* Bruegel represents fallen angels with fish-like features. Take the green sea creature at the lower right near the hellish glow [40], for example: part fish, part crab, and with mussel shells for wings. Fish, like eggs, were often an attribute of fools or jesters, and were brought out at the feasts of Carnival and Mardi Gras because both were served as nourishment during Lent.[29] Mussels, too, feature as boats for the foolish or as the perfect hiding place for a lascivious couple on the central panel of the *Garden of Earthly Delights* (fig. 20).[30] The foolishness of the prideful angels undoubtedly echoes in Bruegel's fish-like creatures, as it does in the sundial-man [30] and the helmed "head-hand-man" [50] that strongly resembles the armored head-footers that populate so many of Bosch's paintings (fig. 90).

The fallen angels are not only foolish, but also pestilent and filthy, like toads.[31] A toad creeps across the bust of a seductive woman in the hell panel of the *Garden of Earthly Delights* (fig. 18). The toad [16] directly under Saint Michael in the *Fall of the Rebel Angels* is so corrupt that it hardly needs transforming: its external appearance is monstrous enough as it is.

*Bruegel as the "New Bosch"*

Bruegel's game of imitation and emulation assumes a public of connoisseurs, the sort of public that is characteristic of Bruegel's earliest admirers. Even before Bruegel's premature death in 1569, the Italian connoisseurs Lodovico Guicciardini (1521-1589) and Giorgio Vasari (1511-1574) celebrated him as a second Bosch.[32] But it was above all Domenicus Lampsonius, the Liège humanist and correspondent of Vasari, who translated the market success of Bruegel and Cock into versified art theory. In the *Pictorum aliquot celebrium Germanicae Inferioris effigies*, a series of twenty-three engravings portraying the most renowned painters since Jan van Eyck, published by Cock in 1572, Lampsonius venerates Bruegel as the "New Bosch," who imitates and even surpasses the master's dreams. This early attempt to portray a local, Netherlandish school of painting went hand in hand with studies of Netherlandish antiquity by Ortelius, Hubert Goltzius (1525-1583), and Lambert Lombard (1505-1566), among others. The first verse of the poem under Bruegel's portrait (fig. 3) in Karel van Mander's translation reads:

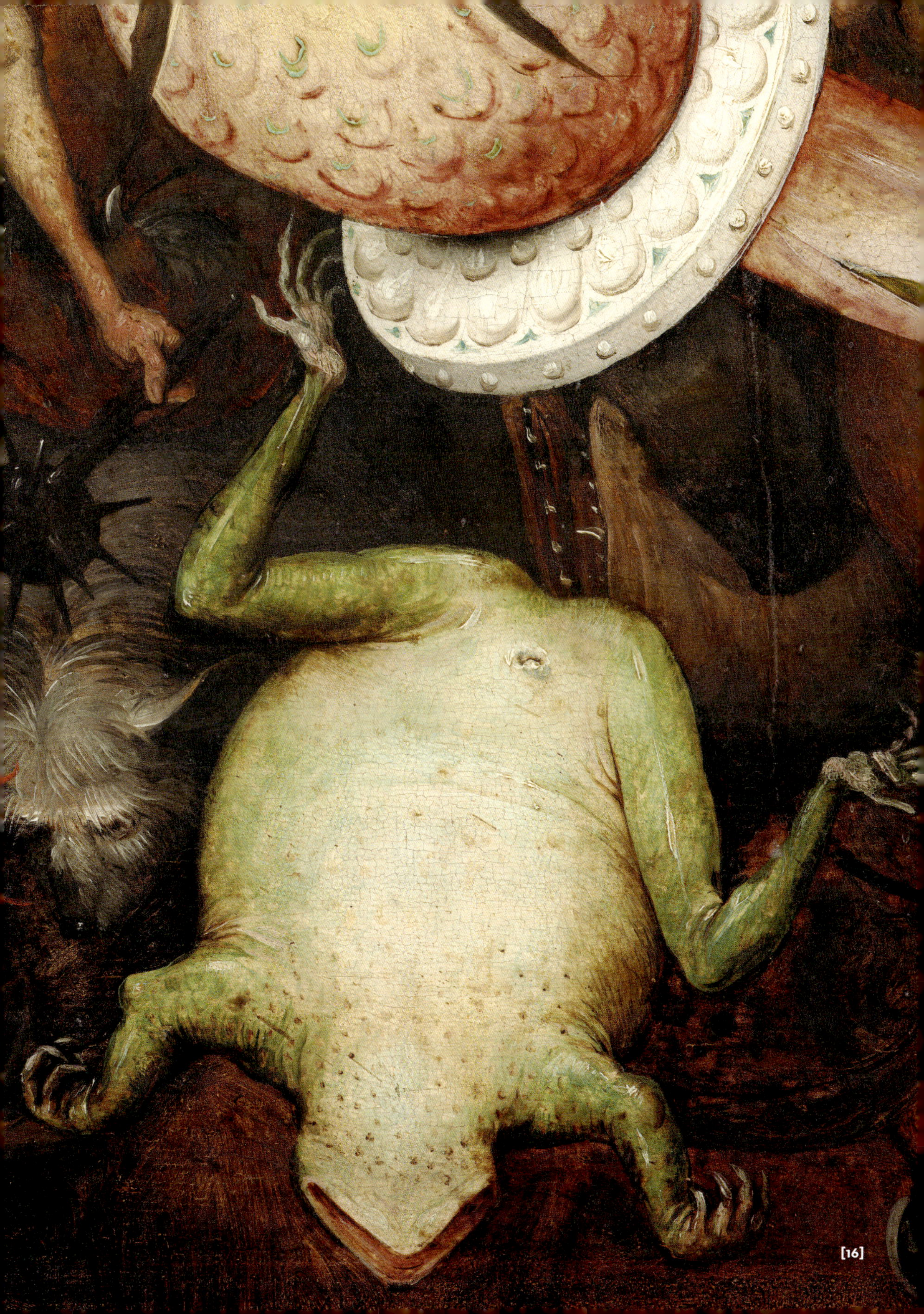

[16]

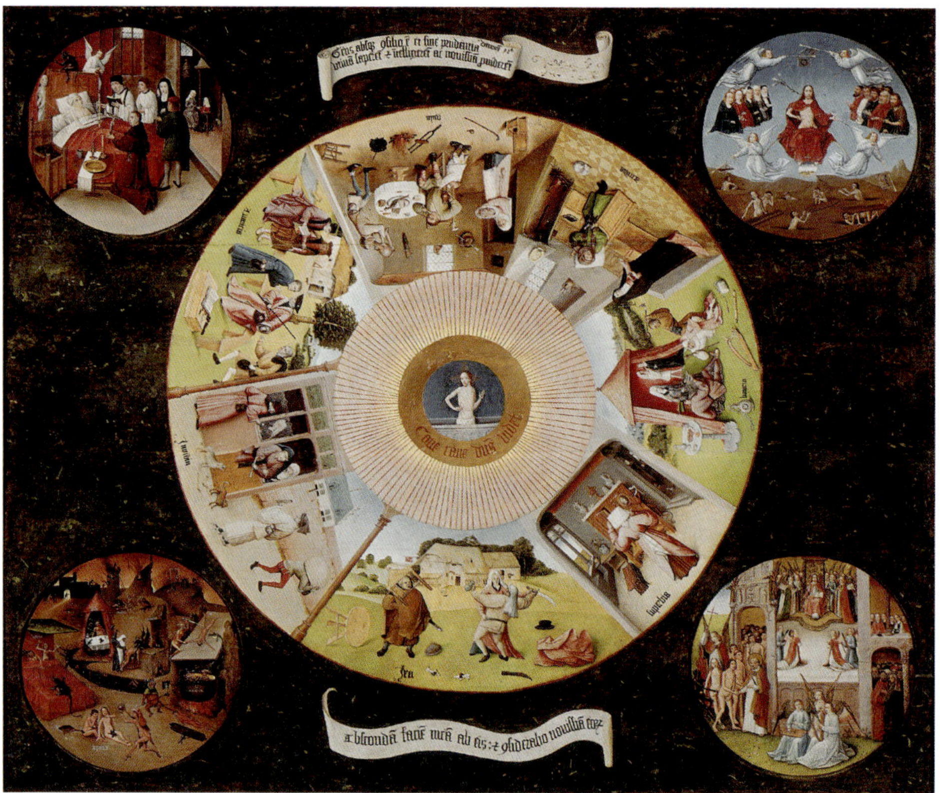

Fig. 19
Hieronymus Bosch, *Seven Deadly Sins*, late 15th century Madrid, Museo Nacional del Prado

> Who is then this Bos? Jeroon once more returned
> To the world, who, trained with the brush and deft with the stylus,
> So imitates for us the dreams of this competent master
> That meanwhile he surpasses him as well?[33]

Bruegel's imitation of Bosch stands out and cannot be overlooked. The real key to Bruegel's work, however, is not so much the question of how he followed Bosch, but rather how, within this framework of imitation and veneration, he distinguished himself from his predecessor. A notable difference is their respective use of perspective. Bosch looks at the world from above. He places the viewer in a position that can be compared to God's, so that he must judge, and in this way turn to God.[34] In his version of the *Seven Deadly Sins,* Bosch paints the sins of men in God's eye - literally (fig. 19). By contrast, Bruegel chooses an earthly perspective. In the print series *Seven Deadly Sins* (fig.14), the observer of human misdeeds stands in the midst of the world. In the *Fall of the Rebel Angels,* evil falls right on to the viewer, as it were: we do not see through the eyes of God, but find ourselves in the midst of a battle between angels and devils, animals and things. Let us look, then, at Bruegel's world and see how it had changed relative to that of Bosch.

## The world in transition

In 1516, the year of Bosch's death, *Utopia,* by Thomas More (1478-1535), first saw the light of day. This book presents the fictional travel account of a Portuguese voyager to an island in the New World. In *Utopia* people live in a kind of earthly paradise, in brotherhood, without dissent, and without possessions. Hans Belting sees parallels between More's *Utopia* and Bosch's *Garden of Earthly Delights,* both Places-that-do-not-Exist.[35] But while More was inspired by the discovery of a new, unspoiled part of the world, the *Garden of Earthly Delights* evokes a utopian paradise prior the discovery of America. The painting is not dated, but one assumes that Bosch painted it in the years 1495-1505. Even if Bosch had heard of America, he would have heard rumors at best, rumors that played on earlier images of ideal places and *terrae incognitae.*

Nevertheless, the *Garden of Earthly Delights,* with its particular blend of naturalistic and fantastic creatures, could easily be ascribed to a general fascination with the exotic and strange from the New World. This was certainly the case in the palace of Hendrik III of Nassau in Brussels, where the *Garden of Earthly Delights* (fig. 20) could be found in 1517, next to the palace of Charles V on the Coudenberg. Here, in the heart of the Habsburg empire, one received not only the first travel accounts - eye witnesses that one could believe or not - but also *realia* from the New World, such as Indian feather headdresses and golden "accouterments" like the ones seen there in 1520 by Albrecht Dürer, which may have formed part of the treasure of Moctezuma, the Aztec leader who was defeated that same year by Hernán Cortéz (fig. 21).[36] Albrecht Dürer, who visited the palace of Nassau in Brussels, does not mention the *Garden of Earthly Delights,* but he does give an account of other artworks in Nassau's possession, and of the "large bed in which 50 people can lie down..." and a "stone that the elements had cast down in the field near the lords of Nassau...," probably a meteorite. Dürer's description gives the impression that Hendrik III of Nassau had a particular interest in *mirabilia* and curiosities. He may have appreciated the *Garden of Earthly Delights* in this context.[37]

Tangible contact with the New World distinguishes the world of Bruegel from that of Bosch. In particular from the second decade of the sixteenth century we see a more physical exploration of America, its fauna, flora, and indigenous peoples. The influx of new species from faraway continents motivated a much more thorough study of the visible world nearby. In botany, zoology, and cartography, attempts were made to understand the exotic through comparison with more familiar natural products from closer to home. The exploration of the world, old and new, was closely allied with trade in raw materials, precious objects, and spices.[38] In 1501 Antwerp became an important depot for Portuguese colonial goods, especially spices. In the interval between Bosch and Bruegel, during the rule of Charles V, who ascended the throne in 1515 and became emperor in 1530, the city was moreover one of the most important financial centers in the emerging capitalist and worldwide

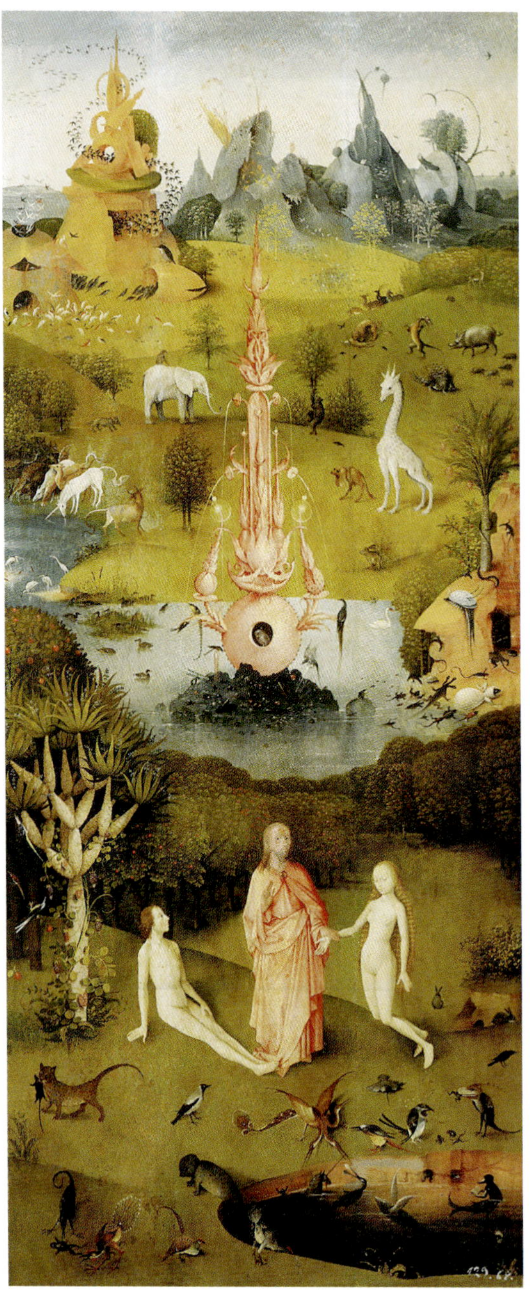

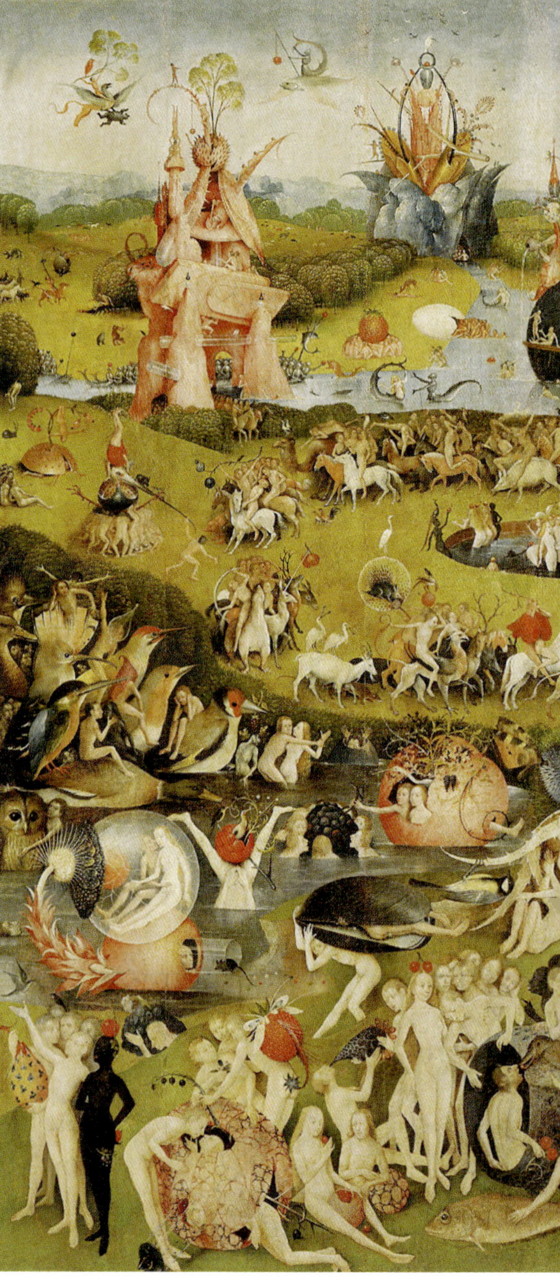

**Fig. 20**
Hieronymus Bosch,
*Garden of Earthly Delights*,
1495-1505
Madrid, Museo Nacional del Prado

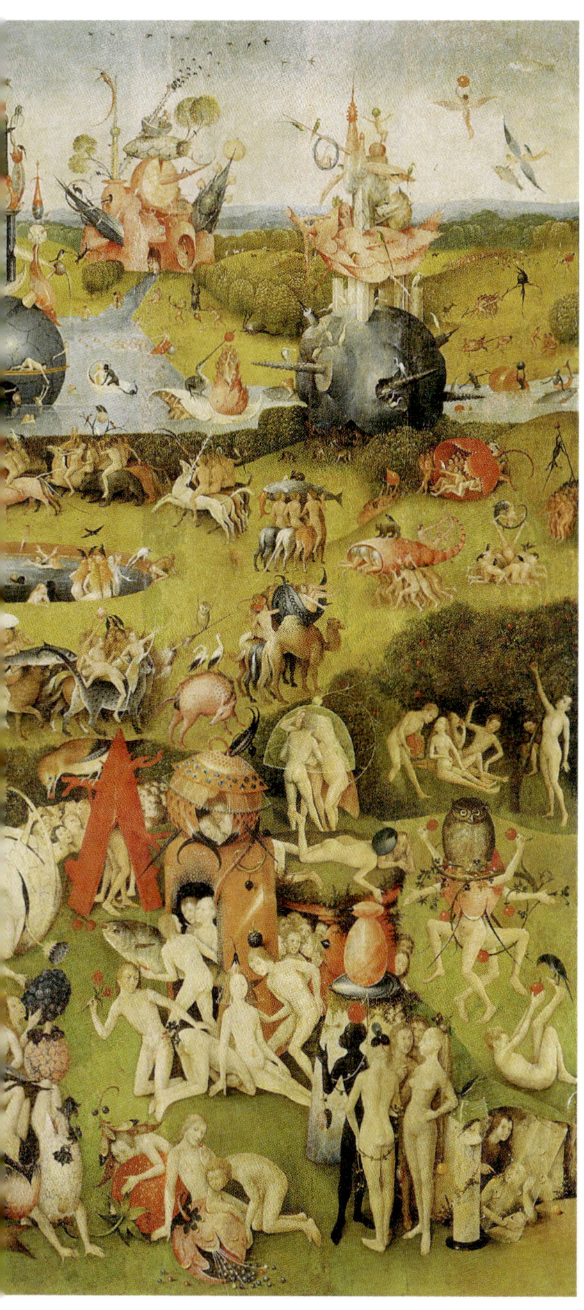

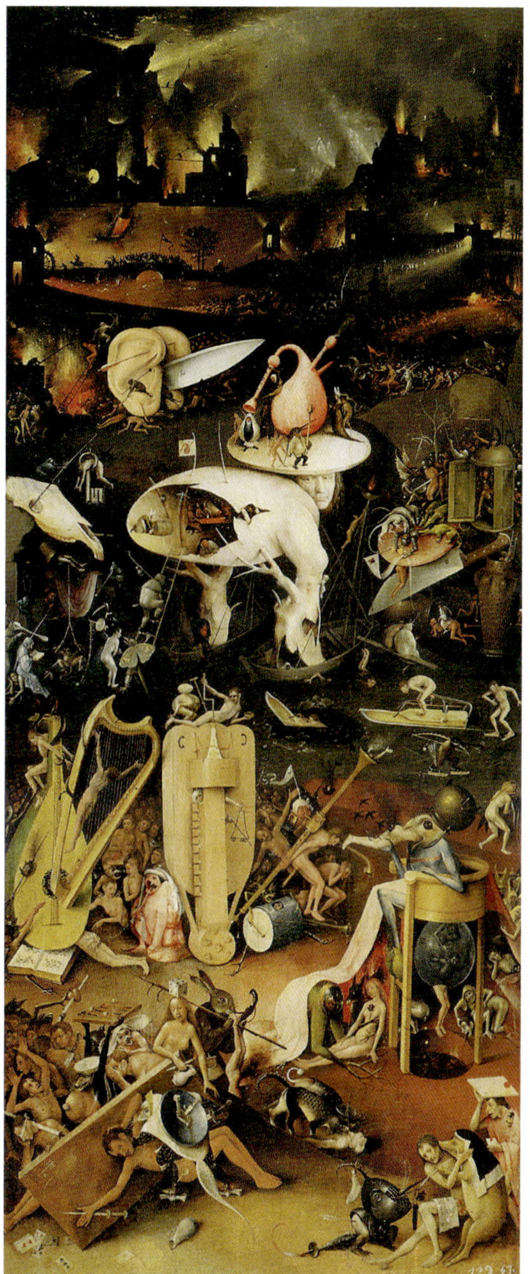

economy.[39] The Fugger, the banking family that helped finance the overseas expeditions of Charles V, opened a branch there in 1508. They provided the Portuguese with copper and silver from Eastern Europe in exchange for malaguetta pepper, but also for exotic goods like ivory, leopard skins, and live monkeys (fig. 36).[40]

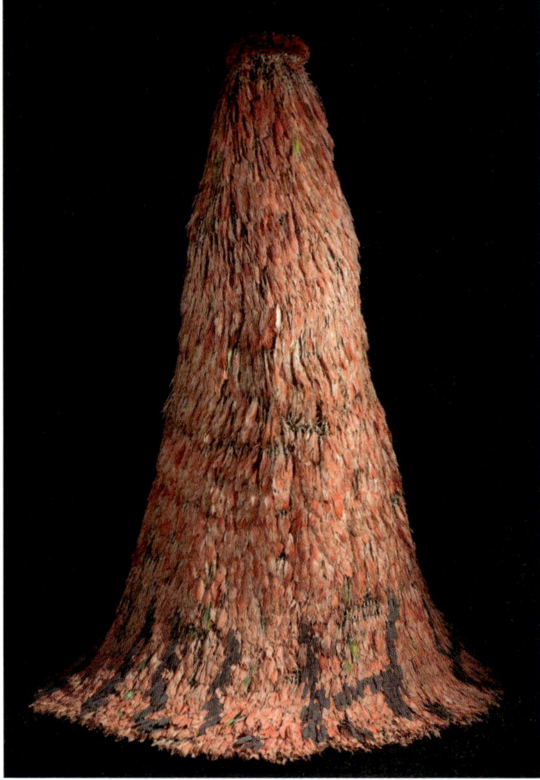

**Fig. 21**
American-Indian feather coat, previously attributed to Moctezuma, probably sixteenth century, made by Tupinamba (Tupi) (Atlantic coast of Brasil)
Brussels, Royal Museums of Art and History

By 1562 Antwerp had lost some of its prominence as a world trade center, among other things because of religious unrest in the Holy Roman Empire and the restoration of the Mediterranean spice trade thanks to the influx of American silver into Spanish ports. But the city on the Scheldt was still specialized in the production and distribution of art and luxury articles. Antwerp exported diamonds, mirrors, paintings, prints, books, and furniture, and imported raw materials, food, and edible luxuries from Iberia and the New World. The world still came to Antwerp, as Daniel Rogers (1538-1591) claimed in his ode on the Antwerp stock market,[41] but Antwerp merchants also went out into the world to build their networks, as well as to collect and disseminate knowledge. The wealthy ship owner Gillis Hooftman (1521-1581), for example, had commercial interests in the Levant and Russia, imported smoked salmon from Eastern Europe and exported Hebrew Bibles for sale to Jews in Morocco.[42] It was Hooftman who convinced Ortelius, the renowned cartographer and friend of Bruegel, then still a young dealer in maps, books, artworks, and antiquities, of the feasibility of a new cartographic product: a compilation of maps that eventually rolled off the presses as the *Theatrum Orbis Terrarum* (1570).[43] Ortelius, in turn, introduced Hooftman to the painter Maerten de Vos (1532-1603), who painted his portrait and decorated his dining room with a series on the life of the apostle Paul (fig. 22).[44]

Ortelius's earliest correspondence illustrates his commercial wanderings to the Frankfurt *Buchmesse* (1556), to Paris (1559), and Italy (1561) to buy and sell maps and antique medals, and to establish business contacts. Ortelius's house in Antwerp functioned as a sort of clearing house, a place where precious objects and learned products - and above all information about them and about the political stage - were exchanged via a European network of correspondents. Already during his early years as a dealer, Ortelius often worked

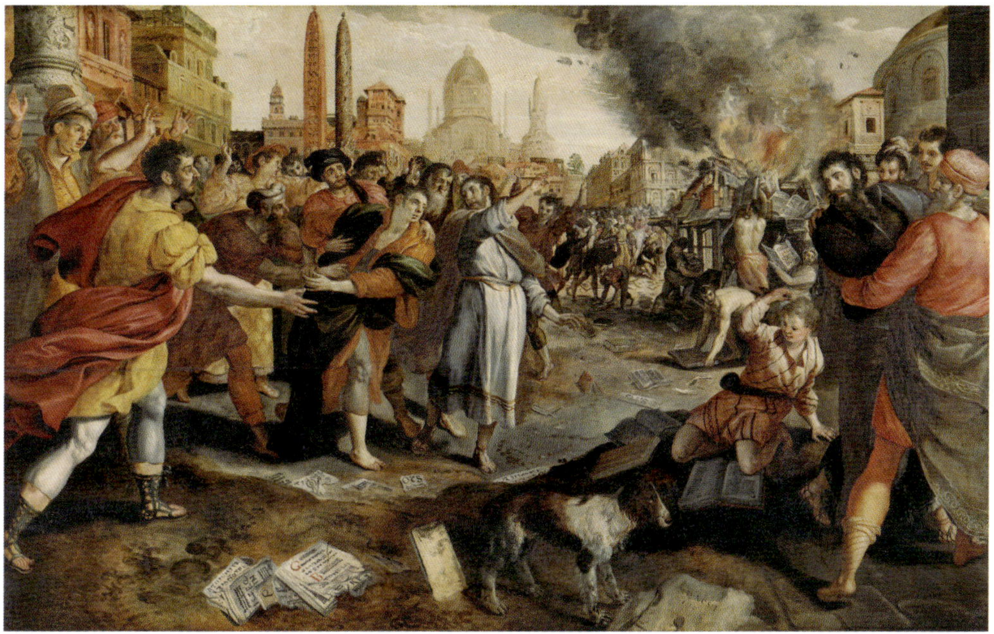

**Fig. 22**
Maarten de Vos,
*Saint Paul in Ephese*,
1568
Brussels, Royal
Museums of Fine
Arts of Belgium

together with the publishing house of Christopher Plantin (1520-1598), itself a model of an international Antwerp *compagnie,* and with Emanuel van Meteren (1535-1612), his cousin and *facteur* in London.[45] In his letters to Van Meteren, Ortelius gives an account of the maps that he has for sale, enquires after rare antique coins in English collections, and reports on political events. In a letter of June 15, 1561, from Joannes Terenumus, alias Vrypenninck, it appears that Ortelius also acted as a provider of art and books from Antwerp to Lisbon. These business contacts frequently informed Ortelius of news concerning geography or exotic products. In the margin of the letter from Vrypenninck, Ortelius noted "To see whether there is any news in geography, and if there is anything unusual from the Indies."[46]

The world between Bosch and Bruegel witnessed not only the expansion of its geographical boundaries, but also the decline of religious stability. In 1519 Luther broke with the church. His followers soon settled in the port city of Antwerp, but were fiercely resisted. But by mid-century Protestantism had gained a sturdy foothold and Calvinists began to establish full-fledged churches of their own.[47] In the Council of Trent (1545-1563) the Catholic Church attempted to formulate an answer to these reformist movements. Ortelius often reported on religious troubles, and emphasized the cruelty shown by all parties in the conflict.[48] A number of artists and merchants opted for a similarly conciliatory position, because war and dissent threatened their affluence, but also out of the conviction that inner spirituality could overcome confessional differences.[49]

## Circa 1562

Bruegel was already part of Ortelius's international circle of friends in the early 1560s, as is evident from two letters sent to the cartographer from Italy. On June 16, 1561, a certain Scipio Fabius, a doctor in Bologna, asked Ortelius about Maerten de Vos and Pieter Bruegel.[50] In a second letter of April 14, 1565, Fabius again sends his regards to these two painters.[51] Both letters are always cited in the Bruegel literature as proof of Bruegel's friendship with Ortelius, and the possibility that he traveled to Italy in the company of Maerten de Vos.[52] However, until now no one has identified this "Fabius." Our research shows that these letters are a unique testament to the contact between Ortelius, Bruegel and De Vos, and the naturalistic milieu in Bologna in the 1550s and 1560s.

### *Bruegel and the Bolognese naturalists*

Scipio Fabius or Scipione Fava (or della Fava) belonged to the noble Fava family, and became a doctor in philosophy in 1550 and a doctor in medicine in 1570 at the university of Bologna. He was married to Virginia di Giovanni Aldrovandi, a relative of the famous Bolognese naturalist Ulisse Aldrovandi (1522-1605).[53] In 1556 and 1559 Fabius competed with Aldrovandi for the appointment to the chair of extraordinary philosophy at the same university.[54] Aldrovandi, like Fabius a physician as well as a jurist and philosopher, was one of the greatest collectors of fauna, flora, and other rarities of his age.[55] He exhibited them in his *Theatrum Naturae* in which he sought to elucidate "the variety of the things of nature."[56] That Fabius possessed a comparable cabinet of rarities is improbable: Aldrovandi's museum was exceptional, and we still know too little about Fabius. But it seems that Fabius too collected *naturalia* and *artificialia.* Ortelius provided Fabius with the world map he published, the *Typus Orbis Terrarum,* and mediated his purchase of a clock for his brother.[57] Perhaps Fabius also owned Egyptian antiquities, or illustrations of them, and of Egyptian fauna, because Ortelius dedicated his *Map of Ancient Egypt* from circa 1565, on which such remains and animals are depicted, to Fabius (fig. 23).[58] Hubert Goltzius includes Fabius among the collectors of antiquities he visited in Bologna between 1558 and 1560.[59] The Fava family, which had become rich in banking and the cloth trade, and of which many members had distinguished themselves as *dottori* at the university, particularly in the medical sciences, was moreover known to be art loving.[60]

Fabius probably met the young Bruegel together with Maerten de Vos, and possibly Ortelius, during a trip to Italy in 1552-54.[61] The naturalistic milieu associated with the university of Bologna undoubtedly inspired the young *fiamminghi,* and one can imagine that they lent their services as painters and draftsmen to these naturalists. We know that Bruegel drew landscapes with animals (fig. 24) in Italy.[62] Maarten de Vos shows his talent as an animal painter in the monumental series for the dukes of Güstrow (fig. 57) and in the print series of the *Four Continents* (fig. 42).[63] Precisely in the years

Fig. 23
Abraham Ortelius,
*Aegyptos*, c. 1565
Basel, Universitäts
bibliothek,
Kartensammlung

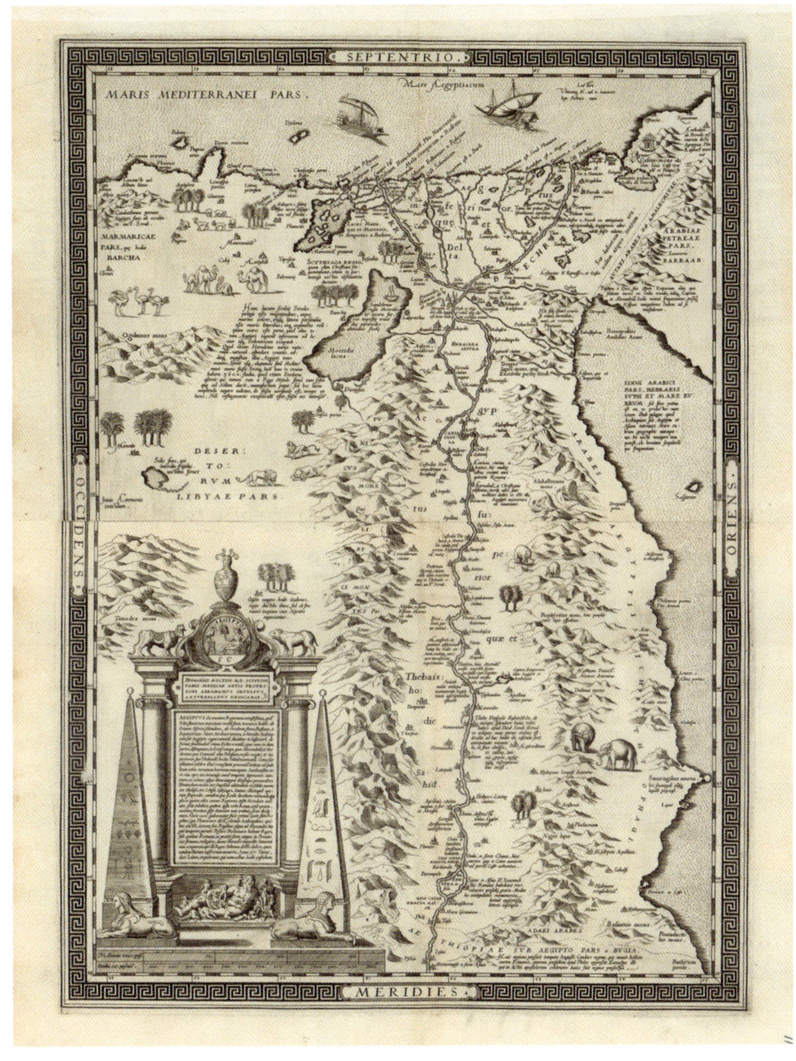


1552-54 Aldrovandi made several excursions through Italy in the company of other scholars and possibly also painters to study and depict local plants, minerals and fish.[64] Aldrovandi's collection was commended early on: Samuel Quiccheberg (1529-1567), the Antwerp medical doctor who was active as a curator and librarian at the court of Albrecht V of Bavaria (r. 1550-76) relates that he visited Aldrovandi in Bologna "while still a young man," and specifically praises his collection of animals, "either in some instances their individual parts, or else dried and stuffed in their entirety or at least depicted in still lifes."[65] Over the years, Aldrovandi collected several thousand depictions of nature (figs. 37, 38, 58), known as the *Natura picta*. Only a few contributing

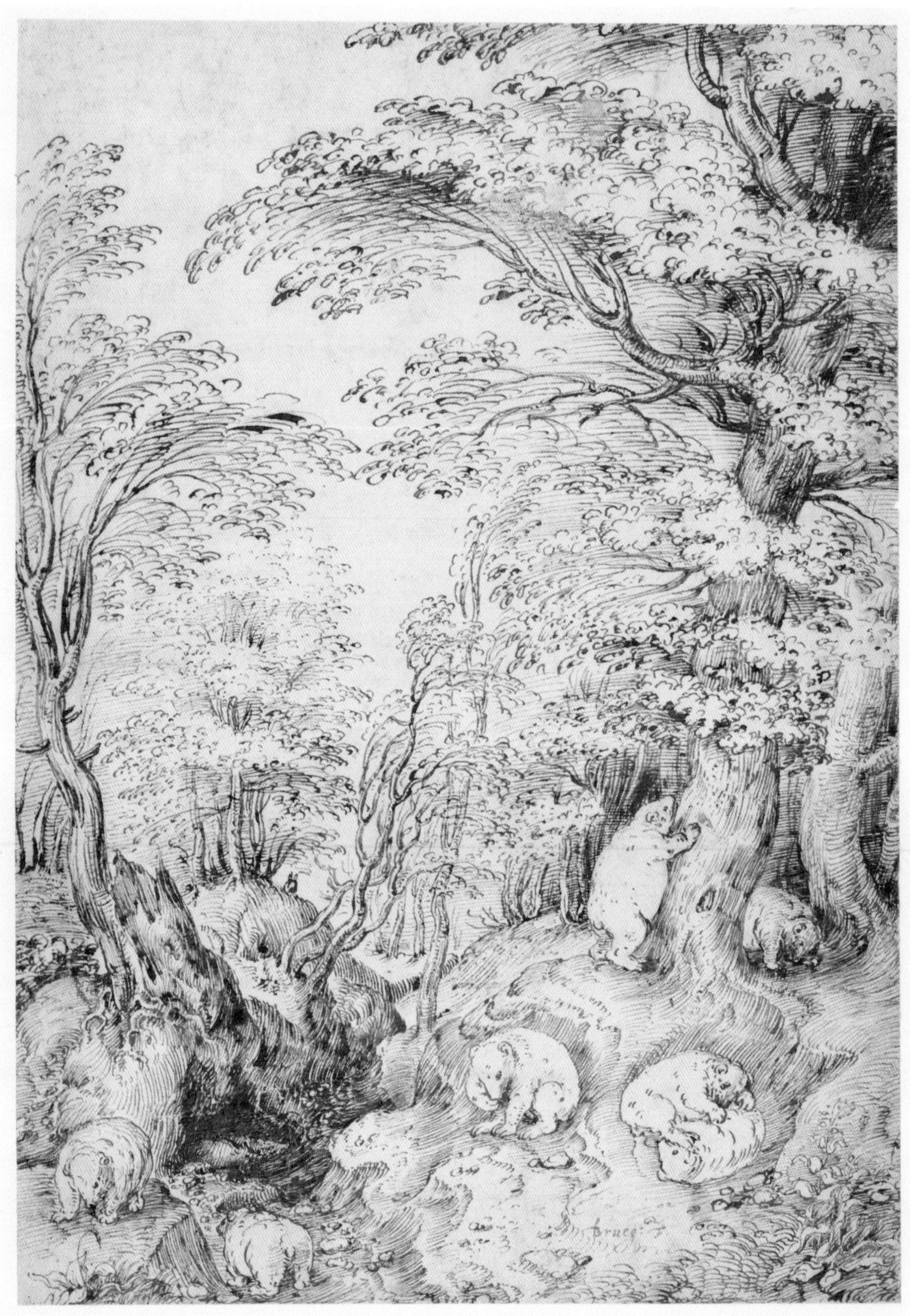

**Fig. 24**
Pieter Bruegel the Elder, *Bears in a Forest*, c. 1554
London, British Museum

**Fig. 25**
Diego Gutiérrez, *America*, wall map, 1562
London, British Library

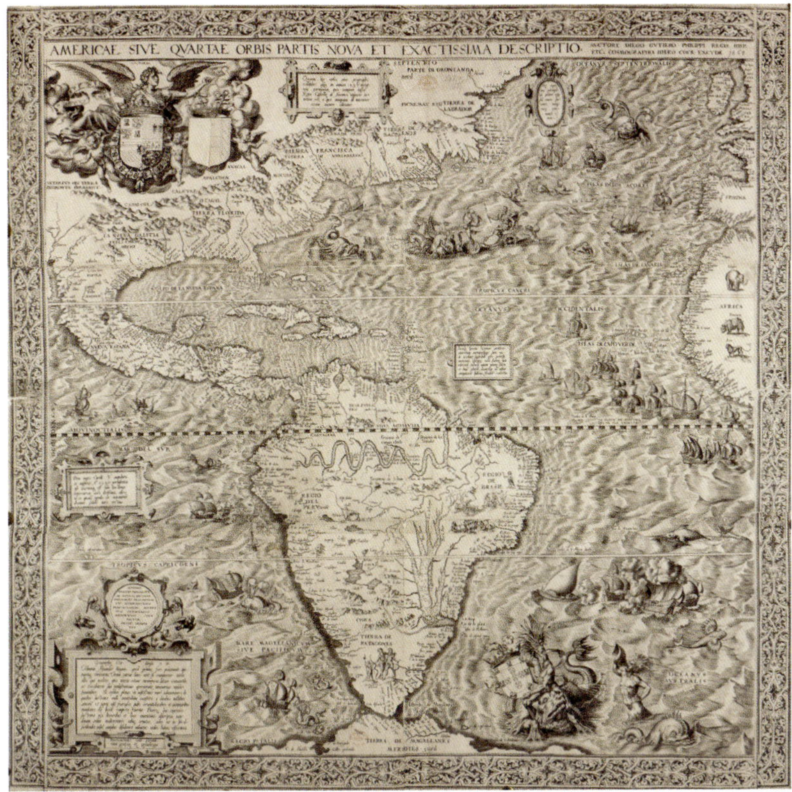


painters, including Jacopo Ligozzi (1547-1627), Giuseppe Arcimboldo (1527-1593), and Hans Hoffmann (1530-1590/91) are known, while many more remain anonymous.[66]

Bruegel's contacts with learned merchants such as Abraham Ortelius and doctors such as Scipio Fabius illustrate his participation in the early modern knowledge economy. How learned he himself may have been is the subject of debate; there are no known letters by his hand and the Latin inscriptions on his prints were added by the publisher. But it is clear that wealthy merchants and learned collectors were particularly interested in his work, and that Bruegel played on their interest while at the same time imbibing it. In Antwerp especially, art and knowledge were considered merchandise and Bruegel was not the only one to profit from its commercialization. The publishing house of Plantin, from which Ortelius often operated, specialized in editions of ancient authors, but also in travel accounts and illustrated scientific studies. In addition to Bruegel's engraved landscapes and Boschian designs, Hieronymus Cock also published humanistic allegories and even maps, such as the map of America by Diego Gutiérrez (fig. 25) from 1562.[67] This wall map, the largest printed map of America until the end of the eighteenth century, is decorated with illustrations of parrots, monkeys, cannibals, and mermaids, with war and merchant ships in the same style as the sailing ships that Bruegel also drew for Cock that same year.[68] Bruegel's prints of sailing ships may be similarly oriented towards a public of learned merchants who were able to appreciate such details.[69]

*Antwerp circa 1562*

Thanks to traveling merchants and artists, but also to learned authors who came to Antwerp for the publication of their studies, the city on the Scheldt became a transit zone for knowledge about distant and newly discovered countries, nature and science, astrology, and even more occult investigations of nature. In 1562 the English magus and court astrologer John Dee (1527-1608) stayed in Antwerp with the printer-publisher Willem Sylvius (ca. 1520-1580) during the preparation of his *Monas Hieroglyphicas,* an obscure search for the linguistic coherence of the cosmos.[70] Perhaps it was in 1562 that Dee first met Ortelius, with whom he was befriended, and possibly Bruegel as well.[71] Bruegel shared Dee's fascination with the idea of a forgotten Ur-language (fig. 2), for magic and alchemy (fig. 10), angels and devils - all of which he translated into vivid images.

1562 was a pivotal year in Bruegel's artistic career. Until then, he had been primarily active as a draftsman of prints published by Hieronymus Cock. Before this date there are only nine known paintings by his hand. In 1562, Bruegel painted not only the *Fall of the Rebel Angels,* but also the *Suicide of Saul* (fig. 26) and *Two Monkeys* (fig. 36). In the six years that followed Bruegel devoted himself primarily to painting: from the period 1563 to 1568, we know of thirty-three paintings by his hand (no work is known from the year of his death, 1569).[72] At the same time, his production of prints and collaboration with Cock gradually tapered off.

In terms of subject matter, the *Fall of the Rebel Angels* marks an end and a beginning in Bruegel's artistic production. Together with *Dulle Griet,* the *Fall* belongs to Bruegel's only painted examples of his contest with Bosch, which during his younger years was concentrated primarily in his work as a draftsman for prints. On the other hand, the *Fall* is Bruegel's first depiction of a story, albeit an apocryphal one, from the Old Testament - a source that he would explore in painting much more frequently after 1562.

Because of their apocalyptic tenor, the *Fall of the Rebel Angels, Dulle Griet* (fig. 27) and the *Triumph of Death* have often been considered an ensemble, although there are no documents to support such an interpretation. Technical investigation has shown that Bruegel painted *Dulle Griet* in 1561.[73] The *Triumph of Death* is not dated. We believe that the *Fall,* with its angels tumbling out of the blue sphere of the heavens and into a foreboding hell-fire at the lower right, and *Dulle Griet,* bathed in a hellish red glow, are related. In both pieces Bruegel incorporates Boschian creatures such as the armored head-footers into the chaos of battle. The protagonist of each of

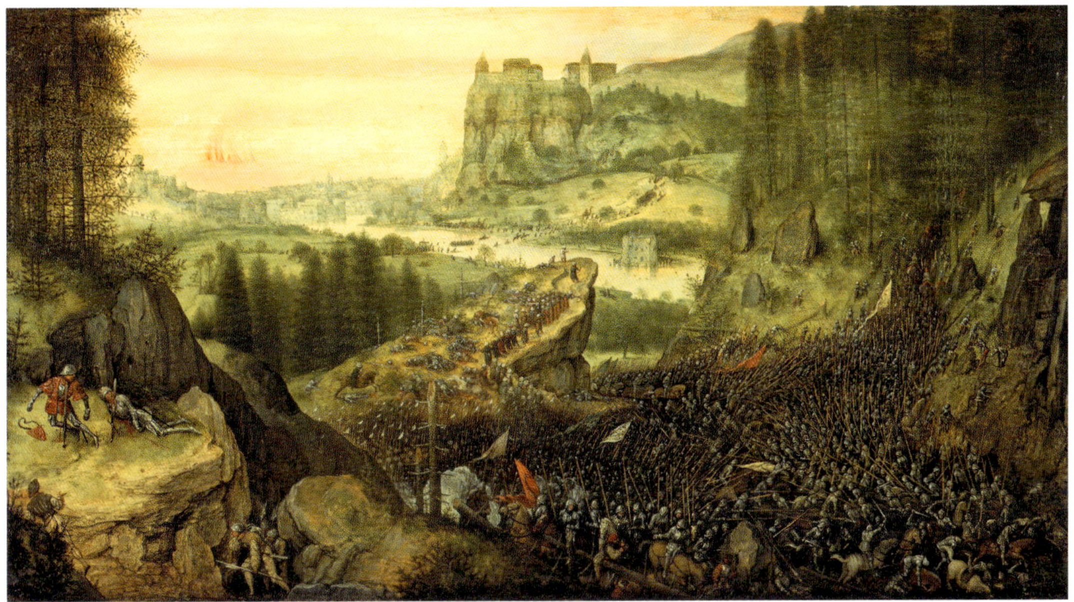

**Fig. 26**
Pieter Bruegel the Elder, *The Suicide of Saul in the Battle against the Philistines at Gilboa*, 1562
Vienna, Kunsthistorisches Museum

these paintings occupies the center of the composition, with Dulle Griet just out of focus. While Saint Michael marches against the devils with martial restraint, Dulle Griet rushes in a frenzy to the very gates of hell, both of them with spread legs: combative, armored, weapon upraised. The enraged woman ("dulle" is an old Flemish word for angry), who strides from country to country scavenging and looting as she goes, a veritable army of housewives in her wake, battles against devils - or are they perhaps the demons in her soul?[74] The *Triumph of Death* (fig. 28) is by comparison much grimmer, and may therefore have been made towards the end of Bruegel's life. Death, mounted on a starved roan horse and with scythe upraised, is a skeleton without armor or protection, indefatigable and inevitable. The battle against evil - which Saint Michael conducts in heaven from the beginning to the end of time, and which Dulle Griet and her female cohorts conduct against imaginary devils at the gates of hell - is at its most hallucinatory when it takes place on earth as a battle between the living and death itself. Death catches everyone in his net, black and white, mother and child, king and cardinal.[75]

In that sense Bruegel's visions of an apocalyptic world made so by the actions of man were truly visionary, because in 1562 the real disasters of war had yet to occur in the Netherlands. The behavior of some religious fanatics, however, left no doubt as to the stupidity and cruelty of human nature, evoked by Ortelius in his letters.[76] Four years later, with the outbreak of the Iconoclasm of 1566 and the rebellion that followed, Bruegel's painted warnings became a painful reality.

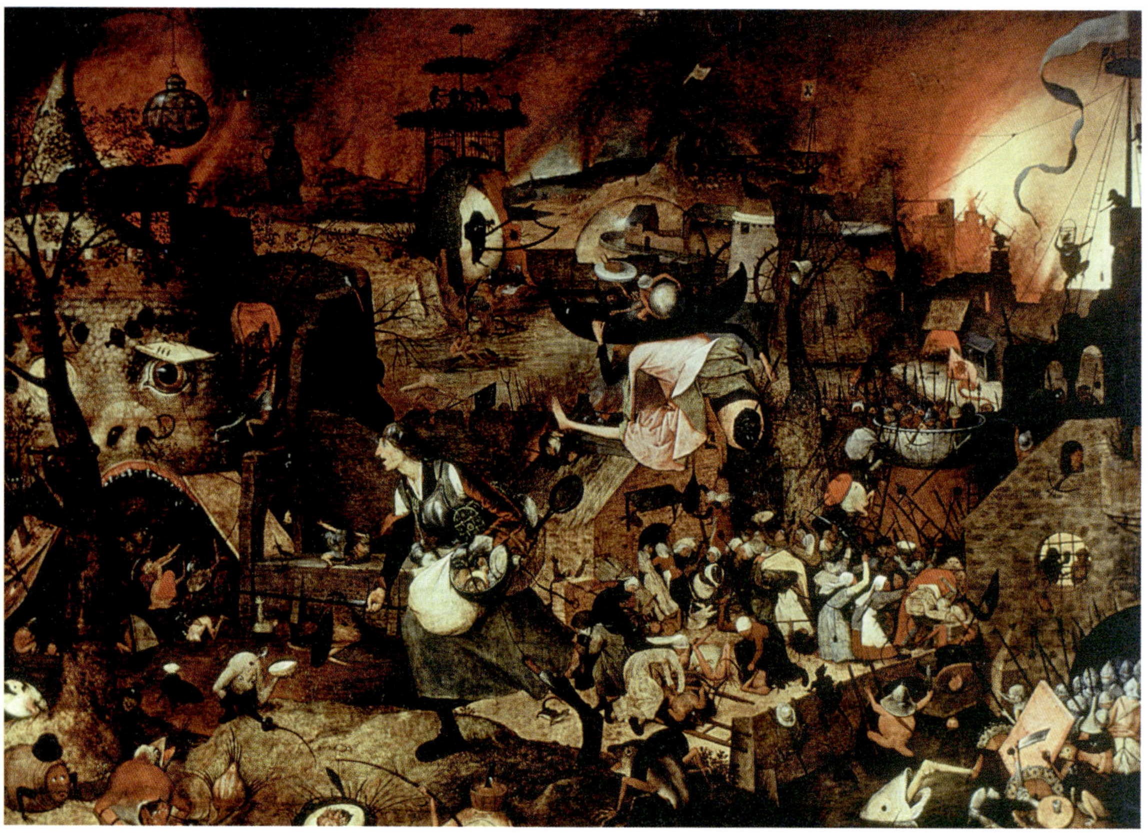

**Fig. 27**
Pieter Bruegel the Elder, *Dulle Griet (Mad Meg )*, 1561
Antwerp, Museum Maeyer van den Bergh

## The move from Antwerp to Brussels

It is probably no coincidence that the shift in Bruegel's output from prints to paintings coincided with his move from Antwerp to Brussels, where he married Mayken Coecke, daughter of Pieter Coecke van Aelst and Mayken Verhulst-Bessemeers in 1563.[77] The registration of this marriage in the parish registers of the Kapellekerk in Brussels is one of the few secure biographical sources concerning the artist.[78] According to Karel van Mander, it was the widow Coecke, from whom, again according to Van Mander, Bruegel had learned his art, who demanded that he move to Brussels in order to forget a love affair in Antwerp. Sometime after her husband's death in 1550, Van Mander writes, Mayken Verhulst herself went to live in Brussels.[79] Recent research shows that Bruegel's ties to the Coecke-Verhulst family were indeed quite close.[80] This sort of "professional" marriage was a common commercial tactic at the time.[81] Thanks to his marriage to Mayken Coecke, Bruegel became part of an established family of artists that was at home in Antwerp's art world while at the same time maintaining strong ties to the court in Brussels.[82] Pieter Coecke even bore the title "Peintre de l'Empereur."[83]

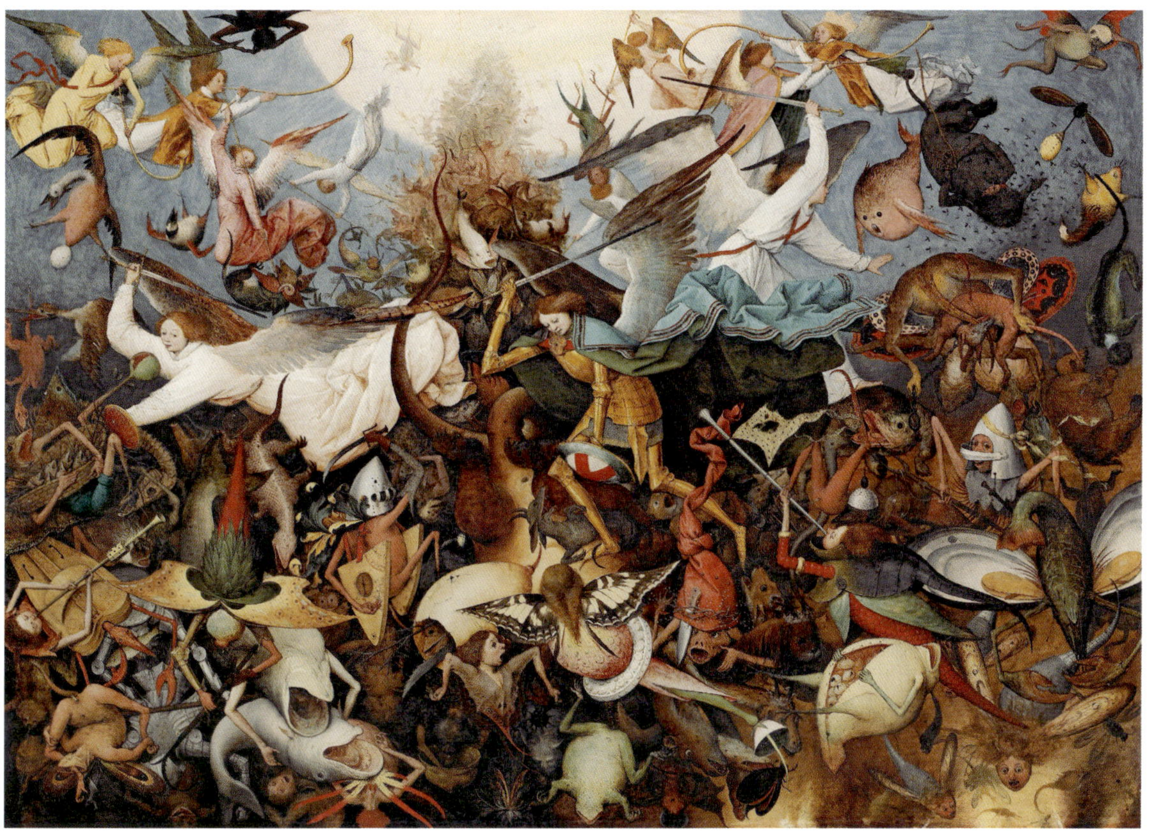

Mayken Verhulst, in turn, undoubtedly saw commercial potential in Bruegel's talent. She was a canny businesswoman with an eye for art: a miniature painter from Mechelen related to the Bessemeers, another family of artists, Mayken published posthumously Pieter Coecke's account of his voyage to Constantinople, *Ces Moeurs et Fachons de Faire des Turcz,* in Antwerp in 1553. Pieter Coecke may have traveled with the imperial ambassador to Constantinople in 1533 to promote Brussels tapestries at the court of Sultan Suleÿman.[84] While artists from Antwerp, Brussels, and even Italy drew designs for tapestries, the weaving workshops were largely based in Brussels. The Brussels court was moreover an important client. Antwerp merchants often financed the Brussels tapestry industry, and commissioned tapestries on spec with an eye toward selling them to courtly customers. Tapestries were more expensive than paintings, and more prestigious as well. Thus the Antwerp merchant Pieter van der Walle sold the tapestries of the *Seven Deadly Sins* designed by Pieter Coecke van Aelst and woven in Brussels to Henry VIII and Mary of Hungary.[85]

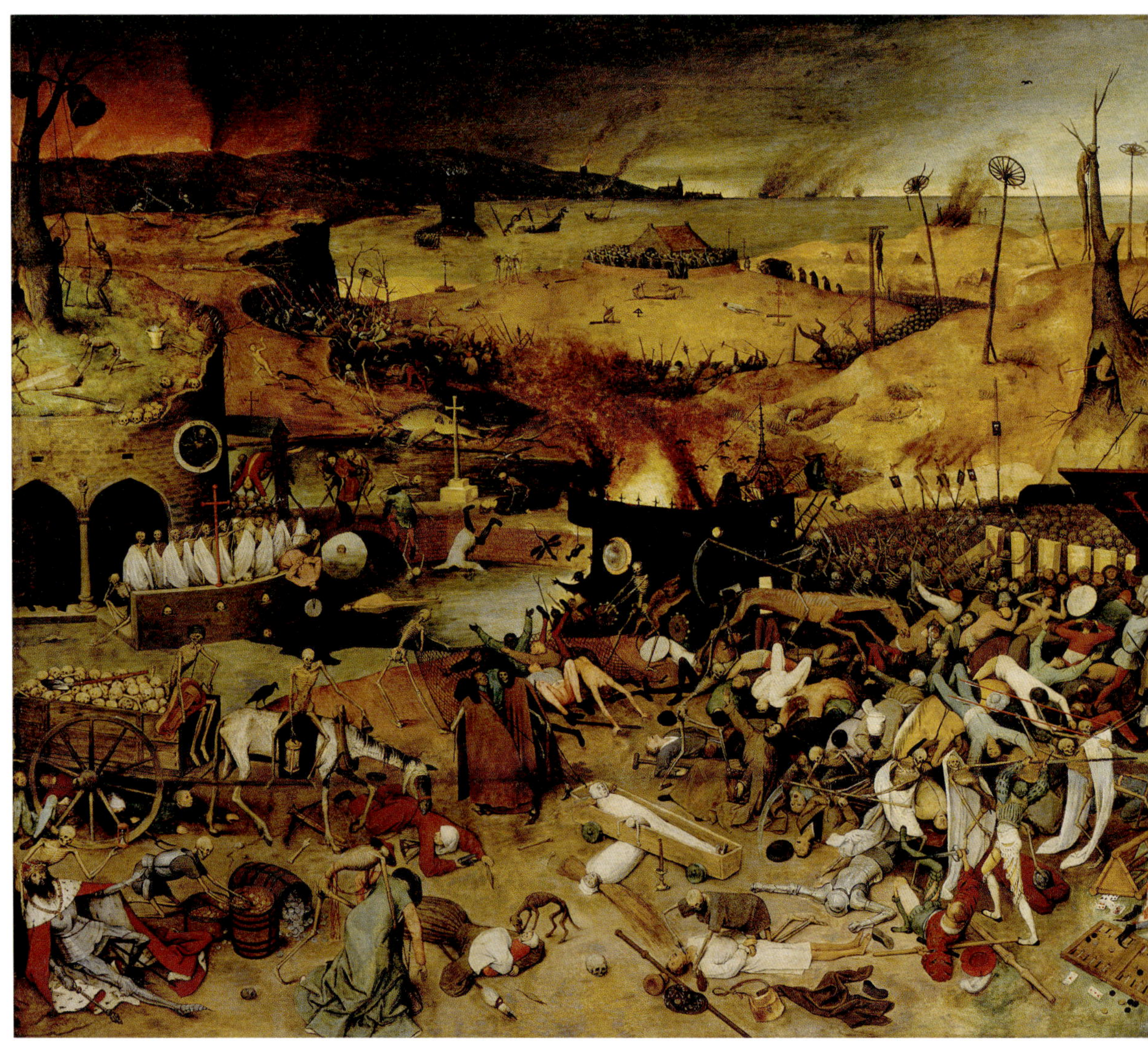

**Fig. 28**
Pieter Bruegel the Elder, *Triumph of Death*, undated
Madrid, Museo Nacional del Prado

Although Bruegel's ties to the Brussels tapestry industry were quite close, they have not been much studied.[86] In particular, the seven-piece set of the *Seven Deadly Sins* seems have been a model for Bruegel's *Fall.* The seven-headed monster of the Apocalypse with the same crowned, horned heads and hairy claws as the central monster [2] in Bruegel's painting draws forth the triumphal carriages of *Pride* and *Lust* (fig. 29). A diabolical fog rises from their tracks, with flames and flying devils or falling angels in the style of Bosch. A warning angel, who like some sort of *deus ex machina* descends from heaven in order to exhort viewers to guard against this kind of sinful

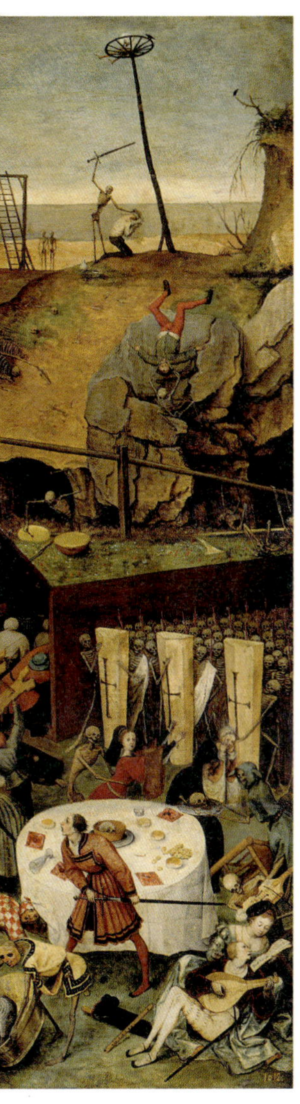

behavior, recalls the central positioning of the archangel Michael in the Bruegel's *Fall.* A standard bearer with on his banner an animal announces each car. A goat, for example, is featured on the banner of Lust.

We have seen how Bruegel too represented each sin as an animal in his print series the *Seven Deadly Sins,* and how this sinful animal symbolism, which goes back to medieval bestiaries, returns in the *Fall of the Rebel Angels.* Perhaps Bruegel was able to examine the original iconographic instructions that Coecke provided to the Brussels weaver Willem de Pannemaker (1512/1514 - 1581) and of which a unique, mid-sixteenth-century copy is still preserved.[87] Bruegel may also have been able to study Coecke's designs. Composition drawings and cartoons were kept ready to hand in the studio, because they often served as models for several weavings. The series of the *Seven Deadly Sins* was particularly popular in court circles. Margaret of Hungary exhibited her set in the castle of Binche on the occasion the visit of Charles V and Philip II in 1549; the count of Egmont owned a series that was confiscated by the duke of Alva in 1568, and another series, still complete, is now preserved in the Kunsthistorisches Museum in Vienna.

There are no known tapestry designs by Bruegel, but we should keep in mind that most of his paintings in water-based paint on canvas, a cheap alternative to tapestries, have been lost. Moreover, Christina Currie proposes that Bruegel made a kind of cartoon, analogous to those used in tapestry weaving, as preparation for his paintings. Only such a procedure could explain the exact copies made by Pieter Bruegel the Younger long after his father's death, when the originals were in foreign collections.[88]

That the shift in Bruegel's production from prints to paintings coincides approximately with his move from Antwerp to Brussels, and his connection to the Coecke-Verhulst workshop suggests further synergies with the tapestry industry. While Bruegel's prints for Cock were destined for the open market, the limited number of paintings suggests that Bruegel made these on commission, or perhaps on spec, but at any rate with a more select public in mind, as was the case for tapestries. Just as the Antwerp merchants and Brussels tapestry workshops negotiated among themselves, Bruegel produced between Antwerp and Brussels, with commissions from Brussels courtiers such as Cardinal Antoine Perrenot de Granvelle and learned Antwerp merchants such as Ortelius and Nicolaes Jongelinck (1517-1570).[89]

Last but not least, Brussels tapestries were famous for their representations of animals, as attested by the so-called *Hunts of Maximilian* and the marvelous tapestries preserved in Wawel castle.[90] Bruegel's master Coecke had been an assistant in the workshop of Barend van Orley, the principal draftsman of the *Hunts of Maximilian.* It is thus not improbable that Bruegel inherited his talent for representing animals from the workshops of Van Orley and Coecke.[91] How he transforms this tradition we shall see in the next chapter.

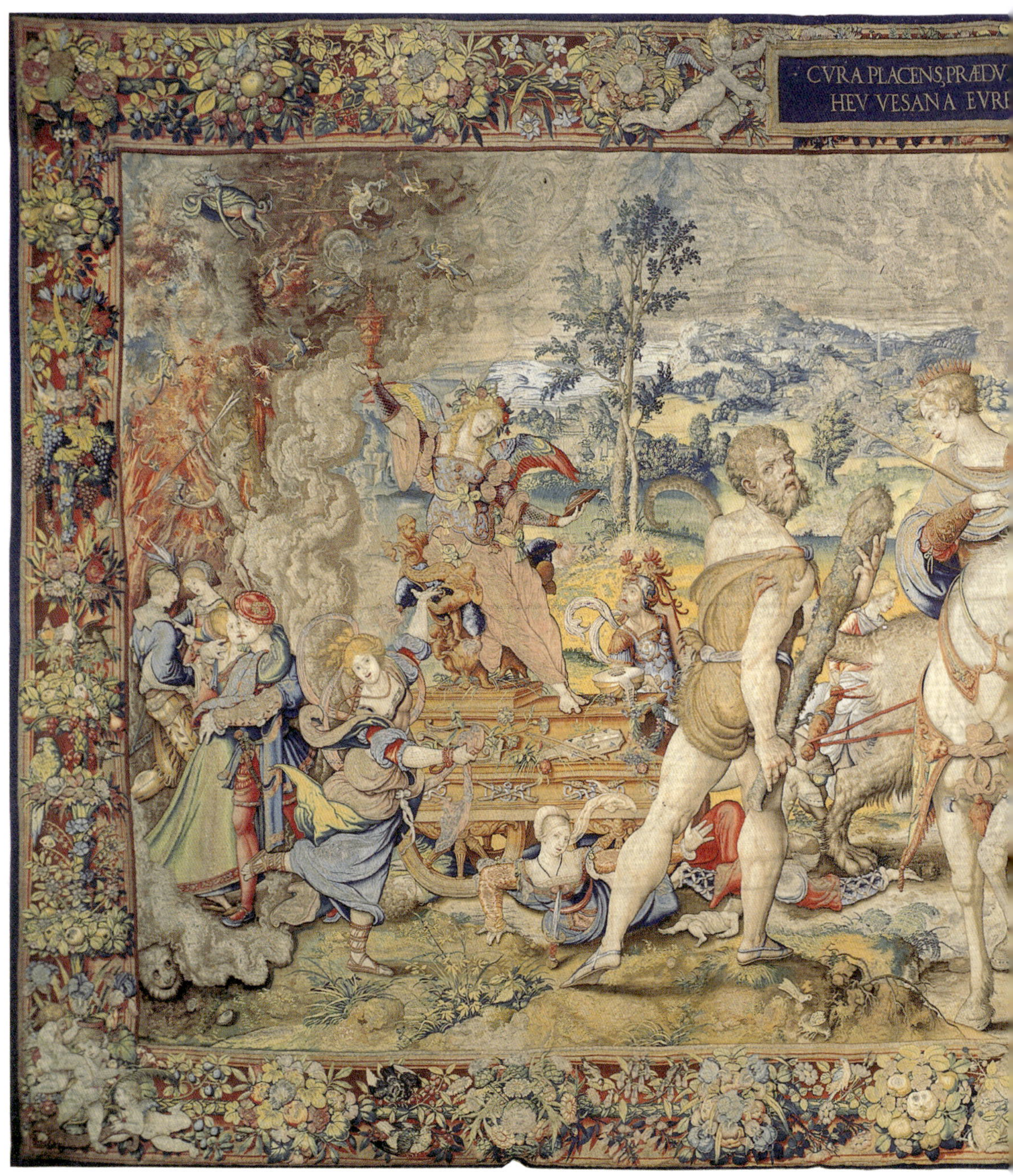


**Fig. 29**
After a design of Pieter Coecke van Aelst (1532-44), *Lust*, from a seven-piece set of the *Seven Deadly Sins*. Woven in Brussels, c. 1542-44
Madrid, Patrimonio Nacional, Palacio Real de Madrid

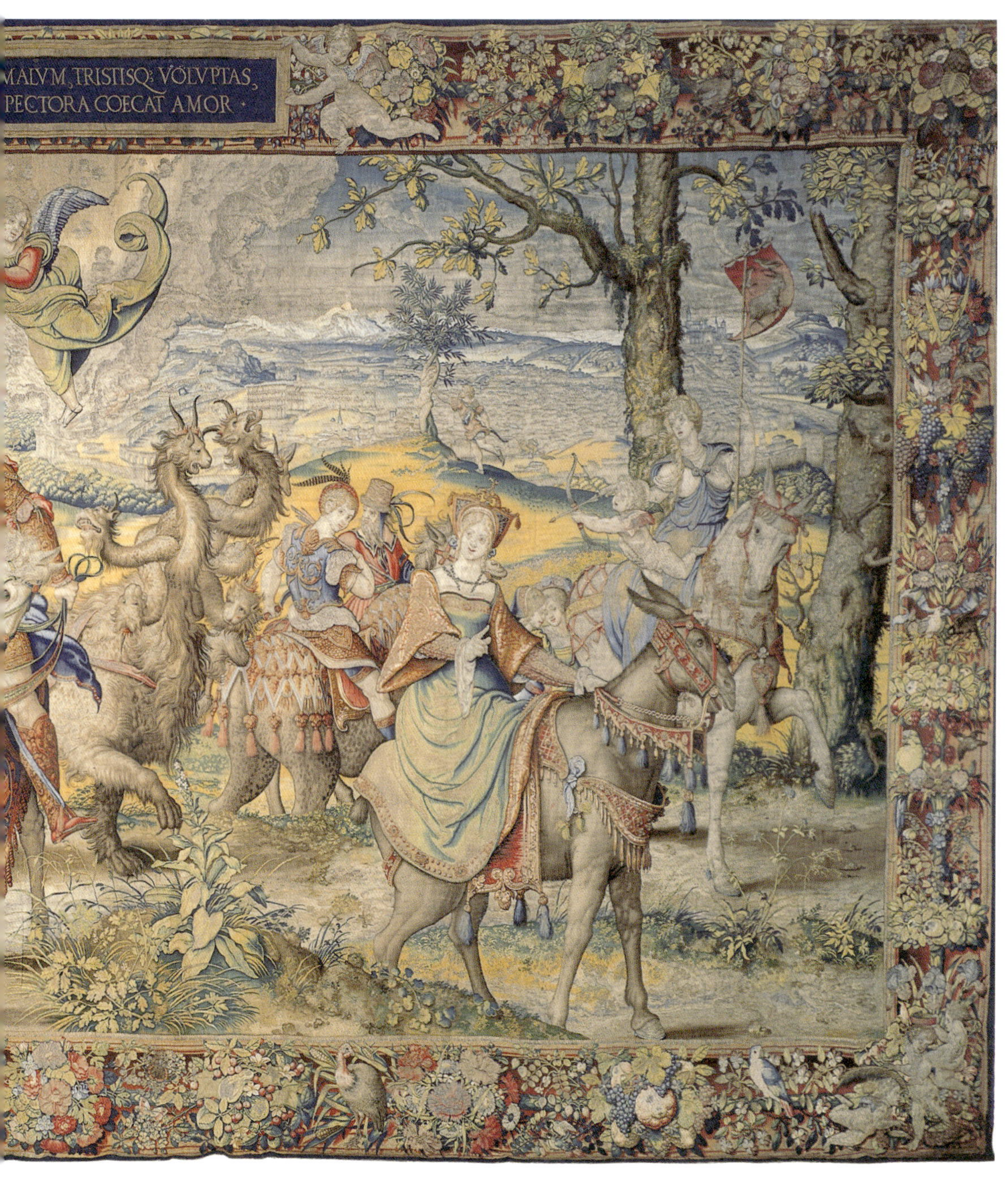
MALVM, TRISTISQ: VOLVPTAS,
PECTORA COECAT AMOR ·

# Chapter II

It is recommended that these things be brought together here in the theater so that by their frequent viewing and handling one might quickly, easily and confidently be able to acquire a unique knowledge and admirable understanding of things.

Samuel Quiccheberg, *Inscriptiones*, 1565, title page[*]

# A marvelous cabinet of curiosities

## New knowledge and the culture of collecting

The early modern discovery of distant lands and ancient cultures created an influx of new knowledge. Learned men articulated their ambition to classify all knowledge systematically as "encyclopedic," derived from the Greek "encyclopedia," which they understood as the "cycle of all knowledge."[1] This encyclopedic impulse is evident among other things from the numerous compilations on natural history and print series that came on the market in the second half of the sixteenth century. Perhaps one of the most striking expressions of this new culture, oriented toward the discovery, collection, observation, and organization of the visible world, were the so-called cabinets of curiosities.[2]

Cabinets of curiosities built on a long tradition of collecting, primarily at princely courts and in church treasuries.[3] The massive influx of collectible objects, however, necessitated new structures for ordering all this knowledge old and new. Most collectors distinguished everything in their cabinets made by human hands, *artificialia,* from everything created by nature herself, *naturalia.* This binary division of art versus nature was rooted in ancient philosophy, and during the sixteenth century it became the main organizing principle for structuring collections.

Although most depictions of art and curiosity cabinets (figs. 30, 39, 43) are of a later date, early modern collections were first formed around 1550. The Bruges painter, antiquarian, and publisher Hubert Goltzius, to whom Bruegel was related through his mother-in-law, writes in his numismatic treatise on *Julius Caesar* (1563) that during his travels through the Netherlands, Germany, Austria, Switzerland, France, and Italy in the years 1558-1560, he visited no less than 968 collections.[4] This figure may be somewhat exaggerated, but Goltzius's list certainly illustrates the rage for collecting that prevailed in those years.

Ortelius, one of Bruegel's earliest supporters, was such an early collector of *artificialia* and *naturalia.*[5] According to his biographer Franciscus Sweertius (1567-1629), he was especially fond of things that nature had made in a particularly artful way, such as exotic seashells, colored marble, or tortoiseshells that were so small or so large that they seemed to have been made by human hands.[6] He also collected antique coins and medals, artefacts made "in the Indies" (a term encompassing America as well as Asia), and modern works of art, among which the best known was Bruegel's grisaille painting of the *Dormition of the Virgin* (fig. 31 ).[7]

Bruegel's splendid painting of the *Fall of the Rebel Angels*, bathed in gold and

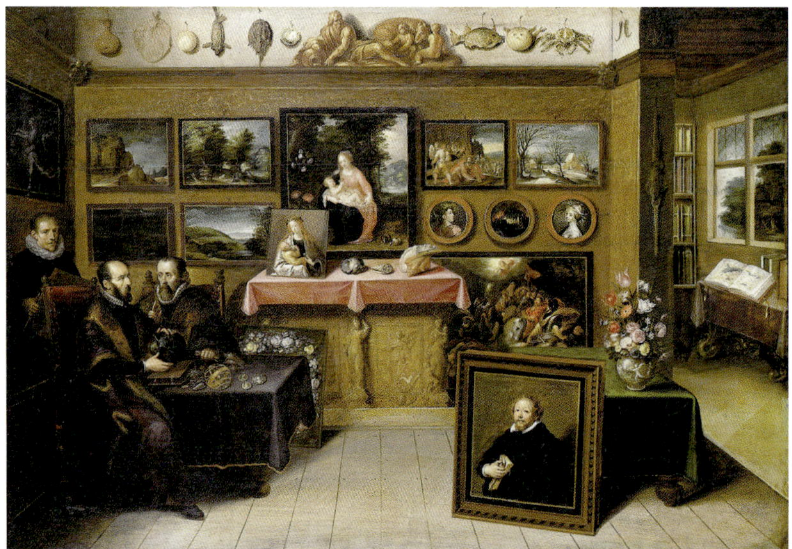

**Fig. 30**
Frans Francken II, *Art Cabinet with Abraham Ortelius and Justus Lipsius*, 1618
Amsterdam, Presented at Christie's Old Master Pictures, Sale 8 November 1999

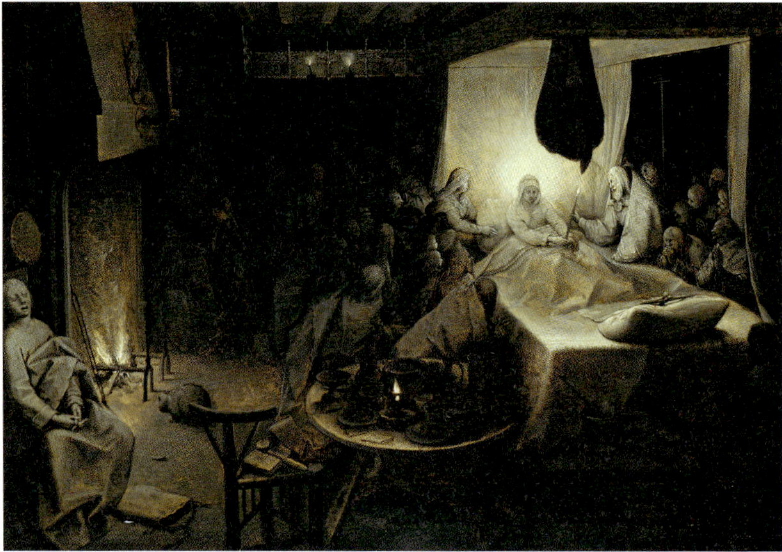

**Fig. 31**
Pieter Bruegel the Elder, *Dormition of the Virgin*, c. 1564
Banbury, Upton House, National Trust

azure, evokes an atmosphere of preciousness, curiosity, and virtuosity - qualities that early modern art-lovers and collectors particularly appreciated. The cropped composition suggests a view into a collector's cabinet: a piece of furniture or an entire room in which art and curiosity collections were housed. The heaping up of the most varied, precious, and strange things also recalls the orderly chaos of early modern cabinets of curiosities. The falling angels in the midst of mutation are inspired by Bosch, but Bruegel's chimerical

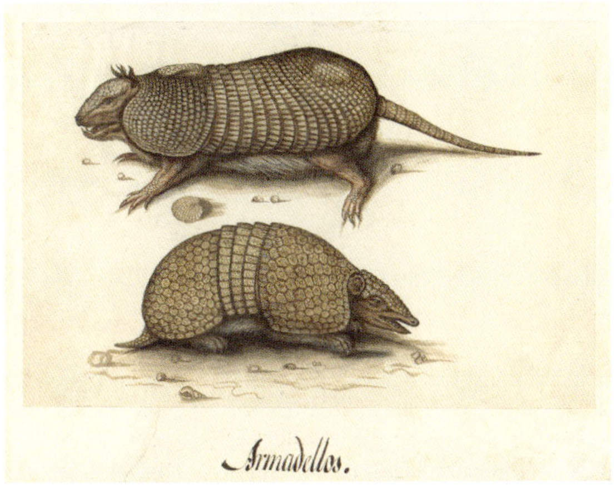


**Fig. 32**
Lambert Lombard (?), *Armadillos*, in: *LIBRO/ De diversos Animales, Aves/ Peçes, y Reptiles,/ QUE EL EMPERADOR CARLOS V/Mandò dibujar a su pintor/ Lamberto Lombardo/ En Bruxelas AÑO/ MDXLII*, 1542 Amsterdam, Rijksmuseum

creatures, even more so than those of Bosch, are assembled from accurately depicted *naturalia* and *artificialia.* They are composed of elements derived from fauna, flora, various instruments, and ethnographic objects that unmistakably reference the variegated interests of contemporary collectors.

Collectors saw the variety of their collections as a reflection of the endless multiplicity of the macrocosm. For this reason Aldrovandi called his impressive collection a "microcosm" of Nature.[8] Behind the apparent disorder of the visible world was concealed the deeper order of God's creation, which collectors hoped to decipher through accumulation and comparison.[9] Samuel Quiccheberg, the author of the first treatise on museums, referred to a collection as a "theater" or an all-encompassing and visual system of knowledge.[10] In his *Inscriptiones vel tituli theatri amplissimi (Inscriptiones or titles of the most ample theatre)* (1565) Quiccheberg proposes a system to organize a collection in five classes, that are each subdivided in ten "inscriptions" or titles. Quiccheberg, a native of Antwerp, proudly describes himself as 'belga' on the title page of his treatise, and was acquainted with the collectors network around Ortelius and Goltzius.[11] He adds a list of collectors explicitly meant to emulate the one of Goltzius.[12] Ortelius later also entitled his compilation of maps a "theater of the whole word," (*Theatrum Orbis Theatrum*, 1570).[13] With references to Seneca and Cicero, he left no doubt about the fact that contemplating, observing, and collecting the visible world was a way to plumb the depths of God's creation.[14]

Collectors brought together objects of art and nature in their cabinets, but because many *naturalia* could not be kept as dried specimens, they often completed their collections with painted depictions. The imperial court of Charles V in Brussels was famous for its collections and its menagerie of exotic animals. It should therefore come as no surprise that one of the earliest albums of animals in the Netherlands was probably commissioned by the emperor from the painter Lambert Lombard in 1542 (fig. 32).[15] Around 1560, the Bruges nobleman Charles de Saint Omer (1533-1569) formed a painted collection of animals and plants known as the *Libri Picturati* (Jagellion Library, Cracow). For the time being we do not know who made these splendid watercolors.[16] Around the same time the Antwerp animal painter Hans Verhagen (b. 1540-1545), known as "the Dumb," painted another animal album (fig. 33).[17] In 1562 the North German painter Ludger tom Ring the Younger (1522-84) traveled to Antwerp and made an exceptional painting depicting sixteen

kinds of animals, among which the exotic civet cat (fig. 34).[18] The albums of Lombard and Verhagen circulated in Antwerp around 1572, and Hans Bol (1534-1593) and Joris Hoefnagel (1542-1601), perhaps the best-known early modern animal painter, copied illustrations from it. That same year Maerten de Vos painted the first monumental animal series for Archduke Albrecht I of Mecklenburg-Güstrow (figs. 56, 57), also in Antwerp. The series comprised only ten animals, but De Vos tellingly labeled it encyclopedic.[19] Antwerp animal painters quickly achieved international renown. Rudolph II (r. 1576-1612), a peerless collector around 1600, acquired animal albums by Bol and Hoefnagel.[20] The emperor later had his own animal album made, known as the bestiary of Rudolph II, with contributions by the Netherlandish artist Dirck van Quade de Ravensteyn (b. 1565/70), among others.[21]
Bruegel was connected to these artistic and scholarly circles through a number of channels. Verhagen had been an apprentice with Anthonis Bessemeers, nephew of Bruegel's mother-in-law Mayken Verhulst-Bessemeers.[22] With Maerten de Vos he may have traveled to Italy; as we saw in chapter I, the Bolognese naturalist Scipio Fabius asked Ortelius to send his regards to both of them in 1561 and again in 1565. Bruegel's friend Ortelius seems to have been a pivotal figure in the Antwerp milieu of animal painters, as he also was for cartography and antiquarian studies.[23] When assembling the *Libri Picturati*, Charles de Saint Omer was advised by the botanist Carolus Clusius (1526-1609) and the collectors Marcus (1521-1581) and Guido Laurinus (1532-1588), all three correspondents

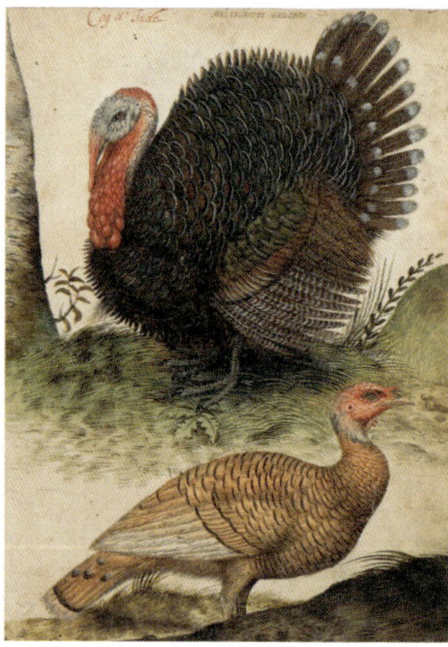

**Fig. 33**
Hans Verhagen, *Turkeys, male and female*, c. 1563
Berlin, Kupferstichkabinett

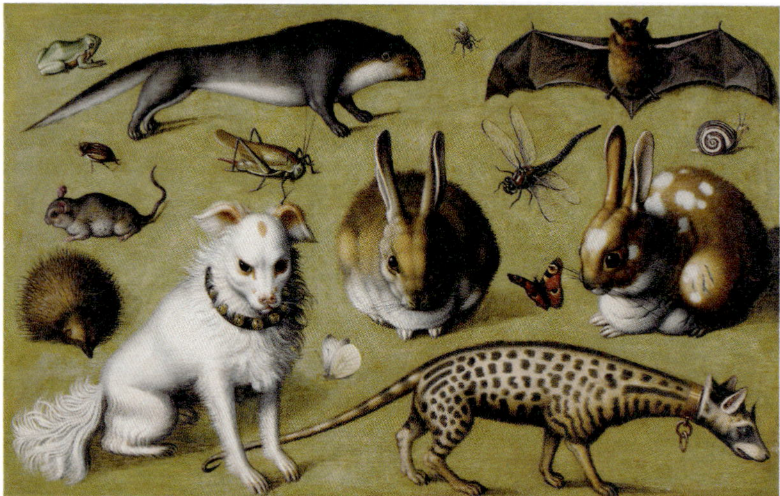

**Fig. 34**
Lutger tom Ring de Jonge *Animal Piece with Genet Cat*, 1562 (?)
Münster Westfälisches Landesmuseum

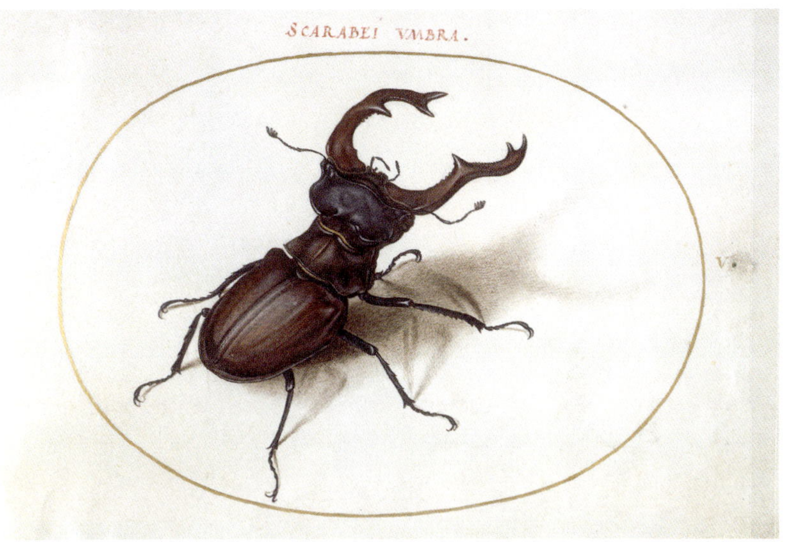


**Fig. 35**
Joris Hoefnagel, *Stag Beetle*, in: *Ignis*/ Fire, plate V, from the *Four Elements*, between 1575-1582 Washington, National Gallery of Art, Collectie Mrs Lessing J. Rosenwald.

of Ortelius.[24] Ludger tom Ring was also familiar with the network linked to Ortelius.[25] Hoefnagel, inspired by Ortelius, profiled himself after Bruegel's death in 1569 as the latter's artistic heir. In his topographic registration of the waterfall on the Tiber at Tivoli, which Hoefnagel recorded in a drawing during his trip to Italy with Ortelius in 1577, he incorporated Bruegel's earlier engraving of the same location.[26] The message of this intervention is clear: imitating Bruegel is the equivalent of imitating nature, precisely as Ortelius claimed in the famous epigraph he wrote on Bruegel, as we shall see further in chapter III.

It is quite possible that Ortelius and Hoefnagel also met the Bolognese naturalist Aldrovandi during their travels through the peninsula. Aldrovandi's *Theatrum Naturae* was a local attraction for erudite travelers. In 1577, moreover, Aldrovandi was in search of painters for his *Natura Picta,* a painted collection of natural objects.[27] Hoefnagel took the album with animal paintings that he had started in the early 1570s in Antwerp with him to Italy.[28] Although there is no documentary evidence that Hoefnagel contributed to the *Natura Picta,* closer study of the Aldrovandi collection could be of interest as this far only a limited number of illustrations have been attributed. Moreover, Aldrovandi was particularly interested in depictions of insects, a specialty of Hoefnagel, whose album *Ignis* (Fire) in the *Four Elements* (1572-92) is one of the first to be dedicated entirely to insects (fig. 35). In this same album he also painted - as one of the first - the Gonzales family, members of which suffered from hirsutism, a medical condition that leads to excessive hair growth on the face and body (fig. 59), and that particularly fascinated Aldrovandi.[29] If they did indeed meet Aldrovandi, Ortelius would undoubtedly have introduced Hoefnagel as the artistic successor of Bruegel, who, as we have seen, was already known among the Bolognese naturalists from an early date, and may also have made paintings from nature for Aldrovandi.

Animal painters used not only the book of nature, but also the books of naturalists as a source.[30] The Swiss naturalist Conrad Gessner (1516-1565), without doubt the most prolific and influential author on animals of the time, advertised his multivolume publications as handbooks for all lovers of the arts, including medical doctors, sculptors, and painters.[31] Gessner's *Icones Animalium* (1553-60) and *Historia Animalium* (1554-87) as well as other printed and illustrated works on natural history by authors such as Pierre Belon (1517?-64) and Guillaume Rondelet (1507-66) were easy to find in the courtly city of Brussels, as well as in Antwerp, a center of publishing and book trade. As we have seen, the Antwerp painters also avidly copied each other's work.[32] Bruegel may further have seen drawings of animals in the workshops of the Brussels tapestry weavers, who had been known for their naturalism since the early sixteenth century.

Whenever we cite books by naturalists and painted collections of natural objects as comparitive material in the pages that follow, we see these not only as sources, but also as witnesses to the encyclopedic interest of Bruegel and the collectors of his time. Indeed, Bruegel's depiction of rare and exotic animals in the *Fall* often predate the painted animal albums. Bruegel stands at the very beginning of a particularly fruitful exchange between art and knowledge, in which artists - thanks to their expertise in the precise depiction of nature - contributed to the scholarly study of the natural world, and at the same time laid the basis for new genres of still life, animal painting, and the painted collector's cabinet.[33]

## Naturalia

Bruegel had depicted animals prior to painting the *Fall*. As we have seen, he rendered the allegorical animals in the print series of the *Seven Deadly Sins* (1556-58) and the print of *Fortitude* (figs. 15) in a strikingly naturalistic way. His drawing of *Bears in a Forest* (fig. 24) and his panel depicting *Two Monkeys* (fig. 36) also suggest that he drew animals directly from life. Most of the animals Bruegel cites in the *Fall*, as befits the theme of mutating angels, are hybrids, combinations of different species as well as composites of art and nature. The components of Bruegel's hybrid inventions, however, are so precise that they betray considerable knowledge. Among the falling angels Bruegel also paints a number of animals in their entirety, including, perhaps not coincidentally, the same kinds that appear in his other inventions.

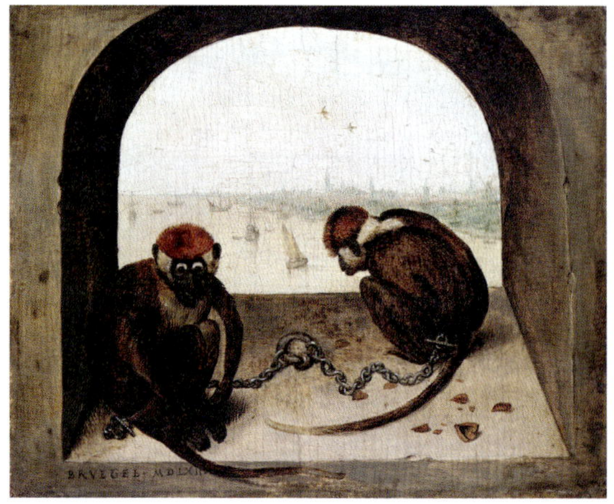

**Fig. 36**
Pieter Bruegel the Elder, *Two Monkeys*, 1562
Berlin, Staatliche Museen zu Berlin, Gemäldegalerie

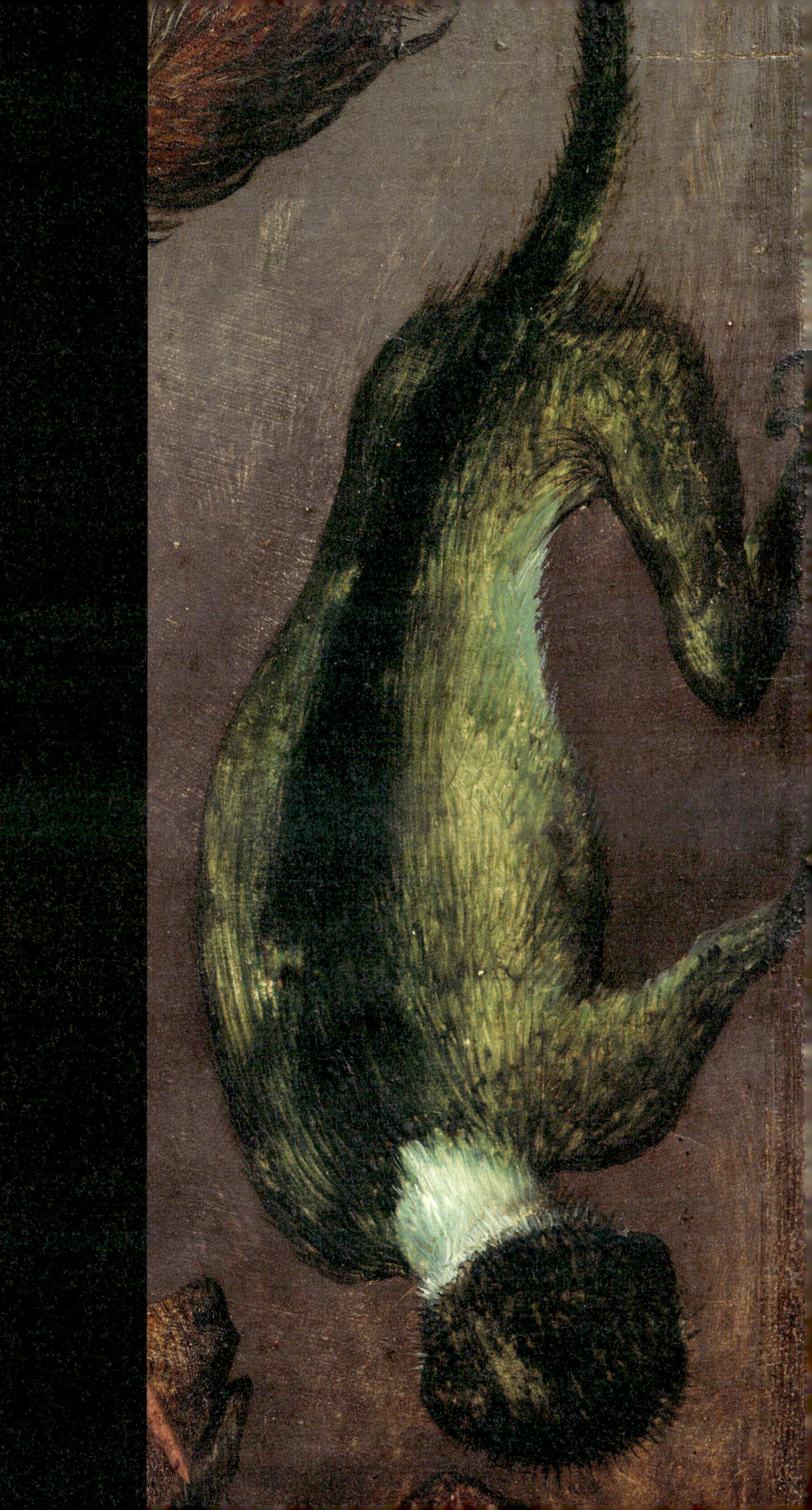

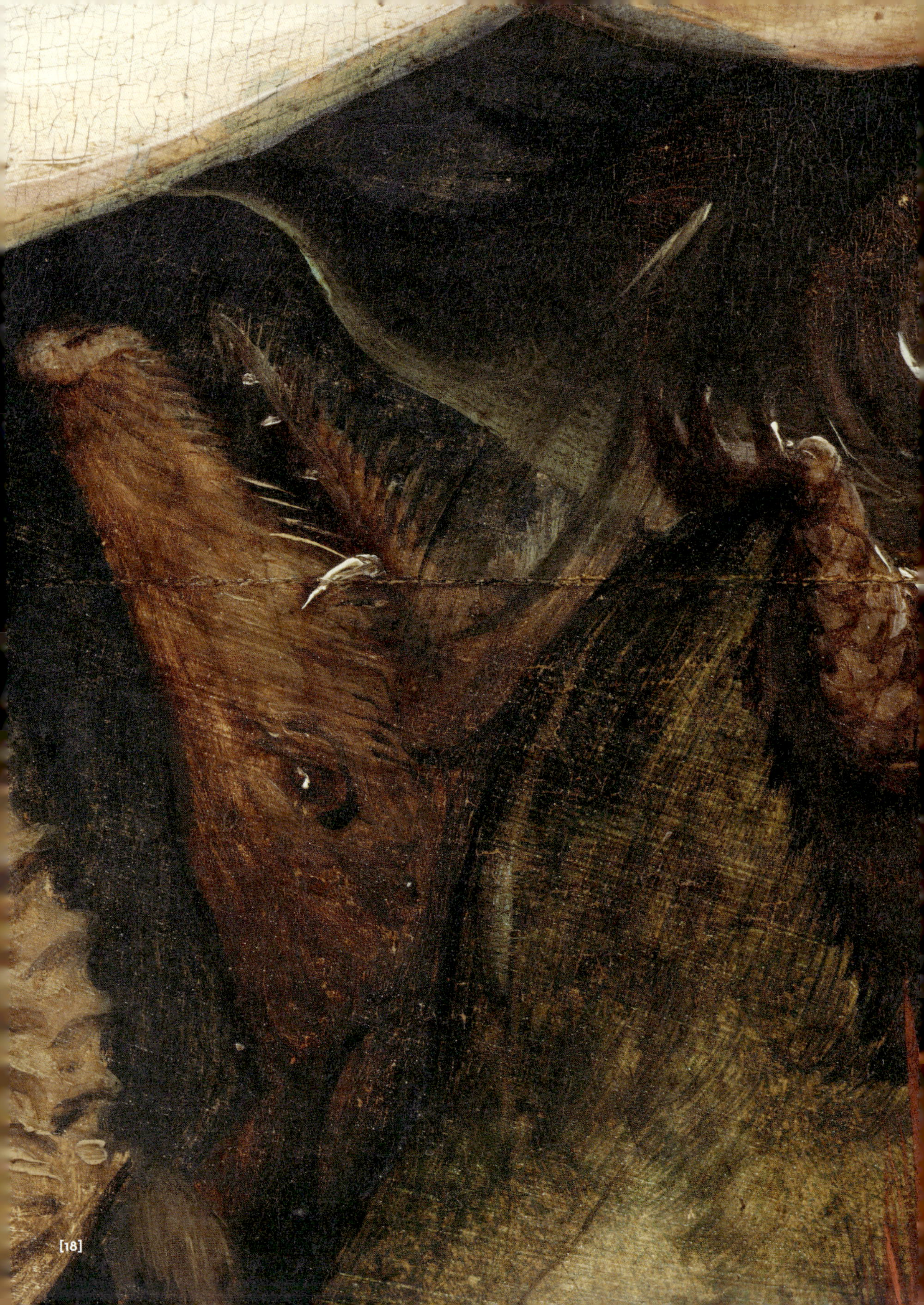

*The bear, the ape, the boar, the toad*

At the center right we see a brown bear (*Ursus arctos*) [9], long familiar in the visual culture of Europe - among other things as the Ursus Maior or Great Bear in the skies of the northern hemisphere.[34] As we have seen, Bruegel also drew brown bears *ad vivum*, probably around 1554 during his stay in Italy, where the animals were still found in the wild (fig. 24).[35]

Immediately above the brown bear in the *Fall* is a primate [17], the same red-capped mangabey (*Cercocebus torquatus*) that Bruegel painted that same year, 1562, in a panel known as the *Two Monkeys* (fig. 36).[36] Bruegel painted the ape in the *Fall* with his back to the viewer and head lowered, but its characteristic white collar and long tail leave no doubt that it is the same sort. Margaret Sullivan has already noted that Bruegel also included two monkeys in the *Dulle Griet* (fig. 27), but no one has remarked that the same ape appears in the *Fall*. According to Sullivan Bruegel often excerpted details from his more elaborate compositions and enlarged them into individual artworks; in this practice she sees the key to the allegorical meaning of the *Two Monkeys*.[37] Much has been written about the meaning of this panel and it is probable that Bruegel, whose paintings were always deliberately charged with layered meanings, also endowed this composition with social, allegorical, or other self-conscious connotations. Fritz Grossmann and Margaret Sullivan see in the *Two Monkeys* a metaphor for the foolish behavior of humanity. Matthijs Ilsink reads the *Two Monkeys* as art about art (art that "apes" nature), and Alfons Montballieu situates the painting, which features a topographic view of Antwerp in the background, in light of contemporary urban developments.[38] In the *Fall of the Rebel Angels*, the falling ape can be associated with the diabolical imitation (or aping) of God.[39]

Without excluding other layers of meaning it is also important to point out the natural-historical character of the *Two Monkeys*. Mangabeys, which come from West Africa, were brought to Northern Europe as curiosities in the wake of the spice trade. Around 1562 they were still fairly rare, exotic animals coveted by learned collectors and naturalists. The painting's format (20 x 23 cm) approaches that of books or drawings of natural objects, and as such makes a perfect collector's item. The reception of Bruegel's *Two Monkeys* confirms the natural-historical interest in the piece. Hans Bol copied Bruegel's *Two Monkeys* in his *Icones quorundum Animalium* (ca. 1572-75), the painted collection of animals that ended up in the possession of Rudolph II.[40] Hoefnagel copied it in an emblem for Albrecht V of Bavaria (1579); and Anselmus de Boodt (1550-1632), a physician from Bruges, in the albums that he made - at least in part - while staying at the court of Rudolph II in Prague.[41] Bruegel's small painting of the *Two Monkeys* clearly enjoyed a status comparable to that of *ad vivum* illustrations by Dürer, which likewise served as models for both artists and scholars.[42]

Directly under the arm of the good angel at the left we see the head of a boar [18], and at the right, under Saint Michael's foot, a toad [16]. Bruegel had drawn a boar as an allegory of *Lust* and a toad to represent *Avarice* in the print series of the *Seven Deadly Sins* (1556-58), in which the brown bear stands for *Wrath*.[43] These three animals also appeared as naturalistic devils who are beaten back by the armed helpers of dame *Fortitude* (fig. 15) from the series of the *Seven Virtues*. In the *Fall of the Rebel Angels*, Bruegel also associated these animals with sinful behavior. At the same time their naturalistic rendering suggests thorough study of the visible world, precisely as such images might have been viewed in the curiosity cabinets of the time.

*Bat and insects*

In the shadow of the falling toad , bottom center, hangs a bat (genus *Vespertilio*) [19] upside down, as if he were sleeping in a cave, but with his wings spread, as bats are often depicted in painted collections of natural objects like Aldrovandi's (fig. 37).[44] The characteristic sharp ears, protruding nostrils and small snout are clearly recognizable. The insect just to the right of the bat features the typical "antlers" (in fact ramified mandibles) of the stag beetle [41] (*Lucanus cervus*), although its beetle-body is not worked out in as much naturalistic detail. Albrecht Dürer's lifelike painting of a stag beetle was an important model for the artistic imitation of nature for Hoefnagel (fig. 36).[45] Bruegel was probably familiar with this model, as the work of Dürer was eagerly collected in the Low Countries, among others by Ortelius and Granvelle, who both also owned paintings by Bruegel. The lower left-hand corner, glowing with the light of hellfire, is crawling with insect-like creatures. Since the time of Aristotle it was believed that insects like flies, beetles, and dragonflies propagated by means of spontaneous generation.[46] Similarly, the stream of winged devils descending behind Saint Michael and his retinue seem to propagate endlessly. The species that serves as the basis for these anthropomorphic insects with crowned heads, butterfly wings, and armored bodies cannot be pinpointed. According to Matthijs Ilsink, the painter must have been inspired by the description of locusts in *Apocalypse* 9:7-10.[47] Behind these hybrid insects flies a garden-variety dragonfly, with its typical transparent wings in double pairs, a long, slender abdomen, and faceted eyes [35]. The dragonfly is another favorite of Hoefnagel, who depicts it in the *Animalia Rationalia et Insecta* (ca. 1575-82), the aforementioned volume on fire (*Ignis*) from his series of the *Four Elements*.[48] Bruegel has painted the most striking insect in the center of the composition: the black and yellow butterfly wings of the hybrid creature directly under Saint Michael's right

**Fig. 37**
Anonymous painter, *Spider, bat, pears, apple, swallow and violet*, in: Aldrovandi Ms, volume 004: animali: volume unico, fol. 35, dated 1599
Bologna, Biblioteca Universitaria

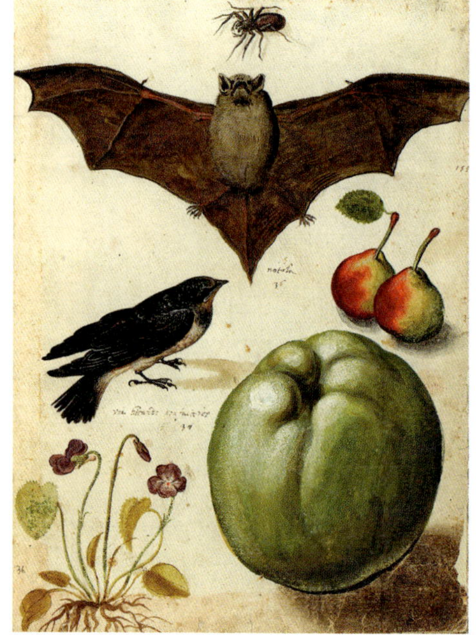

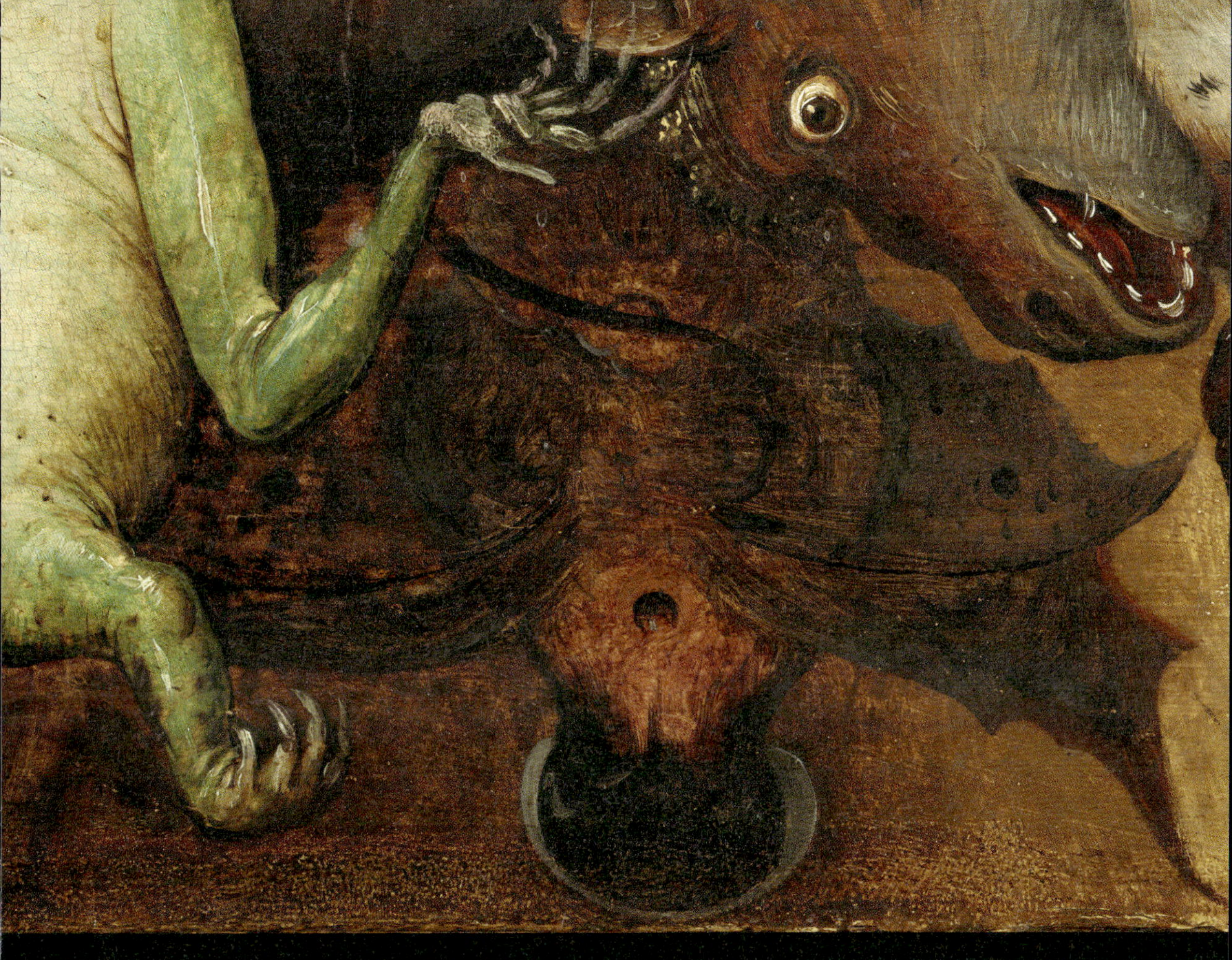

foot are indisputably those of the swallowtail (*Papilio machaon*) [20], a particularly beautiful species of butterfly that lives on the European and American continent (fig. 38).[49] Its beauty, which Bruegel mingles with the softness of angel hair, the sweetness of strawberry and the scent of fantastic flora, makes her one of the most seductive devils in this masterpiece.

*Fish and other aquatic animals*

In addition to insects Bruegel incorporates shellfish, mollusks, and fish into his falling angels, all of which are traditionally associated with the element water. It was under the title *Aqua* that Hoefnagel brought together *Crustacea,* such as lobster and crabs, and *Conchifera,* such as the common mussel (*Mytilus edulis*) in the album of the *Four Elements.*[50] Bruegel combines parts of these species into a Boschian monster [40]. Less ambiguous is the fish at the upper right [21]. It is a blowfish (of the order *Tetraodontiformes*, family *diontonidae*), an exotic fish that occurs in the Pacific and Indian Oceans, and that Hoefnagel would also include in his *Aqua.*[51] Characteristics include spiny scales, two protruding teeth (hence *diontonidae*) and above all the fact that the fish, when threatened, fills up its abdomen with water, as its name suggests. Bruegel has depicted the physiognomy of this fish precisely, as well as its protective mechanism, because he situates it in its inflated state directly opposite the threatening sword of one of the good angels.

Bruegel may have consulted a source such as Guillaume Rondelet's *De piscibus Marinis* (Lyon, 1554), an early and strikingly original fish encyclopedia.[52] It is also possible that he was able to draw directly after a dried specimen in one of the early cabinets of curiosities, such as that of Ortelius or Aldrovandi. It is not known whether either of these collections contained a blowfish - around 1562 both were still in the process of being formed - but we know that in later, well-documented collections of curiosities, blowfish were highly coveted items: a blowfish was mounted on the overstuffed shelves of the museum of Ferrante Imperato (1525-1615?), an apothecary from Naples

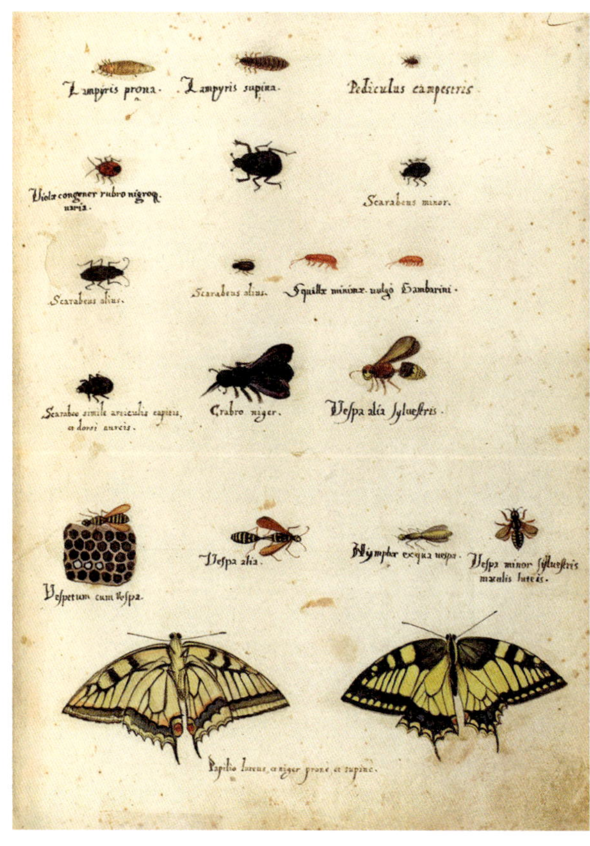

**Fig. 38**
Anonymous painter, *Various insects, with below on the page a papilio machaon* or swallowtail, rectal and dorsal view, in: Aldrovandi Ms, volume 007: animali, fol. 90, between 1550-1605
Bologna, Bibliotheca Universitaria.

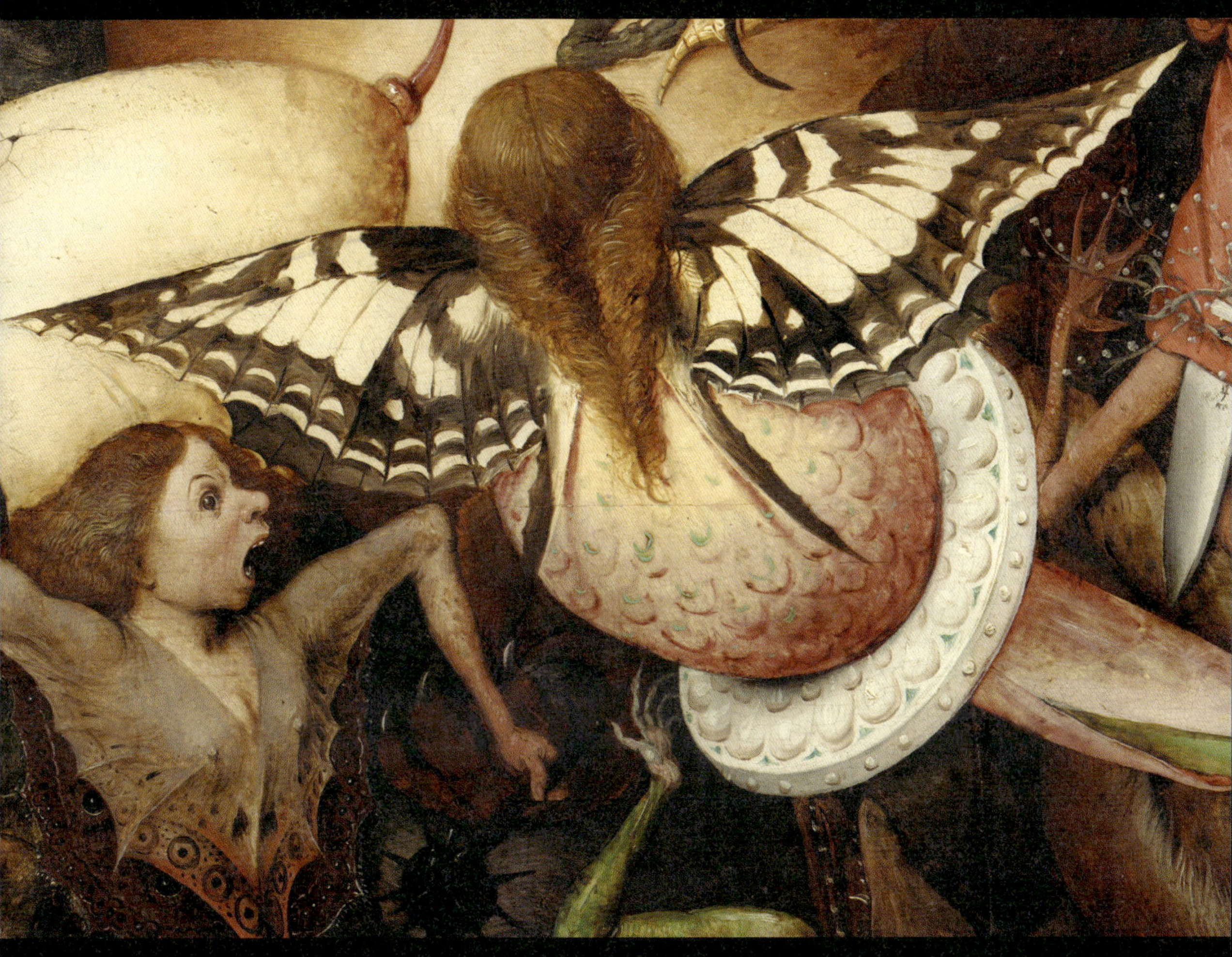

[20]

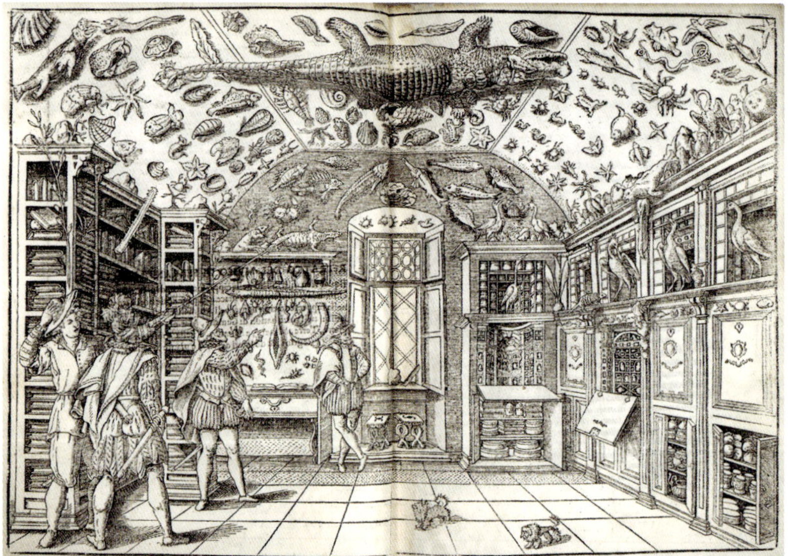

**Fig. 39**
Museum of Ferrante Imperato, in Ferrante Imperato, *Dell' historia naturale libri XXVIII* (Naples, 1599)
Brussels, Royal Library of Belgium

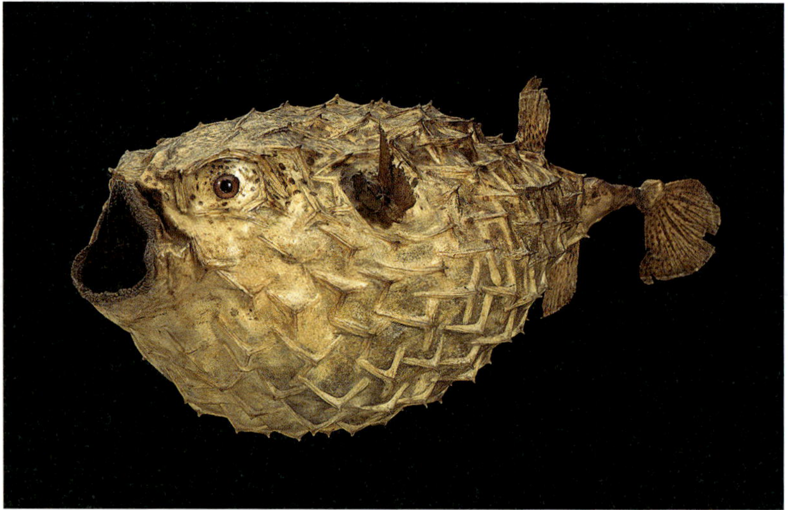

**Fig. 40**
Dried blowfish, early 17th century, possibly from the Tradescant collection
Oxford, History of Science Museum

(fig. 39), and an exemplar was also displayed in the *Hortus Publicus* of the university of Leiden.[53] In the partially imaginary and at any rate posthumous *Cabinet of Curiosities with Abraham Ortelius and Justus Lipsius* by Frans Francken II (fig. 30), we also see a blowfish between the rich collection of dried fish species and *Crustacea.* Aldrovandi's *Natura picta* also contained an illustration of a giant blowfish.[54] A unique example of a dried blowfish, which may have come from the renowned Tradescant collection, can still be admired in the History of Science Museum in Oxford (fig. 40).[55]

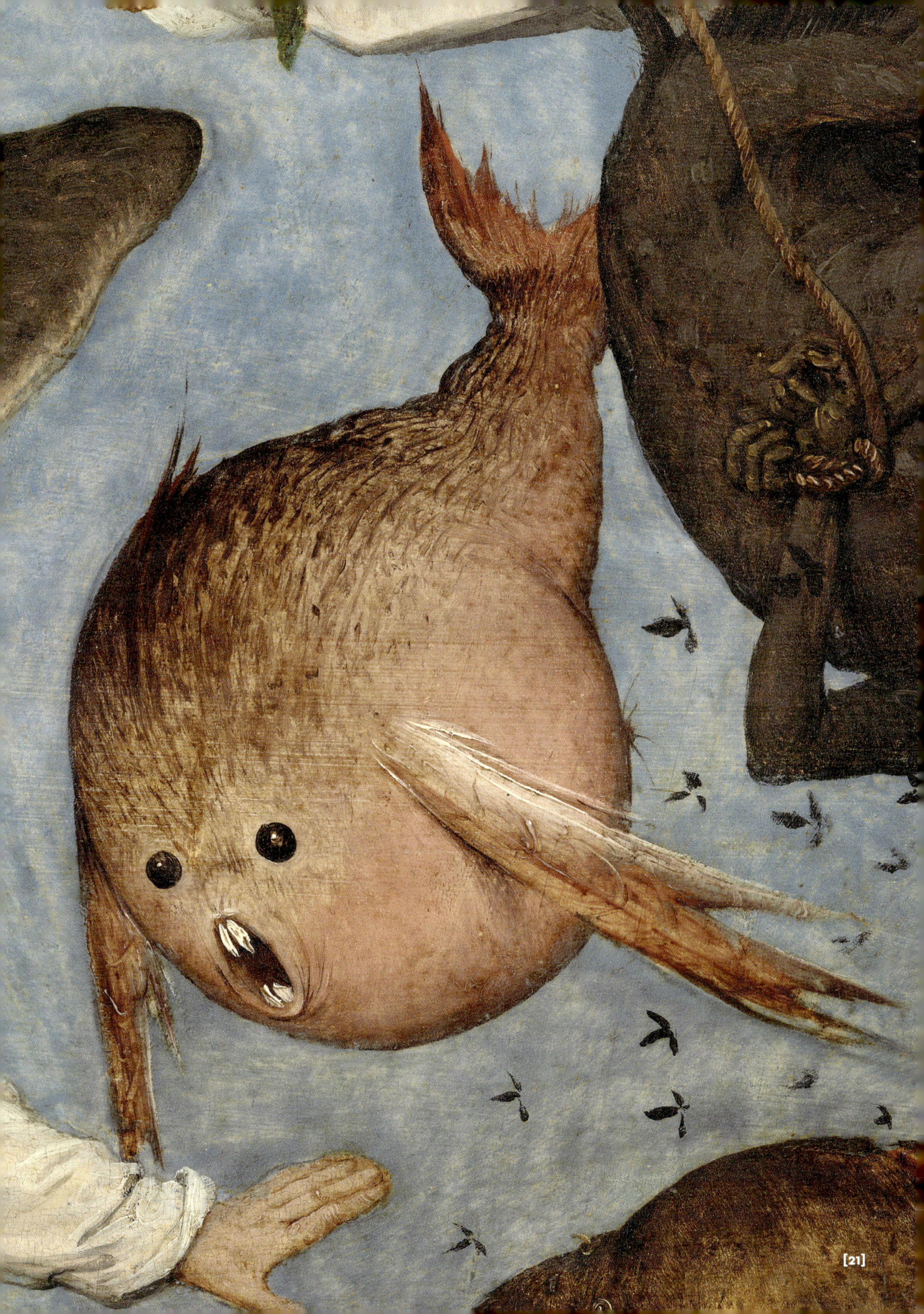

In the *Fall of the Rebel Angels,* various flying fish can also be seen, among which the fish [22] at the end of the endless maelstrom of falling angels from the empyrean realm. We saw that with Bosch, flying fish incarnated the diabolical, the world upside down. Even in the first reports of real flying fish encountered in tropical seas, such as the account of Magellan's voyage by Antonio Pigafetta (1451-1534) and the *Sumario de la natural y general historia de las Indias* by Gonzalo Fernández de Oviedo (1478-1557), flying fish still symbolize danger by air and by sea - and hence the vulnerability of life itself.[56] Many early modern collectors, on the other hand, were fascinated by the strange exterior and special characteristics of flying fish (family *Exocoetidae*), aquatic creatures that flew through the air. Aldrovandi's *Natura picta,* the bestiary of Rudolph II, and the albums of Anselmus de Boodt all contain illustrations of flying fish such as the *Hirundo marino* and the *Dactylopterus volitans.*[57] Like the flying fish that appear next to sirens and imaginary sea monsters on the wall map of *America* published by Hieronymus Cock in Antwerp the same year (fig. 25), Bruegel's flying fish oscillate between symbols of evil and curious species from new-found lands. Among his falling angels, Bruegel painted other aquatic creatures with monstrous features that were popular in curiosity cabinets (fig. 39, 60) while simultaneously evoking a sense of evil, such as the crocodile [39] and the shark [52].[58]

*Animals from the New World*

It should come as no surprise that Bruegel, a sharp observer of the world around him, cites other rare animals from the New World in his *Fall of the Rebel Angels.* Apart from the blowfish and the flying fish, the most striking element is the armor protecting the tender, fruit-like body of the falling angel with the trumpet. It clearly cites the carapace of an armadillo (order *Cingulata*) [23]. Bruegel paints this carapace with its typical bony plates and ribbed tail, which he transforms into a more artificial suit of armor with iron bolts. The armadillo only occurs on the American continent and was a real curiosity around 1562.[59] The album with animals, birds, fish, and reptiles that Charles V may already have commissioned from Lambert Lombard in 1542 depicts several of these exotic creatures (fig. 32).[60]

In Bruegel's time illustrations of armadillos also circulated as prints. The French physician Pierre Belon saw an armadillo at the market in Constantinople and depicted it in his *Les observations de plusieurs singularitéz et choses mémorables* (Paris, 1553), which Plantin published in Antwerp in 1555.[61] Belon notes explicitly that the armadillo was brought from the New World and was therefore not known to the ancients. He also says that the animal could be found as a specimen in cabinets because its hard shell permitted the flesh to be removed without altering its original form.[62] Conrad Gessner included it in his *Animalium Icones* in 1560 (fig. 41).[63] In Adriaen Collaert's iconic print after a drawing by Maerten de Vos (fig. 42), the armadillo is a

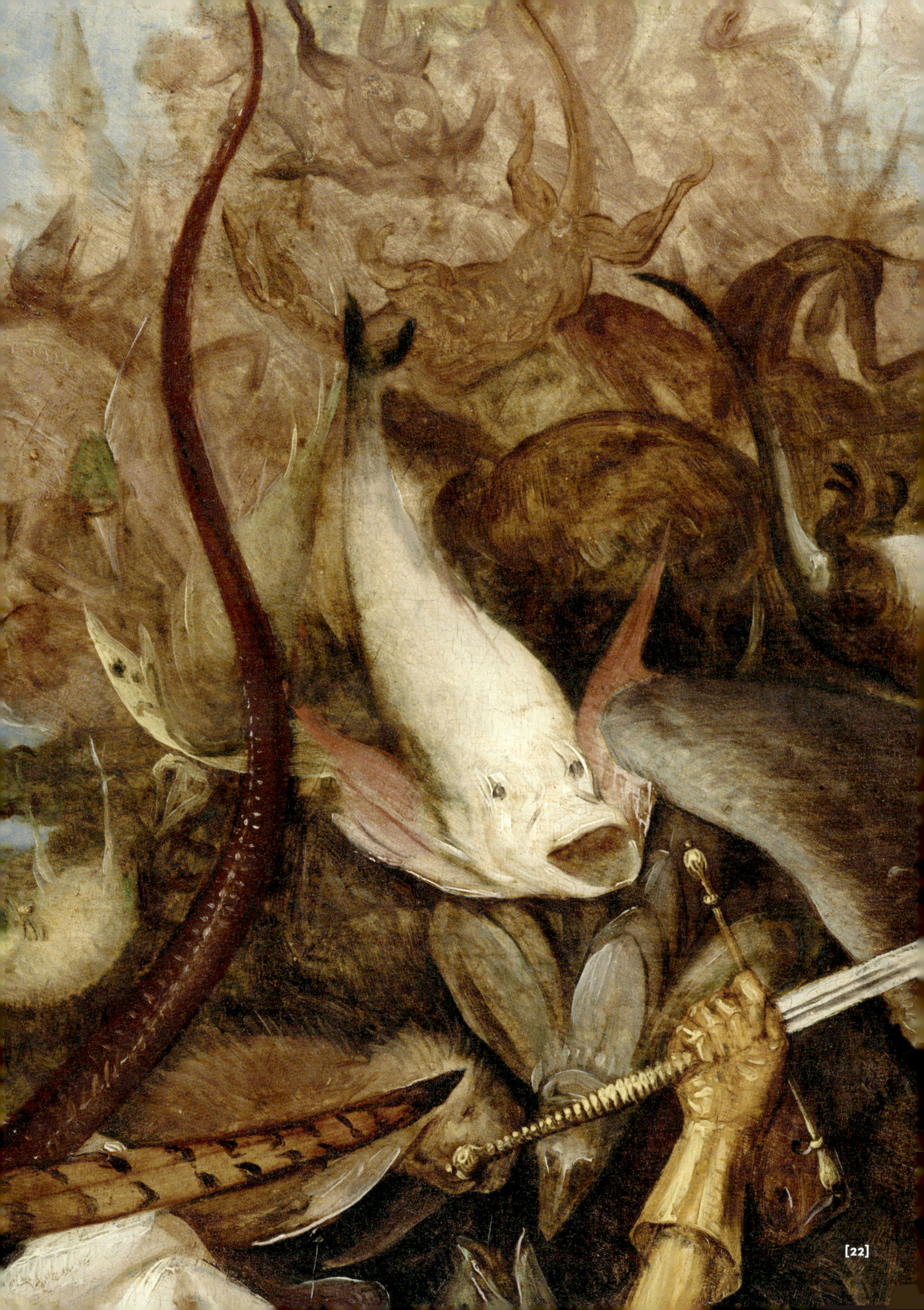

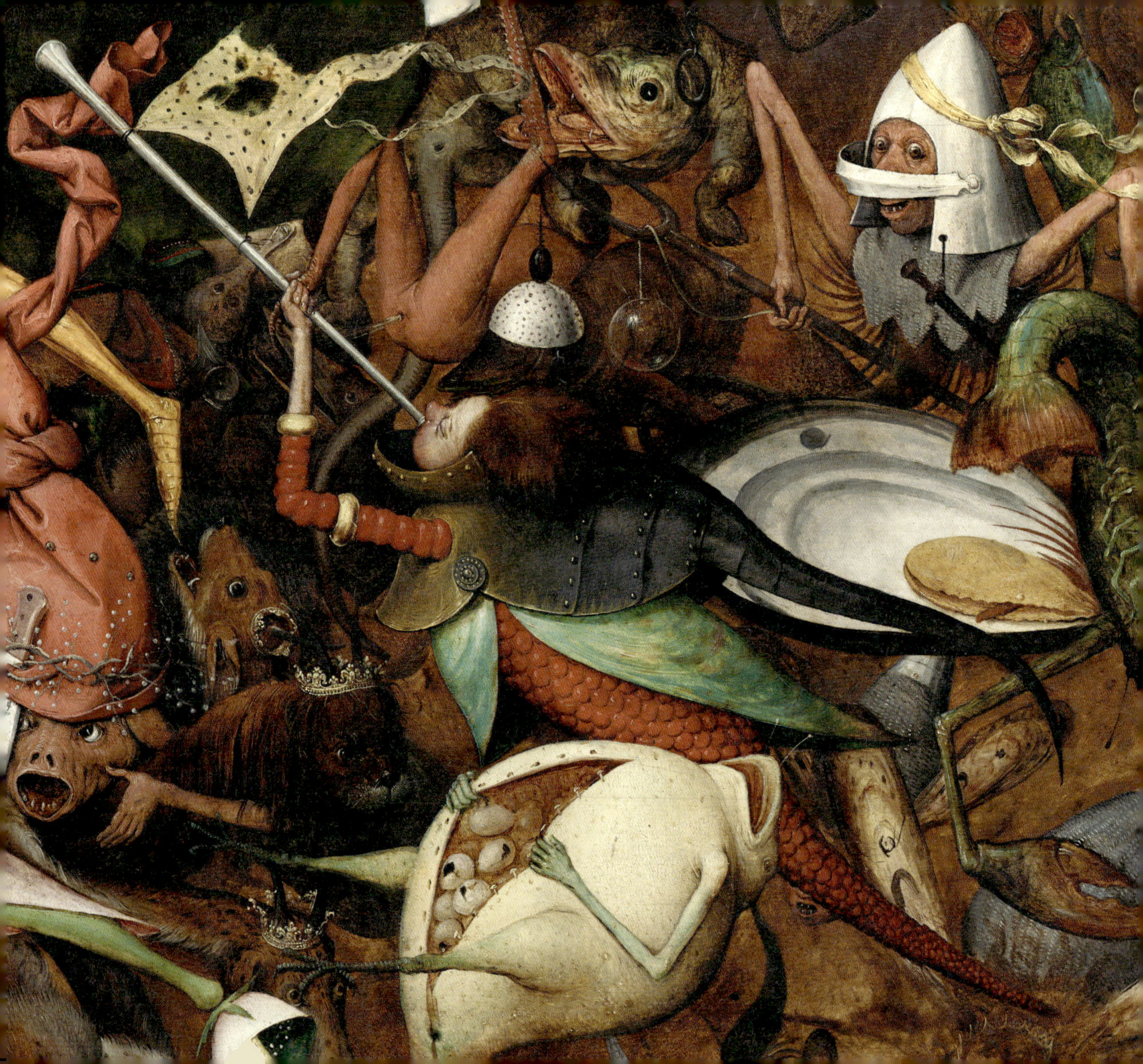

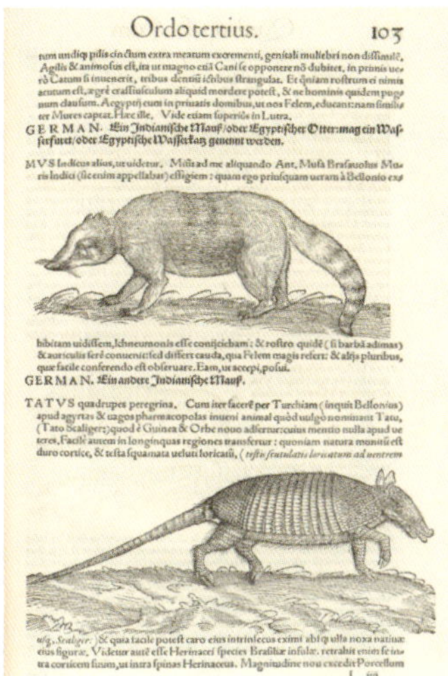
Ordo tertius. 103

rum undiq; pilis cinctum extra meatum excrementi, genitali muliebri non dissimile. Agilis & animosus est, ita ut magno etiã Cani se opponere nõ dubitet, in primis uerò Catum si inuenerit, tribus dentiũ ictibus strangulat. Et quoniam rostrum ei nimis acutum est, ægrè crassiusculum aliquid mordere potest, & ne hominis quidem pugnum clausum. Aegyptij eum in priuatis domibus, ut nos Felem, educant: nam similiter Mures captat. Hæc ille. Vide etiam superiùs in Lutra.

GERMAN. Ein Indianische Mauß / oder Egyptischer Otter: mag ein Wasserfuret / oder Egyptische Wasserkatz genennt werden.

MVS Indicus alius, ut uidetur. Misit ad me aliquando Ant. Musa Brasauolus Muris Indici (sic enim appellabat) effigiem: quam ego priusquam ueram à Bellonio exhibitam uidissem, Ichneumonis esse conijciebam: & rostro quidẽ (si barbã adimas) & auriculis ferè conuenit: sed differt cauda, qua Felem magis refert: & alijs pluribus, quæ facile conferendo est obseruare. Eam, ut accepi, posui.

GERMAN. Ein andere Indianische Mauß.

TATVS quadrupes peregrina. Cum iter facerẽ per Turchiam (inquit Bellonius) apud agyrtas & uagos pharmacopolas inueni animal quòd uulgò nominant Tatu, (Tato Scaliger;) quod è Guinea & Orbe nouo adfertur: cuius mentio nulla apud ueteres. Facilè autem in longinquas regiones transfertur: quoniam natura munitũ est duro cortice, & testa squamata ueluti loricatũ, (testis scutulatis loricatum ad uentrem usq;, Scaliger.) & quia facile potest caro eius intrinsecus eximi absq; ulla noxa natiuæ eius figuræ. Videtur autẽ esse Herinacei species Brasiliæ insulæ. retrahit enim se intra corticem suum, ut intra spinas Herinaceus. Magnitudine non excedit Porcellum

I iiij

**Fig. 41**
Armadillo, in:
Conrad Gessner,
*Icones Animalium Quadrupedum*
(Zurich, 1560), 103
Ghent University Library

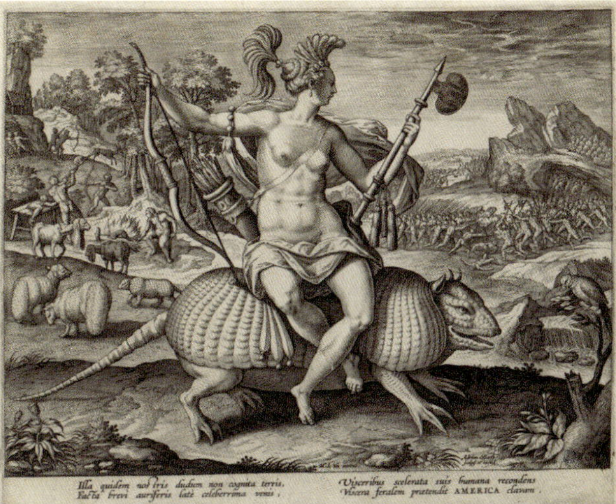


**Fig. 42**
Adriaen Collaert
after Maerten de
Vos, *America*, 1589
Brussels, Royal
Library of Belgium,
Print Cabinet

symbol of *America.* Armadillos are also prominently represented in later depictions of curiosity cabinets, such as that of Basilius Besler (fig. 43). The inventory of the art and curiosity cabinet of Rudolph II (1607-11) mentions no less than three dried specimens and one fine, white armadillo shell.[64]

The manner in which Bruegel cites the armadillo suggests that he was familiar with descriptions by the first travelers to America and by natural historians. Oviedo, for example, notes in the first place the armadillo's carapace, which inspired its European names.[65] Pierre Belon, André Thevet (1516-90)

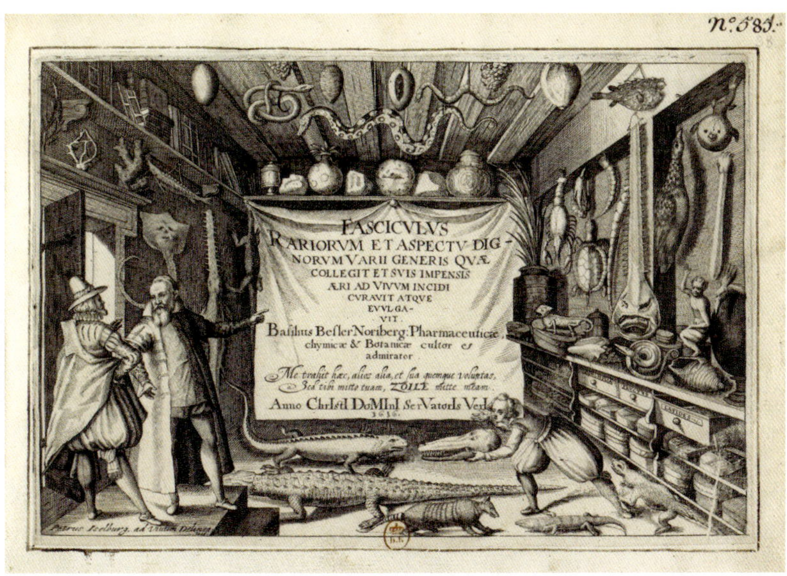


**Fig. 43**
Basilius Besler,
*Fasciculus rariorum et aspectu dignorum varii generis quae collegit et suis impensis ad vivum incidi* (Nuremberg, 1616), titlepage
Paris, Bibliothèque
nationale de France,
département
Estampes et
photographie

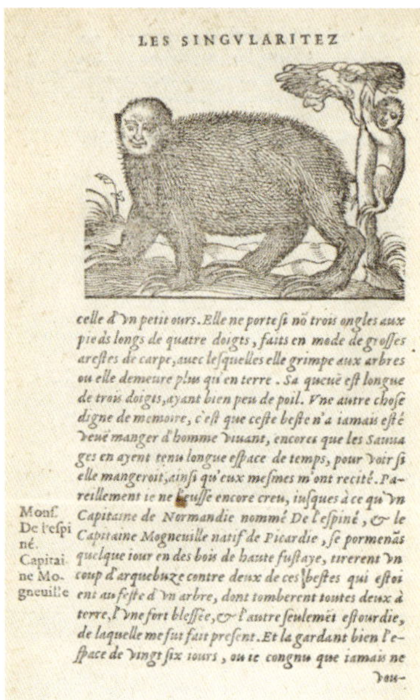

LES SINGVLARITEZ

celle d'vn petit ours. Elle ne porte si nõ trois ongles aux pieds longs de quatre doigts, faits en mode de grosses arestes de carpe, auec lesquelles elle grimpe aux arbres ou elle demeure plus qu'en terre. Sa queuë est longue de trois doigts, ayant bien peu de poil. Vne autre chose digne de memoire, c'est que ceste beste n'a iamais esté veuë manger d'homme viuant, encores que les Sauuages en ayent tenu longue espace de temps, pour voir si elle mangeroit, ainsi qu'eux mesmes m'ont recité. Pareillement ie ne l'eusse encore creu, iusques à ce qu'vn

Monf. De l'espiné. Capitaine Mogneuille

Capitaine de Normandie nommé De l'espiné, & le Capitaine Mogneuille natif de Picardie, se pormenãs quelque iour en des bois de haute fustaye, tirerent vn coup d'arquebuze contre deux de ces bestes qui estoient au feste d'vn arbre, dont tomberent toutes deux à terre, l'vne fort blessée, & l'autre seulemẽt estourdie, de laquelle me fut fait present. Et la gardant bien l'espace de vingt six iours, ou ie congnu que iamais ne vou-

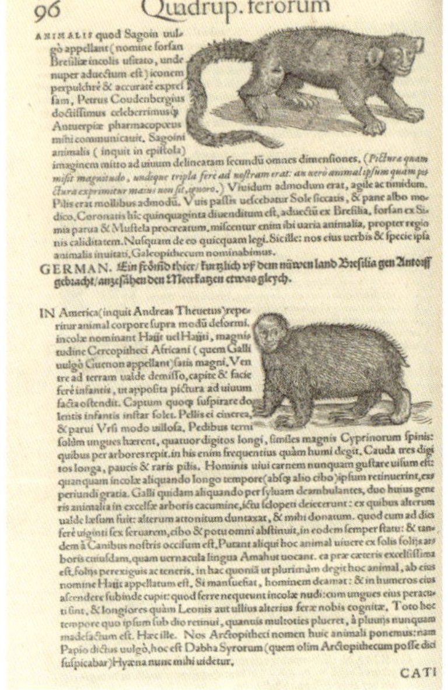

96 Quadrup. ferorum

ANIMALIS quod Sagoin uulgò appellant (nomine forsan Bresiliæ incolis usitato, unde nuper aduectum est) iconem perpulchrè & accuratè expressam, Petrus Coudenbergius doctissimus celeberrimusque Antuerpiæ pharmacopœus mihi communicauit. Sagoini animalis (inquit in epistola) imaginem mitto ad uiuum delineatam secundũ omnes dimensiones. (*Pictura quam misit magnitudo, undique tripla ferè ad nostram erat: an uerò animal ipsum quam pictura exprimitur maius non sit, ignoro.*) Viuidum admodum erat, agile ac timidum. Pilis erat mollibus admodũ. Vuis passis uescebatur Sole siccatis, & pane albo modico. Coronatis hîc quinquaginta diuenditum est, aduectũ ex Bresilia, forsan ex Simia parua & Mustela procreatum, miscentur enim ibi uaria animalia, propter regionis caliditatem. Nusquam de eo quicquam legi. Sic ille: nos eius uerbis & specie ipsa animalis inuitati, Galeopithecum nominabimus.

GERMAN. Ein frömbd thier / kurtzlich vß dem nüwen land Bresilia gen Antorff gebracht / anzesähen den Meerkatzen etwas gleych.

IN America (inquit Andreas Theuetus) reperitur animal corpore supra modũ deformi, incolæ nominant Haüt uel Haüti, magnitudine Cercopitheci Africani (quem Galli uulgò Guenon appellant) satis magni. Ventre ad terram ualde demisso, capite & facie ferè infantis, ut apposita pictura ad uiuum facta ostendit. Captum quoque suspirare dolentis infantis instar solet. Pellis ei cinerea, & parui Vrsi modo uillosa. Pedibus terni solùm ungues hærent, quatuor digitos longi, similes magnis Cyprinorum spinis: quibus per arbores repit. in his enim frequentius quàm humi degit. Cauda tres digitos longa, paucis & raris pilis. Hominis uiui carnem nunquam gustare uisum est: quanquam incolæ aliquando longo tempore (absque alio cibo) ipsum retinuerint, experiundi gratia. Galli quidam aliquando per syluam deambulantes, duo huius generis animalia in excelsæ arboris cacumine, ictu sclopeti deiecerunt: ex quibus alterum ualde læsum fuit: alterum attonitum duntaxat, & mihi donatum. quod cum ad dies ferè uiginti sex seruarem, cibo & potu omni abstinuit, in eodem semper statu: & tandem à Canibus nostris occisum est. Putant aliqui hoc animal uiuere ex solis folijs arboris cuiusdam, quam uernacula lingua Amahut uocant. ea præ cæteris excelsissima est, folijs perexiguis ac teneris. in hac quoniã ut plurimùm degit hoc animal, ab eius nomine Haüt appellatum est. Si mansuefiat, hominem deamat: & in humeros eius ascendere subinde cupit: quod ferre nequeunt incolæ nudi: cum ungues eius peracuti sint, & longiores quàm Leonis aut ullius alterius feræ nobis cognitæ. Toto hoc tempore quo ipsum sub dio retinui, quanuis multoties plueret, à pluuijs nunquam madefactum est. Hæc ille. Nos Arctopitheci nomen huic animali ponemus: nam Papio dictus uulgò, hoc est Dabha Syrorum (quem olim Arctopithecum posse dici suspicabar) Hyæna nunc mihi uidetur.

CATI

**Fig. 44**
Sloth, in: André Thevet, *Les Singularitez de la France Antarctique, autrement nommé Amérique & de plusieurs terres & isles decouverts de nostre temps* (Antwerp, 1558), fol. 99 verso
Antwerp, Plantijn Moretus Museum

**Fig. 45**
Sloth, in: Conrad Gessner, *Icones Animalium Quadrupedum* (Zurich, 1560), fol. 96
Ghent University Library

and Aldrovandi call the armadillo a "tat(o)u(m)," after the name given by the Brazilian Tupi Indians to the animal's hardened carapace.[66] Bruegel's association of an iconic American animal with a devil characterizes the early modern perception of the New World, as we shall see below.

Given Bruegel's knowledge of new natural-historical visual material about the New World, it would come as no surprise if he incorporated even more *americana* into the *Fall of the Rebel Angels.* Another animal that the earliest visitors to the New World never failed to mention, and that for this reason was also often used as a symbol of the newly discovered continent, is the sloth. Thevet adopts the Tupi appellation of the animal, *Haüt,* and illustrates it in his *Les Singularitéz de la France Antarctique* (fig. 44) that first appeared in Paris in 1557. Only a year later, Plantin published a pocket-sized edition of this travel account.[67] Gessner copied the sloth from Thevet in his *Icones Animalium* of 1560 (fig. 45).[68] Bruegel seems to have painted a sloth in the lower left-hand corner of the *Fall* [24]. The hairy body, black snout, and above all the protruding, black, close-set eyes are typical of the three-toed sloth (*Bradypus tridactylus*) from South America (fig. 46). Bruegel has painted this animal hanging head downward, as it does in its natural habitat. This is striking, as only Thevet mentions that the animal hung in the trees, while most early modern illustrations (Gessner, *Bestiaire,* Clusius) show the

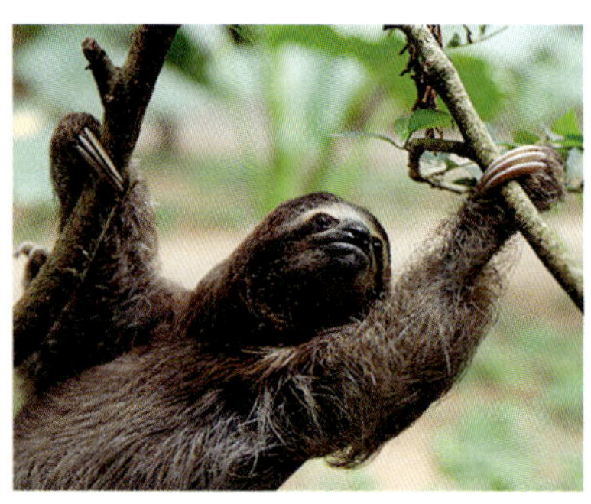

**Fig. 46**
South-American sloth (*bradypus tridactylus*)

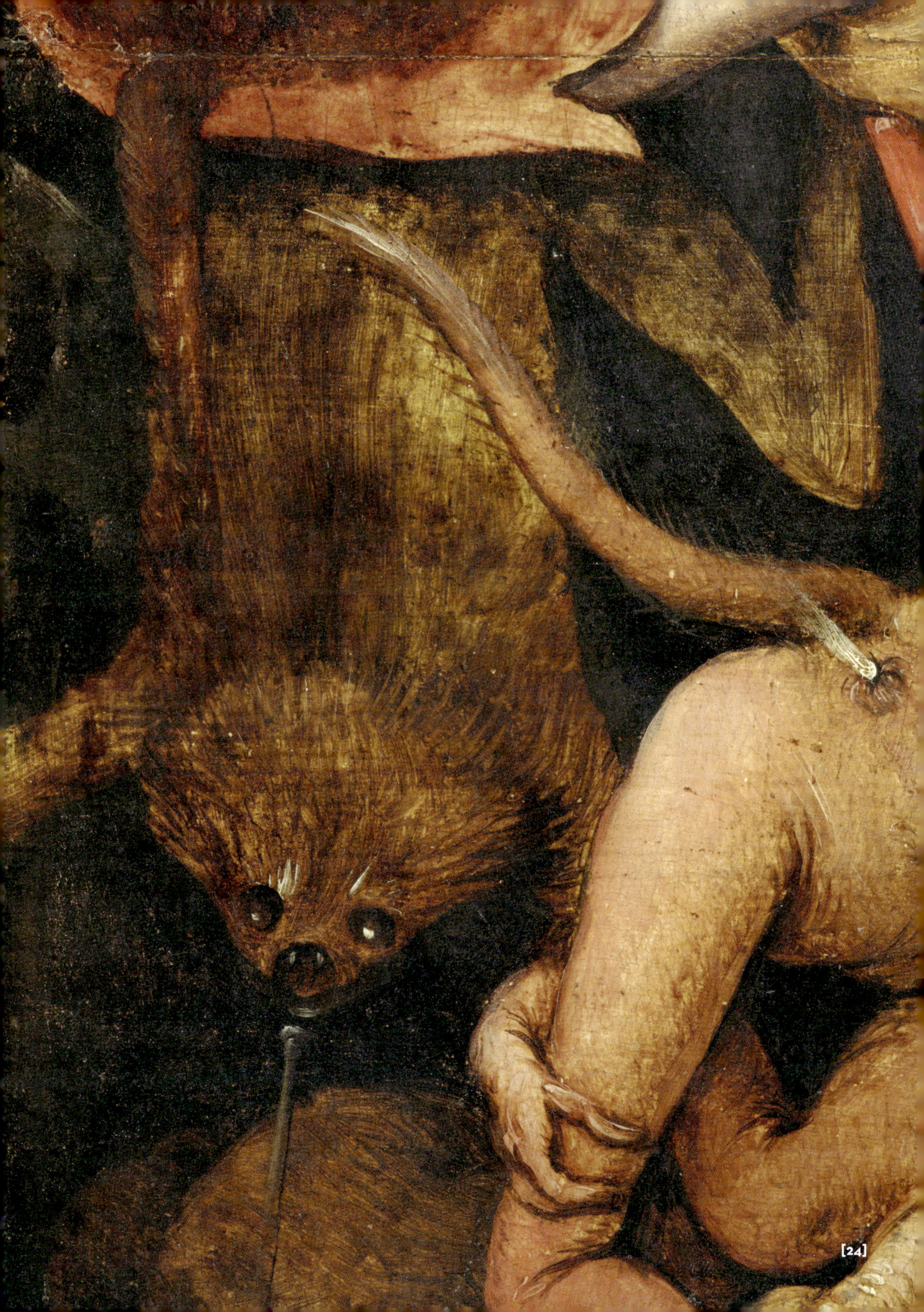

[24]

animal in an unnatural way - standing upright on its four feet, or sometimes sitting.[69] Unlike Thevet, most natural historians had never seen a live sloth. Clusius notes in his *Exoticorum libri decem* that he compared the reports of Oviedo and Thevet with his own examination of a dead sloth that he had acquired from Emmanuel Swerts, a dealer in Amsterdam.[70] This specimen probably ended up later in the collection of Rudolph II.[71]

*From "naer het leven" to "uyt den gheest"*

Other animal elements in Bruegel's swarm of devils, animals, and things, cannot be identified easily. Some of the crowned heads of the seven-headed monster of the Apocalypse [2] have dog-like features; others with their long necks, pointed snouts and ears, and short, black horns are more closely related to goats. Their speckled hides show similarities to the *Antilocapra americana,* or pronghorn, the species of goat depicted in Rudolph II's bestiary.[72] Goats had diabolical connotations, and usually symbolized the vice of Lust.[73] The devil's head [25] protruding between Saint Michael's right leg and the gigantic beast of the Apocalypse is inspired by a species of goat from the region of the Holy Land, the so-called Nubian goat, an exotic sort characterized by soft, hanging ears. In Erhard Reuwich's illustration of Bernard de Breytenbach's *Peregrationes in Terra Sanctam* (1486), a book that Bosch consulted for his depiction of exotic animals in the *Garden of Earthly Delights,* it is labeled a "capra de India."[74] Bruegel has also depicted a sort of spoonbill (genus *Platalea*), a bird that occurs in Europe and America and that is also present in the *Garden of Earthly Delights* (fig. 20), with a plucked member of its own kind in its beak [26].[75] The scaled reptile under one of the good angels [53] is a kind of lizard (genus *Lacerta*), an animal that had also been long associated with sin and decay, and that because of its unusual appearance and the ease with which it could be preserved was also coveted by owners of curiosity cabinets (fig. 39). There are other lizard-like creatures among the fallen angels, such as the winged exemplar [44] in combat with a chained dog [43]. The dog bites the monster's tail, while the monster grabs the dog's tail in a senseless circle of violence, perhaps as a reference to sodomy. To the left, a skeleton (of a horse?) [27], also an item frequently found in cabinets of curiosities, rises up out of the dark depths. In addition to menageries of living animals, skeletons and dried specimens were the natural remains of animal species that could otherwise be collected only as illustrations.[76] In Bruegel's painting the skeleton also recalls the evil atmosphere inhabited by skeletons and teratological forms in various paintings by Bosch.[77]

Overshadowed by a crocodile-like monster, we see a proboscidean [38], which with its elongated, mobile snout recalls an elephant, or perhaps an anteater. It is possible that Bruegel had read about this American proboscidean in Oviedo, but illustrations of anteaters were still extremely rare in 1562.[78] Elephants, on the other hand, had been known since antiquity. Although most Europeans around the middle of the sixteenth century had never

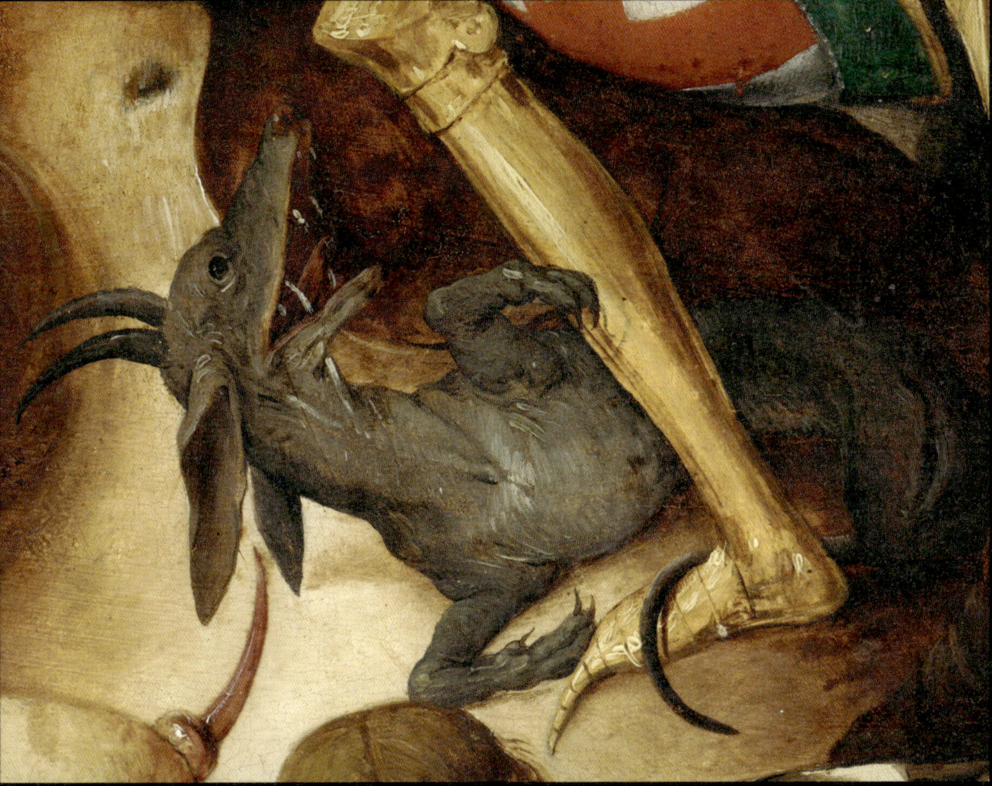

[25]

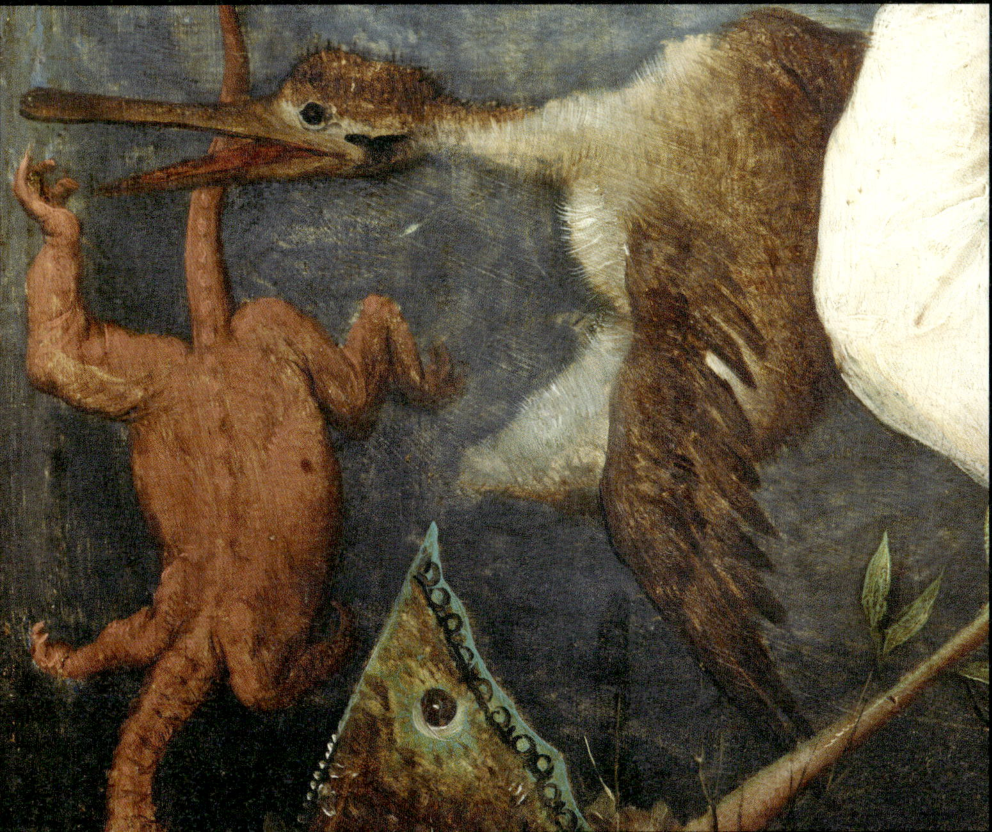

[26]

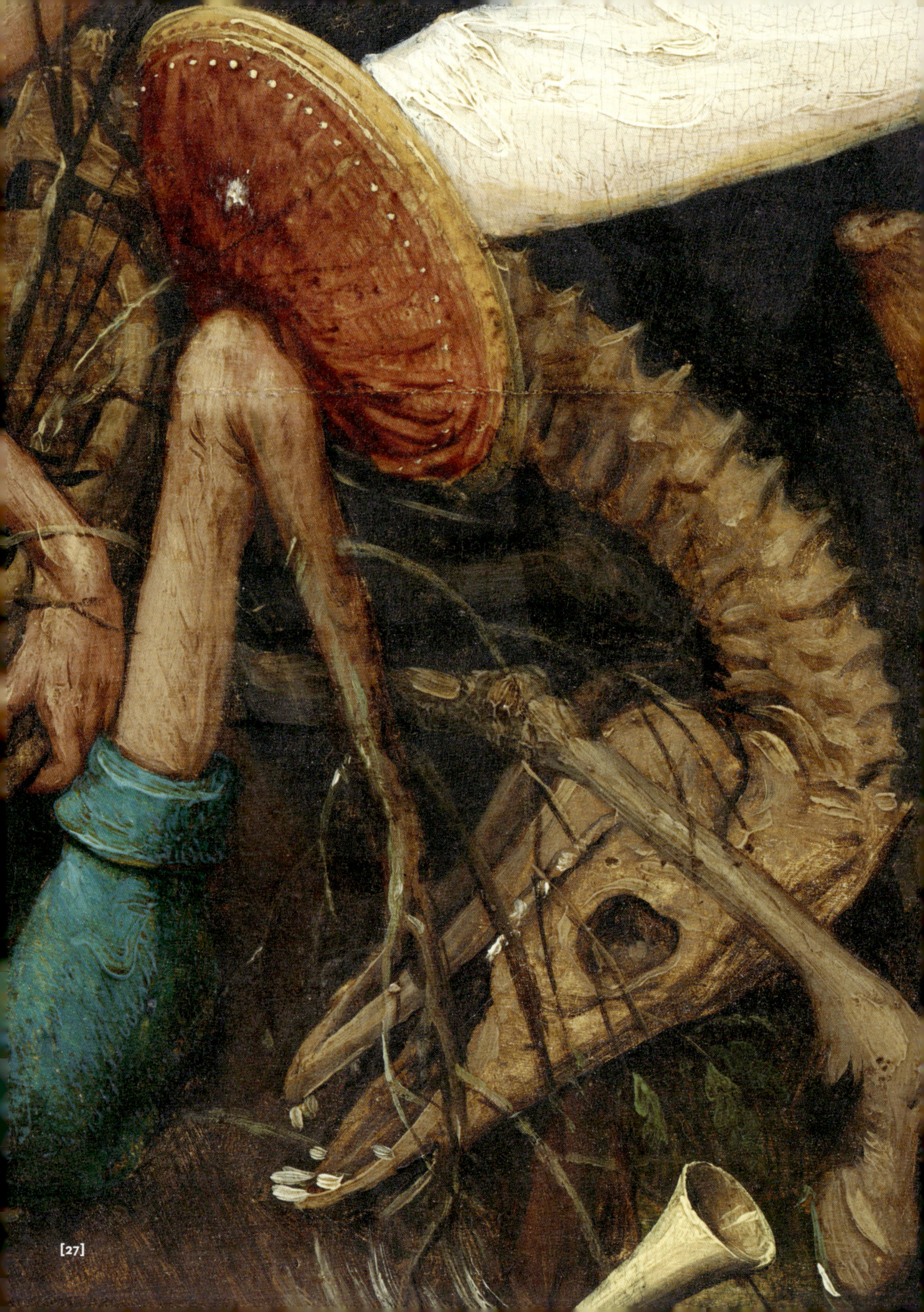

[27]

actually seen a live elephant, they were at least familiar with their appearance from illustrations.[79] An elephant wanders about the earthly paradise in Bosch's *Garden of Earthly Delights*. Of the creature painted by Bruegel in 1562, however, we see little more than a trunk - nor do we see the elephant's characteristic tusks.

The ape-like monster [47] hidden behind the hurdy-gurdy resembles a common marmoset, another popular exotic animal that was a favorite pet of courtiers on account of its minuscule size.[80] Bruegel, however, does not render this species very naturalistically, but rather "creates" it from his own imagination. The influx of exotic animals must have convinced Bruegel more than anything of the endless variety of nature, and provided him with new models on which he as an artist could create endless variations. In his depiction of the proboscidean monster [38] and the ape-like chimera [47] Bruegel shifts the focus from the natural to the imaginary, from what he could draw *naer het leven* (from life) to what he invented *uyt den gheest* (from the mind).[81] Thus, the competition between nature and art that inspired the creation of art and curiosity cabinets also drove Bruegel to imagine fictional species among the falling angels. But before we explore further the natural-philosophical and artistic concepts that inform Bruegel's creative process in chapter III, we will discuss his depiction of manmade objects, or *artificialia*, that formed a counterpart to the *naturalia* in contemporary collectors' cabinets.

## Artificialia

Bruegel has equipped various falling angels with artificial attributes such as scientific and musical instruments, weapons and armor, and ethnographic objects. The detailed depiction of these *artificialia* betray the artist's thorough knowledge of this kind of collector's items.

### *Musical instruments*

The body of the lobster-like monster at the lower left is a hurdy-gurdy [13], a popular instrument associated with beggars, such as Bruegel later depicted in his *Parable of the Blind* (fig. 16). Bruegel renders several typical details of the instrument, such as the four strings, and the decorative pattern on the wooden body with great precision. As mentioned earlier, Bosch depicted a hurdy-gurdy as an instrument of torture in the hell panel of his *Garden of Earthly Delights* (fig. 17), which Bruegel surely references. The falling angel [12] bending over the one with the body of a hurdy-gurdy plays a wind instrument with a fontanelle (a small punched box which covers the key in a shawm), but rendered in metal while the shawm was made of wood.[82] This type of musical instrument is also present in the hell panel of the *Garden of Earthly Delights* (fig. 20), again underscoring its negative connotation. The falling angel with the impressive armor of an armadillo [23] plays a straight trumpet with a blazon, a decorative element often attached at the

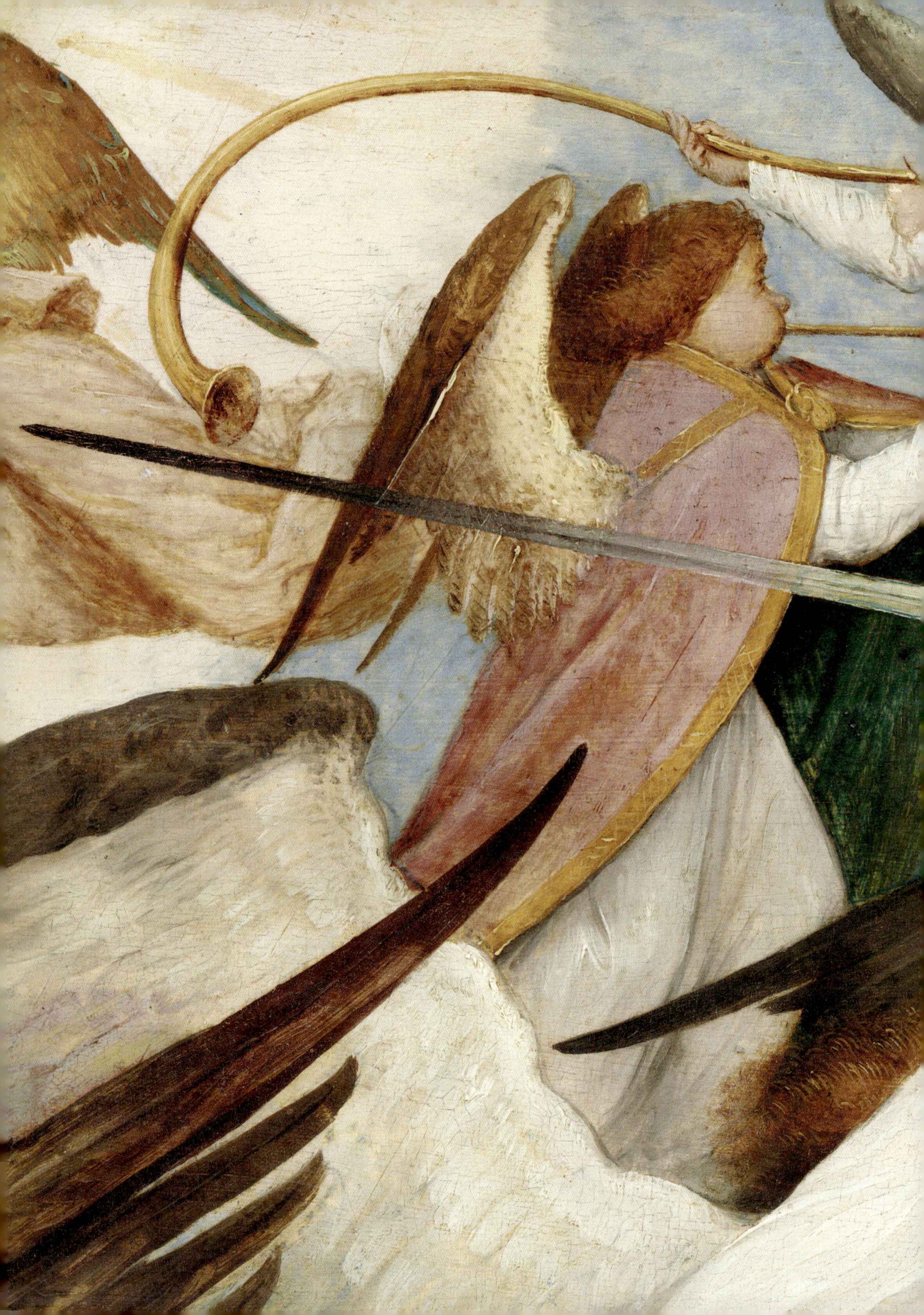

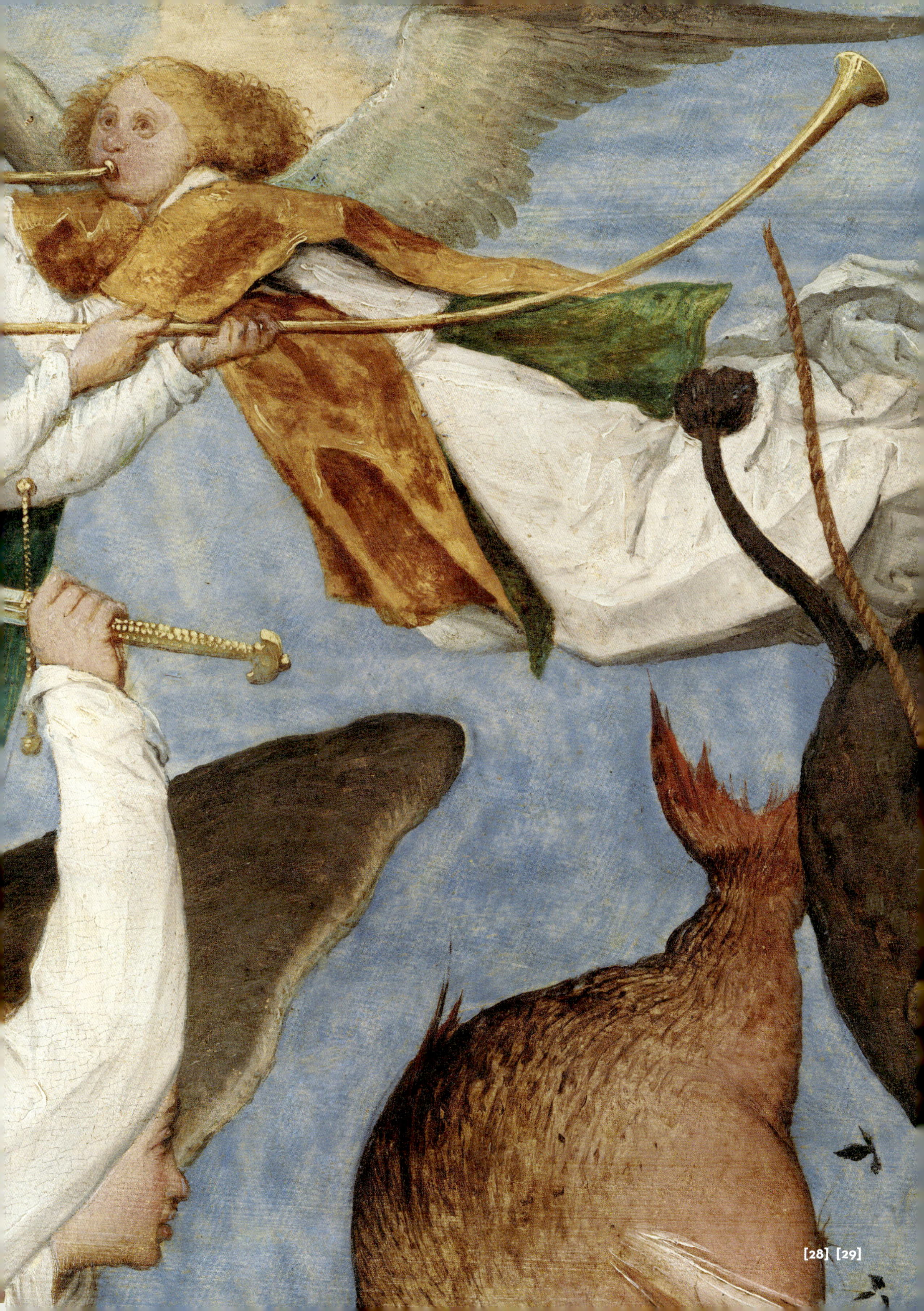
[28] [29]

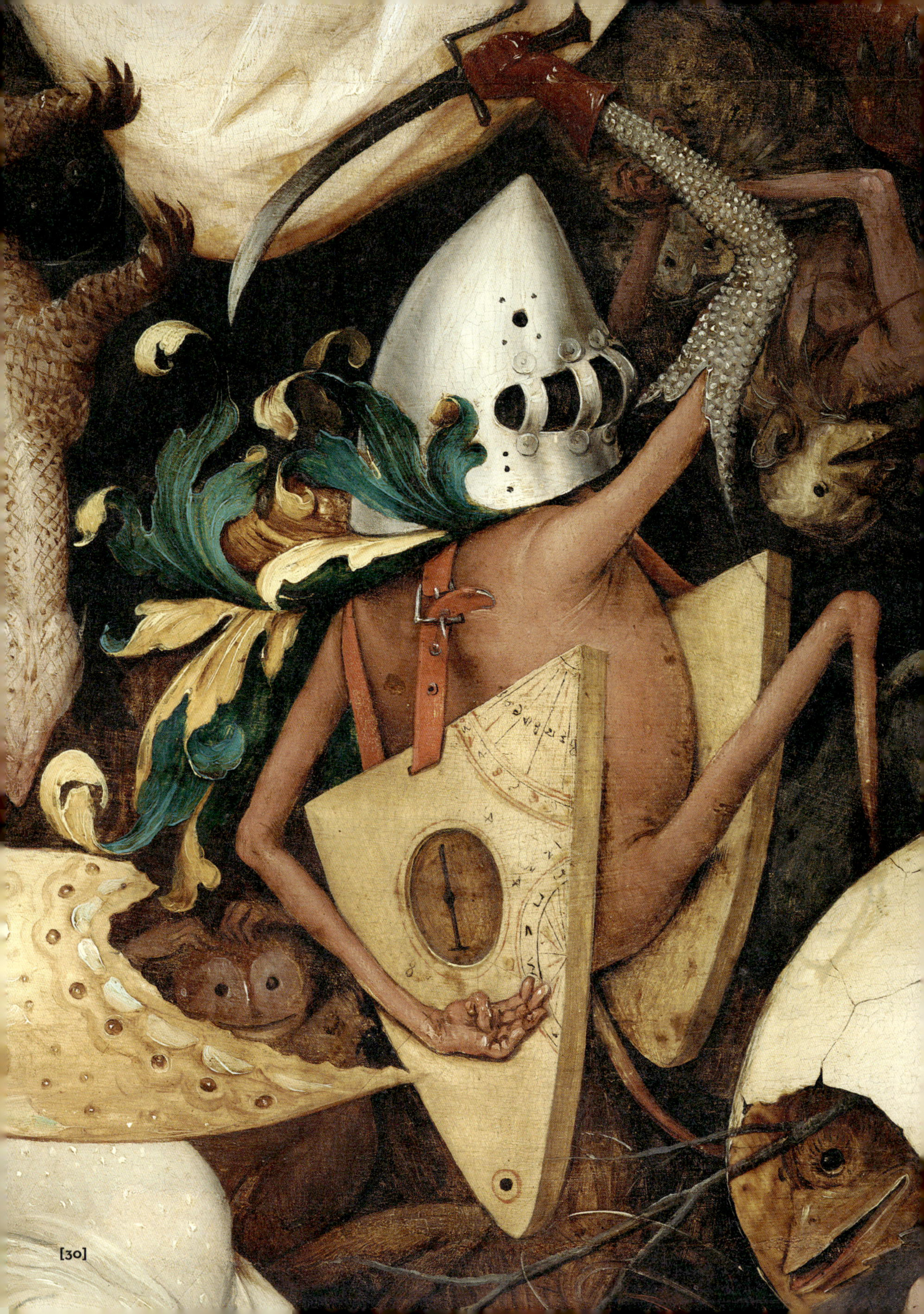

[30]

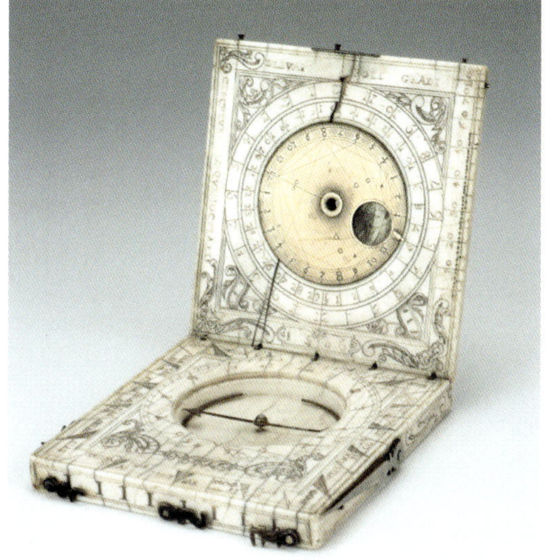

**Fig. 47**
Ivory Diptych Sundial, probably made in Flanders, 1586
Oxford, History of Science Museum

occasion of official ceremonies. The blazon of this falling angel is comically spotted and wielding during its descent, however, accentuating its vain attempts to resist eternal condemnation. In striking contrast with the straight wind instruments of the falling angels, the four music-making good angels sound out their triumph on curved brass trumpets [5, 6, 28, 29] similar to those in Early Netherlandish paintings of the *Last Judgment* by Rogier van der Weyden and others.

*Sundial*

Another falling angel wears a sort of double breastplate worked into a sundial [30]. Although only a fragment is depicted, its whitish-yellow color clearly evokes a particular type of sundial that in the sixteenth century was mainly produced in Nuremberg, but also in Flanders (fig. 47). This type of portable clock is put together like a diptych and is made of ivory from African elephants, with black and red inscriptions. The inside of the lower wing contains an *aspectarium* or compass, consisting of a more deeply embedded bronze plate and needle. A cord indicator or *gnomon* is typically fastened to the lower wing,

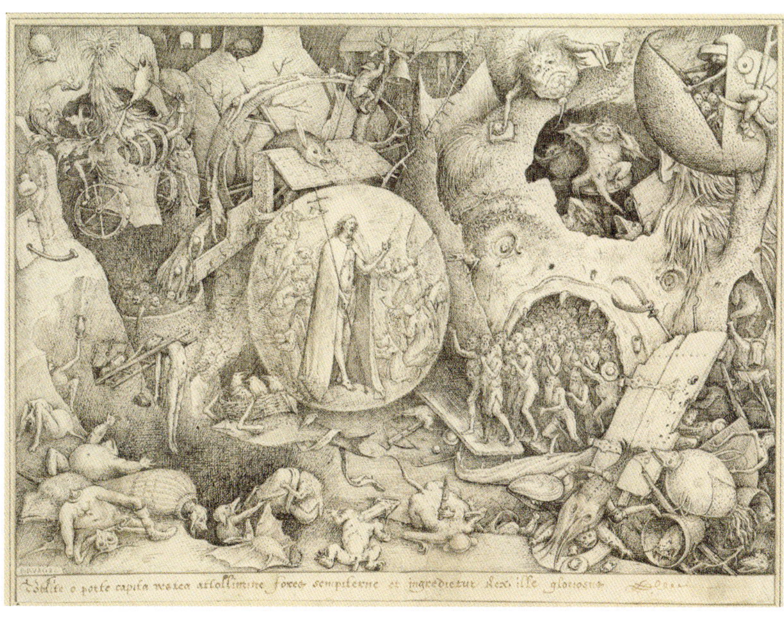

**Fig. 48**
Pieter Bruegel the Elder, *Descent of Christ into Limbo*, (c. 1561?)
Vienna, Graphische Sammlung Albertina

and is used to determine the hours of the day according to the position of the sun as registered by the uppermost inner wing.[83] Bruegel has painted an ivory diptych with a bronze compass, upon which black and red letters indicate the quarters of the sundial in Arabic numbers, and a second circle depicts the signs of the zodiac, a frequently occurring feature on sundials of this sort.[84] He has also clearly marked the knob with which this sort of bilateral sundial was opened and closed. Because it is being used as a breastplate, however, the inscriptions on Bruegel's hybrid sundial are partially obscured.

The incorporation of a portable sundial worn as the armor of one of the falling angels is quite particular and presupposes a specific meaning. It emphasizes the fact that Saint Michael is combatting evil from the beginning to the end of time, and echoes the message that Bruegel suggests by combining the fall of the rebel angels with the monster of the Apocalypse. Like the moralizing inscriptions sometimes found on sundials from the period, this sundial-man reminds the viewer to make good use of his or her time on earth.[85] A sundial was also considered an instrument for recalibrating earth's chaos, with its unpredictable disasters, to be more in tune with the regularity of the universe. The sundial on the back of the falling angel seems to refer to these notions with a healthy dose of irony. At the same time, Bruegel alludes to the boundless appetite for collecting mechanical instruments. Because of their preciousness and technical ingenuity, sundials and clocks were highly coveted collector's items.[86]

*Weapons and armor*

The prominence of weapons and armor in the *Fall of the Rebel Angels* has a narrative logic. After all, the episode portrays the Ur-battle between good and evil, an armed encounter that took place before the creation of mankind.[87] Bruegel's elaboration of the narrative as a sampling of all possible natural and artificial types of armor, however, is unique. Weapons and armor formed an important part of early modern collections, particularly princely collections. The Coudenberg Palace in Brussels housed an armory since the days of the dukes of Brabant. During the reign of Charles V, and later that of Albert and Isabella, it became a splendid display of the suits of armor, shields, and weaponry of the princes and their predecessors that was meant to illustrate dynastic glory to select visitors.[88] The armory has vanished along with Coudenberg Palace, but parts of it were probably absorbed by other Habsburg collections of weapons, in the *Rustkammers* of Vienna and Innsbrück, and the *Real Armeria* of Madrid.[89]

Most striking in Bruegel's painting is the golden armor of its protagonist, Saint Michael [1]. The warlike archangel was frequently depicted in armor, but in contrast to Frans Floris, for example, who dresses Saint Michael in Roman armor *all'antica* (fig. 5), Bruegel has chosen an archaic suit of body armor with an undergarment of chainmail, as was common in the fifteenth

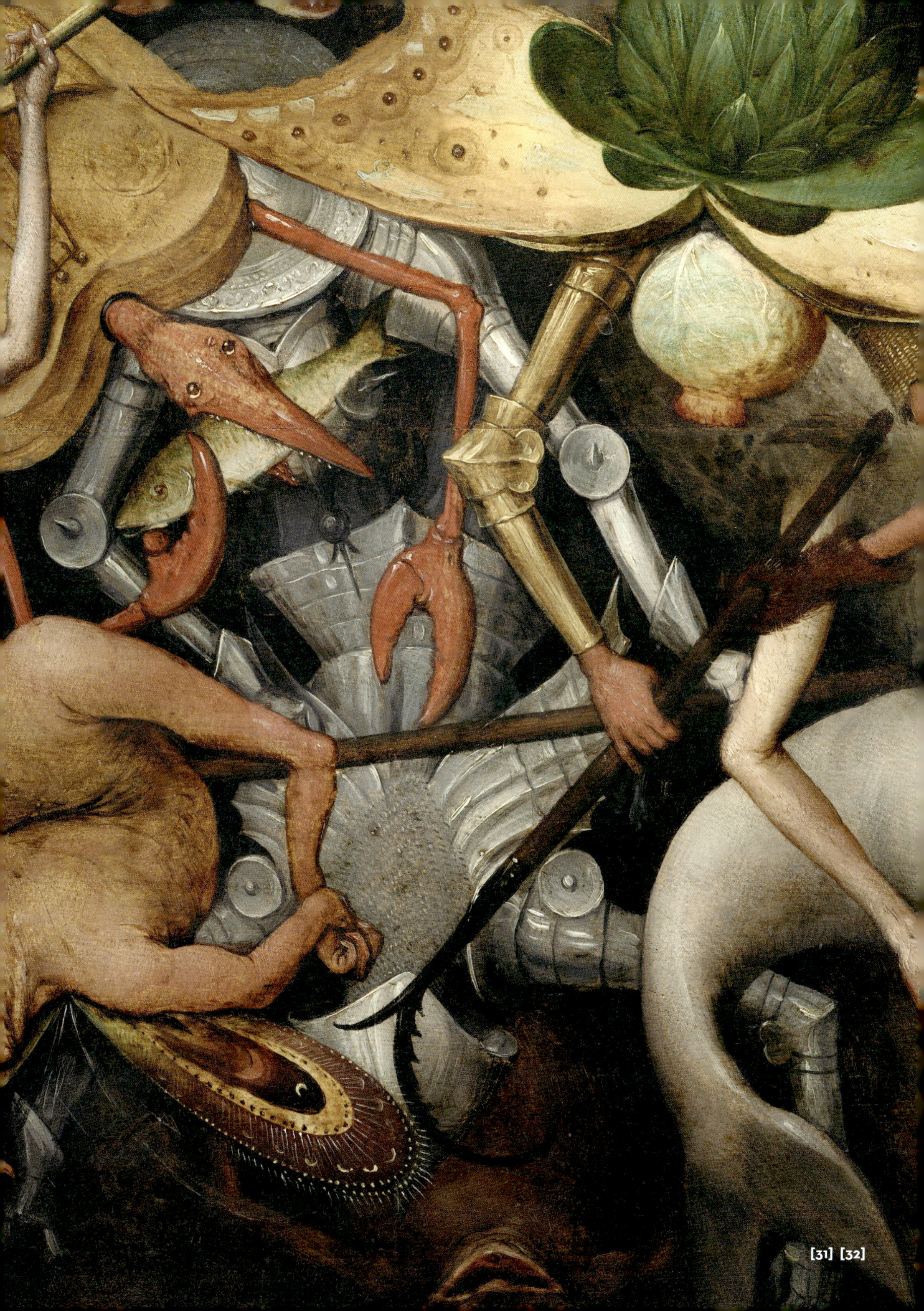

[31] [32]

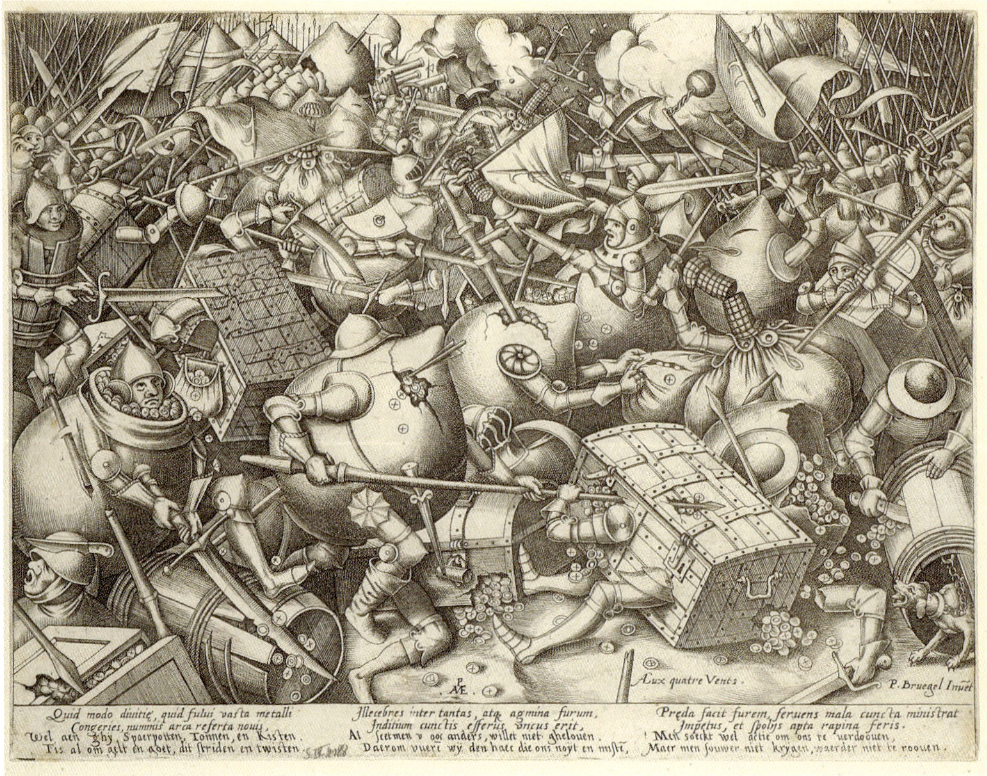


century. Princely suits of parade armor in particular were veritable works of art, often featuring gilded decorations. Bruegel's Saint Michael wears a complete suit of golden armor and so displays his divine nature.

In the lower left-hand corner two devils in armor tumble down one after the other [31, 32]. They are still comparatively well-formed, as if their steel cuirasses were already diabolical enough. Of the gilded armor of the devil falling in front of them, only an arm-piece and torn piece of chainmail remain, while his head has become a cabbage, his body a blooming artichoke, and he has acquired the wings of a moth [49]. The aforementioned devil with the sundial armor [30] wears a helmet with a rounded visor of widely spaced bars, topped with blue and yellow plumes. This is no war helmet, but a helmet used as a heraldic device for jousting or parades.[90] By equipping a diabolical chimera with this sort of tournament gear, Bruegel seems to poke fun at the world of knighthood, where battles were staged for the sake of honor, sport, and entertainment. In his drawing *Christ's Descent into Limbo* (fig. 48), a composition that has much in common with the *Fall of the Rebel Angels*, Bruegel uses a similar parade helmet as a sort of diabolical attribute. And in his later engraving of the *Battle of the Strong-Boxes and Moneybags* (fig. 49), strong-boxes

**Fig. 49**
Pieter Bruegel the Elder, *Battle of the Strong-Boxes and Moneybags* (printed after 1570)
Brussels, Royal Library of Belgium, Print Cabinet

and moneybags likewise battle one another in parade and combat armor in a senseless tournament. The manner in which Bruegel depicts certain confrontations between angels and devils as mock battles recalls masked tournaments of the sort organized at the court of Margaret of Parma on the occasion of the marriage of Ottavio Farnese and Mary of Portugal (fig. 78).[91]
The helmet of the "head-hand-man" [50] may look like proper battle gear, and the rake in his hand like a dangerous weapon, but the ribbon tied in a bow around his helmet makes this warrior just as ridiculous as his brothers-in-arms. The fragile glass sphere that he tries to hold on a silk thread recalls the transparent globe in which Christ and his angels descend towards the gates of hell, or the alchemical vessel - known as an alembic - in which adepts try to distill the golden truth, both of which Bosch incorporated into his *Garden of Earthly Delights* (fig. 20).[92] Perhaps Bruegel wished above all to evoke the fragile existence of good. The breakable glass sphere contrasts sharply with the black club with steel spikes, a so-called morning star, in the hands of a screeching female devil with a butterfly's body [36].

*Non-European* artificialia

Of all the precious objects and curiosities brought together by early modern collectors, exotica were perhaps the most coveted. European princes collected not only armor and weapons from allied dynasties, but also trophies from conquered enemies. The *armeria* of the "Room of Ten" in the Doge's Palace in Venice contained Ottoman helmets and daggers, and so did the Habsburg collection of Ferdinand II of Tyrol (1529-1595) in Innsbrück, among others.[93] Since the fall of the Eastern Roman Empire (1453), the infidel "Turks" - a collective name for various peoples of the Ottoman Empire - formed the greatest threat to Christian Europe. In an age of internal religious conflict they were a common enemy, and their rich culture was looked at with fascination as well as horror. Bruegel was familiar with Turkish customs and habits as recorded by his teacher and father-in-law Pieter Coecke during a trip to

**Fig. 50**
Ottoman saber or *scimitar*, 16th century
New York, Metropolitan Museum of Art. Bequest of George C. Stone, 1935

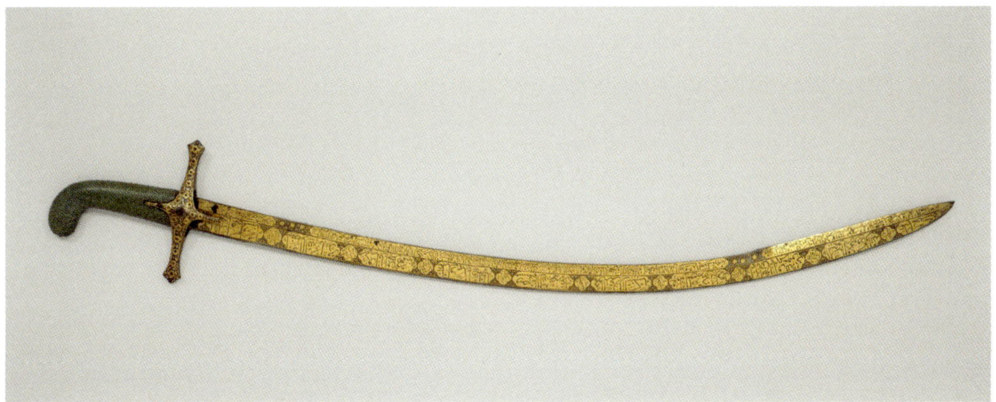

Constantinople.[94] In the *Suicide of Saul* (fig. 26), also dated 1562, Bruegel depicts the biblical battle between the first king of Israel and the Philistines as a confrontation between Western warriors in armor and enemy soldiers in Ottoman garments and turbans. In the *Fall,* Bruegel's devil with the parade helmet and sundial breastplate [30] holds a curved Ottoman sword or scimitar in his right hand (fig. 50). At the very bottom another falling angel [33] loses a typical pointed Ottoman helmet (fig. 51).

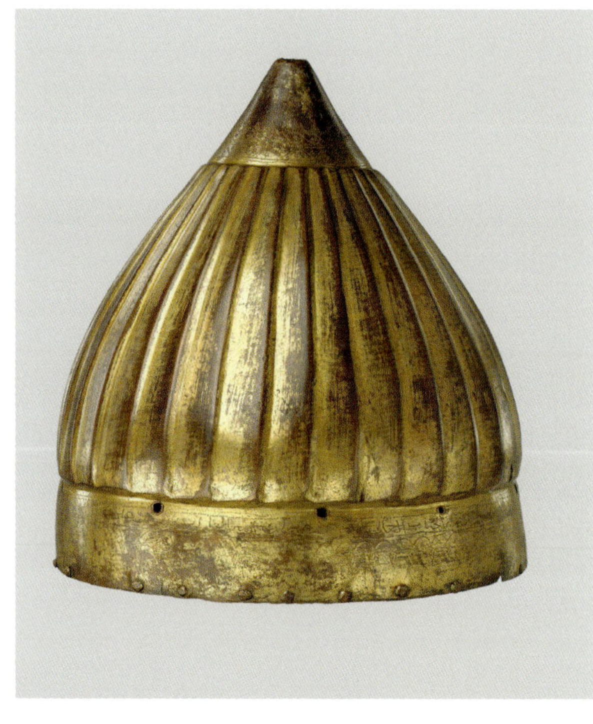

**Fig. 51**
Ottoman pointed helmet, possibly early seventeenth century
New York, Metropolitan Museum of Art. From the collection of Nina and Gordon Bunshaft, Bequest of Nona Bunshaft, 1994

Just to the left of the Ottoman falling angel, Bruegel has painted a nearly nude devil in a red headdress with an ornamental set of colored feathers on his back. These adornments allude to Bruegel's little noticed depiction of that other "other" in early modern European culture: the American Indian [34].[95] That Bruegel must have seen travel accounts and depictions of *americana* is already evident from his incorporation of exotic animals such as the blowfish [21], armadillo [23], and sloth [24] in the *Fall.* It should therefore come as no surprise that he also had some idea of the indigenous peoples of the New World. Bruegel's depiction of an Indian as a falling angel moreover echoes the earliest eye-witness accounts of newly discovered peoples, which regarded the customs and behaviors of the Indians - living in huts, usually nude, and sometimes even as cannibals - as signs of their diabolical nature. In 1558 Plantin published the Dutch translation of the *Wahrhaftige Historia* by Hans Staden, the German sailor who had been captured by the Tupinambà Indians, giving it the impressive title *Een warachtige historie ende beschrijvinge eens lants in America ghelegen, wiens inwoonders wilt, naeckt, seer godloos, ende wreede menschen eeters sijn* (fig. 52).[96] Nudity in particular betrayed their lack of civilization, and it is not by chance that Bruegel's Indian devil is not dressed apart from his headdress and feathers, and in this way echoes the naked, hominoid monster [11] next to him. This is also how André Thevet depicts the Brazilian Tupi Indians in his *Singularitéz de la France Antarctique,* which was also published by Plantin in 1558: as naked savages wearing a few decorative feathers at best.[97]

It was an unfortunate coincidence for the peoples of the New World that

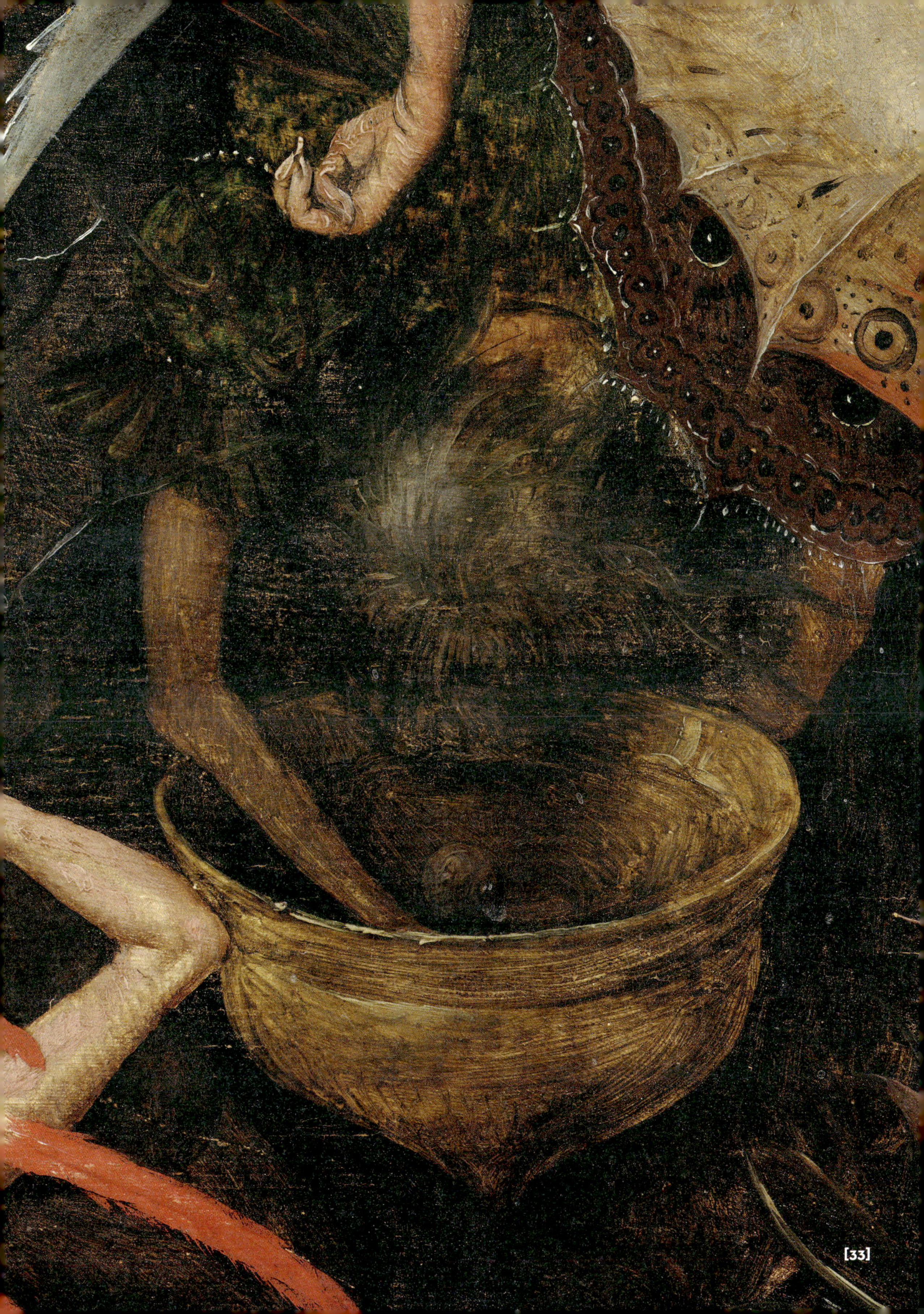

the European exploration of America coincided with the wars of religion that fanned the flames of the battle between orthodoxy and heresy, with the result that all that was unusual or foreign was readily persecuted as witchcraft.[98] According to Thevet, the "poor" Indians, with their own rituals, were possessed by the devil because they lived outside true knowledge of God.[99] The first Franciscan friars in Mexico were similarly concerned with the persistence of the indigenous rituals and ceremonies of the Aztec Indians, which in their view originated with the devil.[100] They even made explicit comparisons between the indigenous gods and fallen angels, and some of them placed their own mission under the patronage of Saint Michael. This acculturation may have been formally inspired: in various indigenous religions, parrots were associated with life after death - and it was precisely for this reason that their colorful feathers (fig. 21) had great ritual value. Consequently, European missionaries were particularly apt to regard the sacred feather ornaments of the indigenous people as demonic.

Because of these associations, and also because they were easily transported and preserved, American feather garments appear in princely collections from an early date.[101] Dürer, as mentioned earlier, saw American feathered crowns at Coudenberg Palace in 1521. He was one of the few at such an early date to praise the "subtle genius" of the makers.[102] The imperial inventory of 1545, which is still held in the Belgian state archives in Brussels, mentions a number of *americana,* including "a turquoise cross made in the Indies; a jade head, probably Mexican; golden jewels in the form of parrots; a cloak made from fish scales; more jewels from Mexico and Peru; American feather art and fans; and a feather painting with three pre-Columbian kings."[103] Besides printed sources, courtly connections may have informed Bruegel as to the appearance and significance of American peoples. Known as a meticulous observer of popular practices and customs in his own country, Bruegel provides a unique painted witness of European reception of the New World in his *Fall of the Rebel Angels.*

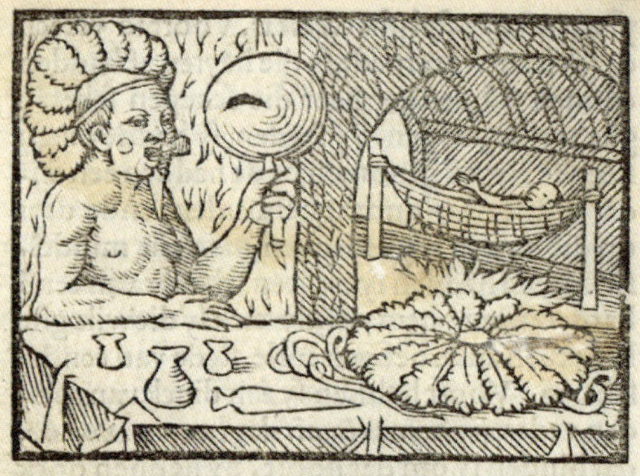

die ſijn ſmal ende lanck. Ende noch hebben ſy
een cieraet dat ſy wt groote zeeſlacken huyſen
maken, ende die heeten ſy *Matte pue*, ende dat
is ghemaeƈt als een half mane, dat hanghen ſy
aenden hals, het is ſneeuwit, eñ wort Bogeſſy
ghenaempt. Oock maken ſy witte cordellen
van witte zeeſlecken, ende is eenen goeden
halm dick, ende het coſtveel arbeyts te maken:
dat hanghen ſy aen den hals. Oock binden ſy
pluymboſſchen aen die armen, ſchilderẽ haer
ſwert, oock met rooden ende witten vederen
ſo bont door malcanderen, ende die vederen
placken ſy opt lijf met materie die wt den boo
men coempt, eñ dat ſtrijckẽ ſy op die plaetſen
daer ſy pluymen hebben willen, ende daer op
legghen ſy dan die pluymen, eñ dat blijft dan
daer

**Fig. 52**
Hans Staden, *Warachtige historie* (Antwerp, 1558), book II: *Een warachtig cort bericht vanden handel ende zeden der Tuppin Imbas, diens ghevangen ick gheweest ben* [...], illustration to chapter XVI: *Wat des mans cieraet is, ende hoe sij haer schilderen* [...] Ghent University Library

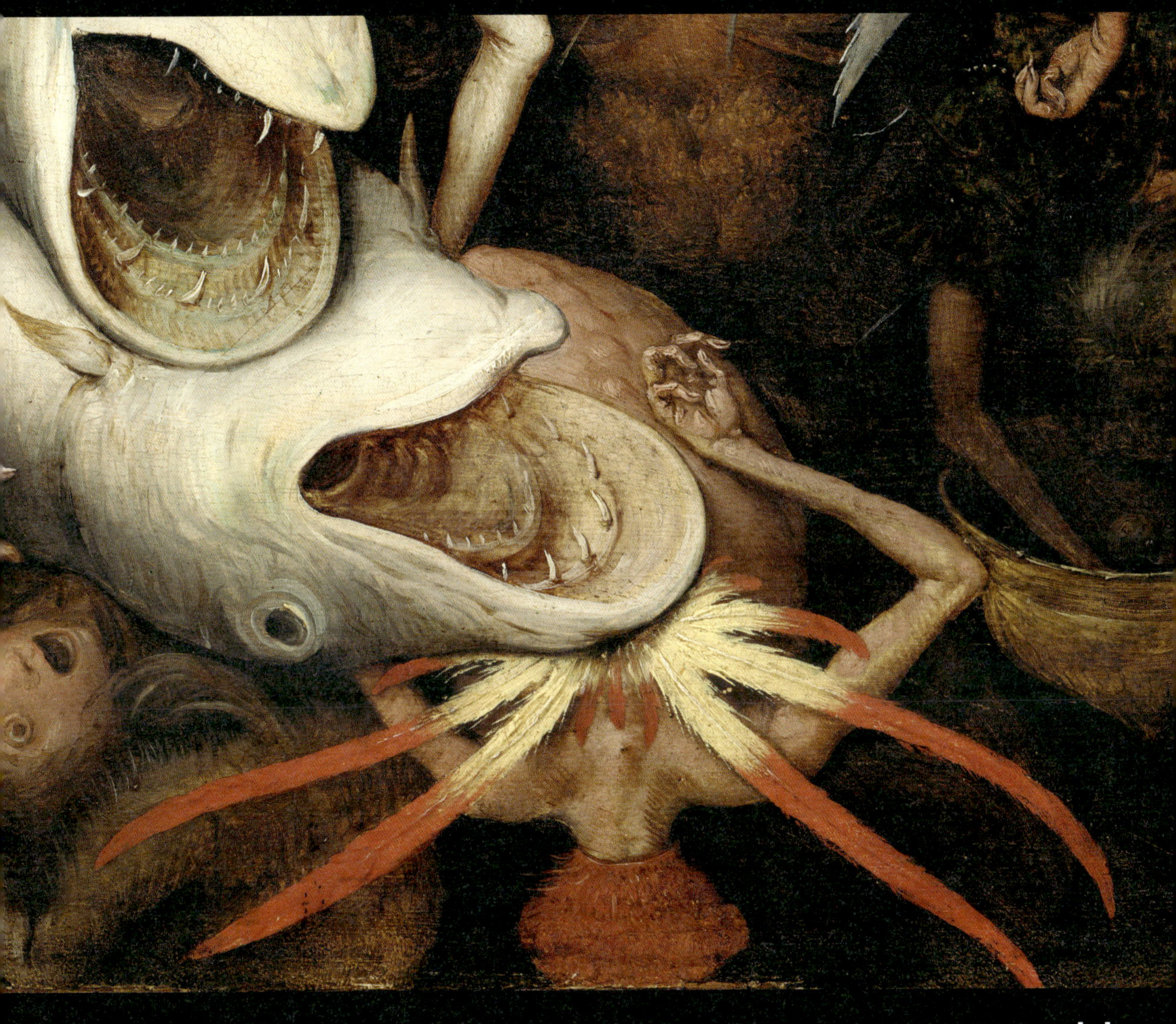

[34]

## Bruegel's painted microcosm

As a reflection of the macrocosm, some encyclopedic collections were further divided according to the four elements. For instance, the renowned *studiolo* of Francesco I (grand duke of Tuscany from 1569 to 1574) in the Palazzo Vecchio in Florence, that housed the princely collection of *naturalia* and *artificialia,* was organized according to this structure.[104] Hoefnagel, we have seen, arranged his watercolour paintings of animals in four albums devoted to each of the *Four Elements.* The ancient doctrine of the four elements held that everything that exists was dominated by one such element: earth, water, air, or fire.[105] Bruegel's painted collection also contains representatives of each element. Plants [49], fish [21, 22], shells [40], and reptiles [53] represent water; birds [26, 42], air; four-footed creatures [9, 17], earth; and *artificialia* such as armor [1, 30, 31, 32, 50], representing fire, which transforms raw metal into works of art.[106] Like Hoefnagel, who classified insects under the element fire (*Ignis*) (fig. 35), Bruegel also paints insects [41, 35] in the glow of the hellfire. According to the prevalent Aristotelian view, insects arose through spontaneous generation, and were therefore associated with fire, the element that brings about the creation and destruction of all that exists.[107] The tumultuous fall of the rebel angels caused some elements to mingle: we see flying fish and falling birds.

Bruegel's use of color strengthens the cosmic structure. In the center, above, Bruegel has painted a half disc of light, the Empyrean realm, the divine world that shines on the sublunary world from above. Underneath it he has rendered concentric disks of blue, the color of the air, which gradually transition into brown tones, the color of the elementary world composed of earth and water. Lower down we see the yellow-gold glow of the hellfire. In this way Bruegel situates the four elements as the innermost spheres of the much greater universe created by God, as is also found in cosmographical diagrams of the Renaissance. In his *De Sphaera, et primis astronomiae rudimentis libellus utilissimus,* for example, published by Plantin in Antwerp in 1561 (fig. 53), Cornelius Valerius shows the cosmos as a series of concentric circles with the elements earth (*terra*) and water (*aqua*) as land and sea in the center; around them the sphere of air (*aer*), followed by that of fire (*ignis*); then come the heavenly spheres of the seven planets; the sphere of the firmament with the zodiac and the fixed stars; the crystalline sphere; and finally the tenth sphere with the *primum mobile,* the boundary of our finite universe. Around it lies the empyrean realm, the dwelling place of God, the angels and and all the saints.[108]

Bruegel skillfully translates these two-dimensional cosmic diagrams into a three-dimensional, painted space. As the angels are cast out of the Empyreum, they begin to lose their transparency and gradually tumble into the elemental world of earth, water, air, and fire; from then on their elemental substance contributes to the speed of their fall.

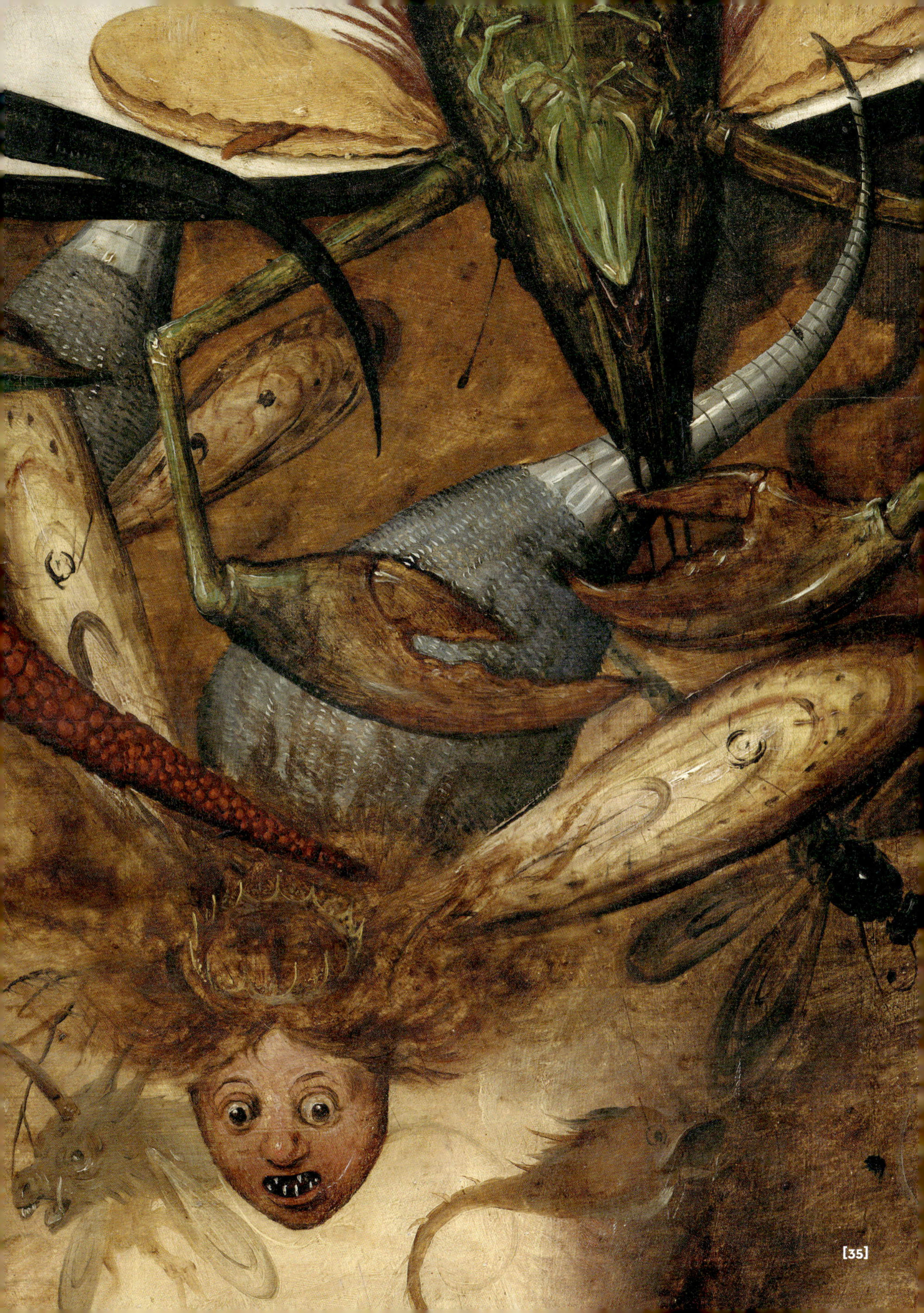

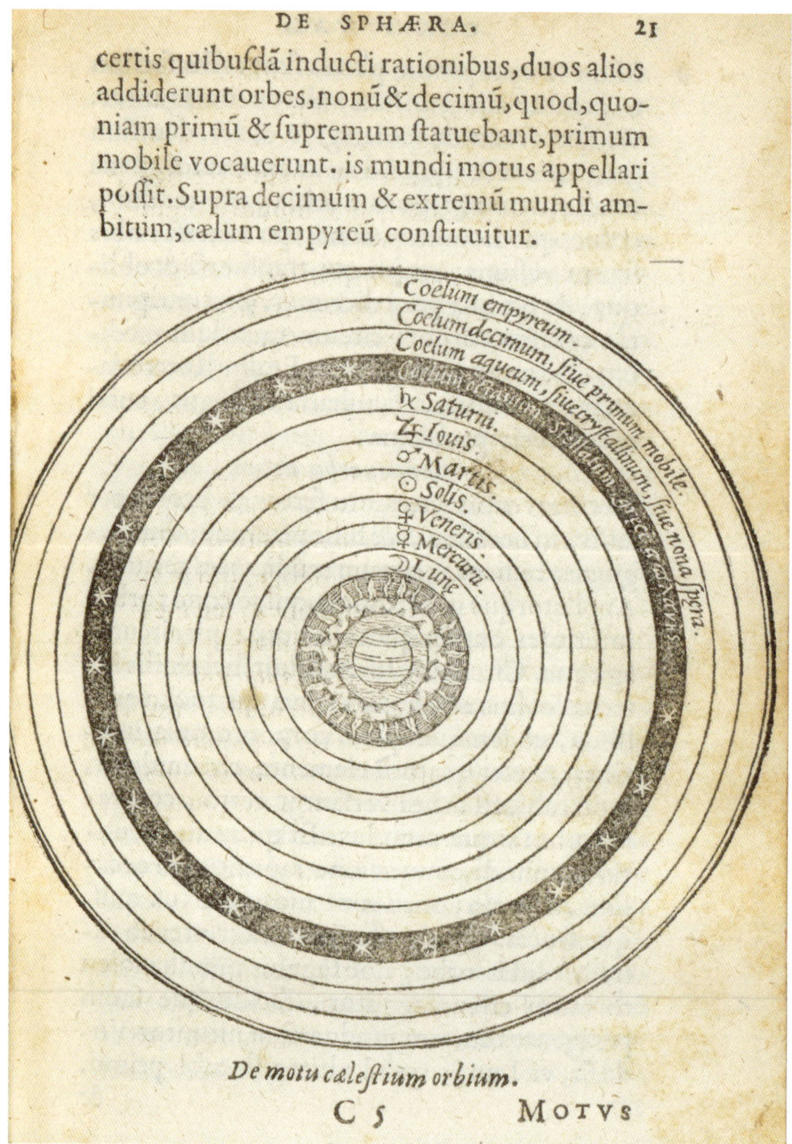

DE SPHÆRA. 21

certis quibuſdã inducti rationibus, duos alios addiderunt orbes, nonũ & decimũ, quod, quoniam primũ & ſupremum ſtatuebant, primum mobile vocauerunt. is mundi motus appellari poſſit. Supra decimum & extremũ mundi ambitum, cælum empyreũ conſtituitur.



De motu cæleſtium orbium.

C 5 MOTVS

**Fig. 53**
Cornelius Valerius
*De Sphaera, et primis astronomiae rudimentis libellus ultilissimus* (Antwerp, 1561), fol. 38
Antwerp, Plantin Moretus Museum

*Collection paintings*

As a commentary on encyclopedic collecting, Bruegel's *Fall of the Rebel Angels* provides an early testament to such practices in the Netherlands. With his striking parody of Hieronymus Bosch, Bruegel moreover refers to a highly specific collecting mania that raged at the time, given that works by Bosch were so highly sought after by erudite collectors. Bruegel's interest in collecting is already evident in his *Proverbs* (fig. 1), *The Battle of Carnival and Lent* (1559), and *Children's Games* (1560), which he conceived as painted collections of popular customs and practices.[109] The print series representing the *Virtues* and *Vices*, and in particular his unsurpassed depiction of cyclical

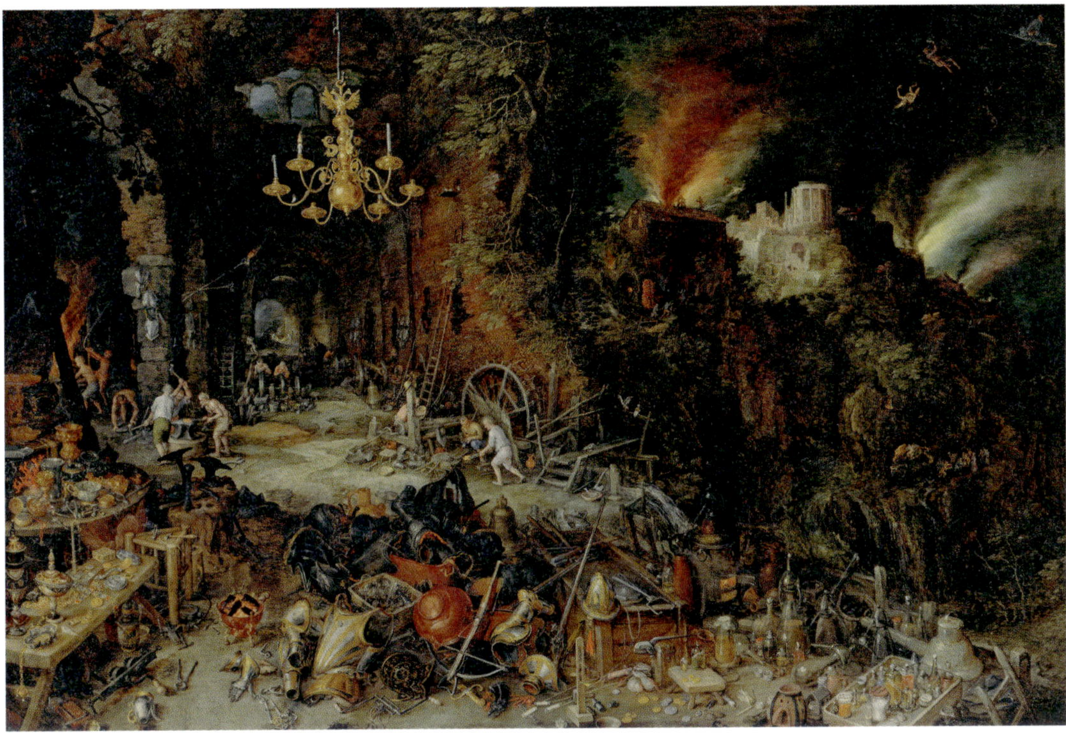

**Fig. 54**
Jan Brueghel the Elder, *The Element of Fire*, 1608
Milan, Biblioteca Ambrosiana

nature in the *Months* (or *Seasons*) (fig. 96), further attest to Bruegel's encyclopedic view of the world.[110]

Bruegel's parallel mapping of erudite collecting in the *Fall of the Rebel Angels*, however, has gone largely unnoticed. We argue that Bruegel's painted collection of *artificialia* and *naturalia* anticipates paintings of collections or *Kunstkammer* paintings, a genre that arose around 1610, and of which, not coincidentally, Bruegel's son Jan (1568-1625) is an important representative.[111] This legacy suggests that Bruegel's sons were in all likelihood familiar with the *Fall of the Rebel Angels* - either the original painting itself or preparatory studies left behind in the studio. Pieter Brueghel the Younger (1564/5-1636) did not paint an exact copy of the *Fall*, as he did with several other works by his father.[112] Yet in light of Pieter the Elder's participation in the contemporary culture of collecting, Jan Bruegel the Elder's collection paintings on themes such as the *Four Elements* (fig. 54) are worthy heirs to his father's iconographic innovation.[113] More than the paintings by Jan Brueghel, however, the *Fall* resonates with a moral warning against the excesses of unbounded collecting. Considering that, in this masterpiece, Bruegel himself acts as a "collector" of the most precious objects of nature and art, it is a reflection that also applies to his own artistic practice, as we shall see in the following chapter.

# Chapter III

In fact, in this work, it is not for the philosophers that we divide all the things of nature strictly conform to nature herself, but for the princes that we classify most of the things that are pleasant to preserve, following orders that are not too difficult. Therefore ... we had to indicate an easier order that follows the form of things.

Samuel Quiccheberg, *Inscriptiones*, 1565, Digression on the First Class.*

Oil painting by all the most eminent artists. So that in these demonstrations of artistic skill it might be observed to what extent one artist seems to have surpassed the other in subject matter, proportion, gesture, optical effects, variety, and ornaments as well as in other respects worthy of note.

Samuel Quiccheberg, *Inscriptiones*, 1565, Fifth Class, Inscription 1.**

# Knowledge becomes art

## Monsters as art

Bruegel's references to the early modern culture of collecting shed new light on his representation of falling angels as monsters. Since antiquity it was believed that monsters inhabited the distant corners of the known world. Monsters were usually represented as hybrids, such as the mermaid, with her womanly body and fish tail, or the griffin, with the feathers and beak of a bird and the body of a lion. We find mermaids and griffins on ancient sarcophagi, as drolleries on the corbels of medieval cathedrals, in the margins of princely manuscripts, and on maps, in the *terrae incognitae* or as yet unknown parts of the earth (fig. 25). In the Christian worldview, the mingling of species was believed to go against the will of God and was therefore seen as a mark of evil.[1]

During the fifteenth and especially the sixteenth century monsters left the margins and turned up in encyclopedic collections and in the cargos of explorers, as well as in apocalyptic pamphlets announcing the imminent end of the world.[2] Exotic animals in particular fascinated contemporaries because of their strange and "monstrous" appearance. With such

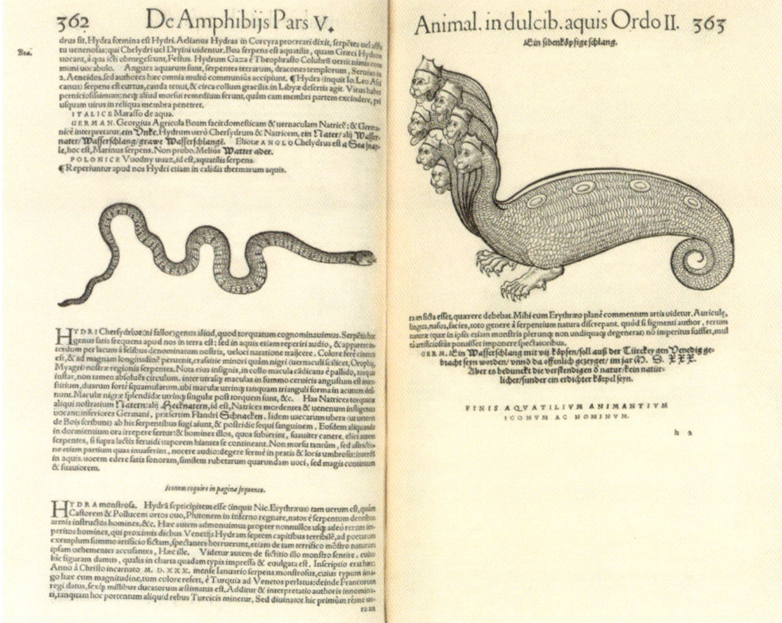

362 De Amphibijs Pars V.

Animal. in dulcib. aquis Ordo II. 363

FINIS AQVATILIVM ANIMANTIVM ICONVM AC NOMINVM.

**Fig. 55**
Seven-headed hydra with crowned heads, in: Conrad Gessner, *Nomenclator aquatilium animantium* (Zurich, 1560), fol. 363
Ghent University Library

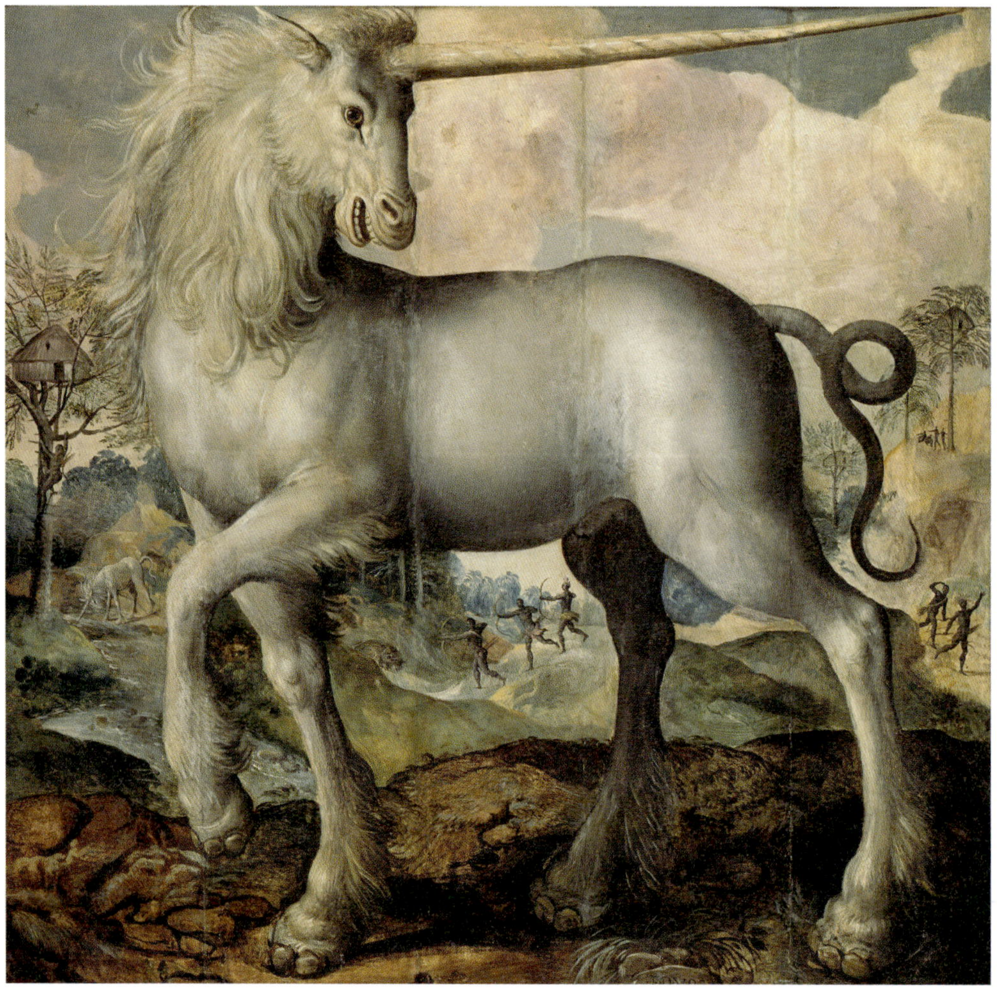

**Fig. 56**
Maerten de Vos,
*Unicorn*, 1572
Schwerin, Staatliche
Museum

an ever-increasing influx of exotic species it was not easy to distinguish a natural being from an imaginary creation. Why should rhinoceroses exist in reality and unicorns only in the imagination?[3] As a result, naturalists and painters often showed living and imaginary animals side by side. Alongside existing animals, Gessner included in his *Nomenclator aquatilium animantium* a unicorn and a seven-headed hydra with crowned heads (fig. 55), which resembles very closely the apocalyptic beast [2] in Bruegel's *Fall.*[4] Bruegel's traveling companion Maerten de Vos painted a unicorn (fig. 56) next to a leopard, an elephant (fig. 57), a dromedary, a lion, and a stag in his monumental "encyclopedia" of animals.[5] Many collectors even exhibited "false" monsters. Aldrovandi, for instance, displayed a so-called "dragon," which was composed of parts of a dried stingray and other fish.[6]

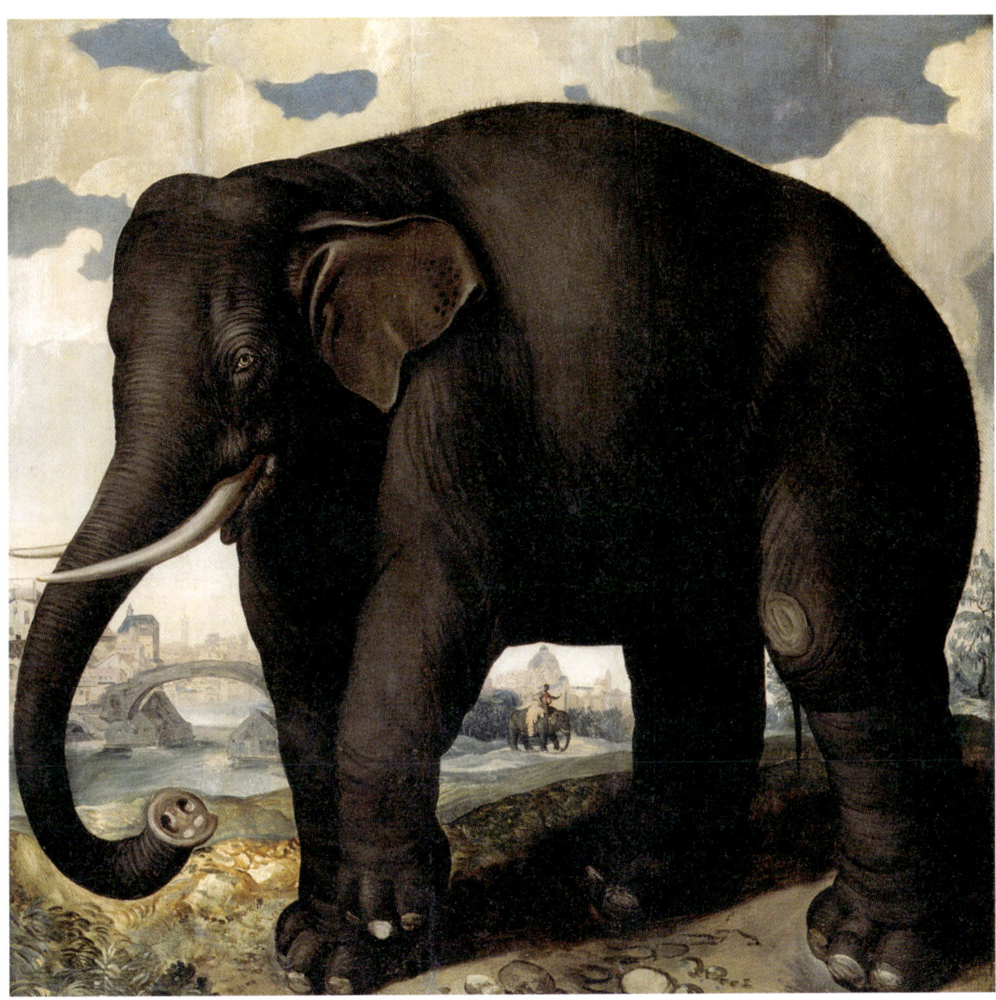

**Fig. 57**
Maerten de Vos,
*Elephant*, 1572
Schwerin, Staatliche
Museum

We further see an increased interest in what were considered natural "monsters, " animals and humans with congenital birth defects such as dwarfs, Siamese twins, and hirsutes. There appeared many reports of cases like these, which were often interpreted as signs of God's wrath, aroused by human sin.[7] The appearance of living "monsters" - the word is etymologically related to the Latin "monstrare," which means "to show" - was often seen as an omen of approaching doom. The early modern obsession with monsters was therefore also intimately connected with the political and religious troubles that plagued the period. In the *Fall*, Bruegel too depicts God's first punishment of sinful behavior as the transformation of angels into monsters. In chapter IV we will see how Bruegel may also have intended the falling angels transformed into monsters as apocalyptic omens of political instability run wild.

In an attempt to understand the natural world around them, early moderns also regarded natural monsters as wonders of nature. Aldrovandi included dwarves, Siamese twins, and the renowned Gonzalez family of hirsutes in his painted microcosm of nature, the *Natura picta* (fig. 58).[8] Hoefnagel also depicts the Gonzalez hirsutes in his painted animal albums of the *Four Elements* and calls them "miracles of nature" (fig. 59).[9] Collectors exhibited hirsutes and dwarves as attractions (fig. 60), sometimes because they were truly considered comical, but mostly because they demonstrated the boundless creativity of nature and her maker. Above all, these extraordinary creations of nature showed the omnipotence of God.[10] Like other creations of nature that crossed the boundaries of existing classes, species, or worlds, such as fossils and coral (fig. 87) (in between animal, vegetable, and mineral, the three Aristotelian realms of nature) monstrous births were also referred to as jokes of nature (*lusus naturae*).[11]

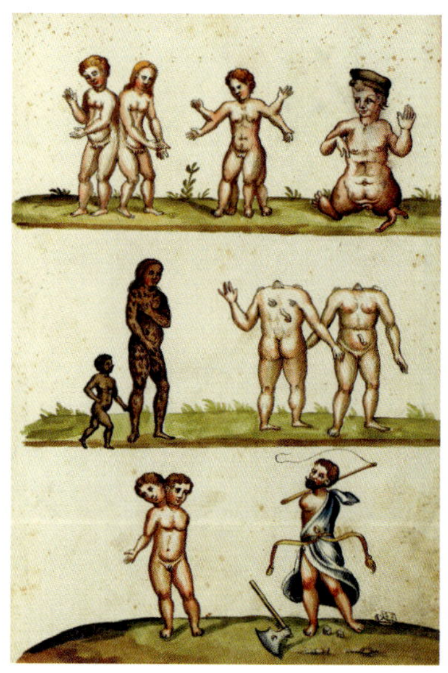

**Fig. 58**
Anonymous painter, *Siamese twins and other misshapen births as well as imaginary human 'monsters,'* in: Aldrovandi Ms, volume 006.2: volume composto da 37 figure di pesci, 32 di mostri humani, 15 di uccelli et 17 di quadrupedi, fol. 68, between 1550-1605 Bologna, Bibliotheca Universitaria.

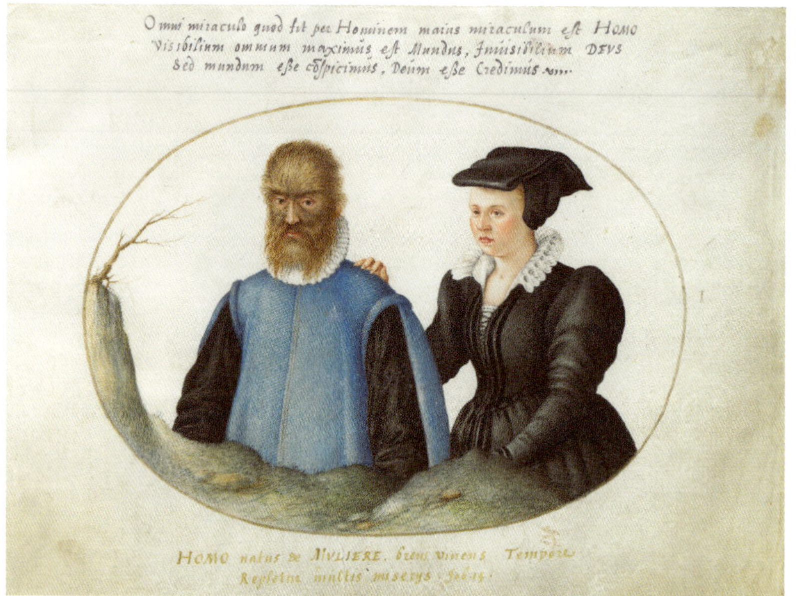


**Fig. 59**
Joris Hoefnagel, *The hirsute Petrus Gonsalus and his wife*, in: *Ignis*/Fire, fol, Ir, from the *Four Elements*, between 1575-1582 Washington, National Gallery of Art, Collection Mrs Lessing J. Rosenwald

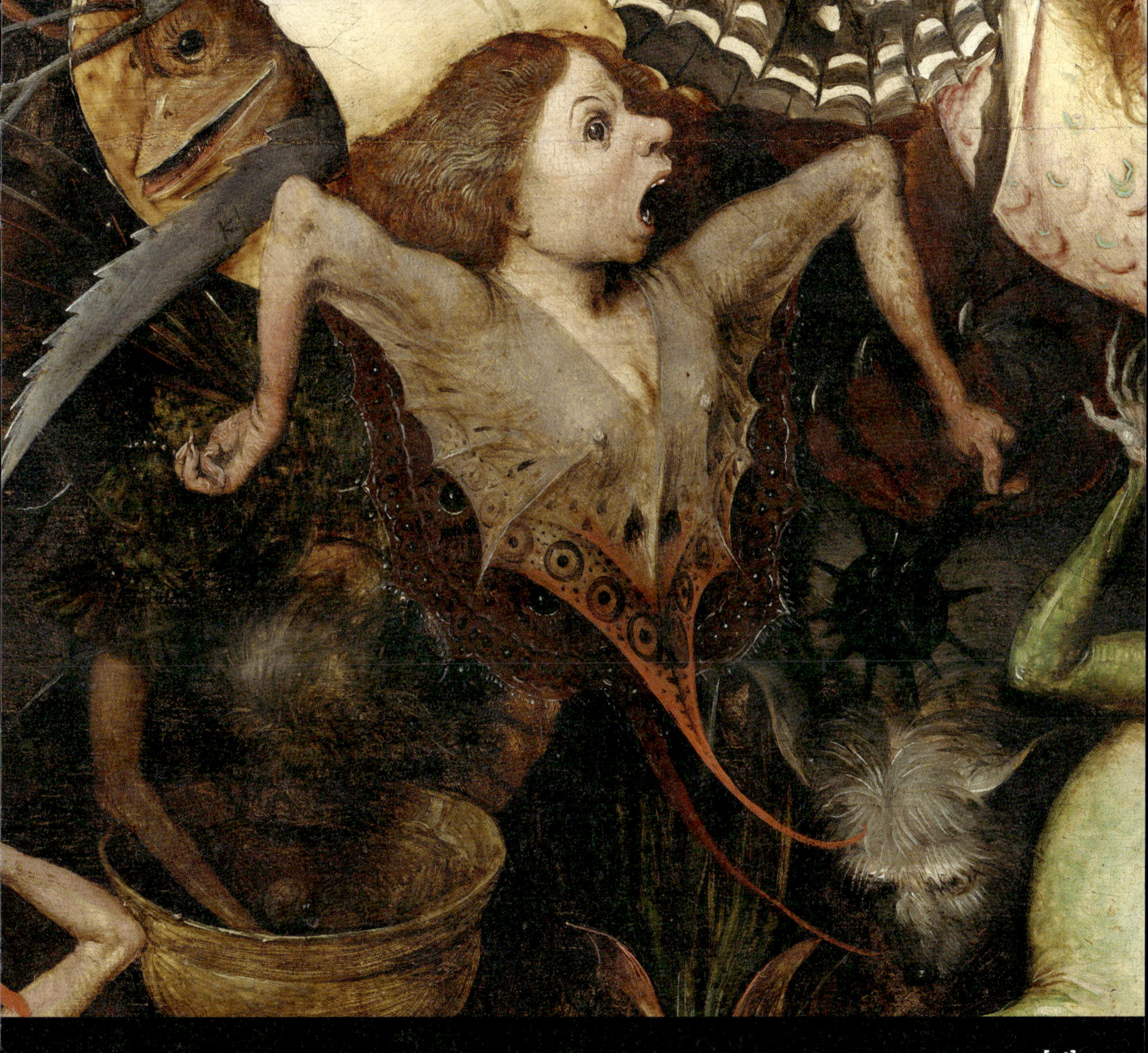

[36]

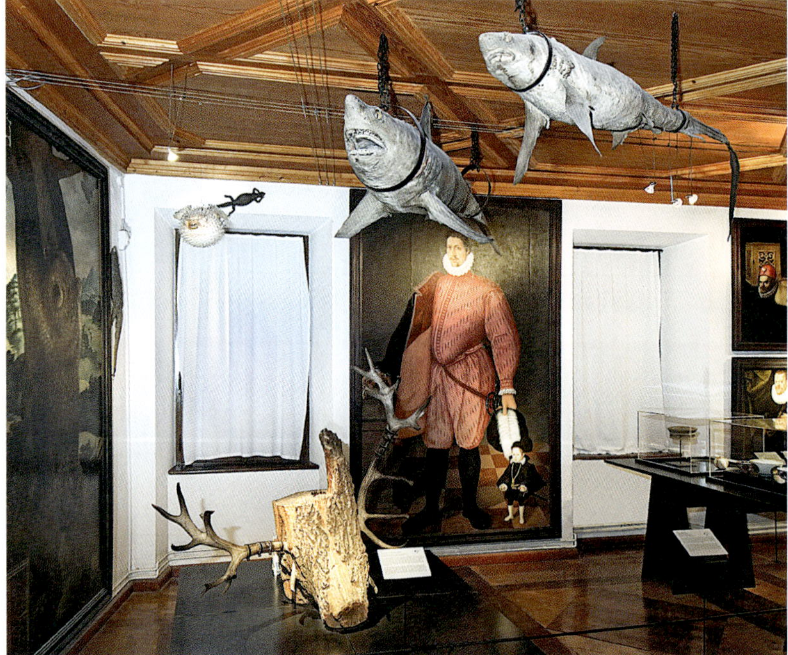

**Fig. 60**
Kunstkammer of Ferdinand van Tyrol, Schloss Ambrass: dried shark, lizard, blowfish and a painting of *A Dwarf and a Giant*, late sixteenth century

Linked with this notion of nature at play, monsters became a central theme in art, above all in the works of Hieronymus Bosch, which Bruegel set out to emulate in the *Fall of the Rebel Angels*.[12] To do so, he transformed a traditional devotion into a painted cabinet of curiosities filled with monsters composed from closely observed *naturalia* and *artificialia*. Bruegel thus created what appear to be natural monsters, but are in fact works of art. His monsters are ominous and wondrous, and at times even funny.

### Bruegel's monsters as serious jokes

The earliest commentaries on the art of Bruegel effectively praise his inventions as jokes. Lampsonius commends Bruegel for his comical and witty art in imitation of Bosch[13] (fig. 3). Van Mander, in a rough translation of Lampsonius's epigram, calls Bruegel's paintings amusing:

> Grow in boldness, Peter, as you do fruitfully in art
> In the manner of your old master by painting lively poses
> Which are most amusing, but you deserve, however, unanimously
> To be royally praised no less than any other master.[14]

According to Van Mander, Bruegel painted many "specters and burlesques" in imitation of Bosch, which earned him the appellation of "Pier den Drol." He writes that many of the master's works cannot be looked upon without laughing, and that even a hardened man cannot but "at least twitch his mouth

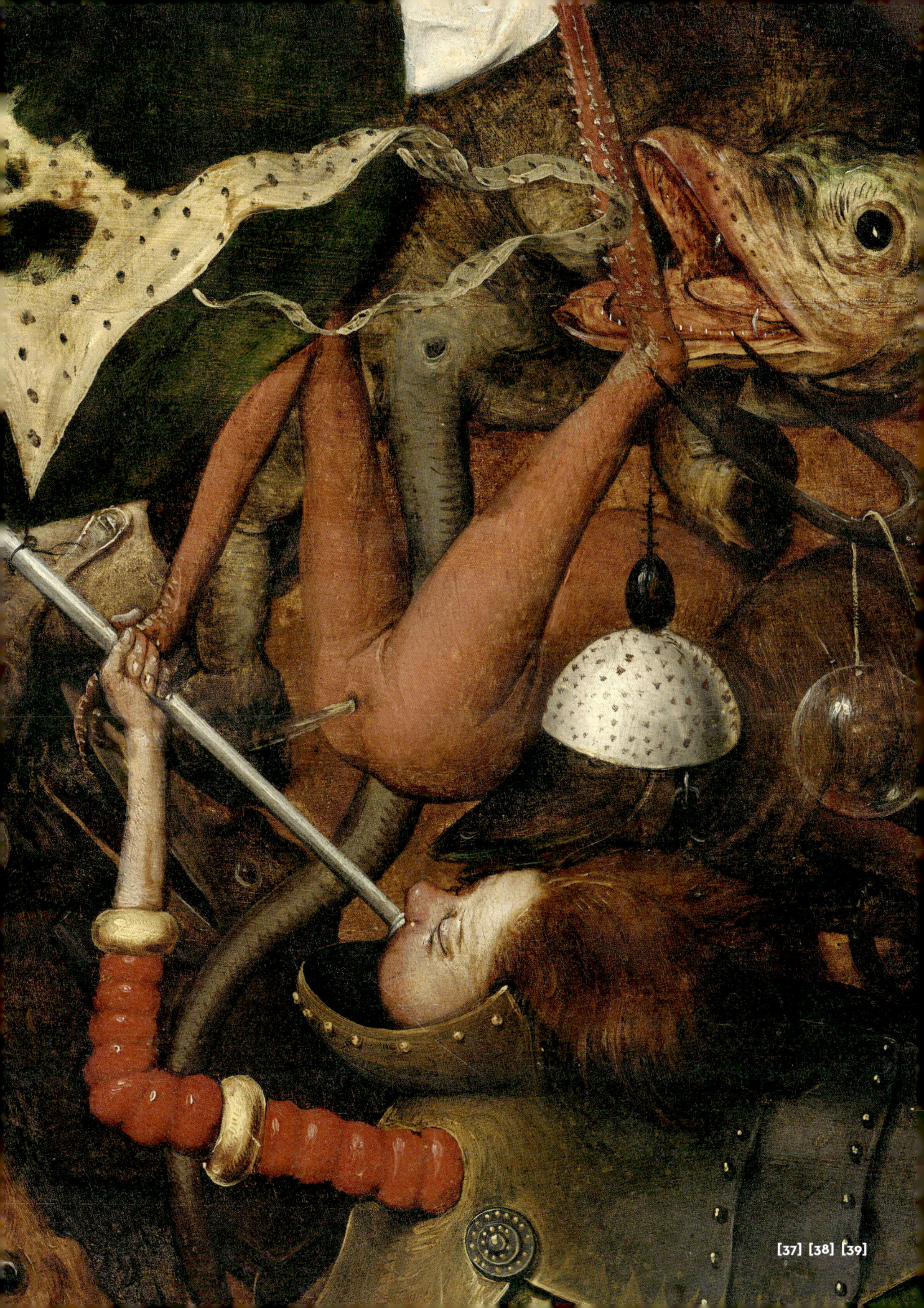

[37] [38] [39]

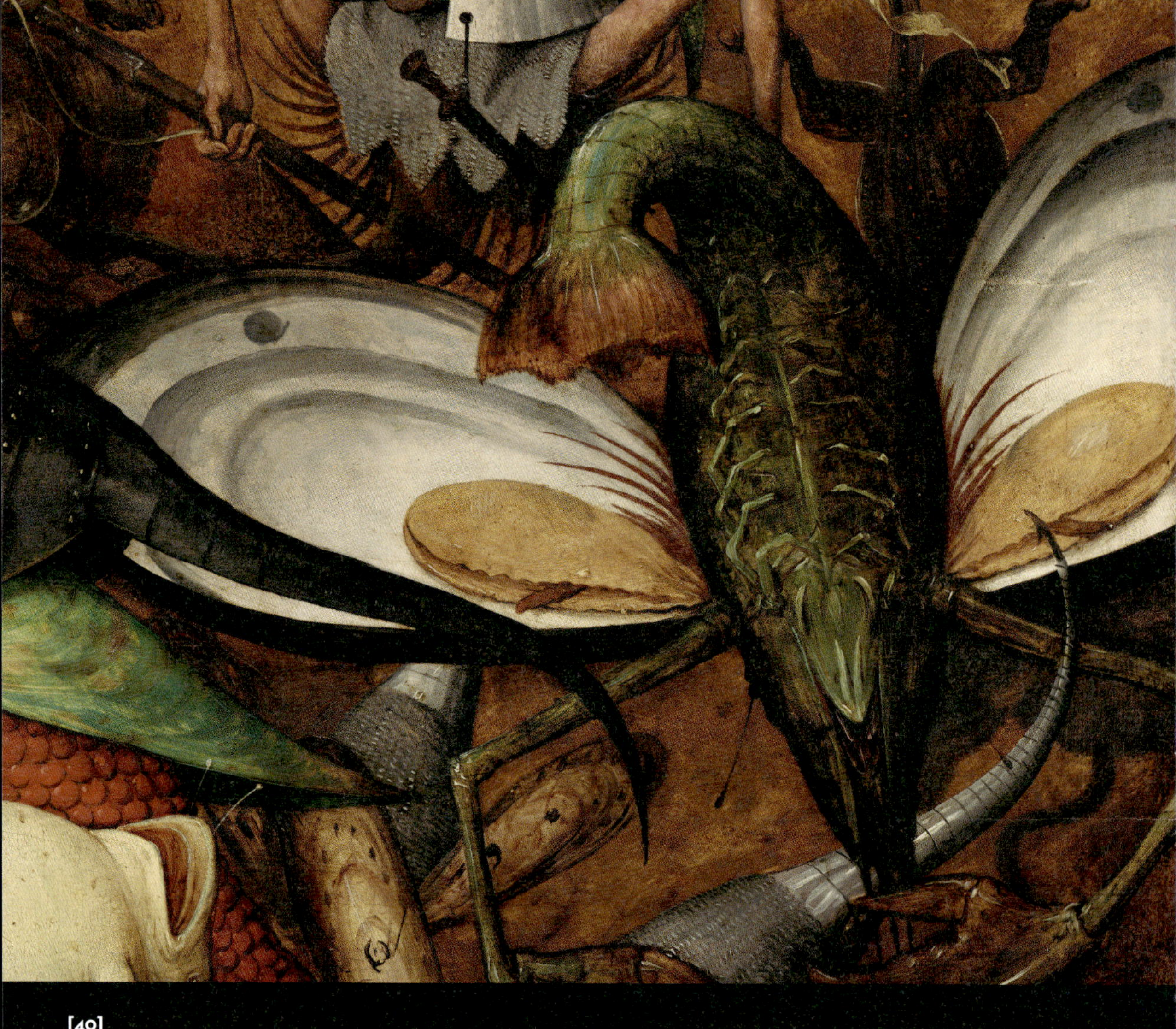

or smile."[15] Van Mander's description launched the image of Bruegel as a painter of comic scenes.[16] Nevertheless, early commentators also suggest that behind the humorous façade often lurked a serious observation. Don Filipe de Guevara, writing circa 1560 on the art of Bosch and his few good imitators - a possible reference to Bruegel - compares the works of Bosch to a genre of paintings the ancients referred to as "grilli." According to Pliny the ancient painter Antiphilus "painted a figure in ridiculous costume who was known by the joking name Gryllus, whence such picture became known as grilli."[17] But De Guevara also emphasizes the "ethical" dimension of Bosch's monstrous creations, which in fact show the customs and affectations of men.[18] Jose de Sigüenza, a monk in the Hieronymus cloister of the Escorial, where various paintings by Bosch could be found, similarly writes that Bosch sketched follies that nevertheless contained profound truths. Hence, Bosch's paintings are not farces, but rather "like books of great wisdom and artifice, and if there are foolish activities to be seen, they are ours, not his; thus let us say it is a painted satire on the sins and inconstancies of humankind."[19] Given that Guevara and Sigüenza were writing when Bruegel was widely praised as the new Bosch, we may assume that this judgment also applies to some extent to Bruegel.

Some details of Bruegel's invention, such as the devils posing as knights or relieving themselves openly [11, 37], are truly funny and arouse laughter. Other falling angels, such as the armored head-hand man [50] and screaming angel with a human face but without limbs [36], recall Bruegel's depiction of cripples.[20] Considering Bruegel's other references to contemporary collecting, they may very well have been meant to play on the collector's fascination with misshapen people as wonders and jokes of nature that could not be reduced to a single species and that therefore were often read as omens.

In a humorous wink at the collector's attempts to classify nature, Bruegel further invents formal "classes."[21] We distinguish a class of armored angels: some wear man-made armor [1, 30, 31, 32, 50], while others are equipped with natural armor, such as mussel shells [40] and lobster claws [13, 37], the carapaces of beetles [41] and, most particularly, the armor of an armadillo [23]. He also depicts a class of winged creatures, including the good angels [1, 3, 54], birds [26, 42], flying fish [22], winged insects [35, 41] and falling angels with wings of butterflies [20, 44, 49], with wings of an opened mussel shell [40] and wearing the wings diptych sundial [30]. As these formal classes visually link things that at first seem disparate, they bring order in the chaos caused by the fall of the rebel angels.

By representing the falling angels as monsters in an ordered chain of being, Bruegel thus anchors his highly amusing creations in a profound reflection on hubris and the origins of evil, the coherence of the cosmos, and its reflection in art and curiosity cabinets. With his depiction of monsters as serious jokes, Bruegel shows himself to be the heir of Erasmus.[22] The *Praise of Folly,* in which lady *Stultitia* jokingly tells the truth, is undoubtedly the best-known

[41]

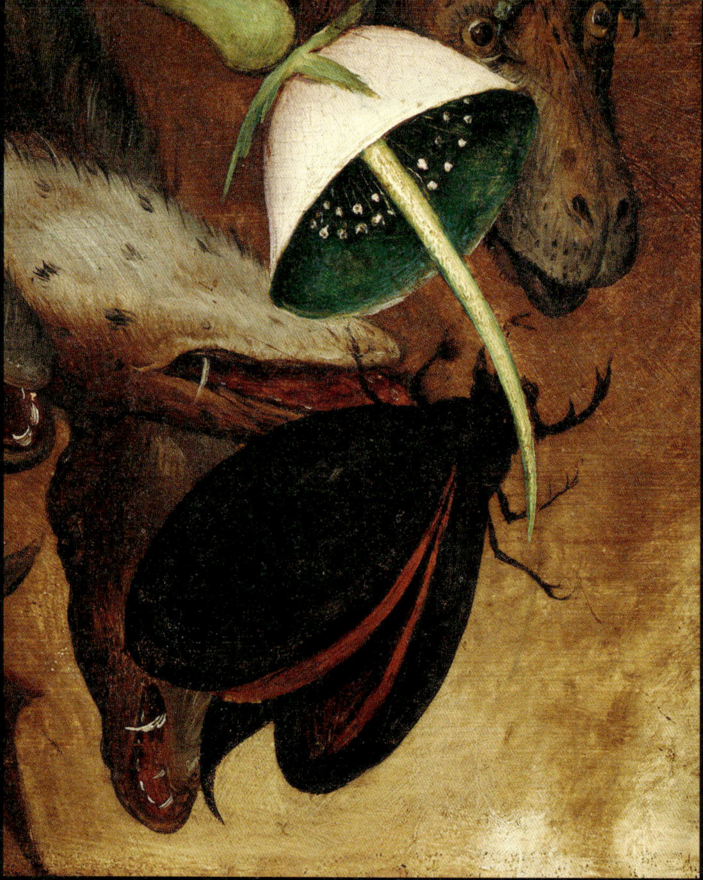

[42]

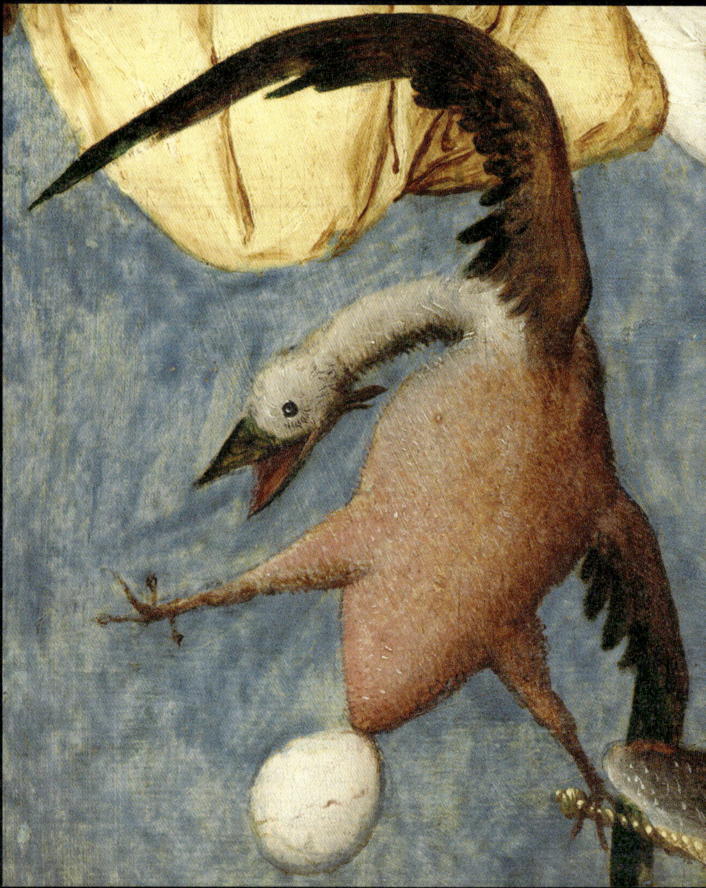

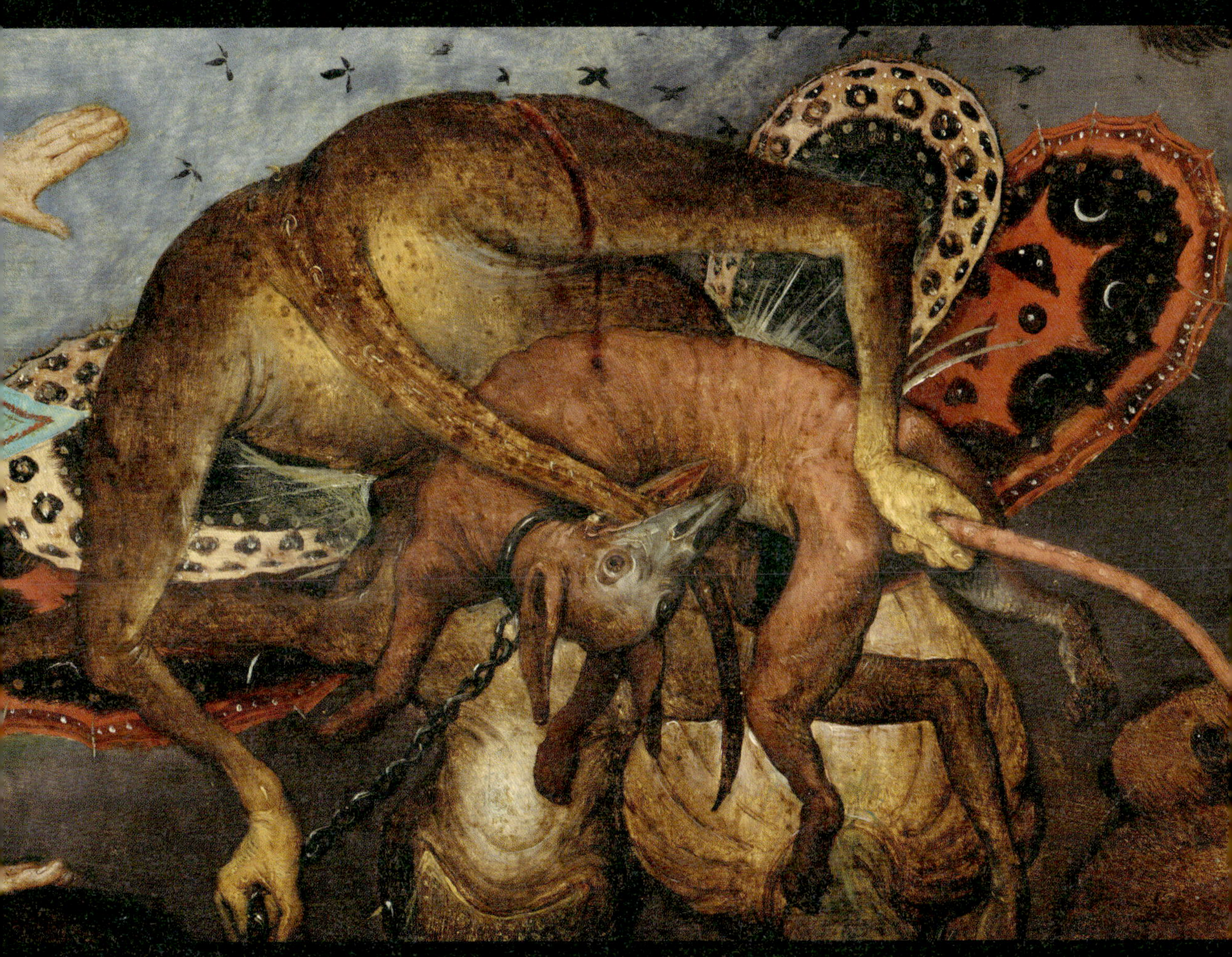

[43] [44]

example of this kind of "serio ludere" (serious play).[23] In a similar fashion, François Rabelais (1494-1563) presents his book *Gargantua* (1534) as a medicine chest that does not contain what the description on the outside actually describes.[24] In this way Bruegel too presents the *Fall* as a kind of cabinet full of wondrous and entertaining things that are not always what they seem at first sight.

## Bruegel as a "Second Nature"

The inventiveness of nature, as demonstrated most pointedly by exotic species and natural monsters, further inspired artists to extend the boundaries of their own creativity. The fascination for the wonders of nature went hand in hand with the greater role that sixteenth-century art critics ascribed to the *ingenium* of the artist, who imitated and even surpassed the creative power of nature.[25]

Shortly after Bruegel's death in 1569, Ortelius wrote an epitaph for his deceased friend in his own *album amicorum.* As was customary this album primarily contained contributions from the geographer's friends, but here Ortelius took up the pen himself in order to pay tribute to his friendship with Bruegel, thereby ensuring it for posterity. In this well-known Latin poem, Ortelius asks whether Bruegel had died so young because Nature, upon seeing Bruegel's artful and ingenious imitations ("artificiosa ingeniusque imitatione"), feared his contempt.[26] Bruegel's imitation of nature is artful, but his works, Ortelius states, are not "artificial" but "natural." In doing so, Ortelius compares Bruegel with the ancient painter Eupompus, of whom Pliny writes that he never imitated another painter, but only Nature herself. Bruegel was not only the best among artists, Ortelius continues, but "Nature among artists, and therefore worthy of being imitated by everyone."[27] Already shortly after Bruegel's death, his works were in fact imitated by a multitude of followers, including Hoefnagel, who succeeded Bruegel as a close friend of Ortelius, with whom he also traveled to Italy.

Ortelius played with the categories art (*ars*) and nature (*natura*) in a way that was similar to the way Bruegel played with them in his paintings. The precise use of the terms "artificiosas" and "naturales" suggests that Ortelius recognized Bruegel's imitation and emulation of nature, which the artist illustrates in a unique way in the *Fall.* Like the curiosity cabinets, which display the contest between art and nature, Bruegel's art measures itself against Nature. Bruegel does not imitate the external characteristics of nature (*natura naturata*), but rather its creative principles (*natura naturans*), and demonstrates this in his unique landscapes as well as in the *Fall,* in which he transforms accurately depicted natural elements into man-made art objects.[28] In this way he transforms the natural armor of the armadillo, for example, into an artificially forged suit of armor held together by metal bolts [23]. In their effort to imitate and even surpass natural wonders with human genius, Bruegel's inventions recall the gold and silver masterpieces constructed as settings for

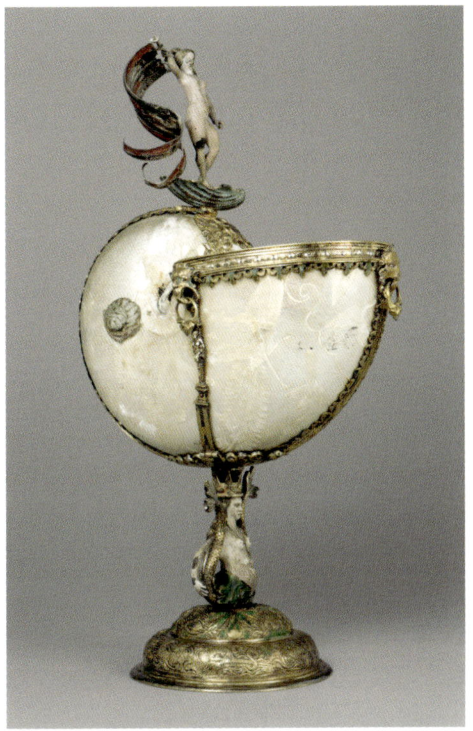

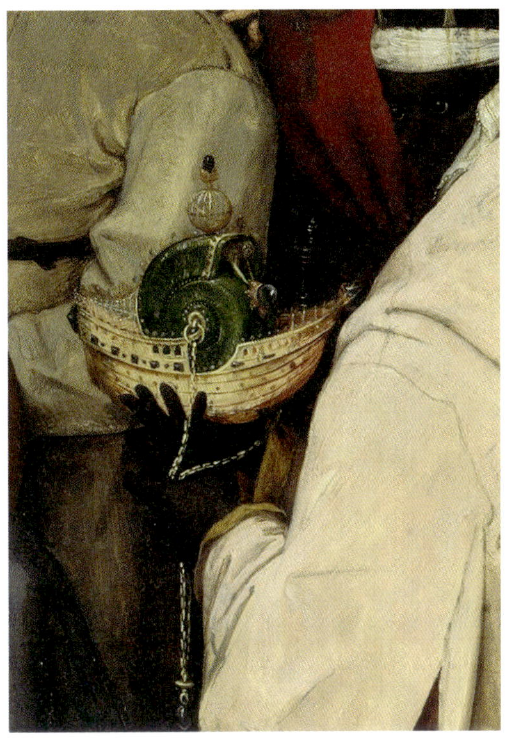

**Fig. 61**
Marx Kornblum, *Nautiluscup*, Vienna, ca. 1580-1590
Nautilus shell, gilded silver, paint
Vienna, Kunsthistorisches Museum, Kunstkammer

**Fig. 62**
Pieter Bruegel the Elder, *Adoration of the Magi*, 1564
London, National Gallery

ostrich eggs, nautilus shells, or sculpted coral (figs. 61, 87, 95), which were often displayed in art and curiosity cabinets.[29] Bruegel again reveals his knowledge of such art objects in his *Adoration of the Magi* (fig. 62).[30]

Bruegel further demonstrates his natural ingenuity in the depiction of light and darkness. As in Dante's description of the ephemeral light of the Empyrean realm, he paints divine light that makes things transparent, and a darkness in which strange devils conceal themselves.[31] The seven-headed beast of the Apocalypse [2], the most revolting of all monsters, is so well concealed in the depths of this darkness that most viewers only perceive it after looking at the painting for a long time. By deliberately hiding a key element of the narrative, Bruegel addresses the erudite connoisseur who appreciated this play of concealing and revealing.[32] Among other things, Ortelius may have been thinking of this painterly quality when he further writes that Bruegel "painted many things that cannot be painted, as Plinius says of Apelles."[33]

Bruegel's exact sources are never easy to trace because he does not cite them; instead, he transforms them. Whether nature or art, Bruegel always transforms what he sees. This is what Van Mander is referring to when he writes that "On his travels he drew many views from life so that it is said that when he was in the Alps he swallowed all those mountains and rocks which, upon returning home, he spat out again onto canvases and panels, so faithfully was

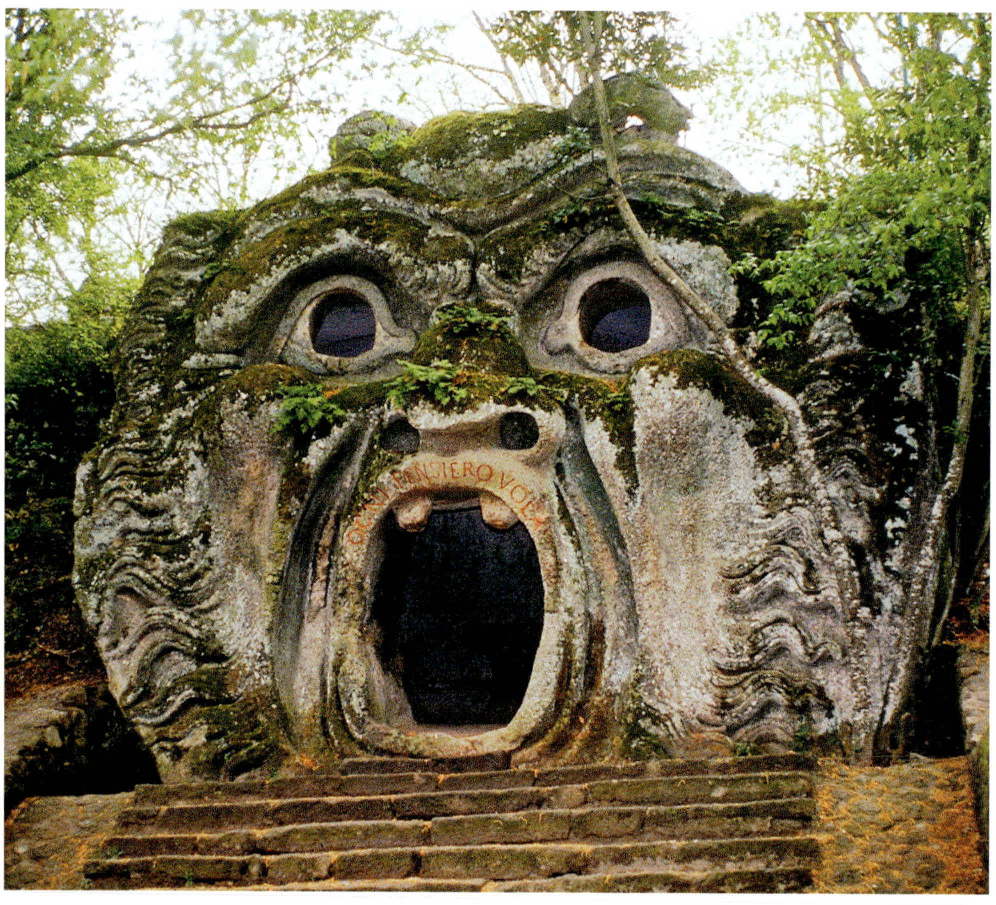

**Fig. 63**
Mouth of Hell, Bomarzo, *Parco dei mostri*, circa 1560

he able, in this respects and others, to follow Nature."[34] Just as the ancients often compared creativity with the work of a bee, which takes nectar from many flowers to produce honey, Van Mander describes Bruegel's creative process in digestive terms.[35] He confirms Ortelius's observation that Bruegel did not imitate the external characteristics of nature, but its creative principles, or *natura naturans.* Bruegel combines natural details in a way that does not occur in nature and thereby creates as an *altera natura,* or "second Nature." He composes a perfectly ordered artwork from the multiplicity of nature, just as artificial Renaissance grottoes conjured a complete building from a combination of natural rock formations, shells, and clay.[36] Bruegel's composite devils are created from nature, like the monsters that appear in the savage forest of Bomarzo (fig. 63), or like human faces that become visible in anthropomorphic landscapes.[37] In this respect it seems to be no coincidence that the mouth of hell in Bruegel's *Dulle Griet* (fig. 27), which he painted in 1561, shortly before the *Fall,* recalls the mouth of hell at Bomarzo.[38]

## Collecting art: Bruegel and his predecessors

As we have seen, collectors often contrasted the wonders of nature with man-made works of art, ancient as well as modern. The Ghent painter and rhetorician Lucas d'Heere (1534-ca. 1584) collected giant bones, a Gallo-Roman sandal, and an antique bronze statue of Mercury, as well as a silverpoint drawing of *Saint Barbara* by Van Eyck.[39] Ortelius, we have seen, had a penchant for the extraordinary creations of nature, such as exotic shell, and also collected antique coins, and modern works of art, such as prints by Dürer and Bruegel's *Dormition of the Virgin* (fig. 31).[40]

The competition between nature and art, as tangibly exhibited in the cabinets of curiosity, further encouraged rivalry among painters, since they tried to surpass one another in their imitation of nature.[41] Although Ortelius depicts Bruegel in the epitaph as an autodidact who only had nature for a master, there is no doubt that Bruegel studied other artists, particularly those predecessors who excelled in the imitation of nature. We have seen how Bruegel attempted to surpass Bosch in the naturalism of his monsters, suggesting that many creations of nature were even more curious than Bosch's strangest fantasy. Bruegel thus emulated Bosch not only in terms of inventiveness, but also in terms of naturalism, another quality for which Bosch is praised. Guevara, for instance, wrote about Bosch that "he never in his life painted anything that was not natural, unless hell or purgatory. His inventions strove to seek out rare but natural things: in such a way that the general rule is that when one or other painting is signed by Bosch but shows only monstrosities, or something that falls beyond the bounds of the natural, one can assume that it is a falsification [...]."[42]

Bruegel also learned from other great masters of Netherlandish painting. The draped alb of the good angel to the right of Saint Michael and the fluttering mantle of the archangel [1 and 48] betray Bruegel's knowledge of Rogier Van der Weyden's art, which was renowned for its dramatically fluttering garments. Like the art of Bosch, the work of Rogier van der Weyden (1399/1400-1464) was much sought after in Bruegel's time. In 1560 Philip II transferred Rogier's *Descent from the Cross* (fig. 73), which had been taken into the Habsburg collection by Mary of Hungary, to Spain.[43] The departure of this masterpiece was deeply regretted in the Netherlands and as early as 1565 Bruegel's publisher Hieronymus Cock issued a commemorative print.[44]

It has been noted that Bruegel emulated the art of Van Eyck and Van der Weyden in other paintings, such as the *Bearing of the Cross* (1564, Vienna, Kunsthistorisches Museum).[45] The art of Jan van Eyck (1390-1441) was also highly coveted in Bruegel's time by the Habsburg rulers as well as learned artists. Philip II, who did not succeed in acquiring Van Eyck's *Adoration of the Mystic Lamb* - commonly known as the Ghent Altarpiece - for his collection in Spain, commissioned a copy from Michiel Coxcie (1499-1592).[46]

In our opinion, the falling angel with the red turban [45] refers to Van Eyck's

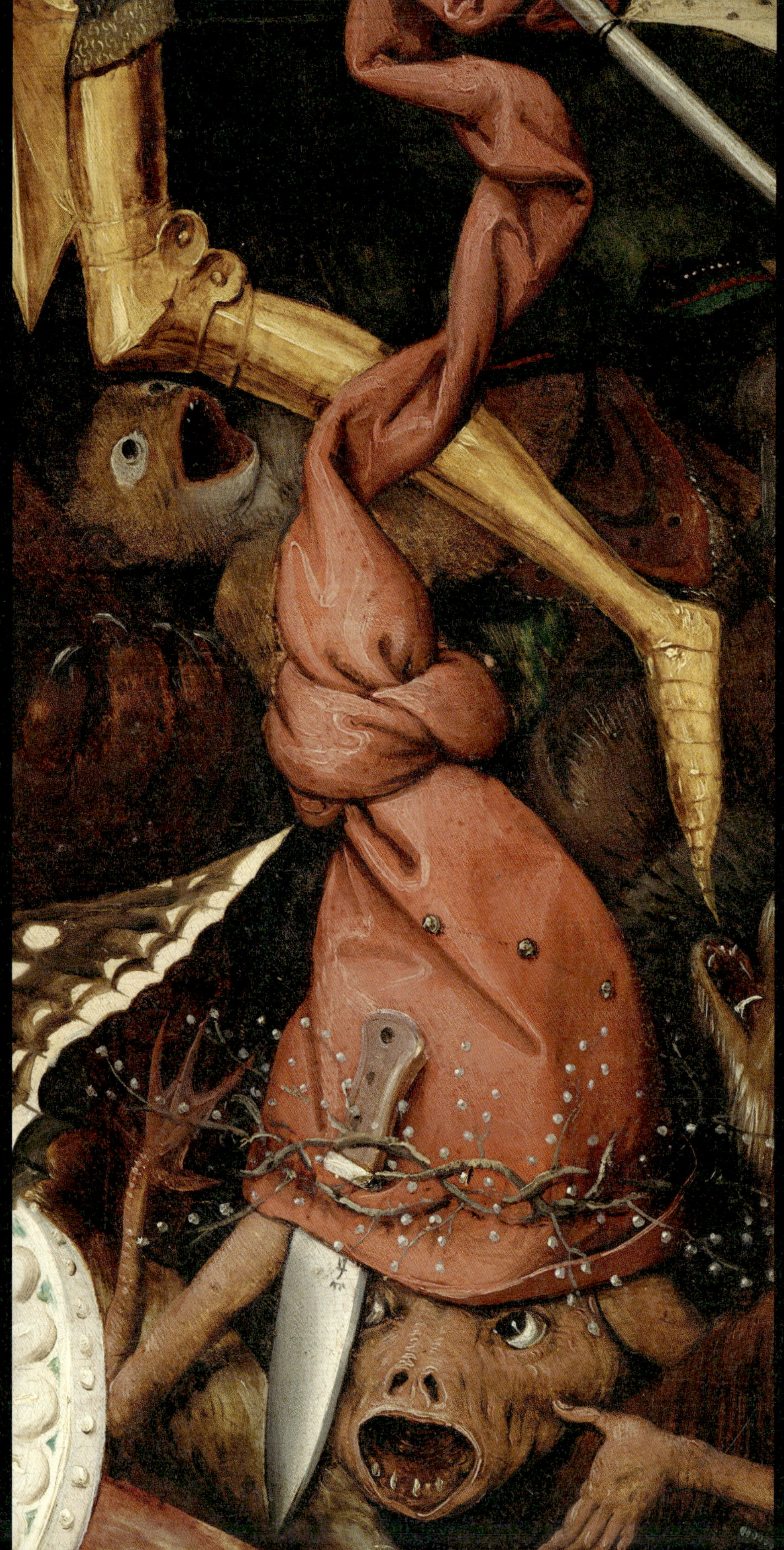

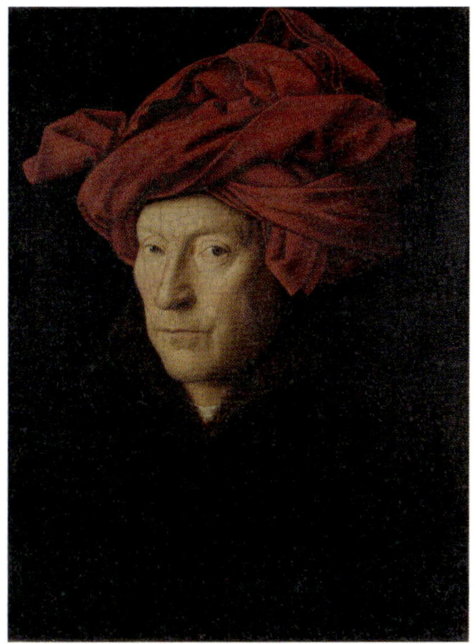

*Man with the Red Turban* (also known as his self-portrait; fig. 64). In citing Van Eyck's famous portrait, which Van Eyck had self-consciously inscribed with the motto "Als Ick Can" (As/If I can), Bruegel on the one hand sanctifies this work, as he rings the turban with Christ's crown of thorns; on the other hand, he gives an ironic spin to this veneration by allowing the turban to unravel during the fall, and adding a sharp knife that will soon cut through the crown of thorns. Bruegel may have been able to admire Van Eyck's portrait in person.[47] At any rate, the idea that Van Eyck wore a turban was widespread in Bruegel's time. Around 1563 the Antwerp merchant and painter Cornelis van Dalem (ca. 1530–1573/76) decorated the façade of his house with sculpted portraits of Van Eyck wearing a turban (fig. 65) and of Albrecht Dürer (fig. 66).[48] The model was based on the panel of the righteous judges in the Ghent Altarpiece, in which it was believed Van Eyck had incorporated a self-portrait wearing a turban.[49] Lampsonius copied the same presumed portrait in the *Effigies* (1572), the series on Netherlandish painters in which the renowned portrait of Bruegel is also included. Indeed, it seems no coincidence that in these same years Lampsonius also wrote his poems for the first published collection of Netherlandish artists' portraits,

**Fig. 64**
Jan van Eyck, *Man with the Red Turban, also called a Self-Portrait*, 1433
London, National Gallery

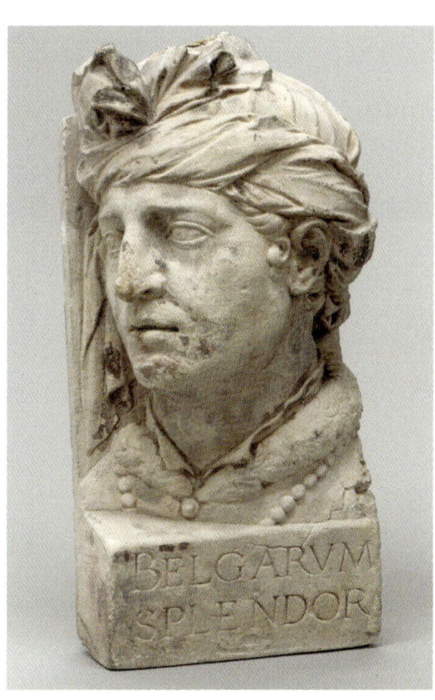


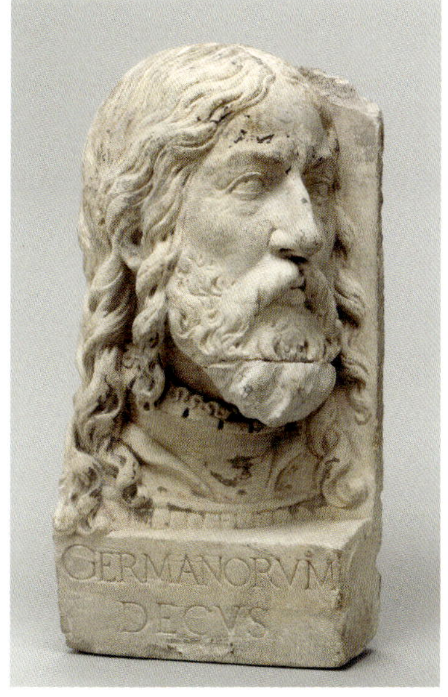


**Fig. 65**
Willem van den Broecke (Paludanus), *Portrait of Jan van Eyck*, c. 1563
Originally from the façade of the house of Cornelis van Dalem in Antwerp, now Antwerp, Museum Vleeshuis/Klank van de Stad

**Fig. 66**
Willem van den Broecke (Paludanus), *Portrait of Albrecht Dürer*, c. 1563
Antwerp, Museum Vleeshuis/Klank van de Stad

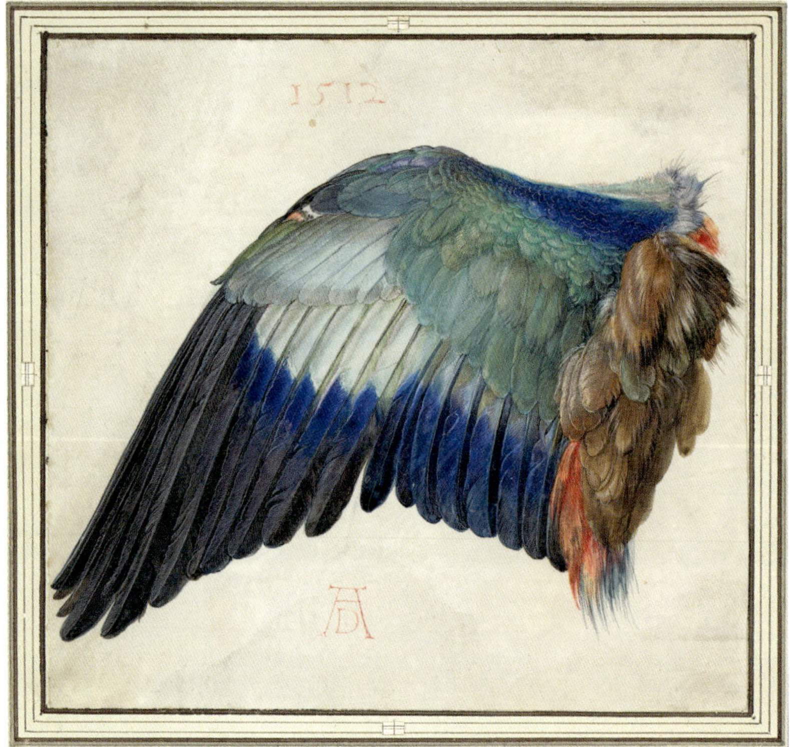

**Fig. 67**
Albrecht Dürer, *Wing of a Eurasian roller (coracais garrulous)*, 1512
Vienna, Graphische Sammlung, Albertina

among which we find the well-known poem describing Bruegel as the new Bosch "who surpassed his master," as well as poetic portraits of Van Eyck, Bosch, Van der Weyden, and Floris.[50]

Bruegel further refers to the art of Albrecht Dürer, an artist who was frequently copied by both artists and naturalists on account of his consummate depiction of nature. As the façade of Van Dalem's house also proclaims, Dürer was already considered one of the founders of the Netherlandish school of painting in Bruegel's time. The remarkably naturalistic wings of Saint Michael [1 and 48] and the good angels [3, 54] are reminiscent of Dürer's paintings of the wings of a Eurasian roller (fig. 67), and part of a collection of drawings by Dürer that Emperor Rudolph had acquired from Cardinal Granvelle.[51] Bruegel may have seen these much-praised watercolors in the collection of the Cardinal during his years in the Netherlands. Dürer's prints were even more widely circulated and avidly collected by learned men such as Ortelius, among others.[52] Not only was Dürer an icon of naturalism, he was also an inventor of monsters.[53] With the seven-headed monster of the Apocalypse [2], Bruegel serves up an innovative yet recognizable adaptation of the monster from Dürer's series of prints on the Apocalypse (fig. 68).[54]

**Fig. 68**
Albrecht Dürer,
*Michael defeating the Apocalyptic Dragon*, 1498
Brussels, Royal Library of Belgium, Print Cabinet

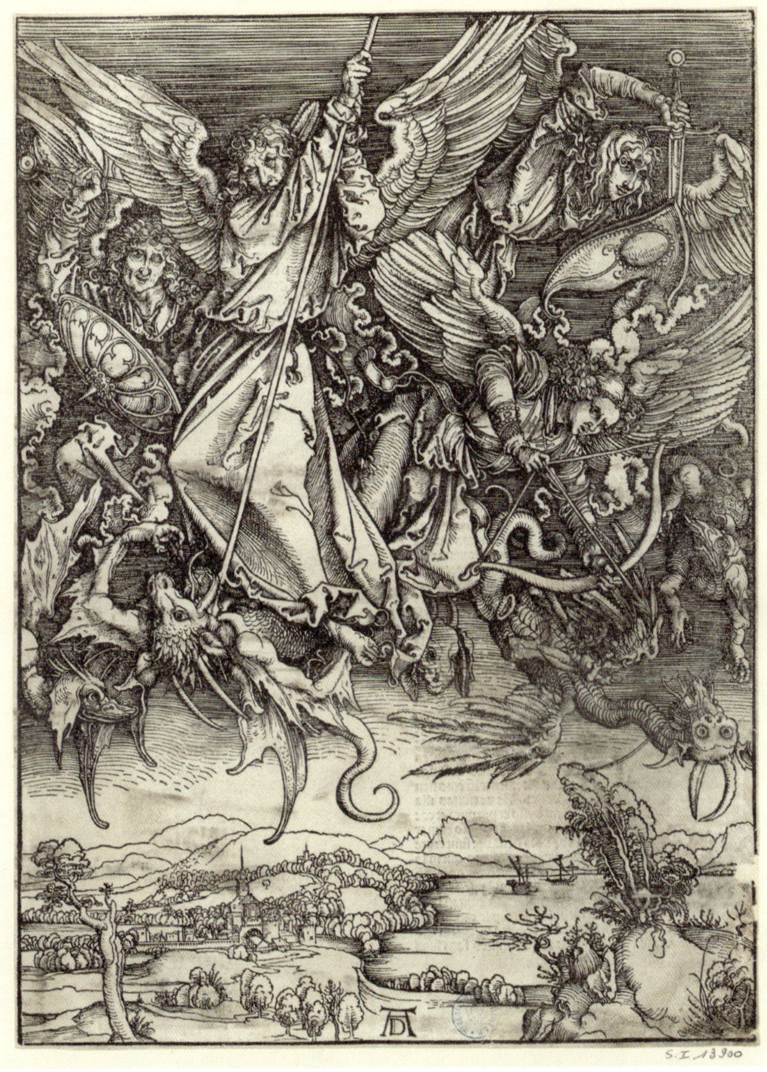

Lastly, Bruegel's armed saint deliberately evokes the archaic cuirasses current in the time of Van Eyck, Van der Weyden, and Bosch, certainly when contrasted to the *all'antica* armor of Saint Michael as painted by his contemporary Frans Floris (fig. 5). There is no doubt that Bruegel was aware of the fame of Floris's invention. In the *Invective, aen enen Quidam Schilder* (1565), written by Lucas d'Heere around the time of the *Fall*, the Ghent rhetorician comments on the rivalry between both painters. D'Heere defends his master Floris against the negative comments that a painter of "carnival puppets" - usually identified as Bruegel - had made on the "sugar figurines" of Floris.[55]

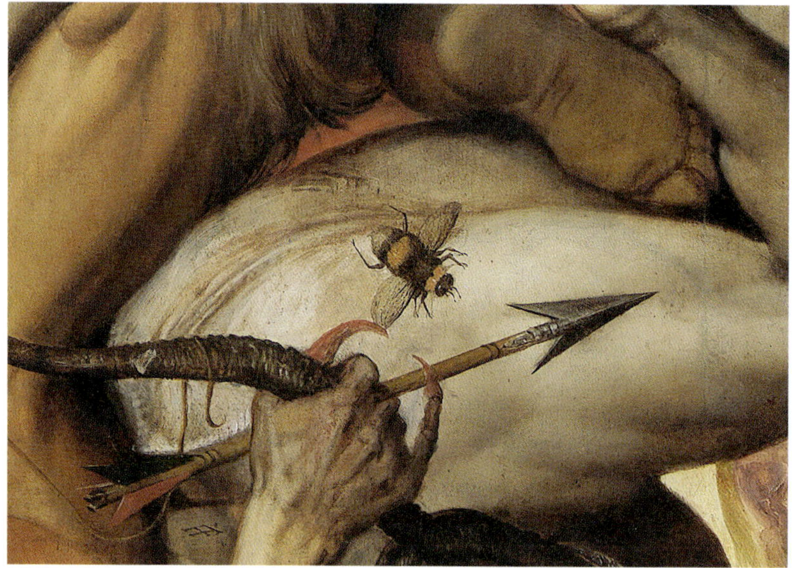

**Fig. 69**
Bee, detail of figure 5 (Frans Floris, *The Fall of the Rebel Angels*, 1554)
Antwerp, Royal Museum of Fine Arts

Whether an indication of true conflict or a rhetorical exercise, the poem indisputably reveals an atmosphere of artistic competition.

The illusionistic fly [46] that Bruegel painted on the left hind leg of the seven-headed monster of the Apocalypse is a subtle reference to the more Michelangelesque interpretation of the same theme by Floris, who had painted an illusionistic bee (fig. 69) on the hind leg of one of his falling angels. The bee, which produces honey from the nectar of many flowers, was in classical rhetoric a familiar example of the selective imitation of nature.[56] Bruegel's fly is more closely related to the hellish atmosphere of the fall of the angels, while at the same time referring to the local artistic tradition of painting flies on the frames of portraits in an optical play of naturalism.[57] Nevertheless, for Bruegel, the frequently noted competition with Floris in the *Fall of the Rebel Angels* was only part of his much broader comment on contemporary practices of collecting and imitating nature *and* art.[58]

For Bruegel, the contest between art and nature, so central to the structure of art and curiosity cabinets, stimulated his artistic self-consciousness. With his painterly transformation of existing collections of art and nature, he entered directly into competition with nature. In this respect it is no coincidence that Bruegel presents his emulation of nature at first sight as an emulation of art. In an attempt to emulate the art of Bosch, Van der Weyden, Van Eyck, Dürer, and Floris, Bruegel imitates the creative powers of Nature. In this way he transforms nature and art into a fantastic artwork that seeks to surpass not only his predecessors, but also Nature itself.

Bruegel's wondrous monsters balance on the edge: between joke and omen, innovation and tradition, art and nature. Like Ovid, Leonardo, and Rabelais,

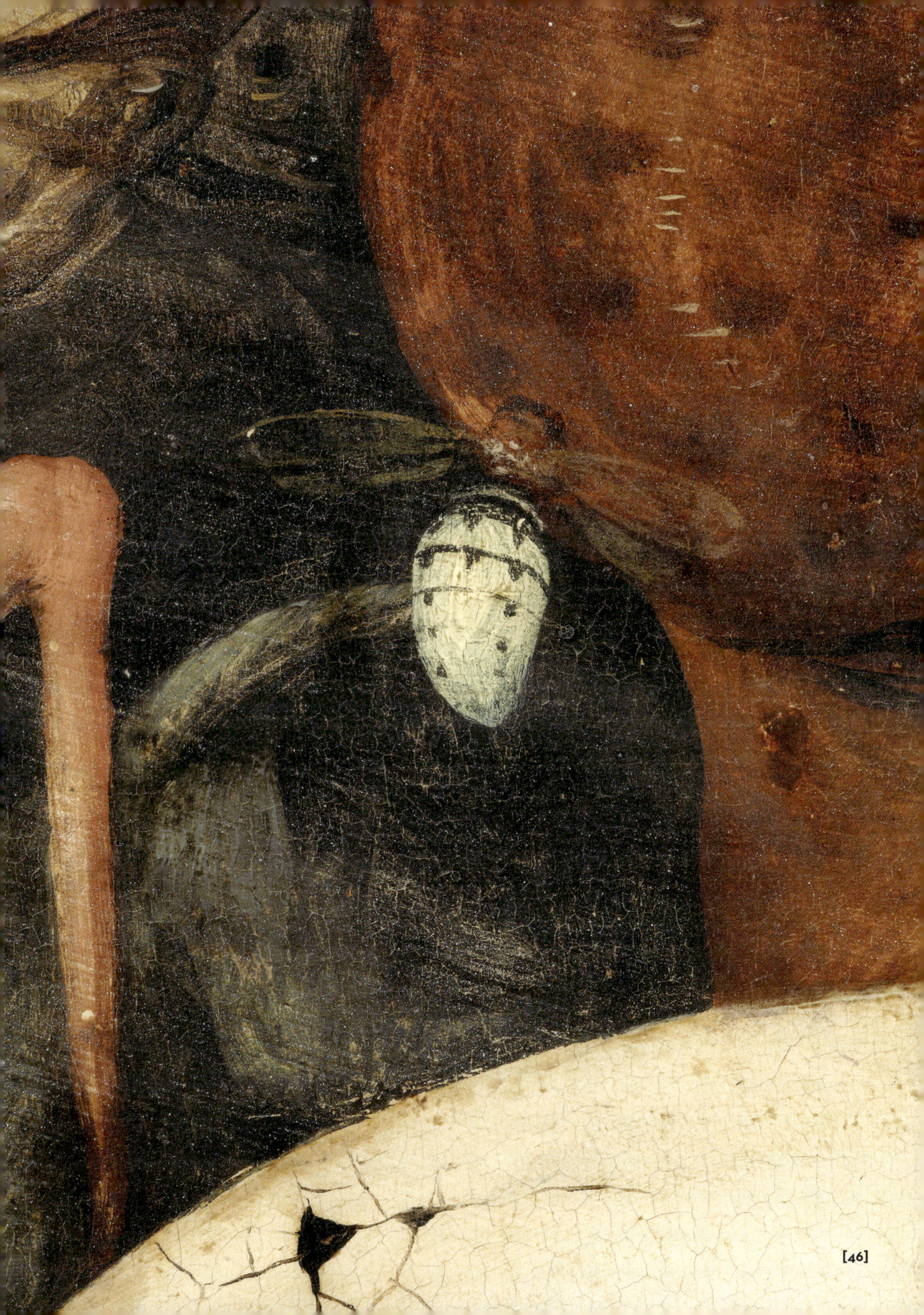

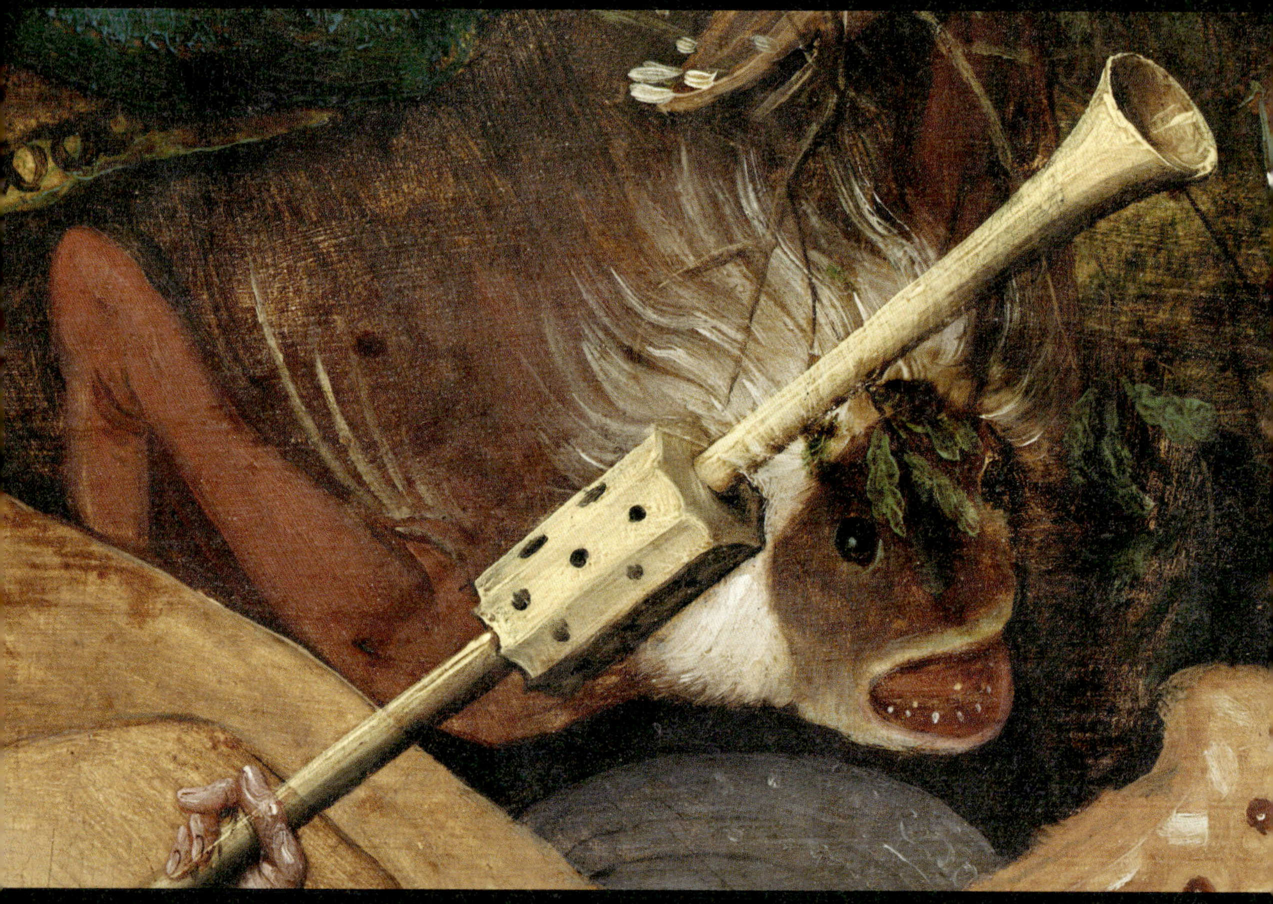

[47]

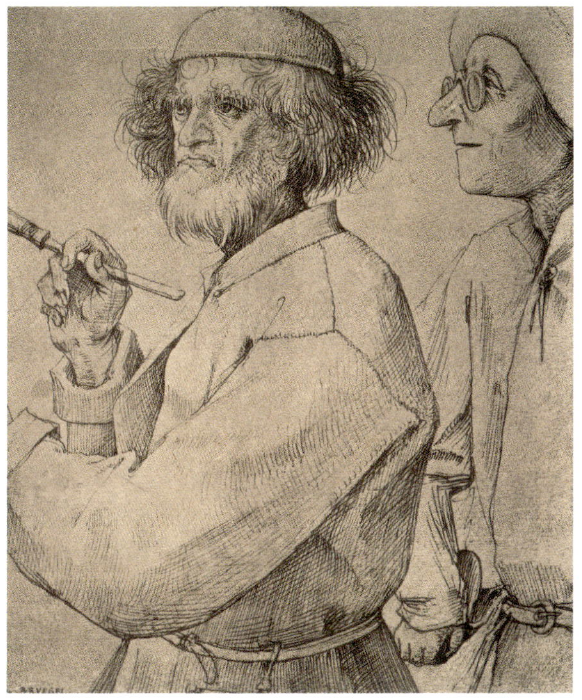

Bruegel shows processes of transformation, not a final product.[59] Later paintings of collections like those of Bruegel's son Jan, which, as we have suggested earlier, proceed from Bruegel's *Fall,* show collections as spaces in which "art-lovers" can display their knowledge of art and nature (fig. 30, fig. 54). Bruegel's miraculous invention betrays his own knowledge of *naturalia* and *artificialia,* and presumes the same knowledge on the part of the collector or viewer of his painting. And yet, while Bruegel demonstrates his own *curiositas* in his carefully composed collection, his depiction of the punishment of pride simultaneously calls into question the unbridled collection of objects of art and knowledge. Bruegel's angels changing into monsters display on the one hand his virtuosity and inventiveness, but they also warn against the dangers of artistic pride. Like Lucifer, who imagined himself equal to God, artists, with their drive to imitate nature, to a certain extent measured themselves against the first Creator, God.

**Fig. 70**
Pieter Bruegel the Elder, *The Painter and the Connoisseur,* ca. 1565
Vienna, Graphische Sammlung Albertina

Bruegel sketches the ambiguity of this almost divine status: it makes the artist supreme, but also dangerously reckless. The falling angels suggest that excessive artistic fantasy can easily devolve into diabolical imaginings, such as those in *Saint James and the Magician* (fig. 10).[60] As in his *Tower of Babel* (fig. 2), a fossil-like structure of natural rock turned into a work of art through human industry, or in the measuring of the stars in *Temperantia* (fig. 76), Bruegel reflects in the *Fall of the Rebel Angels* on the ingenious pursuits of men, whose endless investigations and transformations of nature demonstrate their humanity but can easily be tantamount to hubris.[61] Bruegel's *Fall of the Rebel Angels* truly prefigures the fall of man, brought about by Eve, who could not obey God's prohibition of eating from the tree of knowledge, as Bosch suggests on the left panel of his *Garden of Earthly Delights.*[62] Bruegel typically anchors his representations of timeless human pride in the special interests of the courtly and mercantile collectors toward whom he oriented his work: urban development, scientific instruments, and in the case of the *Fall,* erudite collecting. Yet even though Bruegel evokes the vanity of collecting in the *Fall,* he was well aware that he too created this ingenious work of art to please the greedy eyes of the discerning collector (fig. 70).[63]

# Chapter IV

It is on purpose that one sees the fear of God driven from these countries. Lack of it causes unrest to increase. But where the fear of God reigns in all honesty, great and small shall live together in peace. One shall turn to the severe example of Lucifer: because he did not remain in fear of God. Evil, he chose discordant fighting. Thus becalm yourself and trust in this Word. Fear of God can keep these countries at peace.

*Refereynen ende liedekens van diverschen rhetoricien*, 1563, Refereyn 48*.

# The *Fall of the Rebel Angels* on the eve of the Dutch Revolt

## For whom did Bruegel paint the *Fall of the Rebel Angels*?

There are no known documents that inform us about the patron or, considering that the painting was not necessarily made on commission, the first owner of the *Fall of the Rebel Angels*. This documentary lacuna undoubtedly contributed to the limited attention the work has received, but encourages us to view the painting itself as a kind of document: perhaps the visual references reveal something of the milieu in which it was created, and about the sort of buyer-collector to whom Bruegel addressed his masterpiece.

Bruegel's language was that of paint and brush. There are only a few inscriptions on drawings by his hand, and no known letters or other sample of his writing.[1] The only written word Bruegel has left on the *Fall* is his name in Roman capitals, and - for the first time in his career - the year of its creation in Roman numerals "M.D. LXII/BRUEGEL." The choice of classical letter types suggests a more erudite public, and a self-conscious marking of a new phase in his painting career.[2] As we saw in the first chapter, 1562 was a pivotal year in the life and work of Pieter Bruegel. From then on he designed fewer prints, while painted work began to dominate his production. We have to ask whether this shift from prints to painting indicates that Bruegel, in anticipation of his move to Brussels, hoped to attract a courtly clientele. Perhaps he wanted to settle in Brussels in order to garner more commissions from the court, as had his father-in-law Pieter Coecke.[3] Bruegel's marriage to Mayken Coecke in 1563 must have gained him access to high-level patrons in Brussels.[4]

Most authors have situated the *Fall of the Rebel Angels* in Bruegel's Antwerp period, mainly because it predates his documented period of residence in Brussels (if only by one year), but also because they zoom in on the stylistic differences between Bruegel's interpretation of the theme and the version of that other renowned Antwerp painter, Frans Floris. Floris's monumental *Fall of the Rebel Angels* (1554) for the chapel of the Fencers' Guild in the cathedral of Our Lady in Antwerp probably attracted Bruegel's interest, as we have seen. As early as 1966 Gerhard Menzel suggested a possible connection between Bruegel's *Fall of the Rebel Angels* and Saint Michael as the patron saint of Brussels, but his proposal was not readily embraced.[5] The veneration of Saint Michael was so widespread in early modern Europe that the iconography alone cannot prove that Bruegel made the *Fall* in or for a Brussels milieu. Nevertheless, we believe that the specific rendering of Saint Michael, taken together with its creation in the pivotal year 1562, the atmosphere of precious collecting, and the social and political events in Brussels in 1562 strongly plead in favor of a Brussels context.

## The city of Brussels

*Saint Michael, patron of Brussels*

Saint Michael occupies a special place in Brussels: both the ecclesiastical and municipal powers feature Saint Michael on their banners.[6] A small pilgrimage chapel dedicated to the archangel was situated on a hill near the Zenne, the present site of the Brussels cathedral, as early as the eighth or ninth century. By the eleventh century, it had become the collegiate church of Saint Michael and Saint Gudule. Two centuries later, Saint Michael became the official symbol of the municipal authorities of Brussels as well, as can be seen from the city seal (fig. 71). The most striking expression of this urban identity is the five-meter high gilded statue of Saint Michael (fig. 72), made in 1454 by the renowned bronze founder Martin van Rode and placed as a weathervane on top of the newly completed Brussels city hall. The striking, golden fifteenth-century armor of Saint Michael [1 and 48] in Bruegel's *Fall of the Rebel Angels* recalls this urban icon.[7] Like the statue atop the city hall, the archangel in the painting brandishes his sword as a sign of his omniscient righteousness. The Brussels city hall, built in Brabantine Gothic style, was one of the most prominent sights of the city. Many visitors, among them the painter Albrecht Dürer, praised the building and in particular its "transparent" tower.[8] Dürer also eulogized the famous justice scenes that Rogier van der Weyden had painted for the city hall, still in situ in 1520, but later lost in the bombardments of the central market

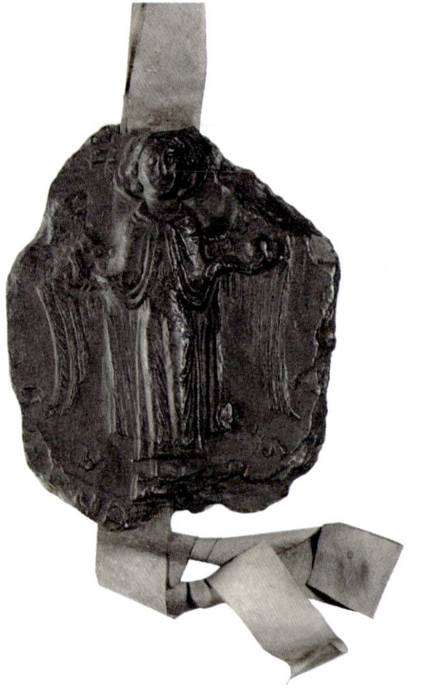

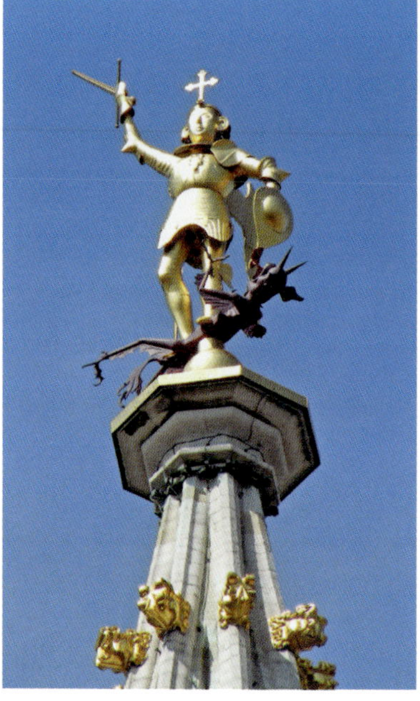

**Fig. 71**
Seal of the city of Brussels, attached to a charter of 1372
Brussels, City Museum

**Fig. 72**
Martin van Rode, *Saint Michael*, 1454
Brussels city hall (copy, twentieth century)

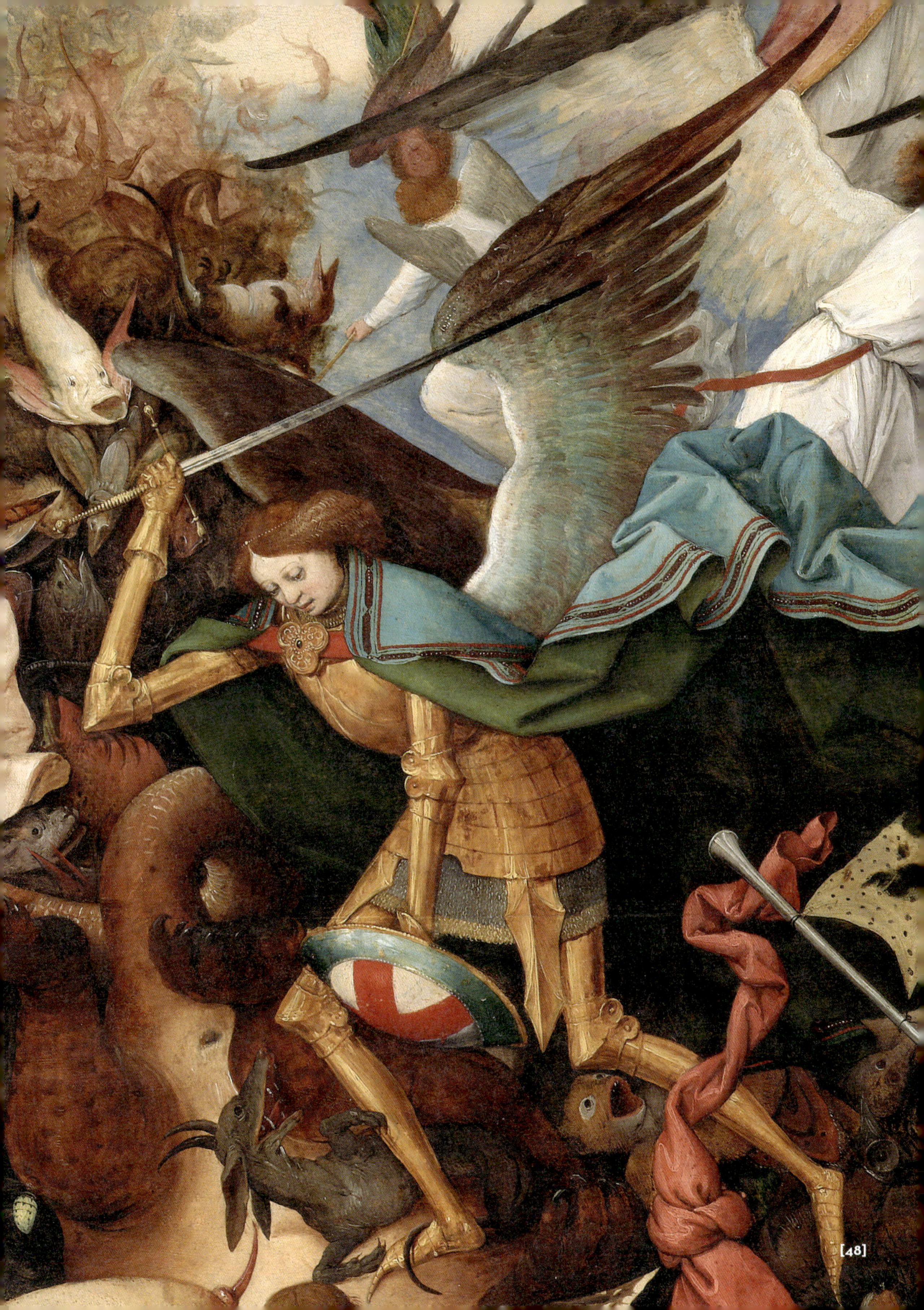

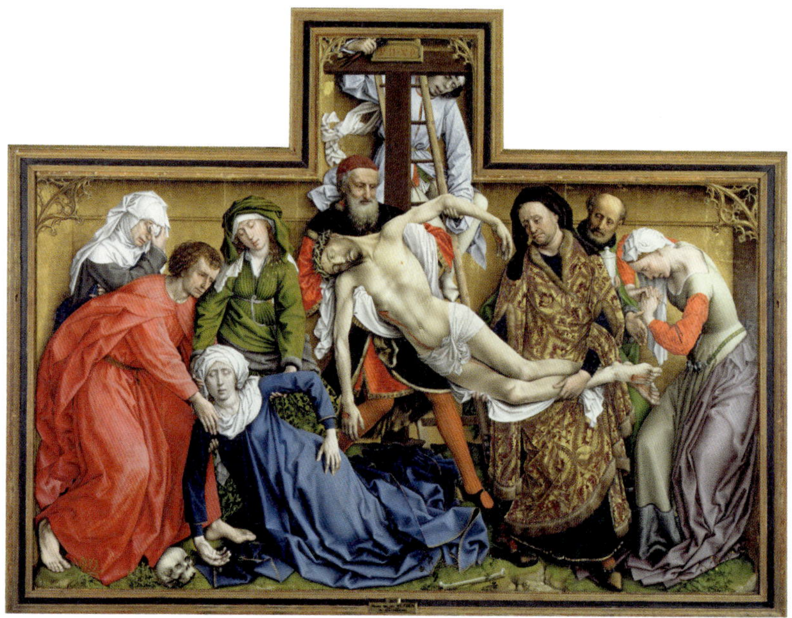

**Fig. 73**
Rogier van der Weyden, *Descent from the Cross*, ca. 1435
Madrid, Museo del Prado

square (Grote Markt) in 1695. We have seen in chapter III that Bruegel emulated the painting style of Van der Weyden (fig. 73), official city painter of Brussels and painter to the court of the Burgundian dukes in the *Fall of the Rebel Angels*, which, maybe not coincidentally, presents also a justice scene. Bruegel's desire to measure himself artistically against his famous predecessor seems therefore imbedded his in his personal experience of the urban culture of Brussels. In contrast to the "Roman" Saint Michael of Frans Floris, which gave shape to the urban, corporate identity of Antwerp, Bruegel addresses the specific urban memory of his new hometown by evoking the glory days of fifteenth century Brussels.[9] With the prospect of settling in the courtly city, Bruegel surely hoped to follow in Rogier's footsteps by garnering both municipal and courtly patronage.[10]

*The Brussels rhetoric contest of 1562*

In 1562, moreover, a rhetoric contest was held in Brussels that had several features in common with Bruegel's painting of the *Fall of the Rebel Angels*. Rhetoricians composed poetry and theatrical performances in the vernacular, and united in "chambers of rhetoric" that frequently organized competitions among them. Members of these chambers were drawn from broad segments of the middle class and included merchants, teachers, and craftsmen as well as numerous artists. Rhetoricians played an important role in organizing and executing festivals and official events, such as joyous entries, for which they designed the stages and produced plays. Often these plays had a political message. In joyous entries they mostly underlined the city's influence and positive relations with the sovereign (fig. 74).[11] Given their broad social basis, the chambers of rhetoric frequently provided a forum for social critique as well, alluding to the religious tensions of the period, the

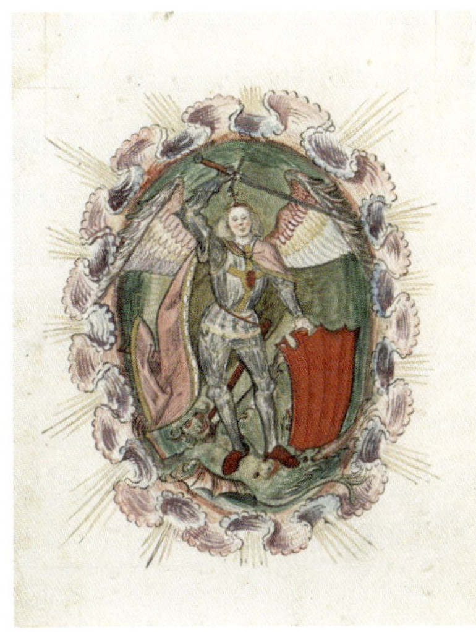

**Fig. 74**
*Blazon with Saint Michael*, in: *Entry of Joanna of Castile in Brussels in 1494*
Berlin, Staatliche Museen, Kupferstichkabinett.

threat of war, civil unrest, food shortages, and rising prices.[12] The rhetoricians played an important role in the construction of an urban culture in the Southern Netherlands.[13]

The central theme of the rhetoric contest that was organized by the Brussels chamber De Corenbloem (The Cornflower) on July 26, 1562, was the precarious political situation. All participants, including the chambers of rhetoric of Brabant, Flanders, Holland, and Zeeland, were asked to compose a refrain or song in answer to the question "What can maintain peace in these countries?"[14] Politics had been particularly turbulent since the regent's principal advisor, Antoine Perrenot de Granvelle, had been appointed the previous year as archbishop of Mechelen, a position that gave him a direct vote in the Council of State. The public announcement by Granvelle and the government in Brussels that the ecclesiastical organization of the Seventeen Provinces would be reorganized, going from four bishoprics to eighteen, had caused a complete crisis.[15] The nobility feared that the ecclesiastical reform would curtail their influence, and the urban patriciate feared that the new structure would strengthen the Inquisition in the Netherlands. Several rhetoricians, known for their sharp tongues, had expressed their dissatisfaction with religious intolerance and lampooned the misbehavior of certain Catholic clergymen. Already in 1559, some members of the Brussels chambers of rhetoric had mocked the clergy and the Holy Spirit.[16] Cardinal Granvelle led the investigation into these "scandalous plays," and on January 26, 1560, governor Margaret of Parma issued a placard requiring that all plays, refrains, and songs with religious content were from then on to be approved by the religious and temporal governments.

The conciliatory theme of the Brussels rhetoric contest of 1562 suggests that it was indeed closely supervised. Like many rhetoricians, Adriaen Van Conincxloo, the Brussels cloth merchant who as "prince" or honorary chairman of the chamber organized the contest, had Calvinist sympathies, but he insisted that the court had supported the event.[17] One year after the performance, he arranged for the contributions to be published. Tellingly, these *Refereynen ende liedekens* (fig. 75) were edited by the official printer of the king and approved by the pastor of the Saint Gudule and Saint Michael.[18]

The most frequently formulated answers to the competition's central question as to what could maintain peace in the Netherlands were wisdom, obedience, fear of God, and unity. At least four of the seventy contributions cite the fall of Lucifer and the rebel angels as a negative example of hubris, one of the greatest threats to peace. A number of refrains and songs cite other negative examples of hubris, themes also painted by Bruegel, including the *Fall of Icarus*, the *Tower of Babel* (fig. 2), and the *Suicide of Saul* (fig. 26). According to a rhetorician from the chamber of the Holy Ghost from Geeraardsbergen with the telling motto *Ubi vult Spirat* (the Spirit goes where it pleases), "Lucifer did not appeal to wisdom, but raised himself as head in order to reign, although he was appointed to serve. Was it not thus that unrest descended for the first time? The entire heavens moved without ceasing until Lucifer was felled."[19] He further insists on the importance of wisdom in politics: "And Wisdom is also good politics, because Wisdom is neither pride nor revulsion, but sweet love, that leads shepherds to rule the community not with prejudice but with a glad heart, not self-seeking and bloodthirsty, but seeking only the welfare of the people, as a father does for his children: these are the good leaders of the lay community."[20]

*Ubi vult Spirat* invokes Lucifer again in refrain 48: "It is on purpose that one sees the fear of God driven from these countries. Lack of it causes unrest to increase. But where the fear of God reigns in all honesty, great and small shall live together in peace. One shall turn to the severe example of Lucifer: because he did not remain in fear of God. Evil, he chose discordant fighting. Thus becalm yourself and trust in this Word. Fear of God can keep these countries at peace."[21] Elsewhere, the rebellious and lusty Lucifer is offered up as a negative example of obedient love and virtue.[22]

Several other participants emphasize the importance of good government and a wise and honest king, who rules with love as a good shepherd, according to the laws of God, and not as a tyrant. Then his subjects will obey him.[23] The advice to the "Prince," to be a wise, honest, loving protector of his country, was undoubtedly not so much meant for the prince of the chamber, but rather for Philip II, a prince with "many townships and countries to rule."[24] Maybe the rhetoricians meant to suggest that the situation was frequently otherwise, but - prudently - they never broadcast their criticisms openly. Instead, they plead for a peaceful society without taking a confessional position. The song to refrain 8 even encourages the prince to put on his armor and battle against evil: "Therefore wise prince, put on the armor of God, in order to better resist the hellish hoards."[25] Here the prince himself becomes Saint Michael.

### *Bruegel and the rhetoricians*

Bruegel's visual language is closely related to the poetic imagery of the rhetoricians. Like these rhymesters, Bruegel often presented a serious message with a dash of mockery, as an inversion of the established order, as the world turned upside down.[26] In Antwerp, the chamber of rhetoric known as De Violieren (The Gillyflowers) had fused with the painters' Guild of Saint Luke, of which Bruegel was a member.[27] In the preparatory drawing for the print *Temperantia* (fig. 76) Bruegel depicts an urban landscape with a public theater performance of the kind produced by the rhetoricians. He also demonstrates his interest in poetical and rhetorical aspects of the Dutch

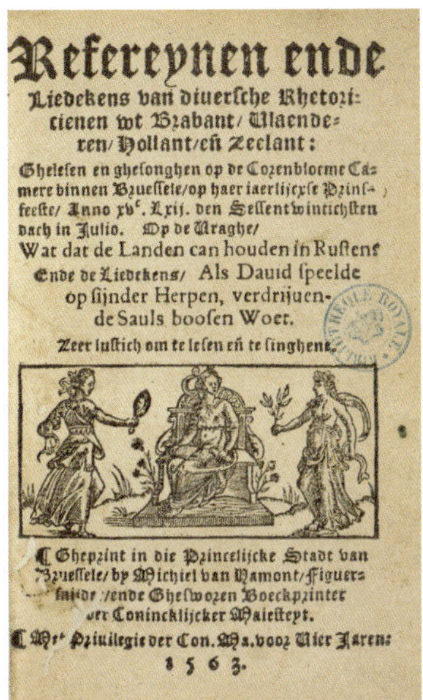

Refereynen ende
Liedekens van diuerſche Rhetori-
cienen wt Brabant/ Vlaende-
ren/ Hollant/ eñ Zeelant:
Ghelesen en ghesonghen op de Corenbloeme Cā-
mere binnen Bruessele/ op haer iaerlijcxse Prins-
feeste/ Anno xv$^{c}$. Lxij. den Sessentwintichsten
dach in Julio. Op de Vraghe/
Wat dat de Landen can houden in Ruſten?
Ende de Liedekens/ Als Dauid ſpeelde
op ſijnder Herpen, verdrijuen-
de Sauls booſen Woet.
Zeer lustich om te lesen eñ te singhene.

Gheprint in die Princelijcke Stadt van
Bruessele/ by Michiel van Hamont/ Figuer-
snider/ ende Gheswozen Boeckprinter
der Coninckllijcker Maiesteyt.
Met Priuilegie der Con. Ma. voor Vier Jaren.
1563.

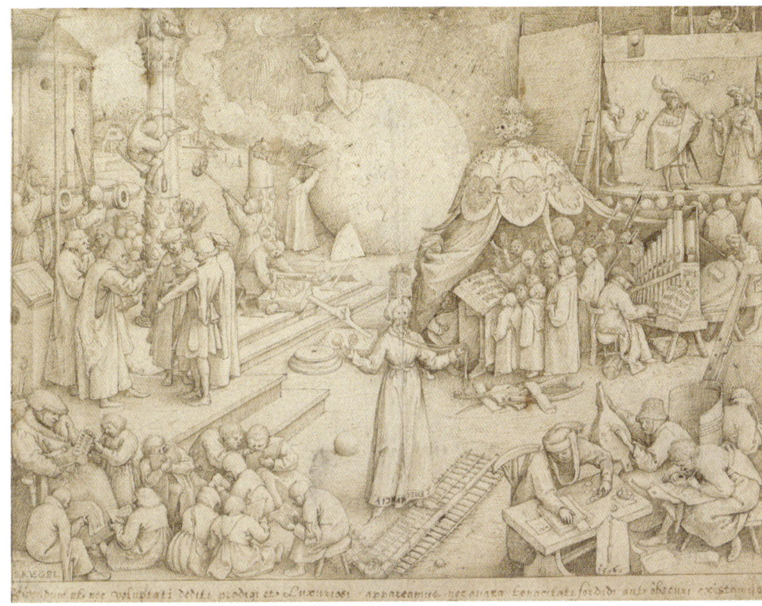

**Fig. 75**
*Refereynen ende liedekens*, 1563, titlepage
Brussels, Royal Library of Belgium

**Fig. 76**
Pieter Bruegel the Elder, *Temperantia*, 1560
Rotterdam, Museum Boijmans Van Beuningen

language in his painting of the *Proverbs* (fig. 1). It has been suggested, moreover, that for his painting of *Dulle Griet* (fig. 27), which is formally related to the *Fall*, he was inspired by a "factie" or comical play performed at the *Landjuweel*, the annual rhetoricians' contest that De Violieren had organized in Antwerp in 1561.[28] It was during this *Landjuweel*, one of the largest and most public of rhetoric contests, that Van Coninxloo had been elected "prince" of De Corenbloem. Many more Brussels prizewinners had a connection to Antwerp and various participants had served as "factors" or jury members in the *Landjuweel* of 1561.[29] Indeed, the Brussels refrain contest of 1562 seems to have been conceived as a continuation of the Antwerp theater festival of the year before, and that had centered on the question of what incites men to art and knowledge.[30]

Although we have no firm indication that Bruegel participated in the Brussels rhetoric contest of 1562, it should be underlined that not all of the participants have been identified. To show their poetical talent, and because they frequently expressed critical views, rhetoricians often signed their poems with a pseudonym or emblematic motto. Furthermore, Bruegel seems to have known several artists who contributed to the Brussels contest. He may have known "prince" Adriaen van Conincxloo: according to Van Mander, Bruegel's son Pieter II later apprenticed with his brother, the painter Gillis van Conincxloo.[31] Michiel Coecke, son from the first marriage of Bruegel's father-in-law Pieter, participated as a member of the Aalst rhetoricians' chamber Catharina with a contribution entitled *D'Betrouwe is al*, or "Trust is everything".[32] Michiel was a poet as well as a painter and was registered as an independent master in the Antwerp Guild of Saint Luke in 1551, the same year as Bruegel. In 1554, he married Margareta, the younger sister of Mayken Verhulst, Bruegel's future mother-in-law. Mayken's two other sisters also married well-known painters: Elisabeth married Hubertus Goltzius; Barbara, Jacob de Pundere, who later in 1562 became a member of De Corenbloem.[33] Two other female rhetoricians who probably belonged to the Coecke family contributed to the 1562 contest: "Catharina per Aelst," possibly the daughter of Jan, brother of Pieter Coecke van Aelst, composed refrains 3 and 38; "Barbara per Aelst" composed refrain 5. Bruegel's in-laws were thus well represented.

The painter, engineer, and architect Hans Vredeman de Vries (1527-1606/9) also turns up among the participants. As a member of the Mechelen chamber De Peoene (The Peony) he refers in his motto to the peaceful reverberations of his own name (*Zijt altijd Vreedman. Vriese*; *Vrede* meaning peace; hence *Vredeman,* a peaceful man).[34] Bruegel and De Vries must have met in the Antwerp print publishing house of Hieronymus Cock, Aux Quatre Vents. In the years during which Bruegel's prints depicting the *Vices* (1559-60) and the *Pedlar Robbed by Monkeys* (1562) rolled from the presses, Cock also published Vredeman's *Scenographia* (1560) and an architectural fantasy (1562), both dedicated to Cardinal Granvelle.[35] The paths of Bruegel and Vredeman also crossed in Brussels. According to Van Mander, Vredeman painted a summer pavilion in perspective in the house of Aert Molckeman, the king's treasurer in Brussels, to which Bruegel, fascinated by the open door in trompe l'oeil, contributed a peasant couple without being asked. This amused the master of the house so much that he refused to have Bruegel's painting removed.[36] Although Van Mander does not assign the correct date to the event, there is every reason to believe his account.[37] Aert Molckeman served the Brussels court and lived in the Putterij, close by the Houtmarkt, in the direct vicinity of the palace of Granvelle. Vredeman settled in Antwerp in 1561, but he must have spent a great deal of time in Brussels, where a canopy depicting *Pluto and Proserpina* was being woven after his designs that year.[38] The Brussels tapestry weavers, a milieu with which Bruegel too had close family and professional ties, were the best-represented professional group among the members of the chamber of De Corenbloem.[39]

## The court at Brussels

Like many sumptuous Brussels tapestries, and like the rhetoricians' contest of 1562, Bruegel's *Fall* addresses the interests and concerns of both city and court. Until 1559, the year in which Philip II returned definitively to Spain after four tormented years in the Netherlands, Brussels was one of the most important residences in the Habsburg realm. Although Charles V and his predecessors, the Burgundian dukes, led an ambulant court life, the peripatetic emperor spent a considerable amount of his time in the Netherlands, particularly in Brussels.[40] In the palace on the Coudenberg, the former residence of the dukes of Brabant, Charles V abdicated the throne in 1555 and

**Fig. 77**
Frans Hogenberg (1535-1590), *Abdication of Charles V on 25 October 1555 in the Brussels Coudenberg Palace*
Brussels, Royal Library of Belgium, Print Cabinet

**Fig. 78**
Masked tournament between wild men (lead by the Count of Egmont) and amazons (lead by the prince of Orange), in: *Pourtraictz au vif des Entrees Festins Joustes & Combatz matrimoniaux celebrees en la Ville de Bruxelles l'an nostre Seigneurs Mille Cincq cens LXV.... Entre Treshaut Trespuyssant & Tresexcellent Prince Monseign. Alexandre Farnese... & entre Treshaute trespuyssante & tresexcellente princesse Donne Marie de Portugal,* c. 1565
Warsaw, Gabinet Rycin Biblioteki Uniwersyteckiej Warszawie, Print Cabinet

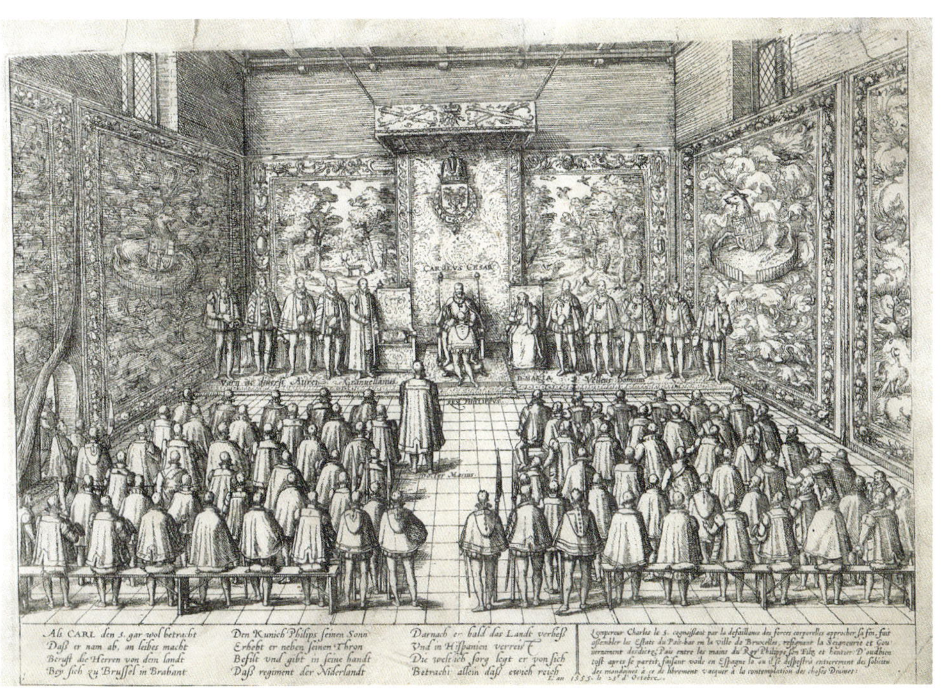
Als CARL den 5. gar wol betracht
Daß er nam ab, an leibes macht
Beruft die Herren von dem landt
Bey sich zu Brussel in Brabant
Den Kunich Philips seinen Sonn
Erhebt er neben seinen Thron
Befilt und gibt in seine handt
Daß regiment der Niderlandt
Darnach er bald das Landt verheß
Und in Hispanien verreist
Die weltlich sorg legt er von sich
Betracht allein daß ewich reich
L'an 1555. le 25e d'Octobre.
Lempereur Charles le 5. cognoissant par la defaillance des forces corporelles approcher sa fin, fait
assembler les Estats du Pais-bas en la ville de Bruxelles, resignant la Seigneurie et Gou
uernement desdictz Pais entre les mains du Roy Philippe son Filz et heritier. D'oubien
tost apres se partit, faisant voile en Espagne la ou il se despestra entierement des sollicitu
des mondaines a ce de librement vacquer a la contemplation des choses Diuines.

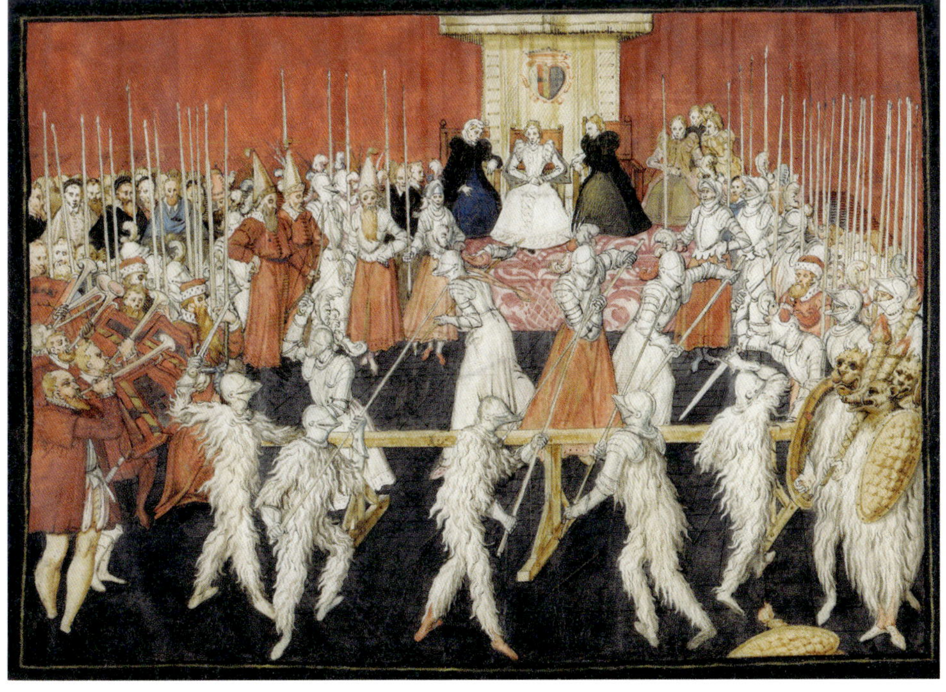

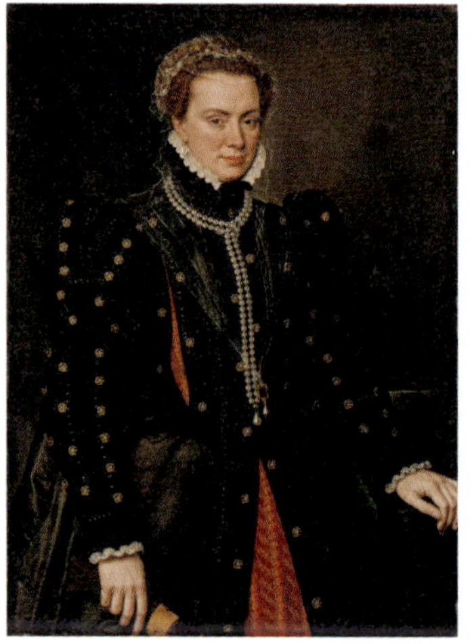

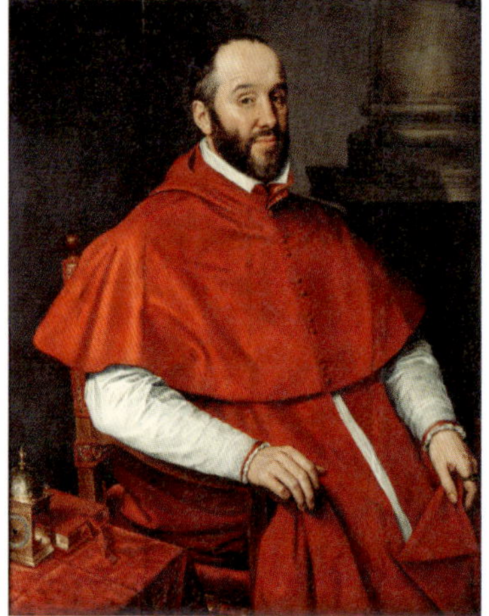

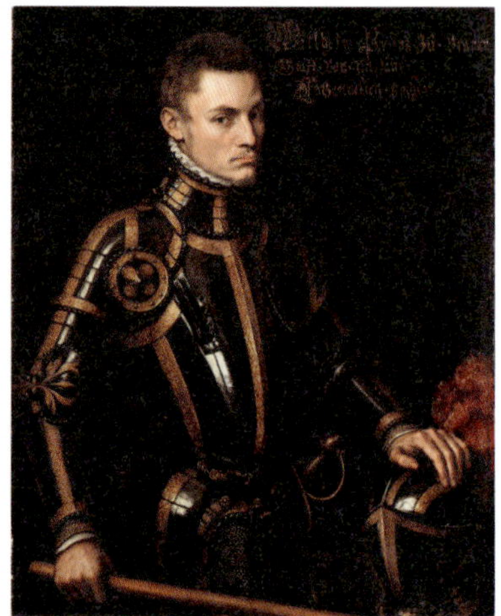

transferred power to his son Philip (fig. 77). The prince, and later the regent of the Netherlands, Margaret of Parma, did not always reside at Coudenberg Palace. Rather, they enjoyed staying at the palaces in Binche, Tervuren, and Mariemont as well. Important political and representative events, however, such as the abdication of Charles V, or the princely marriage of Alexander Farnese, son of Charles V's illegitimate daughter Margaret of Parma, to Maria of Portugal in 1565 (fig. 78), were held at Coudenberg.[41] Representative collectors' items, such as the treasures pouring in from the New World (fig. 21), were kept there as well.[42]

**Fig. 79**
Antonis Mor, *Margaret of Parma*, c. 1562
Berlin, Gemäldegalerie

**Fig. 80**
Willem Key, *Antoine Perrenot, Cardinal Granvelle*, c. 1561
Weimar, Klassik Stiftung Weimar aus Schloß Sonderhausen

**Fig.81**
Anthonis Mor, and studio, *William of Orange*, 1555
Kassel, Staatliche Museen

*Margaret of Parma, Granvelle, Orange*

After the departure of Philip II and during Bruegel's sojourn in Brussels, Margaret of Parma (1522-1586) was regent of the Netherlands (fig. 79) (1559-67, and later in 1580-83). As an illegitimate daughter of Charles V, she had been brought up at the courts of Margaret of Austria and Mary of Hungary. Her marriage to Ottavio Farnese in 1538 brought her prestige and wealth, as well as access to the famous art collection of the Farnese family.[43] An exceptional portrait after Anthonis Mor (1516-1575), who painted Margaret on several occasions, shows her with a painter's palette and brushes in her hand.[44] Remarkably, the artistic interests of the regent have not been the subject of much study, and to this day not one single painting by Bruegel can be traced back to her collections.[45] Perhaps her personal art acquisitions were absorbed into the Farnese collections; nevertheless, she was overshadowed as a patron of the arts - as in politics - by her most important advisor, Antoine Perrenot de Granvelle.[46]

Antoine Perrenot de Granvelle (fig. 80) came from an important family of jurists and councilors. After the death of his father, chancellor Nicholas Perrenot de Granvelle (1484-1550), he followed in the latter's footsteps as

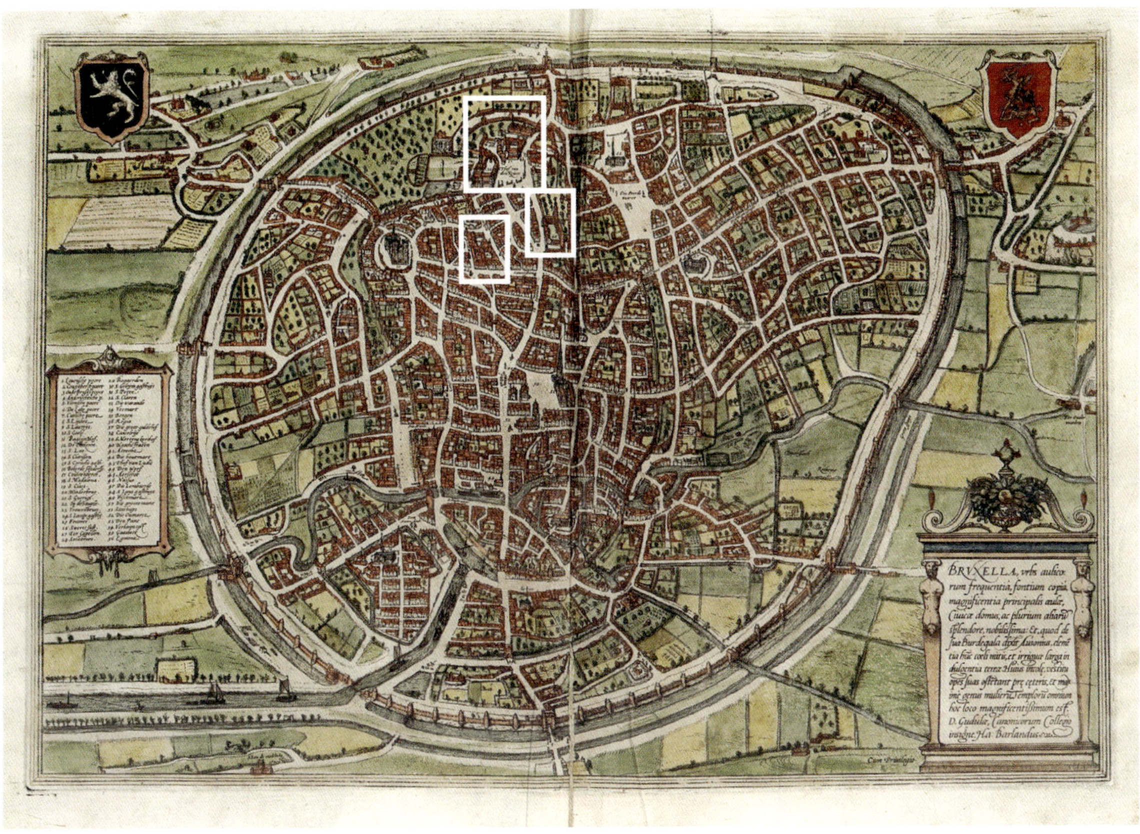


**Fig. 82**
*Bruxella*, in: Georg Braun and Frans Hogenberg, *Civitates Orbis Terrarum* (Cologne, 1572-1612) Brussels, Royal Library of Belgium, Map division, indicated clockwise Coudenberg Palace, Hof van Nassau, Hof van Atrecht (Granvelle's Palace)

principal "minister" of Charles V. In the absence of Charles V, Granvelle advised governor Mary of Hungary and in 1555, at the transfer of power to Philip II at the Coudenberg Palace, he stood at the emperor's right hand (fig. 78).[47] Also present at this solemn event was the young prince William of Orange (1533-1584) (fig. 81). The Spanish historian Sandoval relates that during the ceremony, the exhausted emperor rested on the shoulder of Orange, then a twenty-two-year-old nobleman who was being educated in Brussels and whom Charles V warmly recommended to his son.[48]

In Brussels, Orange lived in the *Hof van Nassau*, situated at a short distance from the Coudenberg Palace (fig. 82). Today only the chapel and a couple of walls survive, and are integrated into the buildings of the Royal Library, but it was once praised as one of the most magnificent buildings in Brussels (fig. 83).[49] The site - the present-day Kunstberg/Mont des Arts, where the Royal Museums of Fine Arts of Belgium are also located - still offers a splendid panorama of the city, with the tower of city hall and its gilded statue of Saint Michael prominently in view (fig. 84).

During the early years of Philip II's reign, William was on good terms with

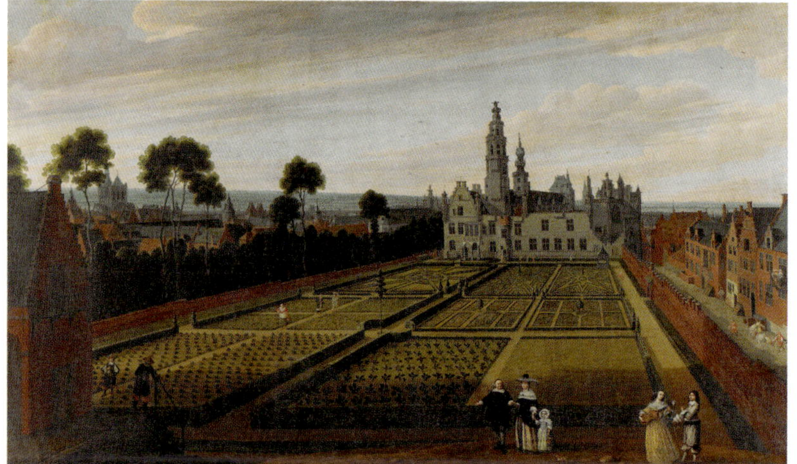

**Fig. 83**
Willem van Schoor, with figures by Gillis van Tilborgh, *The Hotel of Nassau in Brussels*, 1659
Brussels, The Royal Museum of Fine Arts of Belgium

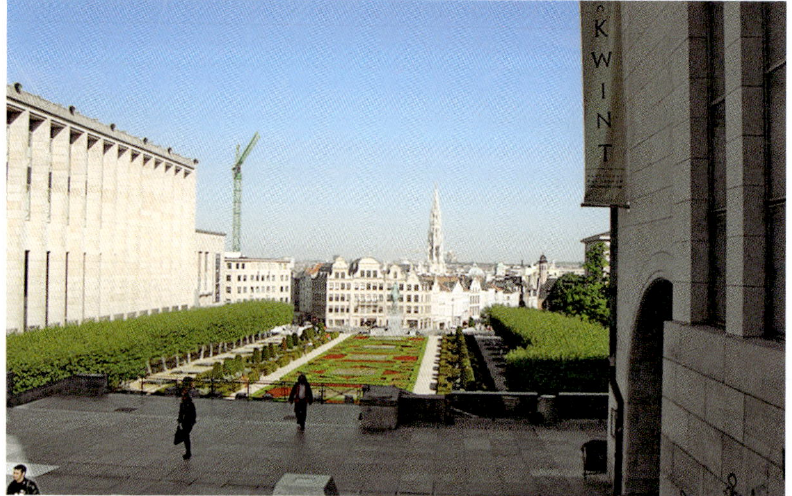


**Fig. 84**
*View on the Spire of the Brussels City Hall viewed from the Coudenberg*, site of present Royal Museums of Fine Art of Belgium.

governor Margaret of Parma and Granvelle. Granvelle even argued in favor of greater freedom for the Low Countries, a demand that was defended by local noblemen such as Orange against the Spanish faction at court. The reason for the deteriorating relations between Granvelle and Orange was not so much a confrontation of ideologies as a question of conflicting positions of power.[50] William of Orange, an independent prince and *seigneur*, expected to play the leading political role in his country.[51] Granvelle's longstanding family tradition of advising the king gave him authority and status, but it did not make him a prince of noble blood. However, Granvelle's position of power changed drastically when Philip II appointed him archbishop of Mechelen in 1561, a function that gave him a direct vote in the Council of

State. It has been argued that this opposition between the increasingly important "noblesse de robe" and the traditional high nobility, the "noblesse d'épée," marks the beginning of what would later become the drama of the Dutch Revolt.[52]

As a member of the Council of State, the central organ that advised on state affairs, government, and the security and defense of the Low Countries, Granvelle entered into a mounting competition with William of Orange. Granvelle and Orange each built up a network of patronage among the upper and lower nobility, the government administration, and the municipal governments in order to exercise the greatest possible influence.[53] In July 1561, the Prince of Orange and Count Lamoral of Egmont (1522-1568) expressed for the first time in a letter to Philip II their dissatisfaction over the fact that political decisions were made without their involvement.[54] Not coincidentally, Granvelle had been appointed archbishop while Orange was abroad for his marriage to Anna of Saxony. However, the king did not receive the letter of the noblemen favorably.

On May 16, 1562, Margaret of Parma convoked the Council of State in connection with eventual military support for France in their fight against the Huguenots. Before reporting to the meeting, ten knights of the Golden Fleece under the leadership of William of Orange, Egmont, and Philip de Montmorency, count of Hornes (1524-1568), met in the Hof van Nassau. During this gathering in the palace of William of Orange, they formed the so-called "League against Granvelle." The most prominent demand of these conspirators was restoring the involvement of the local nobility in the government of the Netherlands, but their discontent coincided with unprecedented public opposition to Catholic repression in the form of the Inquisition, with which Granvelle, as cardinal, was easily identified.[55] Gradually, political and religious discontent were inextricably interwoven. Under increasing pressure from the upper nobility, the king finally dismissed Granvelle on March 13, 1564. Granvelle retreated to the family palace in Besançon, never to return to Brussels.

## Granvelle as connoisseur and collector of art and nature

Granvelle has gone down in history as a despised politician, but in his own time he was also known as great patron of the arts and an insatiable collector. He personally supported the painter Anthonis Mor and the sculptor and medalist Jacques Jonghelinck (1530-1606), whose bronze foundry was established in Granvelle's palace in Brussels.[56] Jacques Jonghelinck may have traveled together with Bruegel to Italy; in any case, they were both on the other side of the Alps in the years 1552-53.[57] Jacques was the brother of Nicolaas Jonghelinck, the art-loving merchant who later commissioned the famous series of the *Months* from Bruegel.[58]

Granvelle's palace in Brussels, on the site of the present-day Ravenstein Gallery, not far from the Coudenberg Palace and the Hof van Nassau (fig. 82), was one of

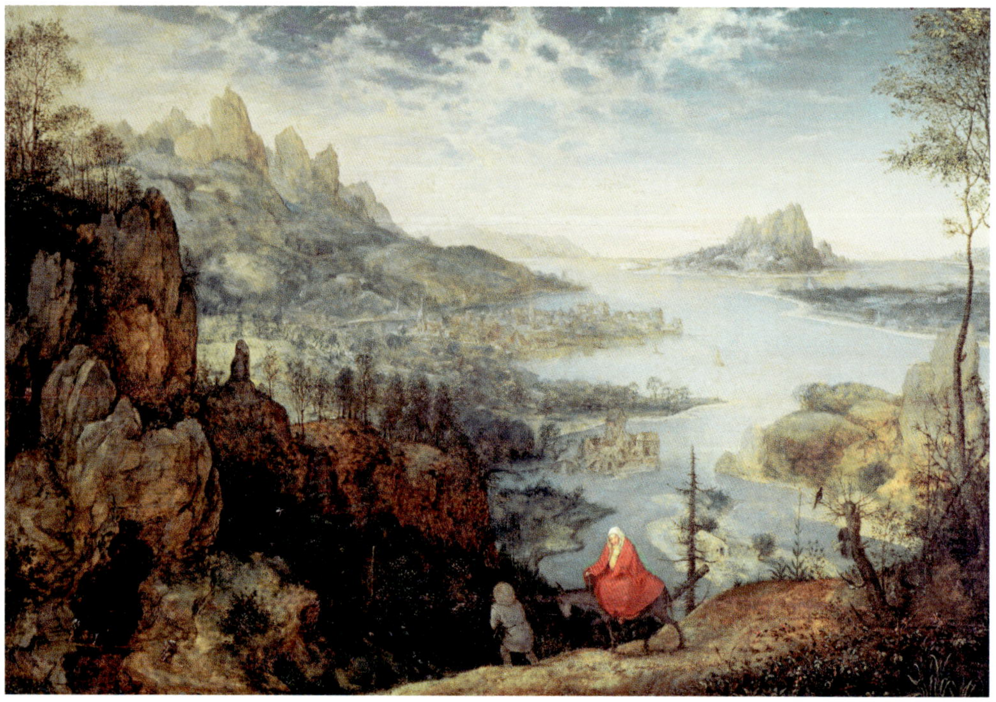

**Fig. 85**
Pieter Bruegel the Elder, *Rest on the Flight into Egypt*, 1563
London, Courtauld Institute of Art, Seilern Collection

the most modern Renaissance designs in the city. Its gardens with medicinal herbs, exotic trees, and unusual animals inspired admiration among many of his contemporaries.[59] The palace contained a "cabinet," an intimate space in which the statesman could study pieces from his collection and show them to visitors.[60] The inventory of this Brussels cabinet has not been found, but a later inventory of the Granvelle family palace in Besançon, to which the cardinal retreated after his stay in Brussels, contains a long list of paintings and ancient and modern sculptures.[61] This inventory was drawn up in 1607, and therefore contains the family's later acquisitions as well, but the lion's share was undoubtedly collected by the cardinal. It is the earliest source and the basis to trace sculptures by Giambologna and paintings by the likes of Titian, Dürer, Pourbus, Floris, and Coxcie to the cardinal's collection - along with Bruegel's *Rest on the Flight into Egypt* (fig. 85).[62] Granvelle is thus one of the few known art-lovers who probably owned paintings by Bruegel during the artist's lifetime.

In addition the inventory of 1607 lists painted depictions of animals, among them the heads of a donkey, dog, fox, South-American guinea pig ("conny d'Inde"), and cat by Frans Pourbus the Elder (ca. 1540-1581), as well as paintings of a bat and a rhinoceros.[63] Granvelle probably also kept the album with Dürer paintings, which included several depictions of nature - among them the *Wings of a Eurasian Roller* (fig. 67) - in the cabinet.[64] Other artworks

**Fig. 86**
Antonis Mor,
*Granvelle's Dwarf and Dog*, c. 1558-1559
Paris, Musée du Louvre

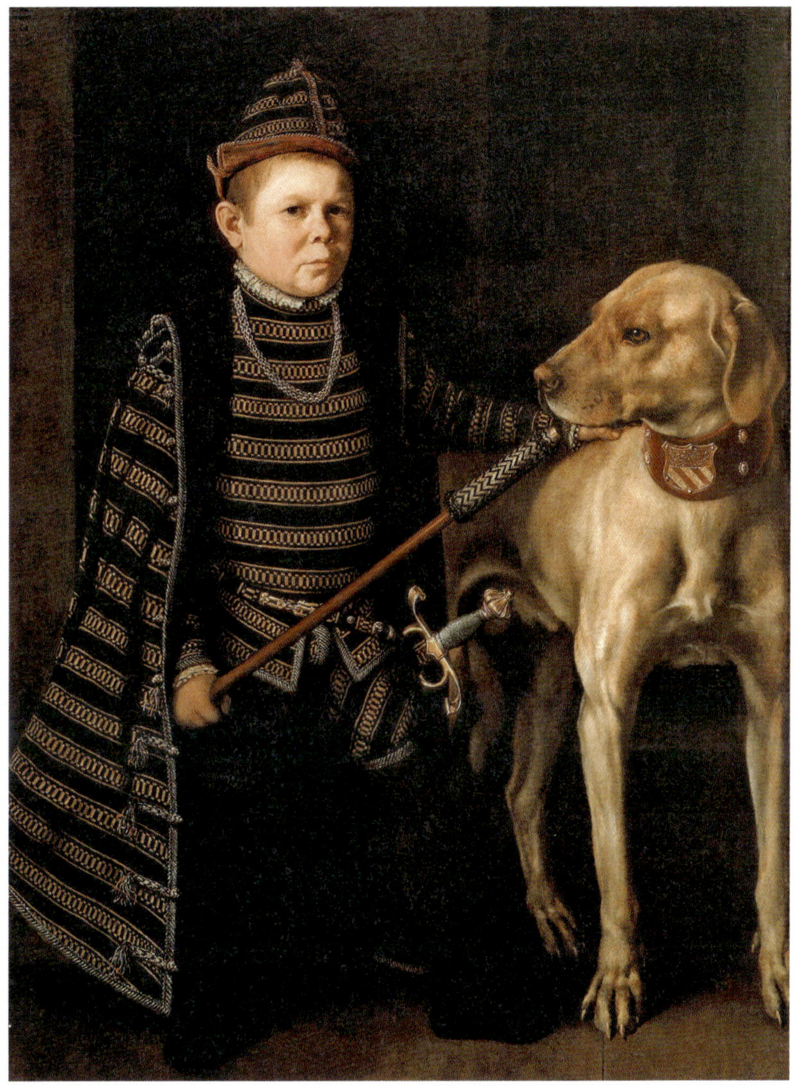

reveal that Granvelle was fascinated by "wonders" of nature: he had his dwarf portrayed by Anthonis Mor (fig. 86) and according to the inventory of 1607 he owned a painting of "woman with a beard" by Willem Key (1516-1568).[65] The inventory also lists artworks in costly materials, with mounted *naturalia*, such as a "Handstein" (fig. 95), a chunk of silver ore featuring a sculpted Ascension; a jasper cup in the form of a shell; a branch of coral partially carved into animals with Orpheus at its base; another branch of coral; a mirror with a copper border; the horn of a wild goat; a coffer made of horn; a jasper crucifix; and three crystal globes.[66] Several of these hybrid artworks (fig. 87), which display the contest between art and nature, ended up in the famous *Kunstkammer* of Rudolph II, whom we know acquired artworks from Granvelle's collection.[67]

The inventory of the Granvelle palace in Besançon from 1607 further mentions a striking number of Turkish carpets, and an "armeria" or arms chamber, a typical element in a princely collection.[68] Remarkably, we also find armor made of tortoiseshell, perhaps made as a shield, but at the same time an exotic and highly sought-after natural specimen.[69] From a letter written by Maximilien Morillon (1517-1586), supervisor of Granvelle's palace in Brussels after his departure, we can deduce that the cardinal's palace in Brussels already had an arms chamber.[70] From a letter by Odet Viron, Granvelle's 'maître de comptes,' we know that his master, a lover of Flemish polyphonic music, kept several musical instruments in cupboards in the gallery, among which a clavichord.[71] Granvelle also arranged the delivery of organs and clavichords made in Antwerp to Philip II in Spain.[72] The cardinal collected scientific instruments as well and was frequently portrayed with a timepiece or clock (fig. 80).[73]

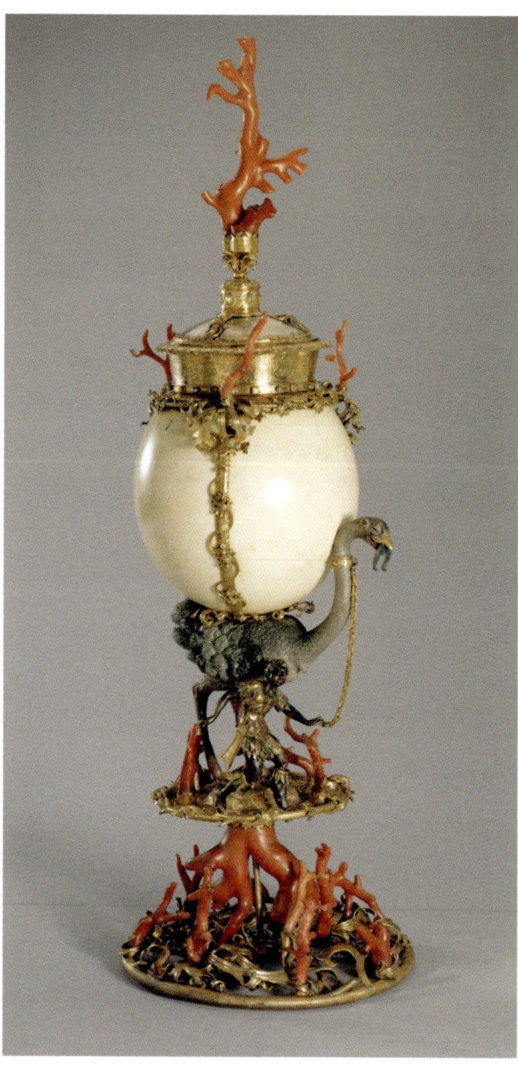

**Fig. 87**
Clement Kicklinger, *Tazza*, c. 1570-1575
Ostrich egg, emerald, gilded silver and coral Habsburg
Vienna, Kunsthistorisches Museum, Kunstkammer

*The Battle for the Garden of Earthly Delights*

In addition to being fond of exotica and preciosa, Granvelle was a great lover of Brussels tapestries. A series now in Vienna featuring exotic animals, including a parrot and a leopard, bears his coat of arms with the cardinal's hat (fig. 88).[74] Probably even before his departure from Brussels, Granvelle commissioned four tapestries in the style of Bosch from Brussels workshops, among them an exact copy after the *Garden of Earthly Delights* (fig. 89). On June 16, 1566 secretary Morillon reports to his master that, on account of the tumult in Brussels, he will send "the new tapestries, *and those of Bosch,*" together with a chest containing the best pieces from the "cabinet" to the cardinal.[75] Morillon clearly sought to ensure the safety of the costly Bosch tapestries.

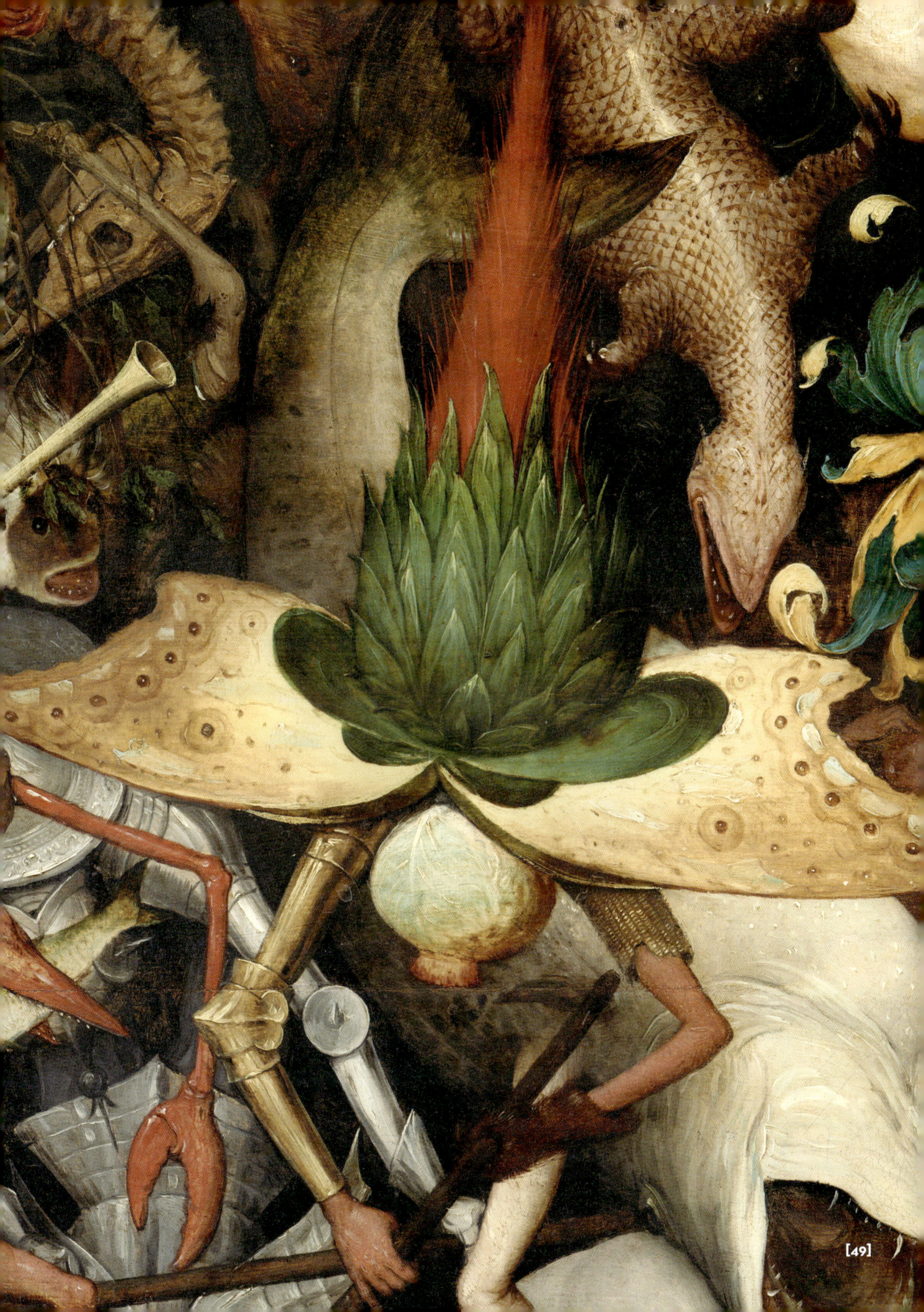

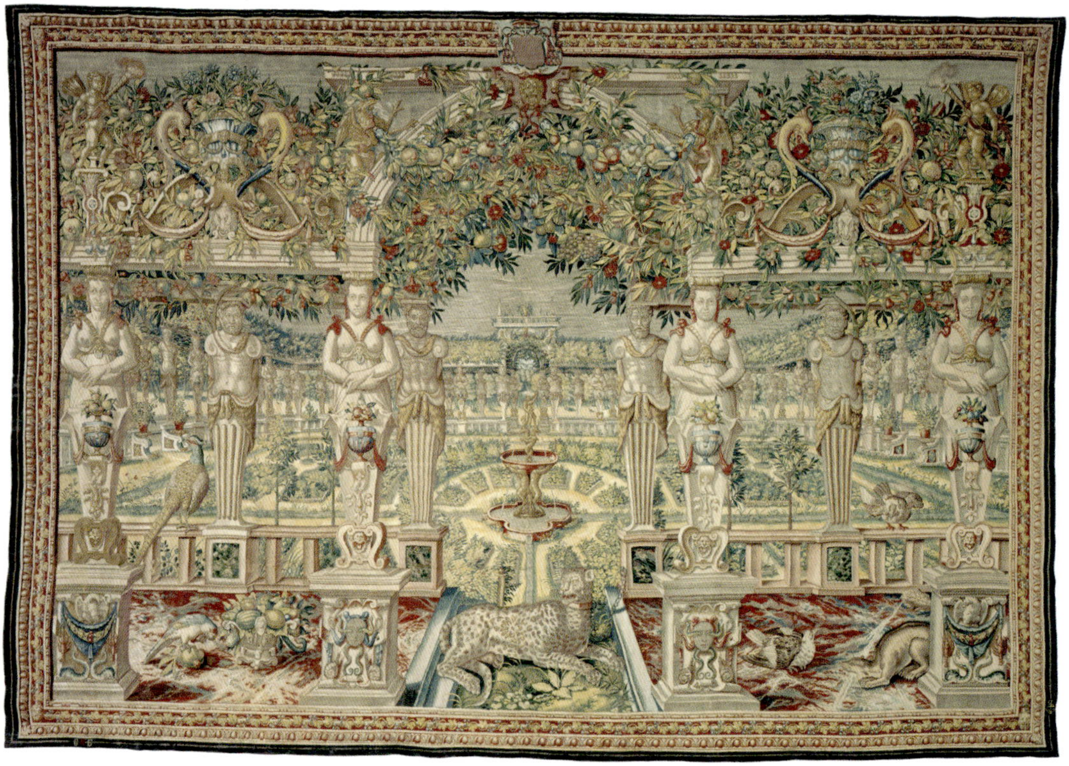

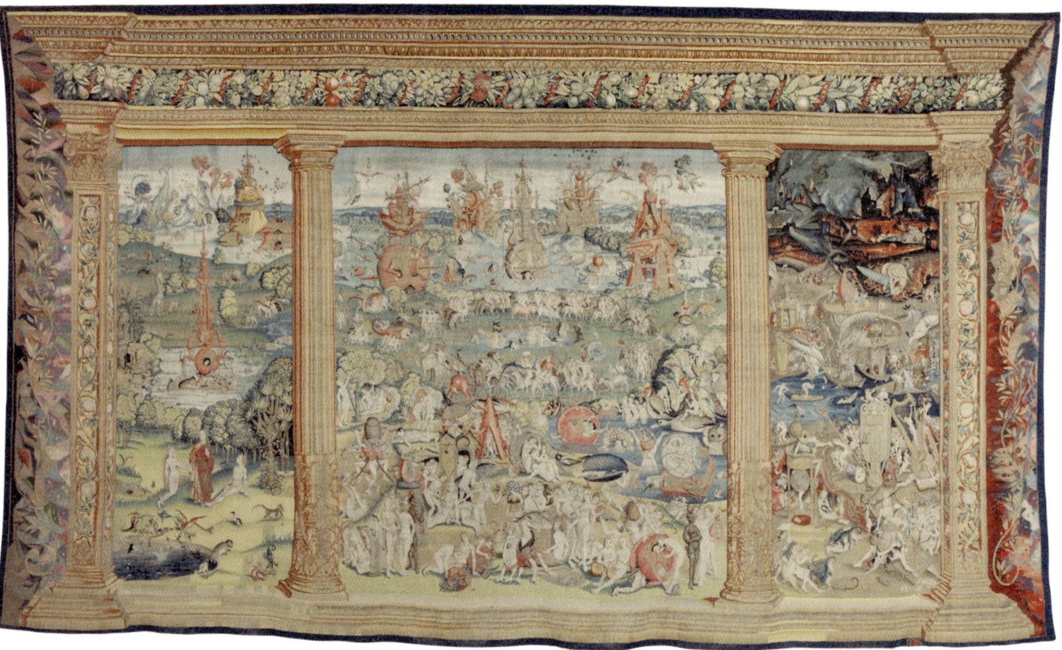

**Fig. 88**
*Garden with herms and with exotic animals, with coat of arms of Cardinal Granvelle*, tapestry woven Brussels, workshop of Willem de Pannemaker, 1564
Vienna, Kunsthistorisches Museum, Tapisseriensammlung

**Fig. 89**
After Bosch, *Garden of Earthly Delights*, tapestry woven in Brussels c. 1560
Madrid, Patrimonio Nacional, Palacio Real Madrid

That Granvelle commissioned tapestries after Bosch should not surprise: the cardinal was particularly fond of Bosch's work, and owned three paintings by the artist that were purchased after his death by Emperor Rudolph II.[76] He shared this taste for Bosch with several courtiers, especially Spaniards, among them Don Filipe de Guevara, and - not least - his sovereign majesty Philip II.[77] Until 1568, moreover, Bosch's most famous painting, the *Garden of Earthly Delights* (fig. 20) was kept in Brussels in the collection of Granvelle's archrival, William of Orange. William's great uncle, Hendrik III of Nassau, had probably commissioned the triptych from Bosch.[78] Although William of Orange himself does not seem to have been a great collector, many undoubtedly envied his possession of the *Garden of Earthly Delights*.
Building on the research of Jan Karel Steppe, Paul Vandenbroeck has drawn attention to the role this artwork played in the political events of 1568, when the Duke of Alba took possession of Orange's palace in Brussels, confiscating its entire contents, including the *Garden of Earthly Delights*.[79] Following this act, the *Garden* was definitively transferred to Spain, and is now one of the highlights in the Museo del Prado in Madrid. Granvelle's prior commission of a tapestry after the *Garden of Earthly Delights*, however, suggests that the battle for possession of the painting was already underway at an earlier date. The fact that Granvelle had an artwork in the collection of the Prince of Orange copied precisely during the years of mounting political competition between the two leaders can hardly be a matter of chance.
When Bruegel painted the *Fall of the Rebel Angels* in 1562, shortly before moving to Brussels, he must have known just how much the courtiers of Brussels - and Granvelle in particular - coveted the work of Bosch. Bruegel's specific references to the *Garden of Earthly Delights*, explained in chapter I, confirm that he must already have seen Bosch's masterpiece before moving to Brussels. Did Bruegel, who was already known as a "New Bosch" on account of his prints, appeal specifically to Cardinal Granvelle, who in those years was one of the most prominent connoisseurs on the Coudenberg? Does Bruegel's imitation and emulation [50] of the most precious work of art in the Orange-Nassau collection (fig. 90) reveal how Granvelle attempted to measure himself against his political opponent in the artistic field as well? From his reading of *Il Cortigiano* Granvelle knew that nothing illuminates a courtier's magnificence more than a splendid work of art.[80] As noted earlier, it is fairly certain that Granvelle owned at least one painting by Pieter Bruegel the Elder, and perhaps even several.[81] Moreover, since 1560 he was in contact with Hieronymus Cock, the publisher who first launched Bruegel's Boschian inventions as prints.[82] Granvelle continued to pursue the paintings of Bruegel throughout his lifetime. In 1572, for example, Morillon informed him from Brussels that paintings by Bruegel had become inordinately expensive - almost priceless - since the painter's death.[83]

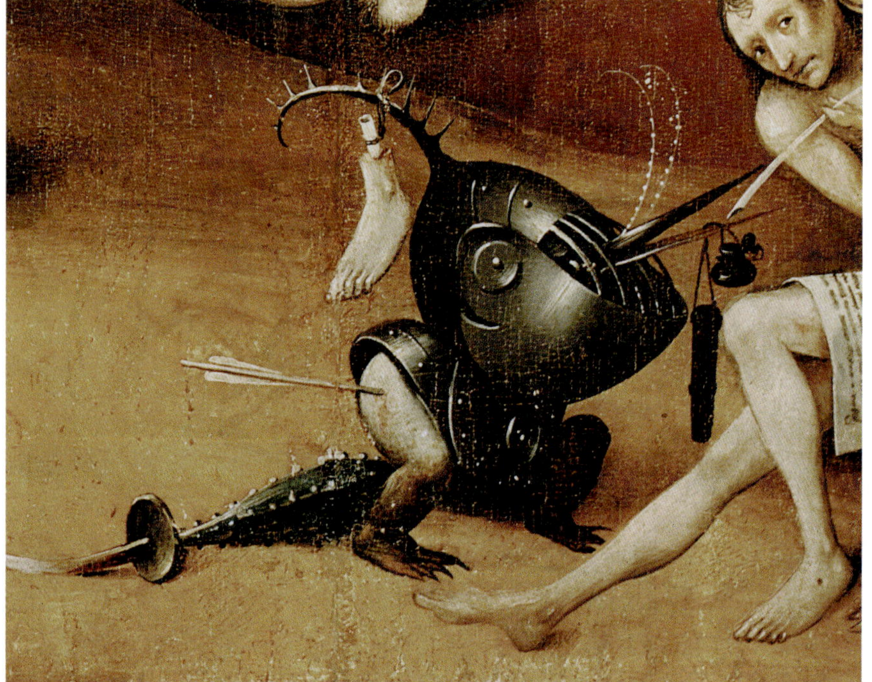

**Fig. 90.**
Headfooter,
detail of figure. 21
(Hieronymus Bosch,
*Garden of Earthly Delights*)
Madrid, Museo
Nacional del Prado

Granvelle moreover profiled himself as the sort of encyclopedic collector of *artificialia* and *naturalia* to whom Bruegel addresses the *Fall of the Rebel Angels*. With the possible exception of Margaret of Parma, few collectors in the Netherlands in 1562 could rival Granvelle. According to Rodríguez-Salgado, Granvelle's role as mediator in the transport of artworks and *naturalia* from the Netherlands to Spain was indeed one of the reasons Philip II postponed Granvelle's resignation for so long.[84] As we have seen, Granvelle collected works of art by Floris, Dürer, and Bosch, among others - painters whom Bruegel cites and emulates - as well as scientific instruments, weaponry, Ottoman pieces, and, unknown until now, costly works of art with mounted natural objects combining exotic and precious materials (figs 87, 95), objects to which Bruegel refers in the *Fall* with his mingling of elements from nature and art [49, 51]. His prestigious collection, a microcosm of art and nature, was undoubtedly meant to display his knowledge of the macrocosm and help underscore those qualities that made him suitable for political leadership.

*Granvelle's apocalyptic visions*

The discontent of the high nobility with respect to Granvelle's autocratic behavior reached a climax precisely in 1562, the year in which Bruegel painted the *Fall*, and consolidated under the leadership of Orange in the

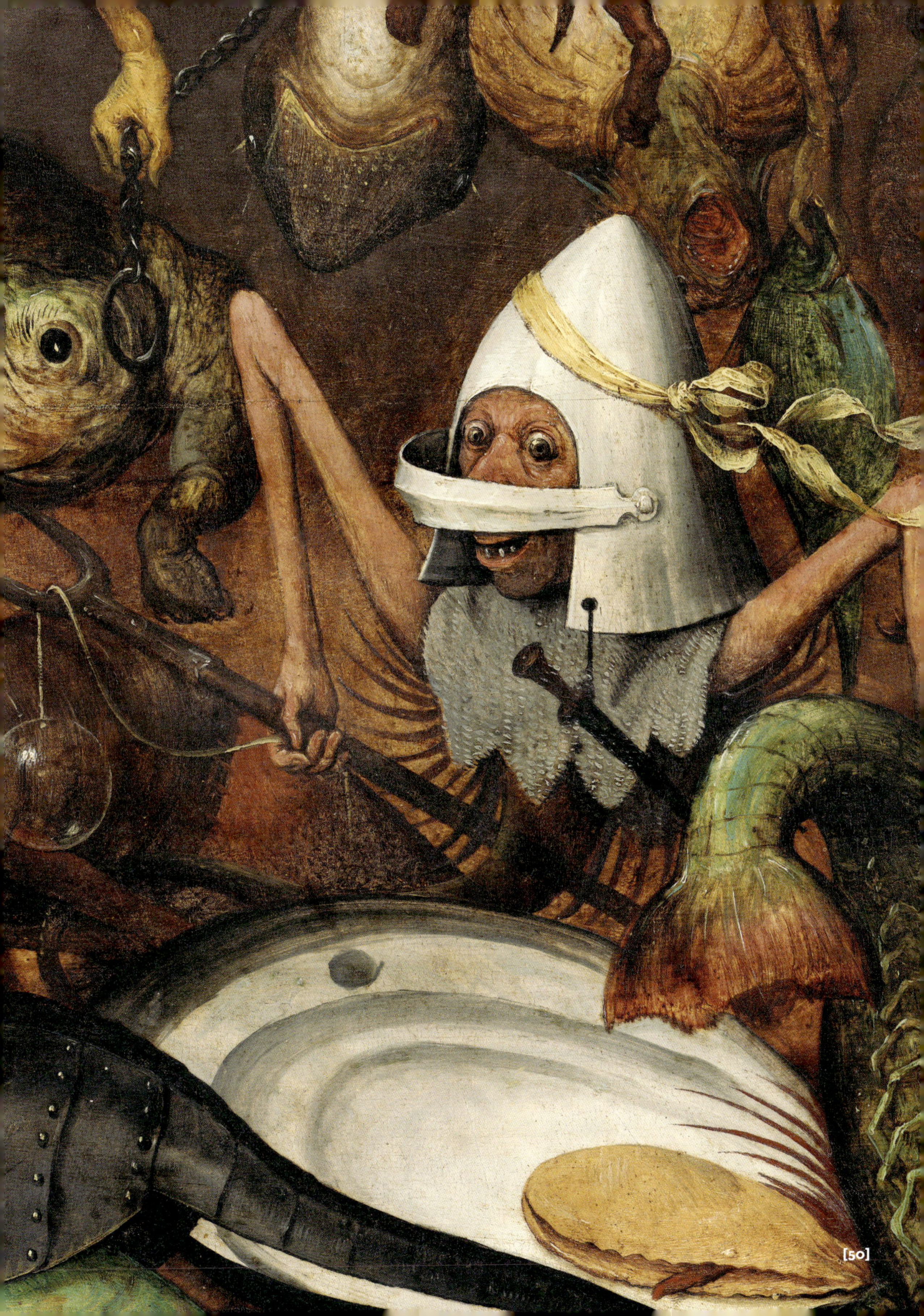

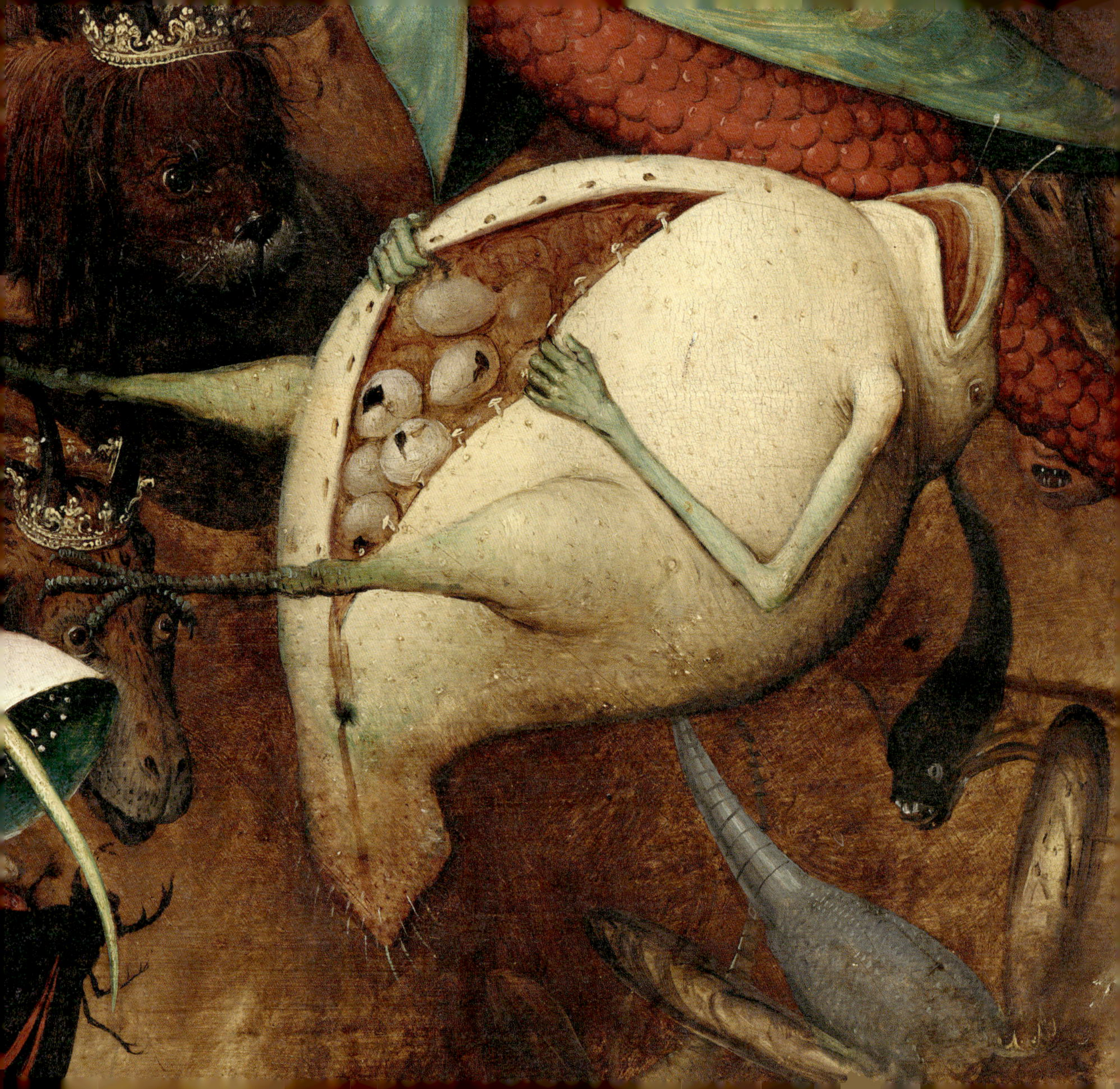

form of the League against Granvelle. From then on, Granvelle began to report, in increasingly sharper words, that the rebellious Netherlandish nobility, with Orange at the forefront, were trying to undermine royal authority. The rise of Protestantism - tolerated, if not directly supported by many nobles - likewise gave Granvelle cause for concern. According to Rodriguez-Salgado, Granvelle's letters to Philip II from 1562-63 read like "apocalyptic visions."[85]

No surviving document can prove beyond doubt that Bruegel painted the *Fall* for Granvelle. The inventory of Granvelle's collection from 1607 mentions a painting with "Saint Michael and the angels, who battle demons," but the dimensions do not correspond to Bruegel's *Fall.*[86] Around 1562, however, apocalyptic scenes appear in other works produced in Granvelle's entourage. One of the most prestigious tapestry series that Philip II commissioned during his stay in the Netherlands was the series of the *Apocalypse.*[87] The original eight-part series, possibly after a design by Barend van Orley, was woven by the Dermoyen brothers in Brussels (1553-56) and transported to Spain by sea in 1559, but the ship sank off the Spanish coast just before arriving.[88] Only two exemplars were saved, one of which is a tapestry depicting *Saint Michael Defeating the Seven-headed Dragon of the Apocalypse* (fig. 91). In 1561 Philip II commissioned a new series of tapestries depicting the *Apocalypse* from Willem de Pannemaker in Brussels, and expressly requested Granvelle to supervise this important commission very closely.[89] The tapestries that could be saved were sent back to the Netherlands to be restored, and to serve as a guide for the replacements for the remaining pieces of the set.

The iconography of the tapestry series of the *Apocalypse* is closely related to that of Bruegel's *Fall,* and some elements, such as the divine Empyrean realm and the seven-headed monster of the Apocalypse inspired by Dürer, are depicted in a similar way. As we have seen, Bruegel was connected with the milieu of Brussels tapestry weavers through the Coecke family, who probably launched him professionally in Brussels. It is quite possible that Bruegel saw the *Apocalypse* tapestries, or at least heard about them while he was painting the *Fall*: at any rate, he refers to this iconographic tradition, which he combines in a unique way with the world of collecting, along with references to the highly sought-after work of Bosch.

The hypothesis that Granvelle commissioned the *Fall,* or that Bruegel addressed the invention specifically to him, can shed new light on its central iconography. In the context of the revolt of the local Netherlandish nobility against Granvelle, the moral of the fall of the rebel angels seems extremely pertinent: those who rebel against the established order will come to ruin. From letters written by Granvelle to the king, it appears that the cardinal clearly felt threatened since the formation of the League against him at the house of Orange, where the *Garden of Earthly Delights* was then held. Inclined to allow his own interests to coincide with those of the king, Granvelle quickly spoke

**Fig.91**
*Saint Michael Overcoming Satan*, from an eight-piece set of the Apocalypse, tapestry woven in Brussels, Dermoyen workshop, c. 1553-56
Madrid, Patrimonio Nacional, Palacio Real de la Granja de San Ildefonso

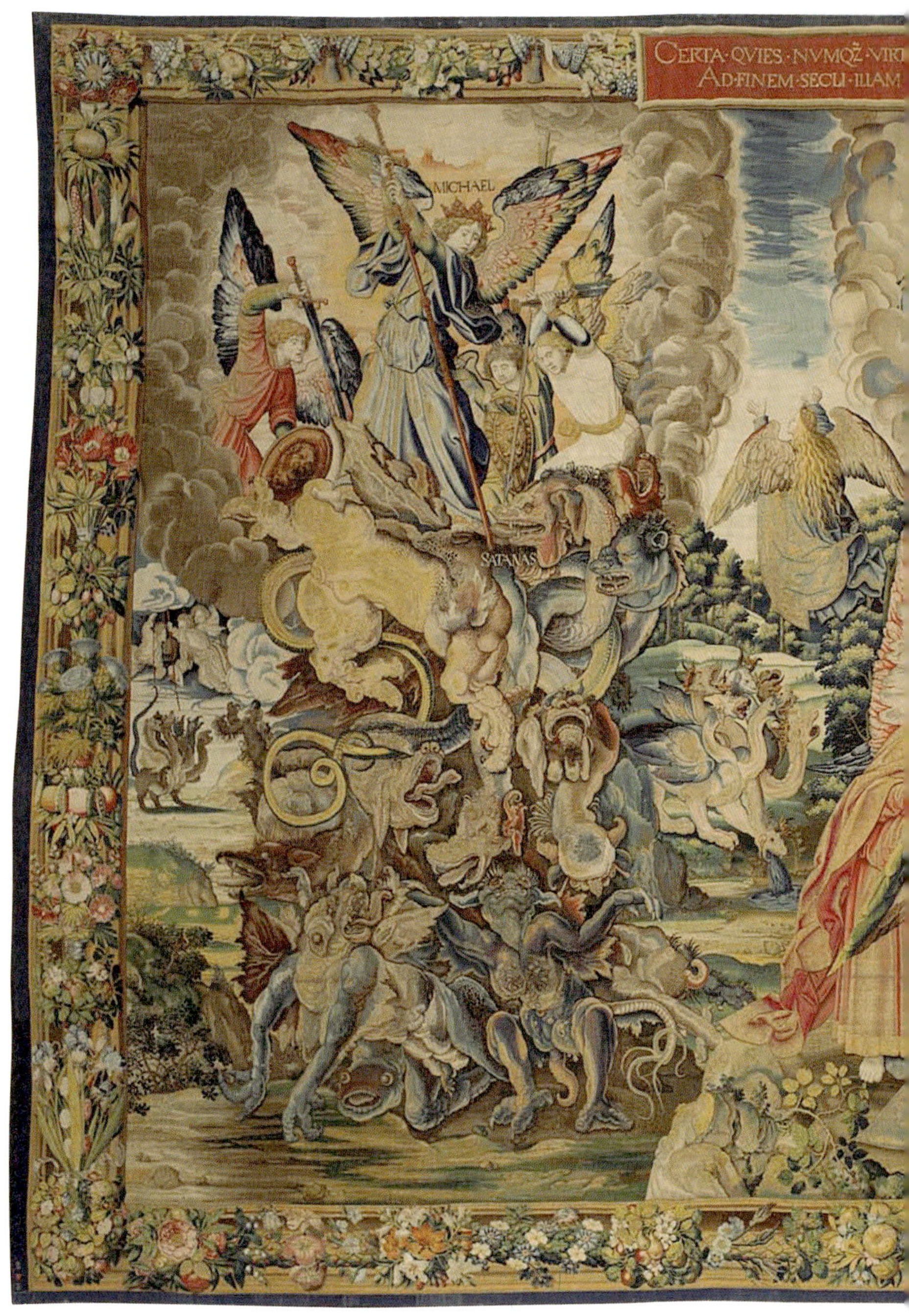

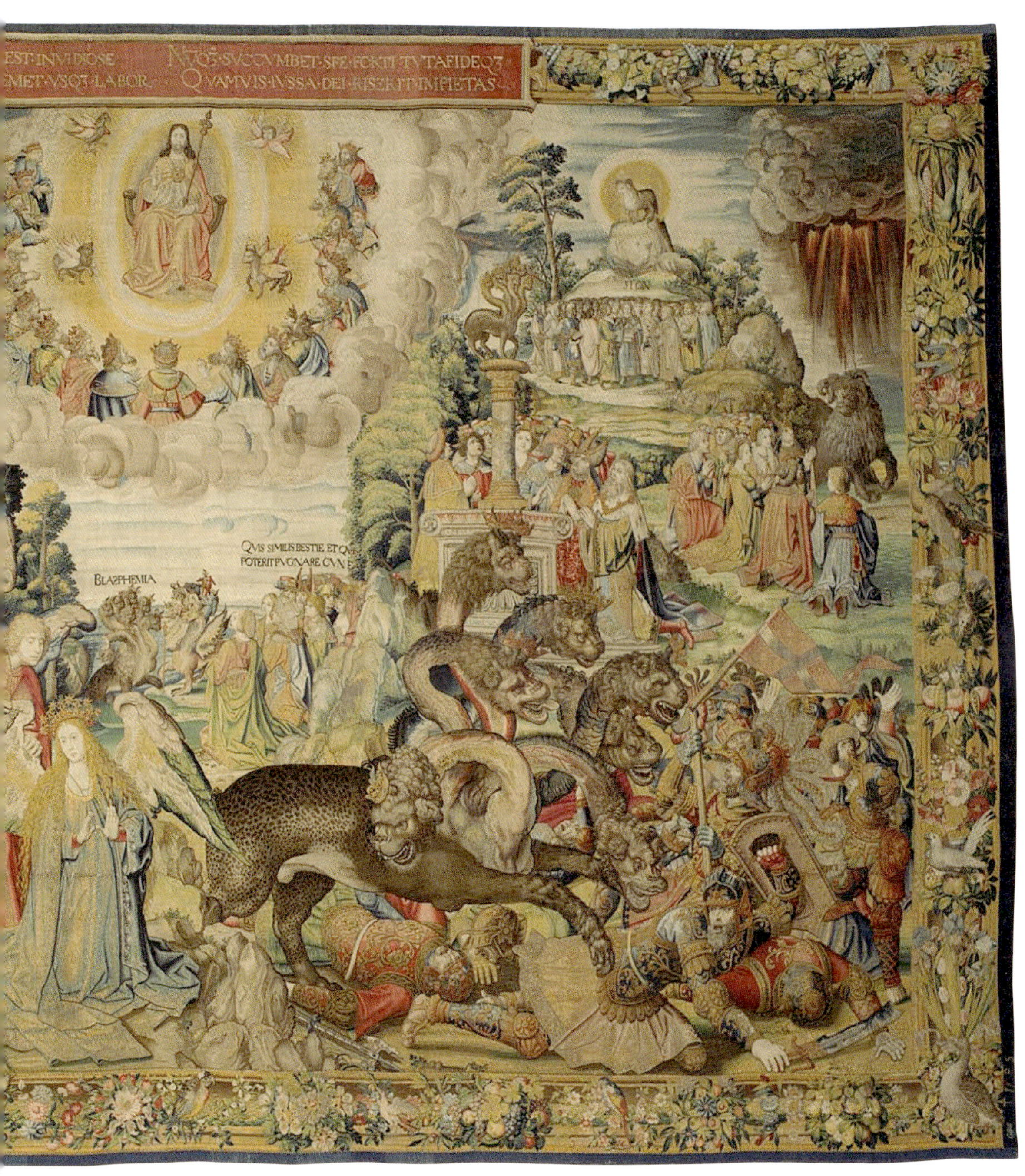
EST·INVIDIOSE
MET·VSQ3·LABOR
NEQ3·SVCCVMBET·SPE·FORTI·TVTA·FIDEQ3
QVAMVIS·IVSSA·DEI·RISERIT·IMPIETAS
QVIS SIMILIS BESTIE ET
POTERIT PVGNARE CVM
BLASPHEMIA

in terms of "betrayal" when discussing the vassals' mutual ties, which had been formed without their sovereign's permission.[90] The Catholic propaganda of the time, with which Granvelle, as cardinal, was undoubtedly familiar, also tended to use Lucifer as a negative example of the rebellious behavior of the heretics. The contemporary rhetorician Anna Bijns (1493-1575), for example, like Bruegel a citizen of Antwerp, portrayed Luther as the "new Lucifer" in her combative *Refreynen*.[91] It is not difficult to see how the many-headed beast of the Apocalypse could turn up as the specter of the divided mother church. The beast's opponent, Saint Michael, may have been an attractive model for Granvelle, who fought for political and religious unity.[92]

## Rebels as rebellious angels?

Around 1562, all the players on the political stage - the political elite, but also the middling groups, such as city dwellers, merchants, and artisans whose livelihood depended on a peaceful environment - tried to avoid open rebellion against the king in spite of the increasing tension. The refrain contest organized that year by the Brussels rhetoricians' chamber De Corenbloem, albeit under close supervision, illustrates how all parties were feverishly in search of solutions in order to restore peace in the Netherlands. The *Refereynen* of 1562 moreover provide insight into how the old narrative of the fall of the rebel angels was given a particularly contemporary twist on the eve of the Dutch revolt. As an answer to the contest's central question as to how peace in the Netherlands was to be maintained, the participants mentioned obedience, unity, and subservience. Disobedience and discord, the undesirable behavior shown by Lucifer and his retinue, were seen as the cause of unrest and turbulence. At least one song proclaims that "Envy, anger and rebellion... always lead to evil."[93]

Later, Orange and his followers would proudly call themselves "rebels," just as some also bore the epithet "geux" or "geuzen" (beggars) with pride.[94] But in 1562, rebellious behavior, particularly when directed against one's own sovereign, was mostly seen as a form of pride, one of the seven deadly sins. Christian kings were crowned and anointed: their authority was thereby empowered by God. Kings were the executors of God's plan on earth. Obedience to God therefore presumed obedience to the king as well; this was at any rate the position advocated by the likes of Justus Lipsius (1547-1606), the influential neo-Stoic from the circle of Ortelius, who as a young man had been introduced to politics by Granvelle.[95] Rebellion against the king was equivalent to rebellion against God himself. Its consequences, after the fall of Lucifer, were well known.

The fact that Bruegel painted Saint Michael and the rebel angels the same year in which they were repeatedly portrayed in a Brussels rhetoricians' competition offers insight into how the painter incorporated images and issues from the urban life of his time. For Brussels rhetoricians and their audiences, the story of Michael, who defeated the rebellious Lucifer, must have evoked highly specific associations. On the one hand, Saint Michael had been the patron of Brussels since time immemorial, and therefore the symbol of urban identity with respect to princely sovereignty, as in the manuscript that the city commissioned on the occasion of the entry of Johanna of Castile in 1496 (fig. 74). On the other hand, Saint Michael's battle against the rebel angels was an intensely current theme given the opposition of certain members of the nobility to Granvelle.

When we consider all of these elements together, it seems quite possible that Granvelle, who was moreover an extraordinary collector and patron of the arts, may have commissioned the *Fall of the Rebel Angels* from Bruegel - or that Bruegel at least addressed Granvelle in his invention. The question arises as to whether the *Fall* could have served as an altarpiece. Although it does depict a devotional theme, its format and dimensions are almost identical to those of the *Children's Games*, the *Proverbs*, and the *Dulle Griet* (fig. 27), all of which are monumental cabinet paintings. Bruegel is not known to have painted altarpieces, apart from his early collaboration with Pieter Baltens on the lost altarpiece of the Mechelen Glover's Guild (1551).[96] This suggests that the *Fall* at any rate also functioned as a conversation piece, in which both universal values and specific political circumstances could be read.

That Bruegel should have given form to Granvelle's propaganda in the *Fall* does not correspond to the prevalent image of Bruegel as a "people's painter." The portrayal of Bruegel as a popular painter usual presumes that he would have chosen the side of the rebels. More than just a standard bearer for one party or another, Bruegel is perhaps best understood as a particularly observant witness of his times. This is especially true of the turbulent period leading up to the Dutch Revolt, when opinions and positions changed rapidly. Accurate positioning in time and space is therefore essential to capturing Bruegel's extremely precise references. Paintings such as the *Murder of the Innocents* (Royal Collection, Her Majesty Queen Elizabeth II) and the *Census at Bethlehem* (fig. 92), made in or around 1566, were maybe interpreted by some of Bruegel's contemporaries as critical of repressive Habsburg policies. In 1562, by contrast, the repression was relatively moderate and the political stage was dominated by rivalry between Orange and Granvelle. In particular, Orange's personal disobedience threatened the political and social order in those years.

Granvelle's plea for the restoration of order by punishing Orange and his cohorts was not received favorably, however. Ironically, the opposite occurred: in 1564, the upper nobility, under the leadership of William of Orange, forced the king to recall Granvelle. From that time onward the situation escalated irrevocably. In 1565 the lower nobility swore the Compromise of Nobles, the most important demand of which was the abolition of the religious placards.[97] Orange himself was only marginally involved in this public demonstration of dissatisfaction, but he did plead openly for freedom of

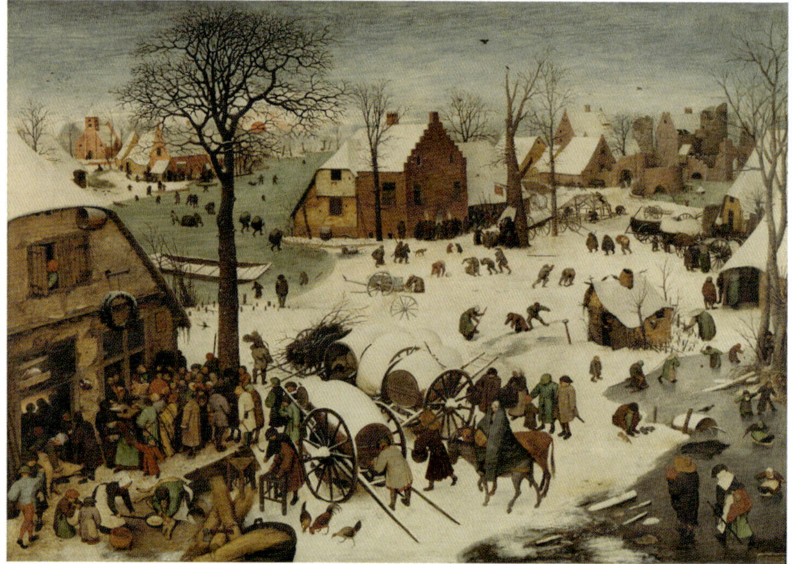

**Fig. 92**
Pieter Bruegel the Elder, *Census at Bethlehem*, 1566
Brussels, The Royal Museum of Fine Arts of Belgium

religion. On April 5, 1566, the nobles marched to Coudenberg Palace with two hundred followers in order to present their petition for tolerance to Margaret of Parma. In August of this so-called "wonder year" (*annus mirabilis*), which got its name from the fact that contemporaries saw political developments take place with lightning speed, iconoclasm broke out in West Flanders.[98]

This time Philip II did not give in: in 1567, Fernando Alvarez de Toledo, duke of Alba (1507-1582) was called in to suppress any and all acts of rebellion. One of his first acts was the confiscation (*in absentia*) of Orange's Brussels palace and collection, including Bosch's *Garden of Earthly Delights*. The work of art that had so fascinated Granvelle, and that Bruegel had tried to surpass in his *Fall,* fell into the hands of Granvelle's merciless successor. In 1568 Alba had the counts Egmont and Hornes executed on the main square in Brussels; the blow of the sword that beheaded them almost seems to materialize the judging Saint Michael towering on top of the city hall.

Orange himself managed to escape on time and became the leader of the rebels. It is in this role, as liberator of his country from a foreign tyrant, that Marcus Gheeraerts (1520-ca. 1590), a political refugee from the Southern Netherlands active in London, portrayed Orange as *Saint George Slaying the Dragon* (fig. 93). The iconography of Orange as Saint George in armor, slaying the dragon with his sword, echoes Bruegel's *Fall,* with Saint Michael killing the seven-headed monster of the Apocalypse. But where Saint Michael strikes down the rebels of heaven, here the roles are reversed: Saint George slays the "barbarian" or - in the original sense of the word - "foreign" tyrant.[99]

In Gheeraerts' print, Orange explains his loyalty to the king of Spain in a

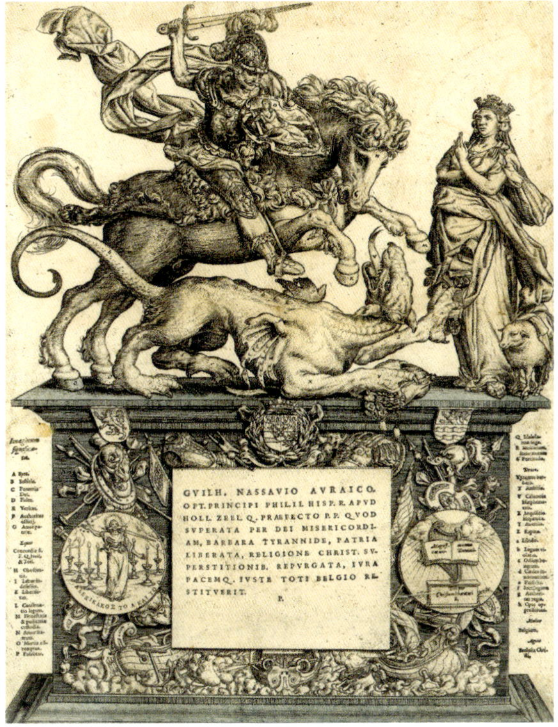


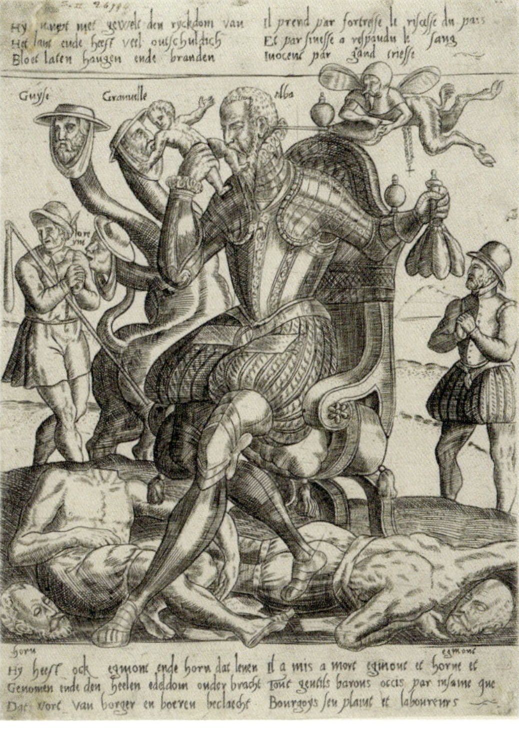


**Fig. 93**
Marcus Gheeraerts, *William of Oranje as Saint George killing the Dragon*, c. 1576
London, British Library

**Fig. 94**
Anonymous, *The Duke of Alba assisted by an Apocalyptic Monster with heads of Granvelle, de Guise and Lorraine*, c. 1572
Brussels, Royal Library of Belgium, Print Cabinet

caption, but in the Dutch version the dragon he is slaying tears the privileges from lady "Nederlant," an unmistakable reference to the fact that according to some, Philip II was trampling the natural, local, social order underfoot. In a satirical pamphlet of 1572, Granvelle himself appears as one of the heads of an apocalyptic monster that, together with the duke of Alba, receives whispered instructions from the devil himself to plunder the riches of the Netherlands, behead her noblemen, and even devour her children (fig. 94).[100] While Granvelle still argued in favor of political and religious freedom in 1562, the propaganda of the Dutch Revolt remembered him only ten years later - not entirely correctly - as a bloodthirsty monster.

The *Fall of the Rebel Angels* does not simply evoke contemporary political and religious questions, however; it also portrays more universal ideas and questions. Can pursuit of the new threaten social, political, and even the God-given natural order by mixing the elements? What are the boundaries of human endeavor in art, knowledge, and politics? Can art serve politics? Even if these urgent questions were directed at the ecclesiastical official, politician, and art-lover Granvelle, they explain at the same time the timeless attraction of Bruegel's painting. Bruegel's art is never unequivocal, and never fails to stimulate introspection.

# Epilogue

Into this wild Abyss,
The Womb of nature and perhaps her Grave,
Of neither Sea, nor Shore, nor Air, nor Fire,
But all these in their pregnant causes mixt
Confus'dly, and which thus must ever fight,
Unless th' Almighty Maker them ordain
His dark materials to create more Worlds,
Into this wild Abyss the wary fiend
Stood on the brink of Hell and look'd a while,
Pondering his Voyage; for no narrow frith
He had to cross.

John Milton, *Paradise Lost*, 1667, II, 910-919

With all those heads pointed downward and legs and paws in the air, with falling birds and flying fish, the *Fall of the Rebel Angels* is perhaps Bruegel's most literal depiction of the world turned upside down. In the *Children's Games* (1559), children behave like adults, and in *The Battle of Carnival and Lent* (1559), a monk and a nun pull the cart for Lent, while a mock king figures in the background. In early modern urban society, carnivalesque inversions existed thanks to a deeply rooted faith in an eternal, unchanging order.[1] The chaos of Carnival demonstrated the necessity of social order, an order that is reflected in nature and given by God.

The elaboration of the *Fall of the Rebel Angels* is less popular in tone, but the moral to the story is highly similar: because Lucifer, bearer of light, created first among the angels, could not adhere to God's established order and orders, God commanded Michael to drive him and his cohorts from heaven. The battle between the good angels and the at times ridiculous falling angels recalls the mock battles of carnival. With his portrayal of pure angels as they morph into the most unimaginable monsters, Bruegel shows very vividly the consequences for those who do not adhere to the established order. Bruegel's devils are monstrous because they combine the four elements of God's cosmos unnaturally. They are assembled from components deriving from earth, water, fire, and air in ways that nature does not allow. Permeated by an atmosphere of *preciositas* and *virtuositas* that recalls costly art objects with mounted *naturalia* in art and curiosity cabinets, Bruegel's monsters are even more incredible than any of the most fantastic creations by Bosch. At the same time, Bruegel's lifelike depiction of their components betrays his thorough knowledge of natural and artistic creations. Incorporated in a narrative about hubris, his artistic masterpiece becomes a meditation on the pride and potential of humanity's quest for knowledge and art, a theme that must have been particularly appealing to the erudite collectors of Bruegel's time, and that has lost little of its pertinence over the centuries. Our information culture continues to debate the boundaries of human intervention in nature: in stem cell research, genetic manipulation, and climate change.[2] The mingling of species often still stands for the ultimate act of evil.[3]

In early modern times, people also saw monsters - particularly wonders of nature, such as hirsutes or six-footed calves - as omens. From this perspective, Bruegel's monstrous falling angels are particularly ominous creatures. Painted in 1562, they seem to announce the advent of the

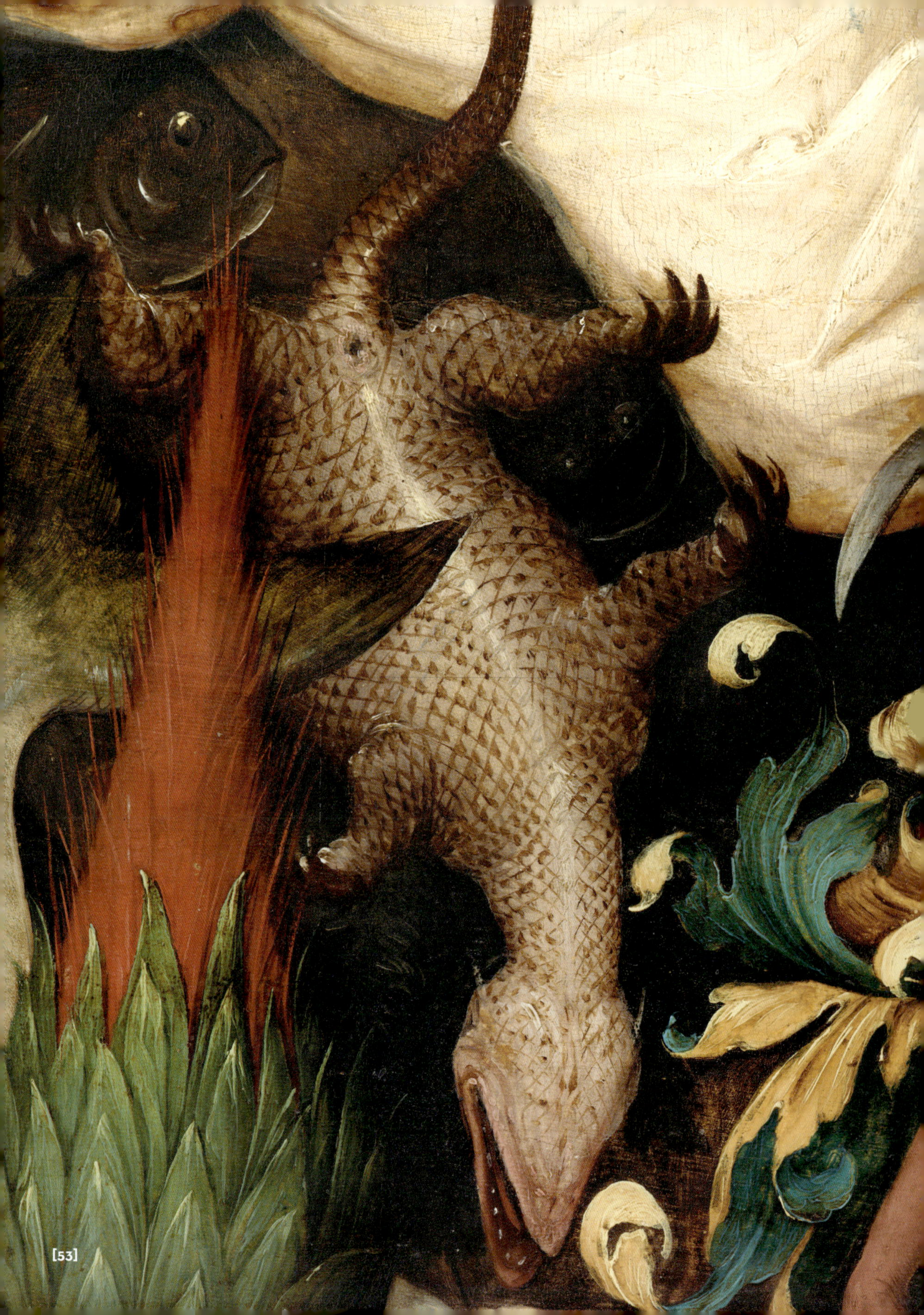

[53]

impending Eighty Years War. That year in Brussels, whose patron had been Saint Michael since time immemorial, a rhetoricians' competition was held that played on the prevailing climate of political and religious unrest. The fall of the rebel angels was mentioned several times in the course of the competition as a negative example of pride, one of the greatest threats to political peace. Also in 1562, at the home of William of Orange, the League against Granvelle was formed; Granvelle, in turn, warned the king in correspondence against the threat of rebellion. Granvelle, who was not only a calculating politician but also an extraordinary collector of art and nature, was moreover particularly fascinated by the *Garden of Earthly Delights* by Bosch, a work that Orange had in his possession and that Bruegel, as the "new Bosch," tried to surpass in the *Fall*. It therefore seems quite possible that Bruegel was addressing Granvelle when he emulated the *Garden of Earthly Delights* (fig. 20), transforming it into an imaginary cabinet of curiosities with princely ambitions. Its message is highly suggestive: the disturbance of political order implies the disturbance of the natural, God-given order of the cosmos.

We do not know what happened to Bruegel's *Fall of the Rebel Angels* after the departure of Granvelle and Orange from Brussels. Shortly after Granvelle's death in 1586, the emperor Rudolph II charged his business agent in Madrid, Johan von Khevenhüller, with purchasing paintings by Bosch and Titian from Granvelle's estate.[4] It is not excluded that the *Fall* also ended up in the emperor's renowned collection. In 1600, Rudolph II purchased various tapestries, among them a tapestry series after Bosch from Granvelle's collection.[5] Karel van Mander reports that in 1604 several important paintings by Bruegel, among them a *Tower of Babel*, a *Crucifixion*, a *Bearing of the Cross*, a *Murder of the Innocents*, a *Conversion of Paul*, a *Temptation of Christ*, and the *Dulle Griet* (fig. 27) (the other Boschian painting by Bruegel!) "as well as other pieces" could be found in the emperor's palace in Prague.[6]

Rudolph II would undoubtedly have appreciated Bruegel's references to the encyclopedic collection of *naturalia* and *artificialia*.[7] The imperial *Kunstkammer* was the richest of all, with paintings, *naturalia*, and precious artworks made by artifice and nature - objects, as we have seen, that Granvelle also collected early on, some of which ended up in the emperor's *Kunstkammer* (fig. 95). After the death of Rudolph II in 1612, his collections were partially dismantled; after the fall of Prague in 1648 another portion came into the possession of Christina of Sweden, who mostly kept the Italian pieces. The remaining works of art ended up being disbursed on the market.

Between 1625 and 1668, the Antwerp collector Peter Stevens noted in his exemplar of Karel van Mander's *Schilder-boeck* that he had seen a *Fall of Lucifer* by Bruegel the Elder. This would suggest that *Fall of the Rebel Angels* was back in the Netherlands once again.[8] Bruegel's son Pieter the

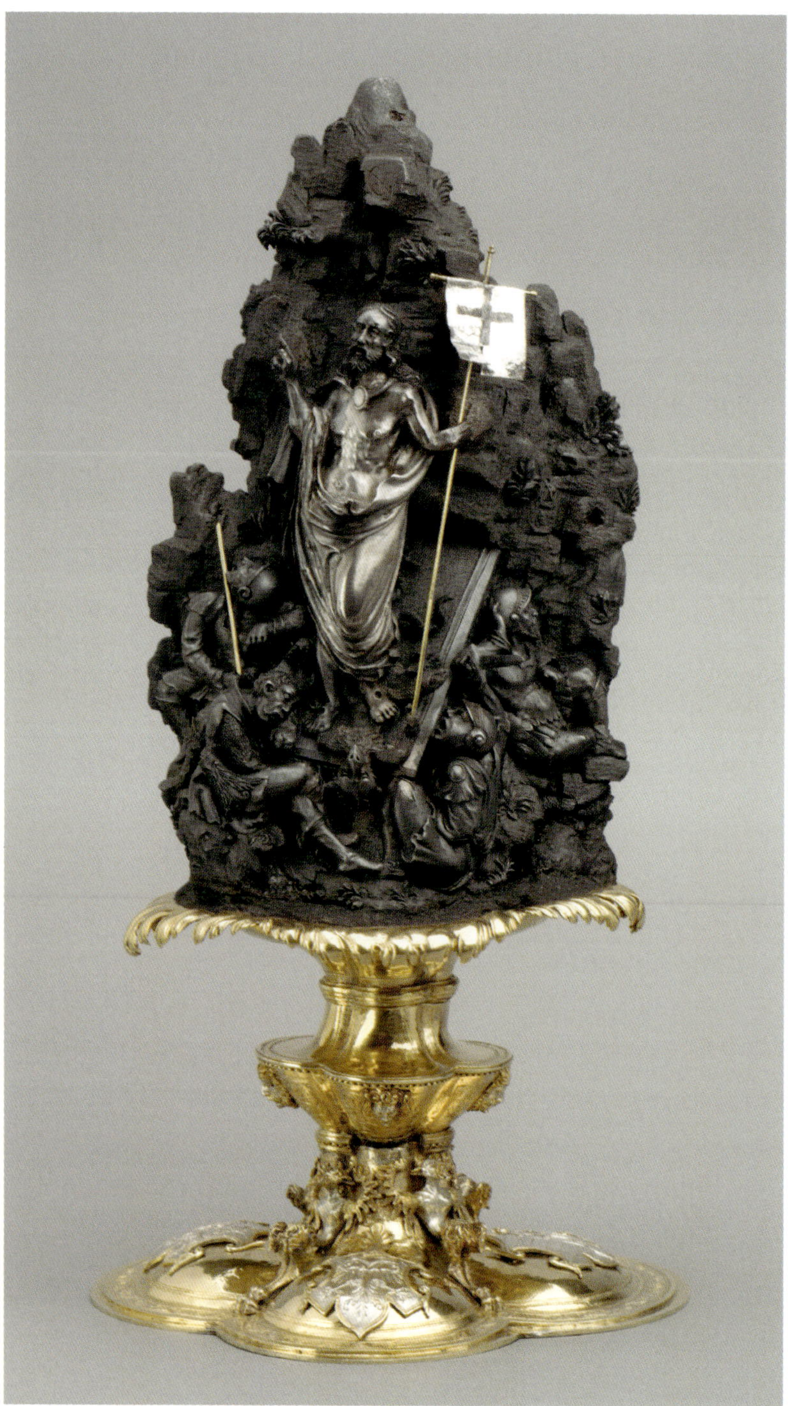

**Fig. 95**
Caspar Ulich,
*So-called "Handstein" with the Resurrection of Christ*, c. 1556/68
Vienna, Kunsthistorisches Museum, Kunstkammer

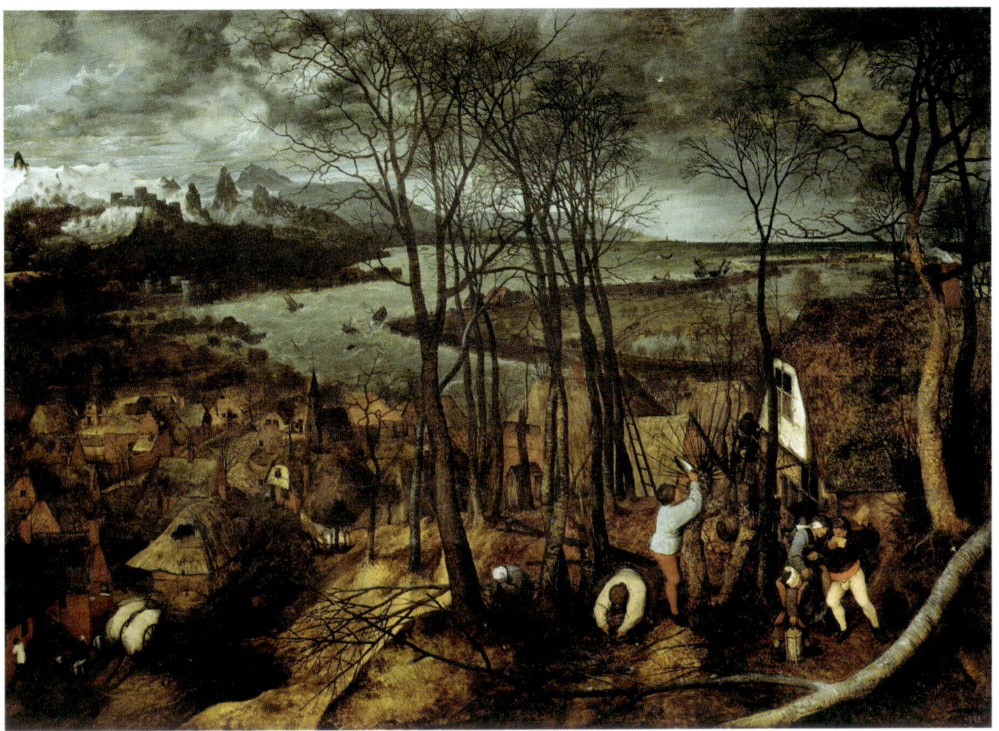

**Fig. 96**
Pieter Bruegel the Elder, *The Somber Day (February/March)*, 1565. From the Series of the Months
Vienna, Kunsthistorisches Museum

Younger never painted a literal copy of the *Fall*, as he did of *Murder of the Innocents* and the *Census at Bethlehem* (fig. 92), in which Bruegel represents episodes from the Bible in the countryland of Brabant.[9] In his paintings of the *Elements* (fig. 55), Bruegel's other son Jan reveals himself to be the true heir of his father in terms of painting collections or collected objects, but without the political undertones. Perhaps the ideal of political and religious unity that Bruegel tried to capture in the *Fall* had since become outmoded, which might explain why there was no longer a demand for such subjects.[10]

Like many of his contemporaries, Bruegel's hopes for a harmonious world were disappointed, but he did not relinquish his belief in an unchanging, divinely created order of nature, as he shows in the renowned cycle depicting the *Months* painted in 1565 (fig. 96). And even though political leaders ignored the message of his *Fall of the Rebel Angels*, the pure beauty of the artwork remains. Most remarkable, but scarcely explained, are the good angels in white albs [3, 54] to the left and right of the protagonist. As is often the case with Bruegel, they are not the principal actors in the traditional narrative, but nevertheless convey the ultimate purpose of the work of art. These nearly transparent beings of light represent absolute good: nameless, timeless, and eternal.

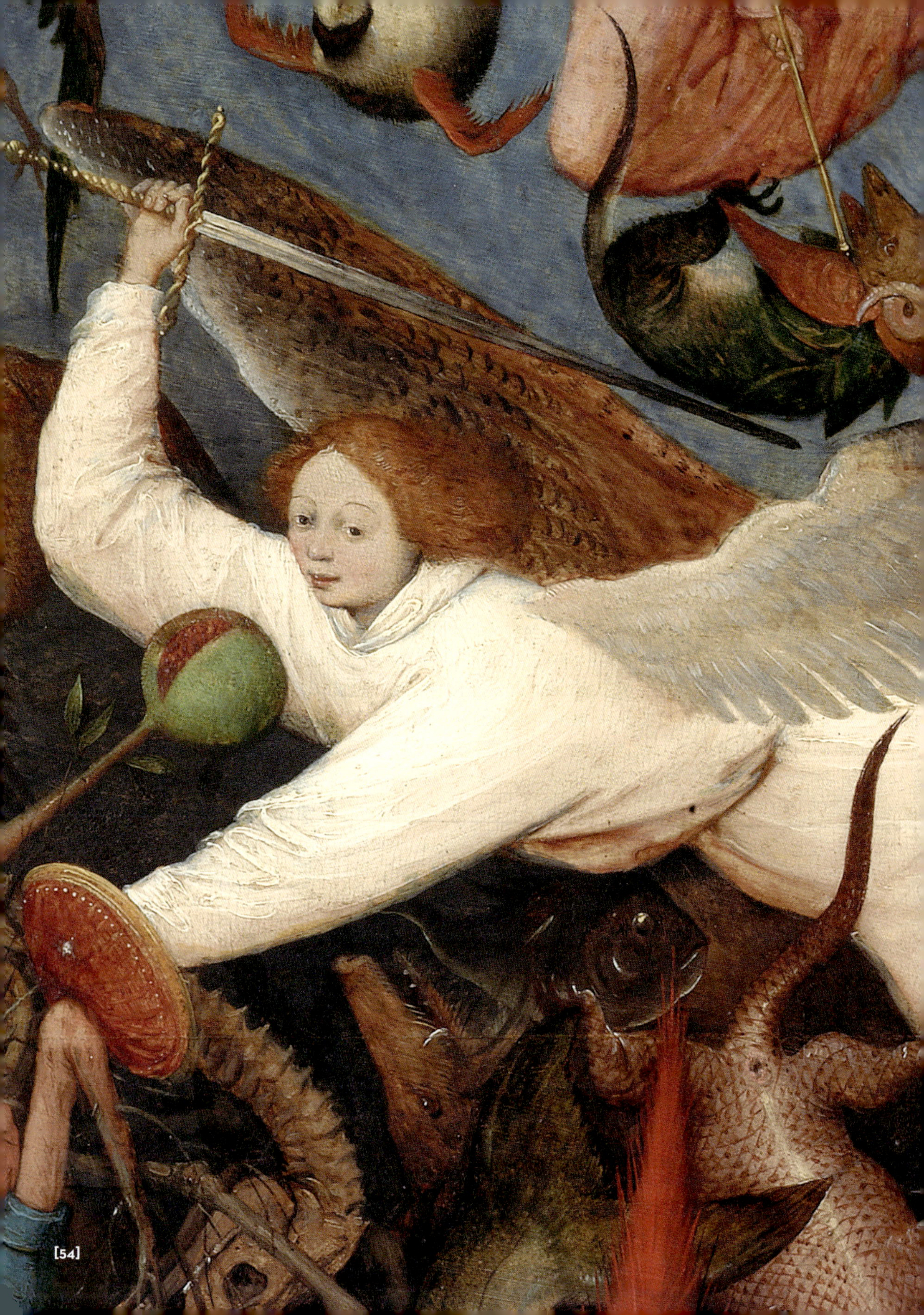

# Notes

## Prologue

* Rabelais, *Gargantua*, Prologue: "C'est pourquoi faut ouvrir le livre et soigneusement peser ce que y est déduit [caché]. Lors connaîtrez que la drogue dedans contenue est bien d'autre valeur que ne promettait la boîte, c'est-à-dire que les matières ici traitées ne sont tant folâtres comme le titre au-dessus prétendait." English edition: *The Histories of Gargantua and Pantagruel*, translated and with introduction by J. M. Cohen (New York, 1955), 38.

** Quiccheberg, *Inscriptiones*, Digression of the Fifth Class, Third inscription. I thank Nicolette Brout for the translation. See Brout, "Le traité muséographique", 109; Meadow and Robertson, *The First Treatise on Museums*, 86.

**1** RMFAB, inv. 584, purchased for the sum of 500 francs from Mr. Félix Stappaerts on March 1, 1846; see museum archive D. Arch. 62. On the modest sum in comparison to prices in the later art market, see Vander Auwera, *Kunst en Financieën*, no. 12. On Jan Bruegel and this genre, see Göttler, "Fire, Smoke and Vapour."

**2** Wouters, *Catalogue*, no. 63.

**3** Lampsonius, *Pictorum*, 19: "Who is that Jerome Bosch, returned to the world anew, who with his brush imitates his master's clever dreams and even surpasses them?". See also chapter I and III.

**4** The only monographic study, largely forgotten in later literature, is Knipping, *Pieter Bruegel*. For discussions in surveys of Bruegel's work, see Gibson, *Pieter Bruegel*, 1977, 99-101; Marijnissen, *Bruegel*, 180-86; Robert-Jones, *Bruegel*, 104-14; Sellink, *Bruegel*, no. 114; Silver, *Bruegel*, 169-74.

**5** In the early museum archives, always in French: "La chute des anges (rebelles)."

**6** The "Life of Pieter Bruegel," in Karel van Mander, *Het Schilder-boeck*, fol. 233-34.

**7** "Van ditto Pr. Bruegel gesien eenen Cruysdraginge, oock een winter beschryvinghe, oock eenen Val van Lucifer, oock een Toren van Babilonien [...]" Stevens's copy of *Het Schilder-boeck* is now held by the Bibliotheca Hertziana in Rome; see Briels, "Amator Pictoriae Artis," 206-207. The *Fall* is not mentioned in the catalogue of Stevens's collection drawn up after his death in 1668. In contrast to other paintings by Bruegel that he mentions, Stevens does not say where he saw the *Fall*.

**8** Sellink, *Bruegel*, no. 114.

**9** For a concise biography, see most recently Sellink, *Bruegel*, 9-39 and 285.

**10** Silver, *Peasant Scenes*, 133-60; Ilsink, *Bosch en Bruegel*.

**11** Museum Mayer van de Bergh, Anwerp, inv. 788. Sellink, *Bruegel*, no. 116, with references to earlier literature.

**12** See especially Ganz, *Neugier und Sammelbild*. Meadow, *Pieter Bruegel*, and Sullivan, *Bruegel*, have connected the *Proverbs* and the *Children's Games* with the practice of *loci communi*, a teaching method that incites pupils to "collect" information on specific commonplace topics. For a monographic study of the *Children's Games* that does not, however, discuss the culture of collecting around Bruegel, see Snow, *Inside Bruegel*.

**13** See chapter III.

**14** De Sigüenza, *Tercera parte*, 837-41: "I would now like to show that his paintings are not farces, but rather as books containing great wisdom, and that if there are silly activities to be seen, they are ours, not his [...]"

**15** My methodology is indebted to those scholars who inspired historical anthropology, among others Geertz, *The Interpretation of Cultures*, 5, and idem, "Art as a Cultural System"

**16** Koerner, "Hieronymus Bosch"; idem, "Unmasking the World."

**17** Jeanneret, *Perpetual Motion*.

**18** Ginzberg, "Microhistory."

## Chapter I

**1** Augustine, *De Civitate Dei*, XI, 15, cited by Link, *The Devil*, 24.

**2** *Ibidem*, XI, 9, cited by Falkenburg, *The Land of Unlikeness*, 107-08.

**3** Galand, *Barend van Orley*, 25.

**4** Ilsink, *Bosch en Bruegel*, 270-302.

**5** Pinson, "Fall of the Angels"; see also Vandenbroeck, *Jheronimus Bosch*, 269-73.

**6** Silver, *Bosch*, no. 308; Sellink, *Bruegel*, no. 114 retitles the work *The Archangel Michael Slaying the Apocalyptic Dragon*.

**7** In his copy of the *Schilder-boeck* by Karel van Mander, now preserved in the Bibliotheca Herziana in Rome; see Briels, "Amator Pictoriae Artis," 206-207, and Allaert, "Pieter Brueghel le Jeune," doc. 16.

**8** Lauterbach, "Plagegeister"; "Fliege," in Dittrich, *Lexikon*, 153-57. My thanks to Bert Schepers for these references.

**9** Someone who "binds the devil" is so enraged that nothing can stop him or her; see Sullivan, *Bruegel*, 38-40 (fig. 14), and 118 (fig. 41).

**10** Danielle Maufort points out that the inscription only mentions a magician, and that there is nothing to indicate that it should be Hermogenes, as is usually presumed. Her research shows that it is probably Faust. I would like thank her for sharing this information. See her lecture *Faust in Antwerpen. Eine bisher unentdeckte, geheime Liaison* (Goethemuseum Düsseldorf 17/04/2013; Knittlingen, Faust-Archiv 29/07/2012).

**11** Link, *The Devil*, 25.

**12** Vandenbroeck, *Jheronimus Bosch*, 218. Independently of this study, Pawlak, *Trilogie*, 25-85, arrived at the same insight. Pawlak, however, interprets Bruegel's *Fall* exclusively as a visual investigation of the theological problem of evil, and does not discuss Bruegel's references to the culture of collecting. Nor does she consider the original context and possible patron of the painting.

**13** Silver, *Peasant Scenes*, 133-59: 140.
**14** *Ibidem*, 137-40, mentions copies in Baltimore and Springfield, MA (by Jan Mandijn).
**15** De Guevara, *Comentarios*, 41-44: "Esto que Hyerónimo Bosco hizo con prudencia y decoro, han hecho y hacen otros sin discrecion y juicio ninguno; porque habiendo visto en Flandes quan accepto fuese aquel género de pintura de Hyerónimo Bosco, acordaron de imitarle, pintando monstruos y desvariadas imaginaciones, dándose á entender que en esto solo consistia la imitacion de Bosco."
**16** Van Grieken/Luijten/Van der Stock, *Hieronymus Cock*, 243.
**17** Sellink, *Bruegel*, no. 42.
**18** Orenstein/Sellinck, *Pieter Bruegel*, no. 55.
**19** Orenstein/Sellinck, *Pieter Bruegel*, nos. 42-54.
**20** *Ibidem*, nos. 64-77.
**21** *Ibidem*, 178.
**22** Silver, *Peasant Scenes*, 283, note 43.
**23** Knipping, *De Val*, 23.
**24** Falkenburg, "The Devil is in the Detail," 64, with references to Pleij, *Het gilde*, 56-62.
**25** Renger, "Bettler und Bauern"; Silver, *Peasant Scenes*, 60.
**26** Bax, *Ontcijfering*, 11-12, and Vervoort, "Bomen en heksen."
**27** Kessler, "Le jardin des délices."
**28** Bax, *Ontcijfering*, 144-46. On drawings of singing fools in an egg, see Silver, *Bosch*, 282-83. In Bruegel's *Carnival and Lent* (1559, Vienna, Kunsthistorisches Museum), various figures wear garlands of eggshells and lay eggs, one of the most important ingredients in waffles, in the path of Prince Carnival.
**29** Bax, *Ontcijfering*, 166-68; Vandenbroeck, *Jheronimus Bosch*, 283-85.
**30** For example, the print Pieter van der Heyden published by Hieronymus Cock as "Hieronimus Bos invenit" and dated 1562; see Silver, *Bosch*, fig. 250.
**31** Vervoort, "The Pestilent Toad."
**32** Guicciardini, *Descrittione*, 100: "Pietro Brueghel de Breda grande imitatore della scienza, & fantasie di Girolamo Bosco, onde n'ha anche acquistato il sopranome di secondo Girolamo Bosco." Vasari, *Vite* (ed. Bettarini / Barocchi), vol. VI (Florence, 1994), 225: "[...] oltre questi... Gillis Mostaeret, che valse assai in fare paesi a olio, fantasticherie, bizzarrie, sogni, e immaginazioni. Girolamo Bos di Ertoghen Bosc, Pietro Brueghel di Breda furono imitatori di costui [...]"
**33** Van Mander, *The Lives*, I, 194. Van Mander, *Het Schilder-Boeck*, fol. 233: "Wie is toch desen Bosch? Ieroon van nieuws ghecomen,
Ter Weerelt, die ons bootst zijns Meesters cloecke droomen,
Ervaren met 't Pinceel, en stijl soo abel daer,
Dat hy hem ondertusch nochtans te boven gaet?"
**34** Falkenburg, "Black Holes in Bosch," 125-28.
**35** Belting, *Hieronymus Bosch*, 98.
**36** Dürer, *1520-1521. Das Tagebuch*, 65; Eichberger, "Naturalia and artefacta." On the treasure of Moctezuma, see Vandenbroeck, "Amerindiaanse kunst- en siervoorwerpen in adellijke verzamelingen. Brussel, Mechelen, Duurstede, 1520-1530," in: Vandenbroeck (ed.), *Amerika, Bruid van de Zon*, 99-119. Some pieces were later brought to the palace of Margaret of Austria in Mechelen; see Eichberger, *Leben mit Kunst*, 179-85.
**37** Dürer, *1520-1521. Das Tagebuch*, 66; Belting, *Hieronymus Bosch*, 77.
**38** Cook, *Matters of Exchange*, 12-17, 49-58; Van der Wee / Materné, "Antwerp as a World Market"; Burke, "Antwerp, a Metropolis."
**39** Wallerstein, "Karel V".
**40** Gorgas, "Animal trade"; Meadow, "Merchants and Marvels".
**41** Rogers' poem appears on the map of Antwerp, 1595, in G. Braun and F. Hogenberg, *Civitates Orbis Terrarum*, V, 2. See also Meganck, *Erudite Eyes*, 213-14.
**42** Hamilton, *Arabische cultuur*, 8.
**43** This is told by Johannes Rotarius (1538-1617), Hooftman's agent and later a merchant himself in London, to Ortelius's nephew Jacob Colius (1563-1628); see *Abrahami Ortelii... epistulae*, no. 330. 18-19.
**44** *Abrahami Ortelii... epistulae*, no. 330. 22-23.
**45** Meganck, *Erudite Eyes*, 26ff and 133-39.
**46** *Abrahami Ortelii ... epistulae*, no. 10: "Te besien ofter niet nieus in geographie en is oft yet vreemts wt Indien." The term "Indies" referred both to Asia (the East Indies) and to America (the West Indies).
**47** Marnef, *Antwerpen in de tijd van de Reformatie*, 11-12.
**48** *Abrahami Ortelii... epistulae*, no. 8 and 9.
**49** Harris, "The religious position of Abraham Ortelius." See also Van Bruaene, *Om beters wille*, 134-35, on the Antwerp rhetorician and instructor Peter Heyns, also a friend of Ortelius, who was himself reform-minded but accepted students of various confessions. Van Bruaene sees the rhetorical competition of 1562, which we will discuss extensively in chapter IV, as "een forum... voor mensen met uiteenlopende ideeën, maar met de gemeenschappelijk verlangen naar religieuze en intellectuele vernieuwing" [a forum... for people with divergent ideas, but with a common desire for religious and intellectual innovation].
**50** *Abrahami Ortelii... epistulae*, no. 11: "de Martino Vulpe pictore excellentissimo [...] ac [...] de Petro Bruochl [...]"; Popham, "Pieter Bruegel and Abraham Ortelius," notes that Fabius may also refer to someone with the same name, the Brussels physician Pieter van Bruegel (ca. 1520-1577) who studied in Padua before 1562. On this Bruglius, see *Abrahami Ortelii... epistula*, no. 47.1-2; 48. 1. Given that Fabius mentions Bruegel in one breath together with De Vos as *pictor*, however, it seems certain that he is referring to the painter, as Popham likewise concludes. Popham was also the first to suggest on the basis of these letters that De Vos and Bruegel traveled to Italy together.
**51** *Abrahami Ortelii... epistulae*, no. 15: "Martino Vulpi ac Petro Brouchel."
**52** On their possible travel to Italy together, see Zweite, *Marten de Vos*, 21-22.
**53** Dolfi, *Cronologia delle familglie nobili di Bologna*, 310-11.
**54** As appears in a document concerning Aldrovandi; see Fondo Ulisse Aldrovandi, Università di Bologna, Ms 064. The Fondo Ulisse Aldrovandi, Università di Bologna, Ms 136.06, also holds a "Catalogus librorum D. Scipionis Fabij," a catalogue of Fabius's works. A survey of the archive in now online: http://www.filosofia.unibo.it/aldrovandi/. Aldrovandi also mentions Scipio Favius in his autobiography; see: Simili, *Il teatro della natura*, 131-43.
**55** Doctors in medicine were among the first to assemble cabinets of curiosities; see Findlen, *Possessing Nature*, 17-31.
**56** Olmi, *l'Inventario del mondo* and idem, "Il museo."
**57** *Abrahami Ortelii... epistulae*, no. 11.4 (1565).
**58** Meganck, *Erudite Eyes*, 24-25, fig. 1.
**59** Goltzius, *J. Julius Caesar*, s.p. (list of collectors added at the end of the book): "Bononiae...: Scipius Fabius Doctor Medicus."
**60** Spezzaferro, "I Carracci e i Fava."
**61** On Bruegel's Italy trip, see Büttner, "Quid siculas sequeris per mille pericula terras?".

**62** Allart, "Sur la piste de Bruegel en Italie."
**63** Zweite, *Marten de* Vos, 237-50. For the series on the Four Continents, see Diels/Leesberg, *The Collaert Dynasty*, VI, 35-39, nos. 1314-17.
**64** "La vita d'Ulisse Adrovandi cominciando dalla sua natività sin' a l'età di 6, anni vivendo ancora," published in Simili, *Il teatro della natura*, 133; Alessandrini/Ceregato, *Natura Picta*, 613-14.
**65** Quiccheberg, *Inscriptiones*, Digression on the Third Class, First Inscription. See Brout, "Le traité muséographique," 105; Meadow/Robertson, *The First Treatise on Museums*, 82.
**66** Olmi, "L'Inventario", 61-64; Olmi, "Il museo"; Staudinger, "Arcimboldo et Ulisse Aldrovandi."
**67** 93 x 86 cm, in six sheets; only two exemplars are known (Washington, Library of Congress, G3290 1562.G7 and London, British Library, Maps VII, col. 102 no. 69810. 18). See Van de Grieken/Luijten/Van der Stock, *Hieronymus Cock.*, no. 102.
**68** On the engravings depicting sailing ships, see Sellink, *Bruegel*, nos. 103-12.
**69** Silver, "The Capital of Capitalism."
**70** Parry, *The Arch-Conjuror of England*, 49-59.
**71** Dee contributed to the Album Amicorum of see Ortelius, *Album Amicorum*, fol. 89.
**72** See Sellink, *Bruegel* for an overview.
**73** Marijnissen, *Bruegel*, 180-86; Van Schoutte/Veroughstraete/Garrido, "La *Dulle Griet* et le *Triomphe de la mort*"; Maximilaan P.J. Martens, "Het realisatieproces in Dulle Griet en de Twaalf spreuken van Pieter Bruegel de Oude," in: Sellink/Martens, *Bruegel ongezien*, 26-59 and idem, "Dulle Griet 1561," in: *ibidem*, 64-67.
**74** On the misogynistic meaning of *Dulle Griet* and links to the persecution of witches, see Gibson, *Pieter Bruegel and the Art of Laughter*, 124-44; Sullivan, "Madness and Folly," and *eadem*, *Bruegel and the Creative Process*, 101-42; Serebrennikov, "On the Surface of Dulle Griet"; Pinson, "Folly and Vanity."
**75** Gibson, *Pieter Bruegel the Elder: Two studies*, 53-86.
**76** See, for example, *Abrahami Ortelii... epistulae*, no. 8.11-12.
**77** Sellink, *Bruegel*, 28-29. Jean Bastiaensen recently found an engagement contract between Bruegel and Mayken Coecke in the registers of the parish of Our Lady in Antwerp (now in the Felix Archief in Antwerp) dated July 25, 1563. This shows that Mayken Coecke then lived in Antwerp. See *De Standaard*, January 9, 2013, with reference to an upcoming publication in *Openbaar Kunstbezit Vlaanderen.*
**78** City Archive Brussels, Onze-Lieve-Vrouw-ter-Kapellekerk, Wedding Register, 1563, fol. 5.
**79** Karel van Mander, *Schilder-boeck*, 1604, fol. 233r-4r.
**80** On this subject see the research of Joost Vander Auwera, which will be published in the *Walraf-Richartz Jahrbuch.*
**81** Brosens/Kelchtermans/Van der Stichelen, *Family Ties.*
**82** Marlier, *La Renaissance flamande*, 42-43; Campbell, *Tapestry in the Renaissance*, 379-91.
**83** De Jonge, "The Court Architect as Artist in the Southern Low Countries 1520-1560."
**84** Campbell, *Tapestry in the Renaissance*, 379-80; Marlier, *La Renaissance flamande*, 55-74.
**85** Campbell, *Tapestry in the Renaissance*, 410-16.
**86** For a *status quaestionis*: N. M. Orenstein, "The elusive life of Pieter Bruegel the Elder," in Orenstein/Sellink, *Pieter Bruegel the Elder*, 3-11.
**87** Madrid, Bibliotheca Nacional, MS 6015; see Bauer/Steppe, *Tapisserien der Renaissance*, 55-99; for Pannemaker's role in Brussels, see Campbell, *Tapestry in the Renaissance*, 279.
**88** Currie, "De ontsluiering van een werkproces."
**89** Granvelle probably owned the *Flight into Egypt* (1563, Courtauld Institute); see Sellink, *Bruegel*, no. 123 and chapter IV. Bruegel painted the *Death of the Virgin* (National Trust, Upton House, Banbury) for Ortelius; see Sellink, *Bruegel*, no. 129. Bruegel painted the famous series of the Months of the Year (1565) for Nicolaas Jongelinck; see Sellink, *Bruegel*, nos. 134-38, with reference to earlier literature.
**90** Niekrasz, *Woven Theatres of Nature.*
**91** Campbell, *Tapestry in the Renaissance*, 379-91: 380.

## Chapter II

* Quiccheberg, *Inscriptiones vel tituli theatri amplissimi, complectentis rerum universitatis singulas materias et imagines eximias, ut idem recte quoque dici possit: Promptuarium artificiosarum miraculosarumque, ac omnia rari thesauri et pretiosae supellectilis, structurae atque picturae quae hic simul in theatro conquiri consuluntur, ut eorum frequenti inspectione tractationeque, singularis aliqua rerum congnitio et prudentia admiranda, cito, facile ac tuto comparari possit.* See Brout, "Le traité muséographique," 84; Meadow and Robertson, *The First Treatise on Museums*, 61.
**1** This interpretation of Greek was not entirely correct, but nevertheless determined the approach of early modern naturalists. See Céard, "Enclyclopédie et encyclopédisme à la Renaissance."
**2** The literature on the early modern culture of collecting is boundless. See, among others, Lugli, *Naturalia e Mirabilia*; Impey/MacGregor, *The Origins of* Museums; Bredekamp, *The Lure of Antiquity*; Kaufmann, "From Treasury to Museum"; Findlen, *Possessing Nature*; Meadow, "Merchants and Marvels"; Bleichmar/Mancall, *Collecting across Cultures.*
**3** Elisabeth Scheicher, "De vorstelijke Kunst- und Wunderkammer," in: Bergvelt et al., *Verzamelen*, 15-36;
**4** Goltzius, *J. Julius Caesar.* A list of 987 collectors is added at the end of the book. Among others Goltzius names Ortelius and Petrus Quicchelberger in Antwerp, Granvelle and Morillon in Brussels, and Scipius Fabius in Bologna. Goltzius was married to Elizabeth Verhulst, sister of Mayken Coecke-Verhulst; see Leloup, *Hubertus Goltzius*, 14-18. On Goltzius's collaboration with Ortelius, see Meganck, "Abraham Ortelius, Hubertus Goltzius en Guido Laurinus."
**5** Büttner, "De verzamelaar."
**6** Sweertius, *Insignium [...] lacrymae*: "Rerum rariorum novatum & antiquarum studiosus erat. Habebat domi suae imagines, statuas, nummos Graecos, Romanos, aureos, argentos, plumbeos, cupreos. Conchas ab ipsis Indis & Antipodibus; marmora omnia coloris. Spiras testiduneas tantae magnitudinis, ut decem ex ijs viri in orbem sendentes, cibum sumere possent: alias rursum ita angustas, ut vix magnitudinem capitelli unius aciculae adaequarent."
**7** Sellink, *Bruegel*, 194; Silver, *Bruegel*, 302-05, with references to earlier literature.
**8** Olmi, *L'Inventario del mondo*, 152-57; Daston and Park, *Wonders and the Order of Nature*, 154.
**9** Kaufmann, "From Mastery of the World to Mastery of Nature. The Kunstkammer, Politics and Science", in his *The Mastery of Nature*, 174-194, especially 181-185 ; Jorink, *Het Boeck der Natuere*, 267-99.

**10** On Quiccheberg see Jansen, "Samuel Quicchebergs Inscriptiones"; Brout, "Le catalogue comme microcosme"; Smith, "Collecting Nature and Art"; Meadow, "Merchant and Marvels"; Meadow and Robertson, *The First Treatise on Museums*.
**11** On contact between Ortelius and the brothers Quiccheberg, see *Epistolae Ortelianae* 53.3; 62.14
**12** Brout, "Le traité muséographique de Quiccheberg," 115-125; and Meadow and Robertson, *The First Treatise on Museums*, 92-103.
**13** Blair, *The Theatre of Nature*, 153-79.
**14** Abraham Ortelius cites Cicero, *De Natura Deorum*, II, 37: ("The horse for riding, the ox for ploughing, the dog for hunting and keeping guard; man himself however came into existence for the purpose of contemplating and imitating the world") on his renowned world map *Typus Orbis Terrarum* (1564). On connections between this Stoic view of the world and Bruegel's landscapes, see Müller Hofstede, "Zur Interpretation von Bruegel's Landschaft." On the importance of Stoicism for natural history and philosophy, see Ogilvie, *The Science of Describing*, 103-05.
**15** This suggests the (seventeenth-century?) inscription: "LIBRO/ De diversos Animales, Aves/ Peçes, y Reptiles,/ QUE EL EMPERADOR CARLOS V/Mandò dibujar a su pintor/ Lamberto Lombardo/En Bruxelas AÑO/ MDXLII" (Amsterdam, Rijksmuseum, Drawings, inv. 52:345). See Boon, *Netherlandish Drawings*, cat. nos 559-606, illustrations in the volume of plates, and in Schaepelhouman, *Nederlandse tekeningen*, supplement. That Hoefnagel copied from this album is found in Rikken, "Conrad Gessners motieven in Antwerpen," 21. See now also Rikken, "A Spanish Album of Drawings of Animals."
**16** Kracow, Jagellonska Lirary, A. 16-30. See Egmont, "Clusius, Cluyt, Saint Omer," especially the volume with animal paintings has not received much study.
**17** Dreyer, "Zeichnungen von Hans Verhagen dem Stummen."
**18** Münster Westfälisches Landesmuseum inv. 1761 LM. The dating is based on similarities to the *Kitchen Piece* by tom Ring that is dated 1562, but is now only known through photos. See Luckhardt, *Das "Küchenstück" von Ludger tom Ringe d. J. (1562)*.
**19** De Vos signed the series of six monumental panels (circa 137 x 136 cm) as "F. Merten de Vos Antverpi ency. 1572." See Zweite, *Maerten de Vos*, cat. nos. 48-53; Blübaum/Erbentraut, *Die Erschaffung der Tiere*.
**20** Hans Bol's manuscripts are now held in Kopenhagen, Det Kongelige Bibliotek, Ms. Gm. Kgl. Saml. 3471 I-III 8°: (I) Icones quorundum animalium quadrupedium (II) Icones quorundum animalium avium (III) Icones animalium quorundum piscem. With thanks to Stefaan Hautekeete, who dates the manuscripts between 1572 and 1575. On the *Four Elements* by Joris Hoefnagel now held in the National Gallery of Art, Washington D.C. Gift of Mrs. Lessing J. Rosenwald, see Hendrix, *Joris Hoefnagel*.
**21** Staudinger, *Le Bestiaire de Rudolphe II*.
**22** Monballieu, "De kunstenaarsfamilie Verhulst Bessemeers," 110.
**23** Rikken, "Abraham Ortelius as intermediary for the Antwerp animal trailblazers." Our investigation was for the most part carried out at the same time as that of Rikken, who does not examine Bruegel's role as a draftsman of animals, but rather goes more deeply into the question of the individual appropriation of particular motifs among animal painters. On Ortelius as a pivotal figure between artists and antiquarians, see Meganck, *Erudite Eyes*.
**24** Meganck, "Abraham Ortelius, Hubertus Goltzius en Guido Laurinus."
**25** Goltzius mentions an encounter with Ring in a letter to Ortelius from 1570; see Hessels, *Epistulae Ortelianae*, no. 28.9
**26** Serebrennikov, "Imitating Nature / Imitating Bruegel."
**27** That year Aldrovandi also met the painter Jacopo Ligozzo; see Olmi, *L'inventario del mondo,* 62. The albums are now online online: http://www.filosofia.unibo.it/aldrovandi/.
**28** On the way to Italy, Ortelius and Hoefnagel stayed briefly at the court of Albrecht V of Bavaria in Munich, where the prince was keen to acquire Hoefnagel's animal paintings. On this see Van Mander, *Schilder-boeck*, fol. 262v-263r: Life of Houfnagel: "Doe sy in hun herbergh waren, sondt den hertogh door sij Hofmeester, oft ander Heer vraghen, wat Houfnaghel begheerde voor dat Verlichterijken van de beestgens..." See also Vignau-Wilberg, "Joris Hoefnagel's Tätigheit in München."
**29** Hendrix, "Of Hirsutes and Insects"; Neri, *The Insect and the Image*, 3-44.
**30** Olmi, *L'inventario del Mondo,* 145.
**31** This advertisment is found in Gessner's German translation of the first book of the *Historia animalium*, dedicated to quadrupeds; see Conrad Gessner, *Thierbuch, das ist ein kurtze beschreibung aller vierfussigen Thieren ... alles su nutz und gutem allen liebhabern der künsten, Artzetem, Maleren, Bildschitzern... gestelt* (Zürich, 1563); Rikken, "Conrad Gessners motieven in Antwerpen," 24 and 32.
**32** Rikken, "Abraham Ortelius as Intermediary."
**33** Kaufmann, *Arcimboldo*.
**34** See, for example, Albrecht Dürer's woodcut of 1515 in Borchert, *Rondom Dürer*, 182.
**35** Sellink, *Bruegel*, no. 20.
**36** Marijnissen, *Bruegel*, 180-81 and Sullivan, "Pieter Bruegel the Elder's Two Monkeys," 115, believe that it is a red Colobus monkey. See also Sellink, *Bruegel*, no. 118, for a *status quaestionis*.
**37** Sullivan, "Pieter Bruegel the Elder's Two Monkeys," 120.
**38** Grossmann, *Pieter Bruegel*, 193; Sullivan "Pieter Bruegel the Elder's *Two Monkeys*"; Ilsink, *Bruegel en Bosch*, 134-213; Montballieu, "De Twee aapjes van P. Bruegel."
**39** For Luther on monkeys as devil and Antichrist, and the devil as "ape" or imitator of God, see Sullivan, "Pieter Bruegel the Elder's Two Monkeys,"117; for an interpretation of the monkeys as imitators in relation to Bruegel's artistic practice of *imitatio,* see Ilsink, *Bosch en Bruegel*, 134-213.
**40** Hans Bol, *Icones*, I, fol. 68 (see note 20).
**41** On Hoefnagel, see Vignau-Wilberg, *In Europa zu Hause*, 102-03. On Anselmus De Boodt, see Maselis/Balis/Marijnissen, *De albums van Anselmus De Boodt*, 70-71; with reference to album II, fol. 60 and 63. De Boodt may have painted the monkeys after Bol or Hoefnagel, or directly from the original, but then probably in the Netherlands. In so far as it is known, Bruegel's painting was never owned by Rudolph II. A certain Elias Verhulst from Mechelen provided some of the nature studies for De Boodt's albums. He may have been related to Mayken Verhulst-Bessemeers, Bruegel's mother-in-law. On this see the research of Joost Vander Auwera, which will be published in the *Wallraf-Richartz-Jahrbuch*.
**42** Eichberger, "Naturalia and artefacta."
**43** See chapter I, pp. 37-41.
**44** Aldrovandi Ms, IV, 35. Clusius, (*Exoticorum Libri Decem*, 94) shows a bat, with reference to Oviedo, *Summarii*, cap. Xxxvi, and Aldrovandi.

**45** Kaufmann, *The Mastery of Nature.* chapter III.
**46** Aristotle writes in the *Historia Animalium*, V.19: "Other insects are not derived from living parentage, but are generated spontaneously: some out of dew falling on leaves, ordinarily in spring-time, but not seldom in winter when there has been a stretch of fair weather and southerly winds; others grow in decaying mud or dung; others in timber, green or dry; some in the hair of animals; some in the flesh of animals; some in excrements: and some from excrement after it has been voided, and some from excrement yet within the living animal, like the helminthes or intestinal worms." See also Smith, *The Body of the Artisan*, 117-20; Janneret, *Perpetual motion*, 20; Jorink *Het Boeck der Natuere*, 187-228.
**47** "In appearance the locusts were like horses equipped for battle. On their heads were what looked like crowns of gold; their faces were like human faces, their hair like women's hair, and their teeth like lions' teeth; they had scales like iron breastplates, and the noise of their wings was like the noise of many chariots with horses rushing into battle. They have tails like scorpions , with stingers, and in their tails is their power to harm people for five months." See Ilsink, *Bosch en Bruegel*, 284.
**48** See note 20.
**49** Aldrovandi depicts the front and back sides of the *Papilio machaon* in Ms Aldrovandi VII, 90. See Alessandrini/Ceregato, *Natura Picta*, 589. The earliest known registration of the American *Papilio glaucus* or tiger swallowtail butterfly is by John White, ca. 1585; see Sloane, *A New World*, no. 63.
**50** It is one of the few miniatures of the *Four Elements* held in Prague, Národní Galerie, *Aqua*; see Vignau-Wilberg, "Joris Hoefnagel's Tätigheit in München," fig. 150. For an early natural historical study of the *Mytulus conchifera*, see Clusius, *Exoticorum* V, cap. XV.
**51** Prague, Národní Galerie, *Aqua*; see Vignau-Wilberg, "Joris Hoefnagel's Tätigheit in München," fig. 149.
**52** Rondelet, *De piscibus marinis*, 419*ff.* Clusius copied the blowfish from Rondelet in his *Exoticorum Libri decem*, V, cap. XXIII and XXVI.
**53** For the *Hortus Publicus*, see Swan, "From Blowfish to Flower Still Life Paintings."
**54** Alessandrini/Ceregato, *Natura Picta*, fig. 349 (Ms Aldrovandi, 004, 43).
**55** Museum of the History of Science, inv. 77644, on loan from the Museum of Natural History, Oxford.
**56** Lestringant, *Sous la leçon des vents*, 247-60.
**57** Alessandrini/Ceregato, *Natura Picta*, fig. 333 (*Dactylopterus volitans*) (Aldrovandi Ms IV, 14); Staudinger (ed.), *Le Bestiaire de Rudolphe II*, fig. 88 (Cod. Min. 129, fol. 89r)(*Poisson volant Exocet*); Maselis/Balis/Marijnissen, *De albums van Anselmus De Boodt*, fig. 46 (VI, 16: *hirundo*)
**58** Knipping, *Pieter Bruegel*, 28, compares this animal with the shark in Clusius, *Exoticorum libri decem*, 137.
**59** Egmond/Mason, "Armadillos in Unlikely Places."
**60** See note 15 of this chapter. For the armadillos, see Boon, *Netherlandish Drawings*, nos. 559-61, and Schaepelhouman, *Nederlandse tekeningen*, 225 (illustrations of the catalogue of 1978, nos. 560-61). Rikken, "Abraham Ortelius as Intermediary," 100-02, and 107-09, finds that some pages of this album were already painted in 1560, and that Ortelius may have been the intermediary who introduced this album among Antwerp animal painters. In that case, Lombard's painting could have been Bruegel's direct source.
**61** Belon, *Observations*, I, 8, and III, 374-75.
**62** Belon, *Observations*, III, 374-5: "Et pource que l'animal [...] qu'on nomme un tatou, est trouvé entre leurs mains, lequel toutesfois est apporté de la Guinée, & de la terre neuve, dont les anciens n'en point parlé, neantmoins nous a semblé bon d'en bailler le portraict. Ce qui fait qu'on voit ceste beste ja commune en plusieurs cabinets, & estre portée en si loingtains pays, est, que nature l'a armée de dure escorce & large escailles à la manière d'un corcelet, & aussi qu'on peut aisément oster la chair de leans sans rien perdre de la naifve figure."
**63** Gessner, *Icones Animalium*, 103.
**64** Staudinger (ed.), *Le Bestiaire*, no. 70.
**65** Oviedo, *Summarii*, cap. xxii, cited in Clusius *Exoticorum libri decem*, XV, 109-11: "bardado [...] hoc est Panoplia, sive integra armature tectum."
**66** Thevet, *Singularitez*, 101: "tattou, qui sont bestes armées [...]"; Ms Aldrovandi, V, 3.
**67** Thevet, *Les singularités de la France antarctique*, 99r-v.
**68** Gessner, *Icones Animalium*, 96. See also Kusukawa Sachiko, "The Sources of Gessner," and Egmond, "A Collection within a Collection."
**69** Joris Hoefnagel may have depicted a sloth on folio 106 of the *Mira callographicae monumenta* (J. Paul Getty Museum, Los Angeles), the calligraphic pattern book made by Georg Bocskay for Ferdinand I that Hoefnagel later illuminated for Rudolph II. See Hendrickx/Vignau-Wilberg, *Mira calligraphiae monumenta*. See also Lowood, "The New World."
**70** Clusius, *Exoticorum libri decem*, 273; see also Mason, "America in the *Exoticorum libri decem* of Charles de l'Écluse," 203-05.
**71** Staudinger (ed.), *Le Bestiaire*, no. 60. A sloth with striking similarities also figures in the *Libri Picturati* (Jagellion Library, Krakow), but according to Peter Mason, *Before Disenchantment*, 199-202, the sloth was added later, in the context of a Dutch expedition to Brazil.
**72** Staudinger (ed.), *Le Bestiaire*, no. 15.
**73** Bax, *Ontcijfering*, 179.
**74** Silver, *Bosch*, 51-52.
**75** Bax, *Ontcijfering*, 24.
**76** See, for example, the skeleton of a dragon or common cat, depicted in the bestiary of Rudolph II; see Staudinger (ed.), *Le Bestiaire*, no. 67.
**77** For example, in Bosch's *Saint Jerome in the Wilderness*, Gent, Museum voor Schone Kunsten; see Reidert Falkenburg in Vergara, *Patinir*, 75.
**78** De Asua/French, *A New World of Animals*, 66.
**79** In 1563 the elephant Emanuel, a gift from King Sebastião I of Portugal to the imperial court in Vienna, made a tour in Antwerp and Brussels. For drawings of the elephant from 1564 by Lambert van Noort, Gerard van Groeningen, and Bernard de Rijckere, among others, see *Wonderlijcke Dieren*, nos. 65-72. Hans Verhagen also reproduces this same elephant in his painted book of animals now in Berlin; see Dreyer, "Zeichnungen von Hans Verhagen," 118-21. Bruegel also depicts an elephant in the print *Saint James and the Sorcerer* (1565); see Vervoort, "De heilige, de heks en de tovenaar."
**80** The most well known is a portrait of Catalina Michaela, daughter of Philip II, with a marmoset, painted by Sofonisba Anguissola; see Pérez de Tudela/Jordan Gschwend, "Renaissance menageries," 439-40. Gessner depicts a marmoset on the basis of a drawing that was sent to him by the Antwerp apothecary Pieter van Coudenberghe (1525-1594), see Gessner,

*Nomenclaturs*, 96 (fig. 45, figure above sloth); Vandewiele, "Wat groeide er in de tuin van Pieter van Coudenberghe."

**81** Parshall, "Imago Contrafacta," 561-62; Dackerman (ed.); *Prints and the Pursuit of Knowledge*, 163-84; Swan, "Ad vivum"; Bakker, "Au vif"; Cook, *Matters of Exchange*, 1-41; Niehr, "Ad vivum." For a critical overview of this literature, see Göttler/Meganck, "Sites of Art, Nature and the Antique in the Spanish Netherlands."

**82** I thank Camilla Cavicchi, Géry Dumoulin and Anne-Emmanuelle Ceulemans for sharing their knowledge about these period instruments.

**83** Gouk, *The ivory sundials.*

**84** See for instance the sundial diptych by Georg Hartmann, Nuremberg 1562, Oxford, Museum of the History of Science, inv. 81528. I thank Jim Bennet for guiding me through the collection of MHS, Oxford.

**85** Oxford, Museum of the History of Science, inv. 49109: diptych sundial by Hans Troschel, Nuremberg 1622, with the inscription "Tempus sumptus est preciosissimus."

**86** Van Cleempoel, "De Leuvense School"; Bennett, "The Mechanical Arts," 681. This is also attested by much correspondence between learned collectors. In the same letter in which he asks that Ortelius greet Bruegel and De Vos, Scipio Fabius asks for help with the purchase of a clock for his brother (Hessels, *Epistulae Ortelianae*, no. 15.4).

**87** This is also why the Antwerp archers' guild, a militia guild, commissioned a *Fall of the Rebel Angels* for its guild chapel from Frans Floris; see Woollett, *The Altarpiece in Antwerp*, 23-49.

**88** Claude Gaier, "La sale d'armes des ducs de Bourgogne et des souverains des Pays-Bas," in Heymans/Cnockaert/Honoré, *Le palais du Coudenberg*, 164-65.

**89** Elisabeth Scheicher, "Twee vorstelijke verzamelingen: van Ferdinand II en Rudolf II," in Bergvelt, *Verzamelen*, 37-56; Del Campo, *Real Armería Palacio Real.*

**90** Kavaler, "Pictorial Satire," 171.

**91** Roobaert, "'Prince van den Onwijzen,'" 44.

**92** Dixon, "Bosch' Garden of Delights."

**93** Howard, "Cultural transfer," 146; Haag/Kirchweger, *Treasures of the Habsburgs*, 20-25.

**94** Van Aelst, *Ces moeurs*; Marlier, *Pierre Coeck*, 55-74; Hamilton, *Arabische Cultuur*, 20-21.

**95** Knipping, *Pieter Bruegel*, 24, notices the American feather headdress but does not investigate further its cultural-historical implications in the sixteenth-century culture of collecting. On exotic people as the other see also Vandenbroeck, *Beeld van de andere*, 21-39.

**96** Staden, *Een warachtige historie.* See also *Amerika, Bruid van de Zon*, no. 195.

**97** Thevet, *Les singularitéz*, XXVI, 50-51: "Elle a esté & est habitée pour le jour d'huy, [...] de gens merveilleusement estrange & sauvages, sans foy, sans loy, sans civilté aucune, ainsi vivans comme bestes irraisonables, ainsi que nature les a produits, mangeans racines, demeurans toujours nuds tant hommes que femmes, jusques à tant, peut estre, qu'ils serons hantez des Chrestiens, dont ils pourront peu à peu despouiller ceste brutalité, pour vestir une façon plus civile & humaine."

**98** Thevet, *Singularitez*, XXXVII, quoted by Grafton/Siraisi, *New Worlds, Ancient Texts*, 92-93.

**99** Thevet, *Singularitez*, XXXVI, 66: "Ce peuple ainsi élongé de la vérité outre les persécutions qu'il reçoit du malin esprit & les erreurs de ses songes, est encore si hors de raison, qu'il adore le Diable par moyen d'aucuns siens ministres, appellez Pagéz [...]"

**100** Cervantes, "Angels conquering and conquered."

**101** Yaya, "Wonders of America."

**102** Chapter I, note 35.

**103** Inventory of the Palace of Brussels, 1545, Brussel, State Archives, Papiers d'Etat et de l'Audience, 1193, fols. 6, 106r-106v, 107r, 122-132r, 132v-133v, published by Perez de Tudela/Gschwend, "Luxury Goods for Royal Collectors," 28. More recently, see also Checa Cremades (dir.), *Los Inventarios de Carlos V*, I: Carlos V, among others no. 6 (Inventario de joyas dejadas en España, 1556, Archives Générales du Royaume, Bruxelles, Chambre des Comptes, leg. 97). This inventory lists jewels that were left behind in Spain, but reported in Brussels in 1556. The inventory (see especially pp. 254-55) contains various jewels from the "Indies," including Peru, and among other things silver pieces and a striking number of feather headdresses.

**104** Madelon Simons, "De studiolo van Francesco I de' Medici," in: Bergvelt et al. (eds.), *Verzamelen*, 21-26.

**105** Krzysztof Pomian, "Histoire Naturelle: de la curiosité à la discipline," in Martin/Moncond'huy, *Curiosité et cabinets de curiosités*, 15-40: 32-33.

**106** Michel de Montaigne calls fire an artist in his *Essais* (1580), hereby referring to the ancient Stoic Zeno of Cition; see Smith, "Sympathy in Eden," 230-33.

**107** Hendrix, "Of Hirsutes and Insects," 282-83.

**108** See the exemplar in the Museum Plantin-Moretus, Antwerp, A 1479. See Heninger, *The Cosmographical Glass*. 37-38.

**109** On the *Proverbs*, see Meadow, *Pieter Bruegel the Elder's Netherlandish Proverbs*; on *Carnival and Lent* and the *Children's Games*, see Sullivan, *Bruegel and the Creative Process*, 53-100; see also Orrock, "Homo Ludens," on the *Children's Games*.

**110** Kaschek, *Weltzeit und Endzeit*; Falkenburg, "Pieter Bruegel's *Series of the Seasons*;" Buchanan, "The collection of Niclaes Jongelinck I," 104, and idem, "The collection of Niclaes Jongelinck II."

**111** There is ample literature on this genre. Recent studies include Van Suchtelen/Van Beneden, *Kamers vol kunst*; Dupré, "Trading Luxury Glass"; Marr, "The Flemish 'Pictures of Collections Genre': An Overview." See also the other essays in this edition of *Intellectual History Review*, 20.1 (2010), devoted to "Picturing Collections in Early Modern Europe." In addition, see Ganz, *Neugier und Sammelbild*, 195-236; Honig, *Painting and the Market*, esp. 196-212; Filipczak, *Picturing Art in Antwerp*, 58-72. Still valuable is: Speth-Holterhoff, *Les peintres flamands*.

**112** Most recently see Currie/Allaert, *The Brueg(H)el Phenomenon.*

**113** Ertz, *Jan Brueghel der Ältere*, 369-84.

## Chapter III

* Brout, "Le traité muséographique, 101; Meadow and Robertson, *The First Treatise on Museums*, 78.

** Brout, "Le traité muséographique, 92; Meadow and Robertson, *The First Treatise on Museums*, 69.

**1** De Hond, *Monsters & Fabeldieren*, 53.

**2** Daston/Park, *Wonders and the Order of Nature*, 173.

**3** Kemp, "Taking it on Trust."

**4** Pignon, "Conrad Gessner," 249-55.
**5** Zweite, *Maerten de Vos*, cat. nos 48-53; Blübaum/Erbentraut, *Die Erschaffung der Tiere.*
**6** Findlen, "Commerce, Art, and Science."
**7** Daston/Park, *Wonders and the Order of Nature*, 255-90; Ghadessi, "Inventoried monsters."
**8** See also Aldrovandi, *Monstrorum Historia* (Bologna: Tebaldinus, 1642), 16-17; Ghadessi, "Inventoried monsters," 270.
**9** Hendrix, "Of Insects and Hirsutes," 376.
**10** Jorink, *Het 'Boecke der Nature,'* 271-72.
**11** Daston/Park, *Wonders and the Order of Nature*; Findlen, "Jokes of Nature and Jokes of Knowledge," esp. 306; Ghadessi, "Inventoried monsters."
**12** Vandenbroeck, *Jheronimus Bosch*, 220-22.
**13** See also chapter I, note 33 and fig. 3.
Lampsonius, *Pictorum...Effigies*, 19.
**14** Van Mander, *Het Schilder-Boeck*, fol. 233.
**15** Van Mander, *Het Schilder-Boeck*, fol. 233: "He had practised a lot after the works of Jeroon van den Bosch and he also made may specters and burlesques in his manner so that he was called by many Pier den Drol. This is why one sees few pictures by him which a spectator can contemplate seriously without laughing, and however straightfaced he may be, he has at least to twitch his mouth or smile." See also Muylle, '"Pier den Drol'. Karel van Mander en Pieter Bruegel."
**16** Serebrennikov, "On the Surface of Dulle Griet,"157-80; Gibson, *The Art of Laughter.*
**17** Guevara, *Comentarios* 41-44; Pliny, *Historia Naturalis* (35: 114: "[...] idem iocoso nomine Gryllum deridiciuli habitus pinxit, unde id genus picturae grylli vocantur"); McHam, *Pliny in the Artistic Culture of the Italian Renaissance*, 50, 298-99, 316, 323. On this *genus grillorum*, see: Muylle, *Genus gryllorum*; Bredekamp, "Grillengänge." One of the most fascinating practitioners of this genre was the Milanese painter Giuseppe Arcimboldo (1526-1593). It seems to be no coincidence that Arcimboldo also painted the earliest of his composite portraits, composed of fruit, flowers, animals, and other natural elements, in 1562. See Kaufmann, *The Mastery of Nature*, 151-57, and Idem, *Arcimboldo*, 105. See also Vandenbroeck, "Zur Herkunft und Verwurzelung der 'Grillen'"; Goettler, "Bootsicheyt."
**18** De Guevara, *Comentarios*, 44, on Bosch's *Seven Deadly Sins*: "el quadro de la invidia á mi jucio es tan raro y ingenioso [...] que puede competir con Aristides, inventors de estas pinturas, que los Griegos llamaron *Ethice*, lo qual en nuestra castellano suena, Pinturas que muestran las costumbres y afectos de los ánimos de los hombres."
**19** De Siguença, *Tercera parte de la Historia de la Orden de S. Geronimo*, 837-841, cited by De Tolnay, *Hieronymus Bosch*, appendix 8: "[...] une peinture comme pour plaisanter et macaronique, en apportant à ces farces beaucoup d'habileté et de curiosités, tant dans l'invention que dans l'exécution de la peinture, en prouvant parfois à quel point il était capable dans cet art, ainsi que faisait aussi Cocayo [alias Teofilo Folengo] quand il parlait sérieusement [...] ainsi prit-il un nom ridicule et se fit-il appeler Merlin Cocayo, ce qui correspond bien à l'aspect de son œuvre, comme chez l'autre qui s'appelait Ysop (sic) dans ses poèmes, il montre avec un art particulier comment on pourrait envisager et saisir le bon dans les poèmes le plus appréciables [...]."
**20** For instance the famous panel of *The Beggars*, dated 1568 (Paris, Musée du Louvre), see Sellink, *Bruegel*, no. 166.
**21** Quiccheberg, *Inscriptiones*, Digression on the First Class, see the first citation introducing this chapter.
**22** Erasmus, *Moriae encomium, sive Stultitiae laus* (1511); Colie, *Paradoxia Epidemica*, 3-40.
**23** Erasmus, *Echiridion militis Christiani* (1503); Müller, *Das Paradox als Bildform*, 90-125.
**24** See Prologue, first quotation.
**25** Kemp, "From 'mimesis' to 'fantasia.'"
**26** Abraham Ortelius, *Album amicorum*, now in Pembroke College, Cambridge University, MS II 113, fols. 12v-13. See also edition by Puraye. For comments on this poem, see: Freedberg, "Allusion"; Muylle, "Pieter Bruegel"; Melion, *Shaping*, 173-82; Meadow, *Pieter Bruegel*, 108-17; Meganck, *Erudite Eyes*, 193-212.
**27** *Ibidem*, "Eupompus pictor interrogator quem sequeretur antecedentium, demonstrata hominum multitudine, dixisse fertur, naturam ipsam imitandam esse, non arteficem. Congruit nostro Brugelio hoc, cuius picturas ego minime artificiosas, at naturales appellare soleam, neque eum optimum pictorum at naturam pictorum vero dixerim. Dignum itaque iudico, quem omnes imitentur." Ortelius is referring to Pliny, *Hist. Nat.* XXXIV.61.
**28** Białostocki, "The Renaissance Concept"; Daston and Park, *Wonders*, 287; Smith, *The Body*, 51-55 Goettler/Meganck, "Sites of Art, Nature and the Antique."
**29** Kemp, '"Wrought by No Artist's Hand."
**30** Sellink, *Bruegel*, no. 130.
**31** I thank Martin Kemp for this comparison.
**32** We may view this close viewing as an extension of the devotional viewing of paintings through visual typology as described by Falkenburg, *The Land of Unlikeness*, 76-95.
**33** In the passage cited by Ortelius, Pliny discusses atmospheric phenomena such as thunder and lightning; Bruegel was also known for his depiction of atmospheric phenomena such as light and snow. See Meadow, *Pieter Bruegel the Elder's Netherlandish Proverbs*, 112.
**34** Van Mander, *Schilder-boeck*, 1604, fol. 233r.
**35** Seneca, letter to Lucilius, 84.5-7. Pigman III, "Versions of Imitation in the Renaissance"; Quiviger, "Honey from Heaven."
**36** Jeanneret, *Perpetual Motion*, 122-43.
**37** For anthropomorphic landscapes, see, for example, KMSKB inv. nos 10827-10828. See most recently Weemans, *Herri met de Bles*, 171-202.
**38** On *Dulle Griet*: Sellink/Martens, *Bruegel Ongezien!* and Pawlak, *Trilogie*, 143-84, with references to earlier literature.
**39** Van Mander, *Schilder-boeck*: Life of Lucas de Heere, 255v. D'Heere himself reports that he also owned giants' bones in his *Corte beschrijvinghe van Engheland Schotland ende Irland*, (British Library Add. Ms. 28330), fol. 36r. See Meganck, "Chorography and Antiquity."
**40** Chapter II, notes 6 and 7; Meganck, *Erudite Eyes*, 157-63.
**41** Quiccheberg, Fifth Class, Inscription 1, see the second citation introducing this chapter. This competition goes back to the rivalry between Zeuxis and Parrhasius, as told by Pliny; see McHam, *Pliny and the Artistic Culture of the Italian Renaissance*, 248-50, 336.
**42** De Guevara, *Comentarios*, 42-43: "Una cosa osa afirmar de Bosco, que nunca pintó cosa fuera del natural en su vida, sino fuese en materia de infierno, ó purgatorio, como dicho tengo. Sus invenciones estrivaron en buscar cosas rarisimas, pero naturales: de manera, que puede ser regla universal, que qualquiera pintura, aunque firmada de Bosco, en que hubiere monstruosidad alguna, ó cosa que passe los limites de la naturaleza, que es adulterada y fingida [...]"

**43** Cambell/Van der Stock, *Rogier van der Weyden*, 36.
**44** Cambell/Van der Stock, *Rogier van der Weyden*, cat. no. 70.
**45** Sellink, *Bruegel*, cat. no. 127; Meadow, "Bruegel's Procession to Calvary."
**46** The Coxcie panels were separated in the nineteenth century and are now in München, Berlin, and Brussels. The panels in the KMSKB are inv. nos 6696-6697-6678-6699-6700-6701.
**47** The Antwerp collector Peter Stevens (1590-1668), also the earliest viewer to comment on the *Fall of the Rebel Angels*, noted in his copy of Van Mander's *Schilder-boeck* that he had seen the portrait in the collection of the Earl of Arundel (1585-1646). Dhaenens, *Hubert en Jan van Eyck*, 188-92; Campbell, *The Fifteenth Century*, 212-17.
**48** Van der Stock, *Antwerp, Story of a Metropolis*, 165-66, cat. 16; see also King, "Artists' Houses."
**49** On the depiction of Jan van Eyck with a turban in Dominicus Lampsonius's *Effigies* (1572), see Göttler/Meganck, "Sites of Art, Nature and the Antique."
**50** Lampsonius, *Pictorum... Effigies*. See Göttler/Meganck, "Sites of Art, Nature and the Antique," forthcoming, with references to the earlier literature.
**51** Koschatzky, *Duerer Zeichnungen. Die geschichte der Dürersammlung der Albertina*, 11; 24-33; Budde, "Das "Kunstbuch des Nürnberger Patrizier Willibald Imhoff," 222.
**52** Buchanan, "Dürer and Abraham Ortelius."
**53** Eichberger, "Naturalia and artefacta."
**54** Hess/Eser, *Der Frühe Dürer*, 434-53.
**55** In his *Hof en Boomgaerd der Poesiën*; Freedberg, "Allusion and Topicality"; Meganck, *Erudite Eyes*, 194-212, and Appendix 1; Richardson, *Pieter Bruegel*, 47-51.
**56** For example, in Petrus Christus, *Portrait of a Carthusian Monk* (1446) in the Metropolitan Museum of Art in New York. See also Ilsink, *Bosch en Bruegel*, 293-94.
**57** Ilsink, *Bosch en Bruegel*, 290-300; Quiviger, "Honey from Heaven."
**58** Melion, *Shaping the Netherlandish Canon*; Ilsink, *Bosch en Bruegel*, 270-302, who does not, however, explore the culture of collecting in which Bruegel's *Fall* was in my opinion created.
**59** Janneret, *Perpetual Motion*, 113.
**60** Vervoort, "De heilige, de heks en de tovenaar." For an interesting interpretation of Bruegel and the history of the imagination, see Milne, *Carnival and Dreams*, esp. 67-80.
**61** For Bruegel's paintings of the *Tower of Babel*, see Sellink, *Bruegel*, nos. 124 and 125, with reference to earlier literature. For his drawing and the print *Temperantia*, see Sellink, *Bruegel*, 86 and 93, with reference to earlier literature.
**62** Falkenburg, *Land of Unlikeness*, 102-16: 107.
**63** On Bruegel and this "paradox of possession," see also Silver, *Peasant Scenes and Landscapes*, 151.

## Chapter IV

* See chapter IV note 21.
**1** See, for example, the *Calumny of Apelles* in the British Museum, Sellink, *Bruegel*, 146.
**2** While various authors have commented on the changing signatures Brueghel/Bruegel (see most recently Sellink, *Bruegel*, 17), the fact that Bruegel only uses Roman numerals for dates from 1562 onward has passed unnoticed. His earliest paintings, the *Proverbs* and *Children's Games*, are signed "BRUEGEL" in Roman capitals, but still dated with Arabic numerals.
**3** Sellink, *Bruegel*, 30.
**4** Chapter I, pages 60-63.
**5** Menzel, *Pieter Bruegel*, 53-55. Particularly since Marijnissen (*Bruegel*, 180-81) radically rejected this hypothesis, without a definite argument, it has rarely been investigated further.
**6** Martens/Vanrie/de Waha, *Sint Michiel en zijn symboliek*, 124-32; Jean-Luc Petit, *Sint Michiel: De Brusselaar*, 8-11.
**7** Now replaced with a copy. The original is still held in the city hall. The gilded bronze statue, five meters in height, seems harmoniously proportioned when seen from the ground - but this is not the case when it is viewed from close by. The optical adjustment bears witness to the mastery of artist Martin Van Rode. See Bonenfant, ed., *Restauration de la tour principale de l'Hôtel de Ville*, 23-26.
**8** Dürer, *Das Tagebuch, 1520.1521*, 64-65: "Jch hab gesehen zu Brüssel jm rathhauß jn der gulden kammer die 4 gemalten materien, die der groß meister Rudier gemacht hat.... Jtem zu Prüssel ist ein fast köstlich rathauß, groß und von schöner maßwerck gehauen, mit einem herrlichen dursichtigen thurn."
**9** In the years 1561-65, the city of Antwerp, an expanding commercial metropolis, was building a new *all'antica* city hall after designs by the brother of Frans Floris, Cornelis. On the immediate afterlife of Van der Weyden see *Bücken/Steyaert, De Erfenis van Rogier van der Weyden*.
**10** Later, Bruegel maintained contact with the Brussels magistracy. According to Van Mander, *Het Schilder-Boeck*, fol. 234, the Brussels magistrates had commissioned "[...] eenighe stucken van het delven van de Brusselse vaert nae Antwerpen [...]" a project which remained unfinished on account of his early death.
**11** Mareel, *Voor Vorst en stad*.
**12** Gibson, "Artists and Rederijkers," 430.
**13** Van Bruaene, "A wonderfull tryumfe, for the wynnyng of a pryse."
**14** "Wat dat de landen can houden in Rusten." See *Refereynen ende liedekens van diverschen rhetoricien uut Brabant, Vlaenderen, Hollant, en [de] Zeelant: ghelesen en ghesonghen op de Corenbloeme camere binnen Bruessele, op haer jaerlijcxse Prinsfeeste*. Gheprint in die Princelijcke stadt van Bruessele by Michel Van Hamont, figuersnijder, ende ghesworen Boeckprinter der Conincklijcker Maiesteyt, 1563. Exemplar in the Royal Library, Brussels: II. 15.122A 5 (RP). See also Van Eeghem, "Het Brussels Rederijkersfeest (1565)"; De Baere, "De Brusselse Refereynen en Liedekens van 1562"; Van Elslander, *Het refrein*, 214-15; Heurer, *The City Rehearsed*, 77-84.
**15** Arnade, *Beggars, Iconoclasts & Civic Patriots*, 57-58.
**16** *Drie Schandaleuse Spelen* (Brussels, 1559). Ed. W. Van Eeghen, Antwerp, 1937; Van Bruaene, *Om beters wille*, chapter 4, esp. 115-16.
**17** Van Bruaene, *Om beters wille*, 132, refers to the Royal Library, Brussels: hs. G. 219, 21v-22r.
**18** *Refereynen ende liedekens*, last page: "[...] elck Refereyn ende Liekeden [...] ghevisiteert ende gheapprobeert by den Eerweerdighen heeren ende meesteren Laurentium Metsium plebaen van Sinte Goedelen kercke binnen de princelijcke Stadt van Brussele int Jaer MDLXIII."
**19** *Refereynen*, refrain 40: "Dat Lucifer gheen Wijsheyt was userende/Maer hem selven als t'Hooft was exalterende/Regerende//daer hy was om dienen ghestelt/Was hier niet eerstmael wt descenderende Onruste? Gheheel den Hemel moverende, niet cesserende//Lucifer en was ghevelt [...]."

**20** *Refereynen*, refrain 40: "Daer Wijsheyt is/oock goede Policije/Daer Wijsheyet is/ en is gheen Hoverdije/Noch eenighe Invije//maer de Liefde soet/ Deur de welcke de Herders niet met Partije Tghemeente regeren/ maer met herten blije Aen elcke sije//en met sinnekens vroet/ Niet om eyghen bate/ oft met evelen moet / Tvleesch en tbloet//ete[n]: maer tvolck welvaert alleene Soekende/als een vader voor sijn kinderen doet:/ Dit zijn goe hoofden voor de Lekens ghemeene [...]."
**21** *Refereynen*, refrain 48: "T'es bij expres//datmen de Vreese des Heeren /Uiten Lande / met schande // nu siet veriaghen./ Tghebreck van haer / claer // doet onruste vermeeren: Maer soo waer // regneert Gods Vreese vol eeren: Salt al groot / en smal // gherustelijck leven: Wilt naer /swaer // exempel van Lucifer keeren: Want hij / bij // Godts vreese niet en is bleven/. Als boos / vercoos // hij het onrustig sneven: Dus stilt u / en wilt nu // op dit Woordt vertrouwen/. Gods Vreese can de Landen in Ruste houwen."
**22** *Refereynen*, refrain 54: "Ongehoorsaem Liefde ... heeft Onrust ghemeckt inden Hemel voorwaer/Waer deur Godt sulcken Enghels heeft verdreven: Ja/ eewich ghepunieert inder Hellen zeer swaer / [...]"; *Refereynen*, refrain 68: "De Godtheyt voorsichtich en van Rade wijs/ Nae dat Lucifer deur t'sondich Afgrijs/ Was ghevallen in het ellendich Tempeest/Heeft gheschape[n] den Mensch net /suyver als een rijs /Vander Eerden [...]."
**23** *Refereynen*, refrains 8, 34 and 56.
**24** *Refereynen*, refrain 56: "Een Prince machtich die heft in handen veel Vlecken enLanden om te regeren. "See also *Liedeken*, or song, to refrain 40. A similar message is embedded in a unique painting depicting *The Good Shepherd (with Philip II?)* in the collection of the RMFAB (inv. 7576), which is based in part on Bruegel's representation of the same theme. See Popelier, "Image des luttes religieuses dans la peintures des Anciens Pays-Bas."
**25** *Refereynen*, *Liedeken* to refrain 8: "Dus Prince vroet/Treckt dan Gods-harnas ane/Om t'Helsch Ghebroet/Beter te wederstane [...]."
**26** Gibson, "Artists and Rederijkers"; Ramakers, "Bruegel en de rederijkers."
**27** Gibson, "Artists and Rederijkers," 431.
**28** Gibson, "Bruegel, Dulle Griet, and Sexist Politics in the sixteenth century," 10.
**29** Van Bruaene, *Om beters wille*, chapter 4, 136-39.
**30** Vandommele, "Mirroring God. Reflecting Man."
**31** Van Mander, *Schilder-boeck*, Life of Pieter Bruegel, 233-34.
**32** *Refereynen*, refrain 67. Monballieu, "De kunstenaarsfamilie Verhulst Bessemeers," 119-20.
**33** Portrait painter Jacob de Pundere alias van Heyst became a member of *De Corenbloem* on 1 october 1562. A Calvinist, he went in to exile with his family in 1568 and in 1570 he was convicted in absentia; see Montballieu, "De kunstenaarsfamilie Verhulst Bessemeers," 118-19; Van Bruaene, *Om beters wille*, 125.
**34** *Refereynen*, refrain 36.
**35** Van Grieken et al., *Hieronymus Cock*, cat. nos 81 and 82.
**36** Van Mander, *Het Schilder-Boeck*, Life of Vredeman de Vries. Van Mander situates this event in 1575-77, but must have been mistaken, since Bruegel had been dead for quite some time by that date.
**37** Montballieu, "Een werk van P. Bruegel en H. Vredeman de Vries voor tresorier Aert Molckeman." Montballieu makes a connection between this commission and Bruegel's print designs for *Spring*, with farmers in a formal garden featuring herms and a pergola that resembles a garden design by Vredeman. For the prints, see Sellink, *Bruegel*, nos. 147-48.
**38** Vienna, Kunsthistorische Museum; see Campbell, *Tapestry in the Renaissance*, 452-57. Bruegel and Vredeman had other mutual acquaintances, among whom Peter Coecke van Aalst and Peter Baltens; Montballieu, "P. Bruegel en het altaar van de Mechelse Handschoenmakers," 97; *idem*, "De 'hand als teken op het kleed'"; Silva Maroto/Sellink, "The rediscovery of Pieter Bruegel the Elder's 'Wine of St Martin's Day,' acquired for the Museo Nacional del Prado," 792.
**39** Roobaert, "'Prince van den Onwijzen': Jan Walraevens, schilder en rederijker te Brussel," 90; Van Bruaene, *Om beters wille*, 123.
**40** In addition, Charles V had spent his entire childhood (1500-1517) in the Netherlands; see Lapeyre, *Charles Quint*, 13; Jacobs, *Een geschiedenis van Brussel*, 130-31.
**41** Bertini, *Le Nozze di Alessandro Farnese.*
**42** See chapter I, note 36, and chapter II, note 103.
**43** Emiliani et al., *Der Glanz der Farnese*; Margaret had moreover been married previously to Alessandro di Medici, from whose illustrious family she inherited a love of art as well as many splendid works of art; see *La Collezione Farnese* (Naples: Museo di Capodimonte, 2009), 13-19.
**44** Woodall, *Anthonis Mor*, 397.
**45** The primary study remains Meijer, *Parma e Bruxelles*; Sabine van Sprang (in: Paredes/van Sprang/Huys, "La magnificence du prince," 163) also notes that it is unusual that the governess of the Netherlands is not known to have commissioned a single work from Bruegel.
**46** Sabine van Sprang (see note, above) and Xander Van Eck, ("Margaret of Parma's gift," 69) propose that Margaret of Parma's limited artistic patronage in the Netherlands also has to do with her preference for her palaces in Parma and Piacenza.
**47** Van Durme, "Les Granvelles au service des Habsburg," 25.
**48** Sandoval, Prudencio de, *Historia de la vida y hechos del emperador Carlos V* (Pamplona, 1618-19), II, 806-07. See also Mörke, *Willem van Oranje*, 61-62.
**49** Meijering, *Het hof van Nassau te Brussel.*
**50** Rodríguez-Salgado, "King, Bishop, Pawn?," esp. 117-18.
**51** Geevers, "Family matters," 471.
**52** Postma, "Granvelle, Viglius en de Adel (1555-1567)."
**53** Koenigsberger, "Orange, Granvelle and Philips II," 583.
**54** Letter of July 23, 1561; see Van Roosbroeck, *Willem de Zwijger*, 114-18; Geevers, *Gevallen gezallen*, 93.
**55** Geevers, *Gevallen gezallen*, 22-23 and 99-115; Arnade, *Beggars, Iconoclasts, & Civic Patriots*, 58, 60, 74.
**56** On Jonghelinck, see the letter of treasurer Odet Viron to Granvelle, Brussels, May 31, 1569, Ms Granvelle 27, fol. 30 r-v, first noted by Tourneur, "Le Médailleur Jacques Jongheling et Cardinal Granvelle 1564-1576," 82. On Mor, see Woodall, *"Patronage and Portrayal."*
**57** Smolderen, "Jonghelinck en Italie."
**58** Buchanan, "The collection of Niclaes Jonghelinck: the "Months" by Pieter Bruegel the Elder."
**59** De Jonge, "De tuinen van kardinaal Granvelle in Brussel en Sint-Joost-ten-Node."
**60** See note 75 for a reference to the "cabinet" in a letter from Morillon to Granvelle (1566, Collection Granvelle, 92, fol. 162). De Jonge, "Le Palais Granvelle à Bruxelles"; on the "cabinet" see Banz, "Zwischen Repräsentation und Humanismus," 395-98.

**61** On the antiquities in the cabinet, see Banz, "Zwischen Repräsentation und Humanismus."

**62** Our knowledge of the Granvelle collection is based on the inventory of the Granvelle palace in Besançon, drawn up in 1607 after the death of François Perrenot, the last male descendant of Cardinal Antoine Perrenot de Granvelle, held in the Bibliothèque municipale de Besançon, Collection Granvelle, Ms Granvelle 50 "Inventaire des meubles de la maison de Granvelle." The entire Granvelle archive is now digitalized: http://www. memoirevive.besancon.fr. For a partial transcription of the "fine arts," primarily paintings but without weapons, armor, and other elements of material culture, see Castan, *Monographie du Palais Granvelle*, doc. IV, 36-67. The inventory mentions an *Our Lady on the Flight to Egypt* by Pieter Bruegel the Elder (*Inventaire*, fol. 93, no. 36: "Peysage d'une Nostre Dame allant en Egypte du Vieux Pierre Brueghel d'haulteur d'un pied quattre polces, large d'un pied treize polces et demy, avec sa molure dorée"). This is probably identical to the painting now at the Courtauld Institute in London, Count Seilern Collection, inv. P. 1978, PG 4751. The inventory is also cited by Allaert, "Pieter Brueghel le Jeune a-t-il pu voir les tableaux de son père?", 49; Banz, *Höfisches Mäzenatentum in Brüssel*, 390-409, and Meijer, *Parma e Bruxelles*, 153-55. For the works by Floris (including a *Calvary*, a *Raising of the Bronze Serpent*, three *Women's Heads*, a *Head of Bacchus*, a *Head of Ceres*, and two portraits) in Granvelle's collection, see Van de Velde, *Frans Floris*, 44, 45, 192, 193, 205, 228, 395, 450, 491.

**63** Besançon, Collection Granvelle, Ms Granvelle 50, Paintings ("*Pourtraictz... et aultres peintures*"), no. 102 ("une chauvesouriz"); no. 109 ("testes d'un asne, d'un chien, d'un renard, conny d'inde et de chat, de la main du vieux Pourbus"); no. 167 ("un rhinocerot").

**64** Chapter III, p. 126.

**65** Besançon, Collection Granvelle, Ms Granvelle 50, Paintings ("*Pourtraictz... et aultres peintures*"), no. 110 ("teste d'une femme pourtant barbe de la main de Guillaume Chayez"). Probably the *Portrait of Marguerite Halseber van Basel*; see Jonckheere, *Willem Key*, 132-35 (A 68). Joanna Woodall, "Patronage and Portrayal,"262-63, dates *Granvelle's Dwarf and Dog* to the early 1560s and reads it as a jocular comment on the political situation (the dwarf is supposed to refer to regent Margaret of Parma, the hound, with Granvelle's arms on its collar, to the cardinal, who surpasses her).

**66** Besançon, Collection Granvelle, Ms Granvelle 50, Sculptures ("*Statues*"), nos. 119-42. These *naturalia* and art objects in precious materials are not listed in full by Castan (1867) and Gauthier (1901), who only transcribed the so-called "fine arts," thereby presenting a distorted image of the original variety of this early modern collection. The complete transcript of the inventory falls outside the scope of this study but is highly desirable. For the unpublished parts, see the online archive http://www. memoirevive.besancon.fr. The pages numbers indicate the digital pagination and the numbers in between brackets the numbers in the manuscript: http://www. memoirevive.besancon.fr (Ms Granvelle 50), 167-70: "un rocher de minne d'argent, au-dessus duquel y a la Résurrection ayant son pied d'argent doré" (no. 118); "une tasse en torque de coquille de jaspe" (no. 119); "une branche de coral ayant au pied un Orphée la branche ... taillez en animaux" (no. 120); "une autre grande branche de coral" (no. 121); "une miroir garni d'un bord de cuivre" (no. 123); "une corne de bouc sauvage" (no. 129); "une coffre de corne" (no. 134); "une croix jaspe christi" (no. 138); "trois globes de cristal" (no. 139).

**67** Haag/Kirschweger, eds., *Treasures of the Habsburgs*, 186-87 ('Handstone' ornament, inv. no. KK 4161); 168-169 (Ostrich egg shell, coral, partly gilt and partly painted silver, inv. no. KK 897) 230-31 (Jasper Jug, inv. no. KK 1866).

**68** http://www. memoirevive.besancon.fr (Ms Granvelle 50), 8-12: "Tapis turcquois," with a list of twenty-two Turkish carpets; http://www. memoirevive.besancon.fr (Ms Granvelle 50), 62, "un tapis turcque"; also http://www. memoirevive.besancon.fr (Ms Granvelle 50), 62: "Armurie."

**69** http://www. memoirevive.besancon.fr (Ms Granvelle 50), 80: "une coquille de tortue de mer."

**70** Picquard, "Le cardinal de Granvelle, amateur de tapisseries," 118: "J'ay faict pendre lesdictctz patrons en l'armurie affin que les ratz n'y puissent advenir" (April 28, 1566). He is referring to cartoons for the *Capture of Tunis* by Jan Cornelisz Vermeyen, woven by Willem de Pannemaker in 1546-54; see Campbell, *Tapestry in the Renaissance*, 269 and 279. Apparently the cartoons ended up in Granvelle's possession, who had additional tapestries woven after them in 1564-66.

**71** Bossuyt, "O Socii Durate: Antoine Perrenot de Granvelle en de Vlaamse Polyfonist Adriaan Willaert." For the reference to the letter of Odet Viron, see 334.

**72** Rodríguez-Salgado, "King, Bishop, Pawn?," 121, and note 66.

**73** For the portrait by Titian (probably 1548, Kansas City, MO, The Nelson-Atkins Museum of Art), by Antonis Mor (1549, Vienna, Kunsthistorisches Museum), and the portrait by Willem Key (1561, Weimar, Staatliche Kunstsammlungen), see Woodall, "Patronage and Portrayal," who only interprets the clock as a vanitas symbol, and does not pursue Granvelle's scientific interests. On Granvelle's interest in scientific instruments, see Van Cleempoel, "De Leuvense school van instrumentenmakers in de 16[de] eeuw," 217-18.

**74** Bauer, "Gartenlandschaften mit Tieren."

**75** Bibliothèque municipale de Besançon, Collection Granvelle, Ms Granvelle 92, fol. 162: letter from Morillon to Granvelle, June 16, 1566. Published by Picquart, "Le cardinal de Granvelle, amateur de tapisseries," 119; Vandenbroeck, *Jheronimus Bosch*, 88, notes that the pieces were not new in 1566, since Morillion notes "je y envoieray les tappisseries nouvelles et de Bosche (sic) avec un coffre des milleures pieces [sic] du *cabinet* selon que vous m'avez escript [...]" Kurz, "Four tapestries after Hieronymus Bosch," asks whether the other three tapestries, now held by the Patrimonio Nacional in Madrid and made in the style of Bosch, are not exact copies but rather after designs by Pieter Bruegel. Given Bruegel's connections with tapestry, through his father-in-law Pieter Coecke, among other things, this is an interesting avenue of exploration.

**76** Vandenbroeck, "Rudolf II als verzamelaar van werk van en naar Jheronimus Bosch," and Elisabeth Scheicher, "Twee vorstelijke verzamelingen van Ferdinand II en Rudolf II," in Bergvelt/Meijers/Rijnders eds., *Verzamelen: Van rariteitenkabinet tot kunstmuseum*, 52-53.

**77** Van Dijck, *Op zoek naar Jheronimus van Aken*, 102-05, for the paintings by Bosch that Philip II could purchase from Guevara's estate. Already prior to 1570, Philip acquired the *Haywain* (fig. 6), and later the tabletop depicting the *Seven Deadly Sins* (fig. 20) and the *Garden of Earthly Delights* (fig. 21), among other things.

**78** Beltung, *Hieronymus Bosch*, 71-84.

**79** Steppe, "Spaans tapijtwerk van de 16de eeuw"; Vandenbroeck, "Hight Stakes in Brussels, 1567."
**80** Picquard, "Les livres du cardinal de Granvelle," 306; Dinard, "La collection du cardinal de Granvelle."
**81** The inventory of 1607 (Besançon, Collection Granvelle, Ms Granvelle 50) also mentions a "peysaged'un Jonas, d'haulteur d'un pied treize polce en large d'un pied dix polces et un quart" (no. 38); "peysage de Peeter Brueghel, sur planche de cuivre, d'haulteur d'un pied et large d'un pied et demy et un quart de polce" (no. 73); "navires en mer tranquille, avec petites figures en icelle et paysage lointain, de Pierre Brueghel, tenant d'hauteur un pied trois polces deux quartz, largeur un pied treize polces" (no. 43); "des aveugles qui se meinent l'un l'autre, de Brueghel; d'haulteur d'un pied douze polces et demy, marge de trois pieds quattre polces" (no. 166). These themes, measurements, and materials do not correspond to surviving works. For a recent discussion of Bruegel's *Rest on the Flight into Egypt,* see Porras, "Rural Memory, Pagan Idolatry."
**82** The archbishop was also a protector of Christopher Plantin, see Van Durme, "Antoon Perrenot van Granvelle: Beschermheer van Christoffel Plantijn," and Voet, *The Golden Compasses*, I, 55 ff. For contacts between Granvelle and Cock, see Wouk, *Frans Floris*, xxxv-xxxviii, and *Hieronymus Cock: the Renaissance in print*, 19, 45-46, cat. nos. 9, 14, 19, 91.
**83** Bibliothèque municipale de Besançon, Collection Granvelle, Ms. Granvelle 28, fols. 211-15: "[...] mais il ne fault que estimiez recouvrer des pièces de Bruegel, sinon fort chèrement: car elles sont plus requisez depuis son trespas que par avant, et s'estiment 50, 100 et 200 escuz, qu'est charge de conscience." Published by Piot/Poullet, *Correspondence du Cardinal Granvelle*, IV, 524; De Tolnay, *Pierre Bruegel l'ancien*, 62.
**84** Rodríguez-Salgado, "King, Bishop, Pawn?," 120-21.
**85** Rodriguez-Salgado, "King, Bishop, Pawn?," 124 (with reference to the Achivio Generale di Simancas E 524, f. 23).
**86** "Saint Michel avec ses anges combattant les démons; 1 pied 6 pouces sur 15 pouces ½ de large" (no. 142). This corresponds to approximately 48 x 38 cm, a much smaller format than Bruegel's *Val.*
**87** Campbell, *Tapestry in the Renaissance*, 435-40.
**88** Buchanan, "The Tapestries Acquired by King Philip II in the Netherlands in 1549-50 and 1555-59," 134-37.
**89** Letter from Philip II to Granvelle from Toledo, March 11, 1561, published by Picquard, "Le cardinal de Granvelle, amateur de tapisseries," 114.
**90** Geevers, *Gevallen gezallen*, 102.
**91** Pleij, *Anna Bijns van Antwerpen*, 99.
**92** Later in the seventeenth century, Saint Michael became a true patron of the Counter-Reformation; see Renger, *Peter Paul Rubens: Altäre für Bayern.*
**93** *Refereynen, Liedeken* to refrain 2: "Men siet nu wel /Dat heden s daechs den vader snel / Tkint bedriecht in alle weghen / En t'kint den vader wreedt en fel /Vol Nijdicheyts boos en rebel / In Sonden pleghen// Altijt tot thet quaet gheneghen"; De Baere, *De Brusselse Refereynen*, 143.
**94** Arnade, *Beggars, Iconoclasts & Civic Patriots*, 91-124.
**95** Oestereich, *Neostoicism and the Early Modern State*, 15-16.
**96** Montballieu, "P. Bruegel en het altaar van de Mechelse Handschoenmakers."
**97** Because of this petition, the authorities called them "geux," *geuzen* or beggars, a mocking epithet that the nobles quickly began to use as a badge of honor. On this example of social inversion, see Arnade, *Beggars, Iconoclasts and Civic Patriots*, 53. On the possible political resonance of Bruegel's depictions of beggars, see Sellink, *Bruegel*, no. 166.
**98** Arnade, *Beggars, Iconoclasts & Civic Patriots*, 76-77; 90-124.
**99** "GUILH. NASSAVIO AURAICO. OPT. PRINCIPI PHIL. II HISP. APUD HOLL. ZEELQ. PRAETECTO P.P. QUOD SUPERATA PER DEI MISERICORDIAM, BARBARA TYRANNIDE, PATRIA LIBERATA, RELIGIONE CHRIST. SUPERSTITIONIB. REPURGATA, IURA PACEMQ. IUSTE TOTI BELGIO RESTITUERIT." The Dutch version (third state) indicates "Coninckliche machte" and the "Spaensche Inquisitie" as the left and right wings of "den Draek"; see Horst, *De Opstand in zwart en wit*, 238-41. Horst thinks the print was made on the occasion of the Pacification of Ghent in 1576.
**100** Horst, *De opstand in zwart en wit*, 115-20 and 323-24.

## Epilogue

**1** Pleij, *Het gilde van de Blauwe Schuit*; De Mooij, ed., *Vastenavond - Carnaval*, which contains, among other things, the essay by Herman Pleij. On children's games, see Snow, *Inside Bruegel*, 1997.
**2** See, for example, "Hybrid human-animal embryo research approved in the UK," *Science Daily*, January 18, 2008.
**3** See, for example, the campaigns of the World Wildlife Foundation against genetic manipulations using manipulated images of "fish people." For a harrowing literary vision of the future in which species are mingled due to climactic change and epidemics created by human agency, see Margaret Atwood, *The Year of the Flood* (2008).
**4** Vandenbroeck, "Rudolf II als verzamelaar van werk van en naar Jheronimus Bosch," 126-33.
**5** *Ibidem*, 119-26.
**6** Van Mander, *Het Schilder-Boeck*, fol. 233v: "Twaer qualijck te verhalen wat hy al ghemaeckt heeft, van tooverijen, Hellen, boerige geschiednissen, en anders... Oock een dulle Griet, die een roof voor de Helle doet, die seer verbijstert siet, en vreemt op zijn schots toeghemaeckt is: *ick acht dees en ander stucken oock in s'Keysers Hof zijn.*"
**7** Kaufmann, *The Mastery of Nature*, 174-94.
**8** Briels, "Amator Pictoriae Artis," 207 and 206; Allaert, "Pieter Brueghel le Jeune a-t-il pu voir les tableaux de son père?," doc. 16
**9** *De Firma Bruegel*, 2001.
**10** The panel painting of an *Apocalyptic Vision* signed ' IS' and dated 1595 (Venice, Palazzo Ducale, inv. 269) may bear witness to Bruegel's painting. It depicts Saint Michael fighting a Boschian sinful world and a semicircle of light that recalls the Empyrian as painted by Bruegel. The atmosphere is much grimmer than the *Fall*, however, and there is no reference to the culture of collecting. See Cecchi e.a. (eds.) *La Renaissance et le rêve*, cat. 60.

# Bibliography


*Abrahami Ortelii (geographi Antverpiensis) et virorum eruditorum ad eundem et ad Jacobum Colium Ortelianum (Abrahami Ortelii sororis filium) epistulae, cum aliquot aliis epistulis et tractatibus quibusdam ab utroque collectis (1524-1628)*, ed. Joannes Henricus Hessels (Cambridge, 1887, reprint Osnabrück, 1969).

Alessandrini, Alessandro and Alessandro Ceregato. *Natura Picta. Ulisse Aldrovandi* (Bologna: Editrice Compositori, 2007).

Allaert, Dominique. "Sur la piste de Bruegel en Italie: les pièces de l'enquête," *Fiamminghi a Roma 1508-1608*. Atti del Convegno Internazionale, Bruxelles 24-15 febbraio 1995 a cura di Nicole Dacos, *Bolletino d'arte*, supplemento al no. 100 (1997), 93-106.

---. "Pieter Brueghel le Jeune a-t-il pu voir les tableaux de son père? Réflexions méthodologiques et critiques," in Van den Brink, *De Firma Brueghel*, 46-57.

Arnade, Peter. *Beggars, Iconoclasts, & Civic Patriots. The Political Culture of the Dutch Revolt* (Ithaca and London: Cornell University Press), 2008.

Bakker, Boudewijn. "Au vif - naer't leven - ad vivum: The Medieval Origin of a Humanist Concept," in *Aemulatio: Imitation, Emulation and Invention in Netherlandish Art from 1500 to 1800: Essays in Honor of Eric Jan Slujter*, ed. Anton W.A. Boschloo et al. (Zwolle: Waanders, 2011), 37-52.

Banz, Claudia. *Höfisches Mäzenatentum in Brüssel. Kardinal Antoine Perrenot de Granvelle (1517-1586) und die Erzherzöge Albrecht (1559-1621) und Isabella (1566-1633)*, (Berlin: Gebr. Mann Verlag, 2000).

---. "Zwischen Repräsentation und Humanismus - zu Funktion und Anspruch von Granvelles Mäzenatum," in De Jonge/Janssens, *Les Granvelle et les Anciens Pays-Bas*, 389-409.

Bauer, Rotraud, and Jan-Karel Steppe. *Tapisserien der Renaissance nach Entwürfen von Pieter Coecke van Aelst*. Ausstellung im Schloss Halbturn 15. Mai bis 26. Oktober 1981 (Eisenstadt: Amt der Burgenländischen Landesregierung, 1981).

Bauer, Rotraud. "Gartenlandschaften mit Tieren. Zur Tapisseriensierie der sogennanten Granvellagärden in Wien," in *Gärten und Höfe der Rubenszeit im Spiegel der Malerfamilie Brueghel under der Künstler um Peter Paul Rubens*, ed. Ursula Härtung (Munich, Hirmer Verlag, 2001), 151-161.

Bax, Dirk. *Ontcijfering van Jeroen Bosch* ('s Gravenhage: Martinus Nijhoff, 1949).

Belon, Pierre. *Observations des plusieurs singularités et choses mémorables, trouvées en Grèce, Asie, Iudée, Egypte, Arabie, & autres pas estranges* (Antwerp: Plantin, 1555).

Belting, Hans. *Hieronymus Bosch. Garden of Earthly Delights* (Munich, Berlin, London, New York: Prestel, 2002).

Bennett, Jim. "The Mechanical Arts," in *The Cambridge History of Science. III: Early Modern Science*, eds. Katherine Park and Lorraine Daston (Cambridge: Cambridge University Press, 2006), 673-695.

Bergvelt, Elinoor; D.J. Meijers and M. Rijnders (eds.). *Verzamelen: Van rariteitenkabinet tot kunstmuseum* (Houten: Open Univeristeit, 1993).

Bertini, Giuseppe. *Le Nozze di Alessandro Farnese. Feste alle corti di Lisbona e Bruxelles* (Milan: Skira, 1997).

Besler, Basilius. *Fasciculus rariorum et aspectu dignorum varii generis quae collegit et suis impensis ad vivum incidi* (Nuremberg: Peter Isselburg, 1616).

Białostocki, Jan. "The Renaissance concept of Nature and Antiquity," *Studies in Western Art. II: Renaissance and Mannerism* (Princeton: Princeton University Press 1963), 19-30.

Blair, Ann. *The Theatre of Nature. Jean Bodin and Renaissance Science* (Princeton: Princeton University Press, 1997).

Bleichmar, Daniela, and Peter C. Mancall (eds.), *Collecting across Cultures: Material Exchanges in the Early Modern Atlantic World* (Philadelphia: University of Pennsylvania Press, 2011).

Blübaum, Dirk and Regina Erbentraut (eds.), *Die Erschaffung der Tiere. Tiere in der niederländischen Kunst des Manierismus und Frühbarock und an den wandfesten Dekorationen des Schlosses zu Güstrow* (Schwerin: Kunstsammlungen, Schlösser und Gärten, Staatlichen Museum Schwerin, 2010).

Boon, Karel G. *Netherlandish Drawings of the Fifteenth and Sixteenth Centuries* (The Hague: Government Publishing Office, 1978).

Borchert, Till-Holger (ed.). *Rondom Durer/ Dürer and his Time. German Prints and Drawings c. 1420-1575 from the Collection of Museum Boijmans Van Beuningen* (Maastricht: Bonnenfantenmuseum and Ghent: Snoeck-Ducajou & zoon, 2000).

Bossuyt, Ignace. "'O Socii Durate': Antoine Perrenot de Granvelle en de Vlaamse Polyfonist Adriaan Willaert (1460-1562). Nieuwe gegevens op basis van de in Madrid bewaarde correspondentie van Granvelle," in De Jonge/Janssens, *Les Granvelle et les Anciens Pays-Bas*, 321-240.

Braun, Georg en Frans Hogenberg, *Civitates orbis terrarum* (Cologne: Peter von Brachel, 1572–1618).

Bredekamp, Horst. *The Lure of Antiquity and the Cult of the Machine. The Kunstkammer and the Evolution of Nature, Art and Technology* (Princeton: Markus Wiener Publishers, 1995).

---. "Grillengänge von Michelangelo bis Goethe," *Marburger Jahrbuch für Kunstwissenschaft*, 22 (1989), 169-180.

Briels, Jan. "Amator Pictoriae Artis. De Antwerpse kunstverzamelaar Peeter Stevens (1590-1668) en zijn Constkamer," *Jaarboek Koninklijk Museum voor Schone Kunsten Antwerpen* (1980), 137-226.

---. *Vlaamse schilders en de dagenraad van Hollands Gouden Eeuw 1585-1630* (Antwerp: Mercatorfonds, 1997).

Brosens, Koenraad; Leen Kelchtermans, and Katelijne Van der Stichelen (eds.). *Family Ties. Art Production and Kinship*

*Patterns in the Early Modern Low Countries* (Turnhout: Brepols 2012).

Brout, Nicolette. "Le traité muséographique de Quiccheberg," in *RTBF 50 ans. L'extraordinaire jardin de la mémoire*, exh. cat. Musée Royal de Mariemont (Morlanwelz: Musée Royal de Mariemont, 2004), 68-135.

---. "Le catalogue comme microcosme entre musée et rhétorique. Les inscriptions de Samuel Quiccheberg," in *Mais raconte-moi en détail*, Odyssée, III, 97. Mélanges de philosophie et de philologie offerts à Lambros Couloubaritsis, eds. M. Broze, B. Decharneux et S. Delcominette (Paris-Brussels: Ousia-Vrin, 2008), 637-649.

Buchanan, Ian. "Dürer and Abraham Ortelius," *The Burlington Magazine*, 124 (December 1982), 732-741.

---. "The collection of Niclaes Jonghelinck: I 'Bacchus and the Planets' by Jacques Jonghelinck, *The Burlington Magazine*, 132 (February 1990), 102-113.

---. "The collection of Niclaes Jonghelinck: II The 'Months' by Pieter Bruegel the Elder," *The Burlington Magazine*, 132 (February 1990), 541-550.

---. "The Tapestries Acquired by King Philip II in the Netherlands in 1549-50 and 1555-59: New Documents," *Gazette des Beaux-Arts*, 6, 134 (October 1999), 131-52.

Bücken, Véronique and Griet Steyaert. *De Erfenis van Rogier van der Weyden. De schilderkunst in Brussel 1540-1520*, exh. cat. Brussels, Royal Museums of Fine Arts of Belgium (Tielt: Lannoo, 2013).

Budde, Hendrik. "Das "Kunstbuch des Nürnberger Patrizier Willibald Imhoff und die Tier-und Pflandstudien Albrecht Dürers und Hans Hoffmans," in *Albrecht Dürer und die Tier- und Pflanzenstudien der Renaissance*. Symposium. Die Beiträge der von der Graphischen Sammlung Albertina vom 7. bis 10 Juni 1985 veranstalteten Tagung, ed. F. Koreny, *Jahrbuch der Kunsthistorischen Sammlungen in Wien*,82/83 (neue Folge Band XVVI/XLVII) (1986/87), 213-241.

Burke, Peter. "Antwerp, a Metropolis in Europe," in Van der Stock, *Antwerp*, 49-57.

Büttner, Nils. "De verzamelaar Abraham Ortelius," *Abraham Ortelius (1527-1598) cartograaf en humanist*, exh. cat. Museum Plantin-Moretus (Turnhout: Brepols, 1998), 169-180.

---. *Die Erfindung der Landschaft. Kosmographie und Landschaftskunst im Zeitalter Bruegels* (Göttingen, Vandenhoeck &Ruprecht, 2000).

---. "Quid siculas sequeris per mille pericula terras? Ein Beitrag zur Biographie Pieter Bruegels d. Ä und zur Kulturgeschichte der niederländischen Italienreise, *Marburger Jahrbuch für Kunstwissenschaft* 27 (2000), 209-242.

Campbell, Lorne and Jan Van der Stock. *Rogier van der Weyden 1400-1464. Master of Passions*, exh. cat. Leuven, Museum M, 2013 (Leuven: Davidsfonds, 2009).

Campbell, Thomas P. *Tapestry in the Renaissance: Art and Magnificence*, exh. cat. New York, Metropolitan Museum of Art (New Haven and London: Yale University Press, 2002).

Castan, Auguste. *Monographie du Palais Granvelle à Besançon* (Paris: Imprimerie impériale, 1867).

Céard, Jean. "Encyclopédie et encyclopédisme à la Renaissance," in Annie Becq (ed.). *Encyclopédisme*. Actes du colloque international de Caen 1987 (Paris: Klincksieck, 1991), 57-67.

Cecchi, Alessandro, Yves Hersant, and Chiara Rabbi Bernard. *La Renaissance et le rêve. Bosch, Véronèse, Greco*, exh. cat. Paris, Musée du Luxembourg, 2013 (Paris: Réunion des musées nationaux, 2013).

Cervantes, Fernando. "Angels conquering and conquered: changing perceptions in Spanish America," in Marshall/Walsham (ed.). *Angels in the Early Modern World* (Cambridge: Cambridge University Press, 2006), 104-33.

Checa Cremades, Fernando (dir.), *Los Inventarios de Carlos V y la familia imperial/The Inventories of Charles V and the Imperial Family* (Madrid: Fernando Villaverde Editiones, 2010).

Clusius, Carolus. *Exoticorum Libri decem* (Leiden: Officina Plantiniana Raphelengii, 1605).

Colie, Rosalie L. *Paradoxia Epidemica. The Renaissance Tradition of Paradox* (Princeton: Princeton University Press, 1966).

Cook, Harold J. *Matters of Exchange. Commerce, Medicine, and Science in the Dutch Golden Age* (New Haven and London: Yale University Press, 2007).

Currie, Christina. "De ontsluiering van een werkproces: de Volkstelling te Bethlehem van Pieter Brueghel de Jonge, in Van den Brink, *De Firma Brueghel*, 81-124.

Currie, Christina and Dominique Allaert. *The Brueg(H)el Phenomenon. Paintings by Pieter Bruegel the Elder and Pieter Brueghel the Younger. With a special Focus on Painting technique and Copying Practice* (Brussels: Royal Institute for Cultural Heritage, 2012).

Dackerman, Susan (ed.). *Prints and the Pursuit of Knowledge in Early Modern Europe*, exh. cat. Harvard Art Museums, Cambridge, MA (New Haven and London: Yale University Press, 2011).

Daston, Lorraine and Katharine Park. *Wonders and the Order of Nature* 1150-1750 (New York: Zone Books, 2001).

De Asuá Miguel and Roger French. *A New World of Animals. Early Modern Europeans on the Creatures of Iberian America* (Aldershot: Ashgate, 2005).

De Baere, Cyriel. "De Brusselse Refereynen en Liedekens van 1562," *Koninklijke Vlaamse Academie voor Taal- en Letterkunde Verslagen en Mededelingen* (1948), 119-55.

De Guevara, Don Filipe. *Comentarios de la Pintura* (Madrid, 1788).

De Hond, Jan (ed.). *Monsters & Fabeldieren. 2500 jaar geschiedenis van randgevallen* (Amsterdam: Ludium and s'Hertogenbosch: Noordbrabants Museum, 2004).

De Jong, Jan and Dulcia Meijers e.a. (eds.). *Virtus. Virtuositeit en kunstliefhebbers in de Nederlanden 1500-1700*, Nederlands Kunsthistorisch Jaarboek, 54 (2003).

De Jonge, Krista. "De tuinen van kardinaal Granvelle in Brussel en Sint-Joost-ten-Node. Kanttekening bij zijn briefwisseling," *Tijdschrift van Dexia Bank*, 218, 4 (2001), 69-77.

---. "Le Palais Granvelle à Bruxelles: premier exemple de la Renaissance Romaine dans les anciens Pays-Bas," in De Jonge/Janssens, *Les Granvelle et les Anciens Pays-Bas*, 341-387.

---. "The Court Architect as Artist in the Southern Low Countries 1520-1560," in *Envisioning the Artist in the Early Modern Netherlands*, eds. H. Perry Chapman and Joanna Woodall, Nederlands Kunsthistorisch Jaarboek 59 (2010), 110-135.

De Jonge, Krista and Gustaaf Janssens (eds.). *Les Granvelle et les Anciens Pays-Bas. Liber doctori Mauricio Van Durme dedicans* (Leuven: Universitaire Pers, 2000).

Del Campo, Alvaro Soler. *Real Armería Palacio Real* (Madrid, Patrimonio Nacional, 2000).

Del Monte, Alvaro Soler, *Real Armería del Palacio Real* (Madrid: Patrimonio Nacional, 2000).

De Ligne, Chloé. *Brussel Boven Water. De relatie van de stad met haar waterlopen van de Middeleeuwen tot vandaag* (Brussels: Historia Bruxellae, 7, 2005).

De Mooij, C. (ed.). *Vastenavond - Carnaval. Feesten van de omgekeerde wereld* (Zwolle: Waanders, 1992).

De Siguença, Fray José. *Tercera parte de la Historia de la Orden de S. Geronimo* (Madrid, 1605).

De Tolnay, Charles. *Hieronymus Bosch* (Basel: Les Éditions Holbein, 1937).

---. *Pierre Bruegel l'ancien* (Brussels: Nouvelle société d'éditions, 1935).

Dhaenens, Elisabeth. *Hubert en Jan Van Eyck* (Antwerp: Mercatorfonds, 1980).

Diels, Ann and Marjolein Leesberg. *The Collaert Dynasty*, The New Hollstein. Dutch and Flemish Etching, Engravings and Woodcuts 1450-1700, ed. Ger Luijten en Arnout Balis, 8 vols. (Ouderkerk and Ijssel: Sound and Vision Publishers, 2005-2006).

Dinard, Simon-Pierre. "La collection du cardinal Antoine de Granvelle (1517-1586). L'inventaire du palais Granvelle de 1607," in *Les Cardinaux de la Renaissance et la modernité artistique*, Villeneuve d'Ascq, eds. Frédérique Lemerle, Yves Pauwels et Gennaro Toscano, IRHiS-Institut de Recherches Historiques du Septentrion, Histoire et littérature de l'Europe du Nord-Ouest, 40 (2009), 157-168 [Online: http://hleno.revues.org/229].

Dittrich, Sigrid and Lothar. *Lexikon der Tiersymbole. Tiere als Sinnbilder in der Malerei des 14-17. Jahrhunderts* (Petersberg: Michael Imhof Verlag, 2004).

Dixon, Lauren S. "Bosch' Garden of Delights Tryptich: Remnants of a "Fossil" Science," *The Art Bulletin*, 63, 1 (1981), 98-113.

Dolfi, Pompeo Scipione. *Cronologia delle famiglie nobili di Bologna. Con le loro insigne, e nel fine i Cimieri. Centuria prima. Con un breve discorso della medesima città* (Bologna: Gio. Battista Ferroni, 1670).

Dreyer, Peter. "Zeichnungen von Hans Verhagen dem Stummen von Antwerpen. Ein Beitrag zu den Vorlagen der Tierminiaturen Hans Bols und Georg Hoefnagels,' in *Albrecht Dürer und die Tier- und Pflanzenstudien der Renaissance*. Symposium. Die Beiträge der von der Graphischen Sammlung Albertina vom 7. bis 10 Juni 1985 veranstalteten Tagung, ed. F. Koreny, *Jahrbuch der Kunsthistorischen Sammlungen in Wien*, 82/83 (neue Folge Band XVVI/XLVII) (1986/87), 115-144.

Dupré, Sven. "Trading Luxury Glass, Picturing Collections and Consuming Objects of Knowledge in Early Seventeenth-Century Europe," *Intellectual History Review*, 20.1 (2010), 53-78.

Dürer, Albrecht. *1520-1521 Das Tagebuch der Niederländischen Reise*. Mit dem Silberstift-Skizzenbuch und den während der Reise Ausgeführten Bildern und Zeichnungen. Einleitung und Anmerkungen van J.-A. Goris und G. Marlier (Brussels: La Connaissance, 1970).

Egmond, Florike. "Clusius, Cluyt, Saint Omer. The Origins of the Sixteenth-Century Botanical and Zoological Watercolours in Libri Picturati A 16.30," *Nuncius*, XX (2005), 11-67.

---. "A Collection within a Collection. Rediscovered Animal Drawings from the Collection of Conrad Gessner and Felix Platter," *Journal of the History of Collections*, 25, 2 (2013), 149-170.

Egmond, Florike and Peter Mason. "Armadillos in Unlikely Places. Some Unpublished Sixteenth-Century Sources for New World Rezeptionsgeschichte in Northern Europe," *Ibero-Amerikanisches Archiv. Zeitschrift für Sozialwissenschaften und Geschichte*, 20, 1-2 (1994), 3-52.

Eichberger, Dagmar. "Naturalia and artefacta: Durer's nature drawings and early collecting," in *Dürer and His Culture*, ed. Dagmar Eichberger and Charles Zika (Cambridge: Cambridge University Press, 1998), 13-37.

---. *Leben mit Kunst. Wirken durch Kunst. Sammelwesen und Hofkunst undter Margarete von Osterreich, Regentin der Niederlande* (Turnhout: Brepols, 2002).

Ertz, Klaus, and Christa Nitze-Ertz. *Jan Brueghel der Ältere(1568-1625): Kritischer Katalog der Gemälde* (Lingen: Luca Verlag, 2008-2010).

Falkenburg, Reindert L. "Pieter Bruegel's *Series of the Seasons*: on the perception of divine order," in *Liber Amicorum Raphael De Smedt*, ed. Joost Vander Auwera et al. (Leuven: Peeters, 2001), II, 253-275.

---. "The Devil is in the Detail', in Vergara, Alejandro (ed.). *Patinir: Essays and Critical Catalogue* (Madrid: Museo Nacional del Prado, 2007), 64-79.

---. "Black Holes in Bosch: Visual Typology in the Garden of Earthly Delights," in *Image and Imagination of the Religious Self in Late Medieval and Early Modern Europe*, eds. Reindert Falkenburg, Walter S. Melion and Todd M. Richardson (Turnhout: Brepols, 2007), 105-132.

---. *The Land of Unlikeness: Hieronymus Bosch, The Garden of Earthly Delights* ([s.l.]: WBooks, 2011).

Filipczak, Zirka Zaremba. *Picturing Art in Antwerp: 1500-1700* (Princeton: Princeton University Press, 1987).

Findlen, Paula. *Possessing Nature: Museums, Collecting, and Scientific Culture in Early Modern Italy* (Berkeley, et al.: University of California Press, 1996).

---. "Jokes of Nature and Jokes of Knowledge: the Playfulness of Scientific Discourse in early Modern Europe," *Renaissance Quarterly*, 43/2, 1990, 292-331.

---. "Commerce, Art, and Science in the Early Modern Cabinet of Curiosities," Smith/Findlen, *Merchants & Marvels*, 297-323.

Freedberg, David. "Allusion and Topicality in the Work of Pieter Bruegel: The Implications of a Forgotten Polemic," *The Prints of Pieter Bruegel the Elder*, ed. David Freedberg (Tokyo: s.l., 1989), 53-65.

Galand, Alexandre, with a contribution by John Hand and Carole Christensen. *Bernard van Orley Group*, The Flemish Primitives. Catalogue of Early Netherlandish painting in the Royal Museums of Fine Arts of Belgium, VI (Turnhout: Brepols, 2013).

Ganz, Ulrike Dorothea. *Neugier und Sammelbild. Rezeptionsästetische Studien zu gemalten Sammlungen in der Niederlandischen Malerie ca 1550-1650* (Weimar: VDG, 2006).

Gasparri, Carlo (ed.). *La collezione Farnese*. Museo Archeologico Nazionale di Napoli (Verona: Electa), 2009.

Gauthier, Jules. "Le Cardinal de Granvelle et les artistes de son temps," *Mémoires de la Société d'émulation du Doubs*, VI, Série VII (1901), 305-351.

Geertz, Clifford. *The Interpretation of Cultures* (New York: Basic Books, 1973).

---. "Art as a Cultural System," *Modern Language Notes*, 91, 6 (1976), 1473-1499.

Geevers, Liesbeth. "Family matters: William of Orange and the Habsburgs after the Abdication of Charles V (1555-67)," *Renaissance Quarterly*, 63, 2 (Summer 2010), 459-90.

--- . *Gevallen vazallen. De integratie van Oranje, Egmont en Horn in de Spaans-Habsburgse monarchie (1559-1567)* (Amsterdam: Amsterdam University Press, 2008).

Gessner, Conrad. *Historia animalium libri I-IV*. Cum iconibus (Zurich: C. Froschauer, 1551-1558).

---. *Icones animalium quadrupedum viviparorum et oviparorum, quae in historiae animalium Conradi Gesneri libro I. et II. describuntur*, editio secunda auctior (Zurich: C. Froschauer, 1560).

---. *Nomenclator aquatilium animantium. Icones animalium in mari & dulcibus aquis degentium* (Zürich: C. Froschauer 1560).

Ghadessi, Touba. "Inventoried monsters. Dwarves and Hirsutes at court," *Journal of the History of Collections*, 23, 2 (2011), 267-281.

Gibson, Walter S. *Pieter Bruegel* (London: Thames and Hudson Ltd., 1977).

---. "Bruegel, Dulle Griet, and Sexist Politics in the sixteenth century," *Pieter Bruegel und seine Welt*, eds. Otto von Simson and Matthias Winner (Berlin: Gebr. Mann Verlag, 1979), 9-15.

---. "Artists and Rederijkers in the Age of Bruegel," *The Art Bulletin*, 63/3 (1981), 426-446.

---. *Pieter Bruegel the Elder: Two studies*. The Franklin D. Murphy Lectures, XI, Spencer Museum of Art. The University of Kansas (Lawrence, Kansas, 1991).

---. *The Art of Laughter in the Age of Bosch and Bruegel*, The Twelfth Gerson Lecture held in memory of Horst Gerson (1907-1978) (Groningen: The Gerson Lectures Foundation, 2003).

Ginzberg, Carlo. "Microhistory: Two or Three Things that I know about It," *Critical Inquiry*, 20 (Autumn 1993), 10-35.

Goltzius, Hubertus. *J. Julius Caesar* (Bruges: Hubertus Goltz, 1563).

Goossens, A. (ed.). *Restauration de la tour principale de l'Hotel de Ville.*, rapport no. 3, Etude Historique, City Archives, Brussels (september 1990).

Gorgas, Michael. "Animal trade between India and Western Eurasia in the Sixteenth Century-The Role of the Fuggers in Animal Trading" in *Indo-Portuguese Trade and the Fuggers of the Sixteenth Century*, ed. K.S. Matthew (New Delhi: Manohar Pubns, 1997), 195-225.

Göttler, Christine. "Fire, Smoke and Vapour. Jan Brueghel's 'Poetic Hells': 'Ghespoock' in Early Modern European Art," in *Spirits Unseen: The Representation of Subtle Bodies in Early Modern European Culture*, eds. Christine Göttler and Wolfgang Neuber, *Intersections*, vol. 9 (Leiden: Brill, 2007), 19-46.

---. "'Bootsicheyt': Malerei, Mythologie und Alchemie im Antwerpen des frühen 17. Jahrhunderts: Zu Rubens' Silen in der Akademie der Bildenden Künste in Wien," in *Erosionen der Rhetorik? Strategien der Ambiguität in den Künsten der Frühen Neuzeit*, ed. Valeska von Rosen, *Culturae*, 4 (Wiesbaden: Harassowitz Verlag, 2012), 259-301.

Göttler, Christine and Tine Meganck. "Sites of Art, Nature and the Antique in the Spanish Netherlands," in *Embattled Territory. The Circulation of Knowledge in the Spanish Netherlands*, Sven Dupré, Bert De Munck e.a., (Ghent: Academia Press, forthcoming).

Grafton, Anthony with April Shelford and Nancy Siraisi, *New Worlds, Ancient Texts. The Power of Tradition and the Shock of Discovery* (Cambridge, MA and London: Harvard University Press, 2000).

Groenveld, Simon and H.L.Ph. Van Leeuwenbergh e.a. (eds.), *De Tachtigjarige Oorlog. Opstand en consolidatie in de Nederlanden (ca. 1560-1650)* (Zutphen: Walburg pers, 2008).

Grossmann, Fritz. *Pieter Bruegel, Complete Edition of the Paintings* (London: Phaidon Press, 1955).

Gouk, Penelope. *The Ivory Sundials of Nuremberg 1500-1700* (Cambridge: Whipple Museum of the History of Science, 1988).

Guicciardini, Lodovico. *Descrittione di tutti i Paesi Bassi, altrimenti detti Germania inferiore* (Antwerp: Guglielmo Silvio, 1567).

Haag, Sabine and Franz Kirschweger. *Habsburg Treasures at the Kunsthistorisches Museum, Vienna* (London: Thames and Hudson, 2013).

Hamilton, Alistair. *Arabische cultuur en Ottomaanse pracht in Antwerpens Gouden Eeuw* (Antwerp: Plantijn Moretus Museum, 2001).

Harris, Jason. "The religious position of Abraham Ortelius," in *The Low Countries at the Crossroads of Religious Belief*, eds. Arie-Jan Gelderblom, Jan L. de Jong and Marc Van Vaeck, *Intersections*, vol. 3 (Leiden: Brill, 2004), 89-139.

Heere, Lucas D'. *Hof en Boomgaerd der Poesien* (Ghent: Matthys de Casteleyn, 1565).

---. *Hof en Boomgaerd der Poësien*, ed. Walter Waterschoot (Zwolle: Tjeenk Willinck, 1969).

Hendrix, Marjorie Lee. *Joris Hoefnagel and the Four Elements. A Study in Sixteenth Century Nature Painting* (Princeton, PhD Dissertation Princeton University, 1983).

---. "Of Hirsutes and Insects: Joris Hoefnagel and the Art of the Wondrous," *Word and /Image* 11 (October-December, 1995), 373-90.

Hendrix, Marjorie Lee and Thea Vignau-Wilberg. *Mira calligraphiae monument. A Sixteenth-Century Calligraphic Manuscript inscribed by Georg Bocsay and illuminated*

*by Joris Hoefnagel* (Los Angeles: CA: The J. Paul Getty Museum, 1997).
Heninger, S.k. jr. *The Cosmographical Glass: Renaissance Diagrams of the Universe* (Oakland, CA, University of California Press, 2005).
Hess, Daniel and Thomas Eser (eds.), *Der Frühe Dürer*, exh. cat. Germanischen Nationalmuseum (Nuremberg: Verlag der Germanischen Nationalmuseums, 2012).
Heuer, Christopher P. *The City Rehearsed: Object, Architecture, and Print in the Worlds of Hans Vredeman de Vries* (London and New York: Routledge, 2009).
Heymans, Vincent, Laetitia Cnockaert and Frédérique Honoré, (eds.). *Le palais du Coudenberg à Bruxelles. Du château médiéval au site archéologique* (Brussels: Mardaga, 2014).
Honig, Elizabeth Alice. *Painting and the Market in Early Modern Antwerp* (New Haven: Yale University Press, 1998).
Horst, Daniel R. *De Opstand in zwart-wit. Propagandaprenten uit de Nederlandse Opstand 1566-1584* (Zutphen: Walburg Pers, 2003).
Howard, Deborah. "Cultural transfer between Venice and the Ottomans in the Fifteenth and Sixteenth Centuries," in *Cultural Exchange in Early Modern Europe*, volume 4: *Forging European identities*, ed. Herman Roodenburg (Cambridge: Cambridge University Press, 2007), 138-177.
Ilsink, Matthijs. *Bosch en Bruegel als Bosch; kunst over kunst bij Pieter Bruegel (c. 1528-1569) en Jheronimus Bosch (c. 1450-1516)* (Nijmegen: Uitgeverij Orange House, 2009).
Impey, Oliver and MacGregor Arthur (eds.). *The Origins of Museums: The Cabinet of Curiosities in Sixteenth and Seventeenth-Century Europe* (Oxford: Clarendon Press, 1985).
Jacobs, Roel. *Een geschiedenis van Brussel* (Tielt: Lannoo, 2004).
Jansen, Dirk J. "Samuel Quicchebergs 'Inscriptiones': de encyclopedische verzameling als hulpmiddel voor de wetenschap, in. Bergvelt/Meijers/Rijnders, *Verzamelen*, 57-76.
Jeanneret, *Perpetual Motion. Transforming Shapes in the Renaissance from da Vinci to Montaigne*, transl. Nidra Poller (Baltimore and London: The John Hopkins University Press, 2001).
Jonckheere, Koenraad, in collaboration with Gijs Key. *Willem Key (1516-1568). Portrait of a Humanist Painter* (Turnhout: Brepols, 2011).
Jorink, Erik. *Het 'Boeck der Natuere.' Nederlandse geleerden en de wonderen van Gods schepping 1575-1715* (Leiden: Primavera Pers, 2006).
Kaschek, Bertram. *Weltzeit und Endzeit. Die "Monatsbilder" Pieter Bruegels d. Ä.* (Munich: Wilhelm Fink Verlag, 2012).
Kaufmann, Thomas DaCosta. *The School of Prague. Painting at the Court of Rudolf II* (Chicago: Chicago University Press, 1988).
---. "From Treasury to Museum," in *The Cultures of Collecting*, eds. John Elsner and Roger Cardinal (London: Reaktion Books Ltd, 1994), 137-154.
---. *The Mastery of Nature, Aspects of Art, Science and Humanism in the Renaissance* (Princeton: Princeton University Press, 1993).
---. *Arcimboldo. Visual Jokes, Natural History and Stil-Life Painting* (Chicago: Chicago University Press), 2010.
Kavaler, Ethan Matt. "Pictorial Satire, Ironic Inversion, and Ideological Conflict," in Meadow e.a. *Pieter Bruegel*, Nederlands Kunsthistorisch Jaarboek 47 (1997), 155-179.
---. Pieter Bruegel. *Parables of Order and Enterprise* (Cambridge: Cambridge University Press, 1999).
Kemp, Martin. "From 'mimesis' to 'fantasia'. The Quattrocento Vocabulary of Creation, Inspiration and Genius in the Visual Arts," *Viator* 8 (1977), 347-98.
---. "Taking it on Trust: Form and Meaning in Naturalistic Representation," *Archives of Natural History*, 17, 2 (June 1990), 127-188.
---. '"Wrought by no artist's hand." The Natural, the Artificial, the Exotic and the Scientific in some Artifacts from the Renaissance," in *Reframing the Renaissance. Visual Culture in Europe and Latin America 1450-1650*, ed. Claire Farrago (New Haven: Yale University Press, 1995), 177-196.
Kessler, Erwin. "Le jardin des délices et les fruits du mal, " *Cahier du Léopard d'or*, 6 (1997), 177-198.
King, Catherine. "Artists's houses: mass-advertising artistic status and theory in Antwerp c. 1565," in *Théorie des Arts et Création Artistique dans l'Europe du Nord du XVI^e au début du XVIII^e siècle*, eds. Michèle-Caroline Heck, Frédérique Lemerle and Yves Pauwels (Villeneuve d'Ascq: Université Charles-de-Gaulle Lille 3. Centre de Gestion de l'Edition Scientifique 2002), 173-189.
Knipping, John B. *Pieter Bruegel de Oude. De val der opstandige engelen* (Paneel en doek, 1, 4) (Leiden, Uitgave L. Stafleu, 1949).
Koenigsberger, Helmut G. "Orange, Granvelle and Philips II," *Bijdragen en mededelingen betreffende de geschiedenis der Nederlanden*, 99, 4 (1984), 573-95.
Koerner, Joseph Leo. "Hieronymus Bosch's World Picture," in *Picturing Science, Producing Art*, eds. C. A. Jones and P. Galison (New York and London: Routledge, 1998), 297-323.
---. "Unmasking the World. Bruegel's Ethnography," *Common Knowledge*, 10, 2 (2004), 221-251.
Koschatzky, *Duerer Zeichnungen. Die geschichte der Dürersammlung der Albertina* (Salzburg and Vienna: Residenz Verlag, 1985).
Kurz, Otto. "Four tapestries after Hieronymus Bosch," *Journal of the Warburg and Courtauld Institutes*, 30 (1967), 150-162.
Kusukawa, Sachiko. "The Sources of Gessner's Pictures for the *Historia animalium*," *Annals of Science*, 67 (2012), 303-328.
Lampsonius, Dominicus. *Pictorum aliquot Celebrium Germaniae Inferioris Effigies* (Antwerp: apud viduam Hieronymi Cock, 1572).
Lapeyre, Henri. *Charles Quint* (Paris: Presse Universitaire de France, 1971).
Lauterbach, Christiane. "Plagegeister. Fliegen in der christlichen Kunst um 1500," in *Vom Ansehen der Tiere.* Kulturgeschichtliche Spaziergänge im Germanischen Nationalmuseum, Band 11 (Nuremberg, 2009), 47-57.
Le Loup, Willy (ed.). *Hubertus Goltzius en Brugge* 1583-1983, exh. cat. Bruges Gruuthusemuseum (Bruges: Stad Brugge, 1983).
Lestringant, Frank. *Sous la leçon des vents. Le monde d'André Thevet cosmographe de la Renaissance* (Paris: Presses de l'Université de Paris-Sorbonne, 2003).
Link, Luther. *The Devil. A Mask without a Face* (London: Reaktion Books Ltd, 1995).

Lowood, Henry. "The New World and the European Catalogue of Nature," in *America in European Consciousness 1493-1750*, ed. K.O. Kupperman (Chapel Hill and London: The University of North Carolina Press, 1995).

Luckhardt, Jochen. *Das "Küchenstück" von Ludger tom Ringe d. J. (1562). Kunst in Antwerpen zwischen Münster und Braunschweig* (Braunschweig: Herzog Anton Ulrich-Museum, 2013).

Lugli, Adalgisa. *Naturalia e Mirabilia. Il collezionismo enciclopedico nelle Wunderkammern d'Europa* (Milan: Gabriele Mazzotta, 1983).

Mareel, Samuel. *Voor Vorst en Stad. Rederijkersliteratuur in Vlaanderen en Brabant* (Amsterdam: Amsterdam University Press, 2010).

Marijnissen, Roger H. *Bruegel. Het volledige oeuvre* (Antwerp: Mercatorfonds, 1988).

---. *Ter aanvulling: De Bruegelstudie sinds 1988* (s.l..2003).

Marlier, Georges. *La Renaissance Flamande. Pierre Coeck d'Alost* (Brussels: Éditions Robert Finck, 1966).

Marnef, Guido. *Antwerpen in de tijd van de Reformatie. Ondergronds protestantisme in een handelsmetropool* (Amsterdam: Meulenhof/Antwerpen: Kritak, 1996).

Marr, Alexander. "The Flemish 'Pictures of Collections' Genre. An Overview," *Intellectual History Review*, 20/1 (2010), 5-25.

Martens, Mina; André Vanrie and Michel de Waha. *Sint Michiel en zijn symboliek* (Brussels: Editions d'Art Lucien De Meyer, 1979).

Martin, Pierre and Dominique Moncond'huy (eds.). *Curiosité et cabinets de curiosités* (Neuilly: Éditions Atlande, 2004).

Mason, Peter. *Before Disenchantment. Images of Exotic Animals and Plants in the Early Modern* World (London: Reaktion Books, 2009).

Mauriès, Patrick. *Cabinets of Curiosities* (London: Thames and Hudson, London).

McHam, Sarah Blake. *Pliny and the Artistic Culture of the Italian Renaissance. The Legacy of the "Natural History"* (New Haven: Yale University Press, 2013).

Meadow, Mark A. "*Bruegel's Procession to Calvary*: Aemulatio and the Space of Vernacular Style," in Meadow e.a. *Pieter Bruegel*, Nederlands Kunsthistorisch Jaarboek 47 (1996), 181-205.

---. *Pieter Bruegel the Elder's Netherlandish Proverbs and the Practice of Rhetoric* (Zwolle: Waanders, 2002).

---. "Merchants and Marvels. Hans Jacob Fugger and the Origins of the Wunderkammer," in Smith/Findlen, *Merchants & Marvels*, 182-200.

Meadow, Mark A. e.a. *Pieter Bruegel*, Nederlands Kunsthistorisch Jaarboek 47 (1996).

Meadow, Mark A. and Bruce Robertson (eds.). *The First Treatise on Museums. Samuel Quiccheberg's Inscriptiones, 1565*. Translation by Mark A. Meadow and Bruce Robertson. Introduction by Mark A. Meadow (Los Angeles: The Getty Research Institute, 2013).

Meganck, Tine L. "Abraham Ortelius, Hubertus Goltzius en Guido Laurinus en de studie van de Arx Britannica," *Koninklijke Nederlandse Oudheidkundige Bond Bulletin*, 98 (1999), 5/6, 226-236.

---. *Erudite Eyes: Artists and Antiquarians in the Circle of Abraham Ortelius* (1527-1598) (PhD Dissertation Princeton University, 2003).

---. "Chorography and Antiquity between the Low Countries and the British Isles, 1568-1606," in *Antiquarianism and Science in Early Modern Urban Networks*, ed. Vittoria Feola (Paris: Blanchard, 2014), 55-81.

Meijer, Bert W. *Parma e Bruxelles. Committenza e collezionismo farnesiani alle due corti* (Parma: Silvana Editoriale, 1988).

Meijering, Stefan. *Het hof van Nassau te Brussel. Een bouwgeschiedenis en reconstructie van een middeleeuws stadspaleis* (Masterscriptie UGent, 2009).

Melion, Walter. *Shaping the Netherlandish Canon. Karel van Mander's Schilder-Boeck* (Chicago and London: Chicago University Press, 1991).

Menzel, Gerhard W. *Pieter Bruegel der Ältere* (Leipzig: E.A. Seemann Verlag, 1966).

Miedema, Hessel. "*Kinship and Network in Karel van Mander,*" in Brosens/Kelchtermans/Van der Stighelen *Family Ties: On Art Production, Kinship Patterns and Connections, 1600-1800*, 11-19.

Milne, Louise S. *Carnivals and Dreams: Pieter Bruegel and the History of the Imagination* (London: Monochrome, 2011).

Monballieu, Adolf. "P. Bruegel en het altaar van de Mechelse Handschoenmakers (1551)," *Handelingen van de Koninklijke Kring voor Oudheidkunde, Letteren en Kunst van Mechelen*, 68 (1964), 92-110.

---. "Een werk van P. Bruegel en H. Vredeman de Vries voor tresorier Aert Molckeman," *Jaarboek van het Koninklijk Museum voor Schone kunsten* (1969), 113-135.

---. "De kunstenaarsfamilie Verhulst Bessemeers," *Handelingen van de Koninklijke Kring voor Oudheidkunde, Letteren en Kunst van Mechelen*, 78 (1974), 105-212.

---. "De 'hand als teken op het kleed' bij Bruegel en Baltens," *Jaarboek Koninklijk Museum voor Schone Kunsten Antwerpen* (1979), 197-209.

---. "De Twee aapjes van P. Bruegel of de Singerie (seigneurie) over de Schelde te Antwerpen in 1562," *Jaarboek Koninklijk Museum voor Schone Kunsten Antwerpen* (1983), 119-211.

Mori, Yoko. "The Prints of Pieter Bruegel the Elder as Pictorial Sources for his Paintings," in *The World of Bruegel in Black and White from the Collection of the Royal Library of Belgium*, exh. cat. Bunkamura Museum of Art; Niigata City Art Museum and Museum [Eki] Kyoto (Bunkamura: The Yomiuri Shimbun 2010), Essays, 6-22.

Mörke, Olaf. *Willem van Oranje (1533-1584). Vorst en 'vader' van de Republiek* (Amsterdam/Antwerp: Uitgeverij Atlas, 2010).

Müller, Jürgen, *Das Paradox als Bildform. Studien zur Ikonologie Pieter Bruegels d. A.* (Munich: Wilhelm Fink Verlag, 1999).

Müller-Hofstede, Justus. "Zur Interpretation von Bruegel's Landschaft. Ästhetischer Landschapftsbegriff und Stoische Weltbetrachtung," *Pieter Bruegel und seine Welt*, eds. Otto Von Simson and Matthias Winner, Matthias, (Berlin: Gebr. Mann Verlag: 1979), 73-142.

Muylle, Jan. "Pieter Bruegel en Abraham Ortelius: Bijdrage tot de literaire receptie van Pieter Bruegel's Werk," *Archivum Artis Lovaniense. Bijdragen tot de geschiedenis van de kunst de Nederlanden opgedragen aan Prof. Em. J. K. Steppe*, ed. Maurice Smeyers (Leuven: Peeters, 1981), 319-337.

---. '"Pier den Drol". Karel van Mander en Pieter Bruegel. Bijdragen tot de literaire receptie van Pieter Bruegel's werk ca. 1600,' in *Wort und Bild in der Niederländischen*

*Kunst und Literatur des 16. Und 17.* Jahrhundert, eds. Herman Vekeman, Justus Müller Hofstede (Erfstadt: Lukassen Verlag, 1984), 137-138.
---. *Genus gryllorum, gryllorum pictores: legetimatie, evaluatie en interpretatie van genre-iconografie en van de biografieën van genreschilders in de Nederlandsce kunstliteratuur (ca. 1550-ca1750)* (PhD Dissertation, KULeuven, 1986).
Niehr, Klaus, "'Ad vivum - al vif': Begriffs- und kunstgeschichtliche Anmerkungen zur Auseinandersetzung mit der Natur in Mittelalter und früher Neuzeit," in *Natur im Mittelalter: Konzeptionen - Erfahrungen - Wirkungen.* Akten des 9. Symposiums des Mediävistenverbandes, Marburg, 14-17 March 2001, ed. Peter Dilg (Berlin: Akademie Verlag 2003), 472-487.
Niekrasz, Carmen. *Woven Theatres of Nature: Flemish Tapestry and Natural History 1550-1600* (PhD Dissertation Northwestern University, 2007).
Oestereich, Gerhard. *Neostoicism and the Early Modern State* (Cambridge, Cambridge Universtiy Press, 2008).
Ogilvie, Brian W. *The Science of Describing. Natural History in Renaissance Europe* (Chicago and London: Chicago University Press, 2006).
Olmi, Giuseppe. *Ulisse Aldrovandi. Scienza e natura nel secondo Cinquecento* (Trento: Università di Trento, 1976).
---. "Il museo o 'microcosmo di natura'", in Alessandrini/ Ceregato, *Natura Picta*, 19-37.
---. *L'Inventario del Mondo. Catalogazione della natura e luoghi del sapere nella prima età moderna* (Bologna: Il Mulino, 1992).
Orenstein, Nadine and Sellink, Manfred (eds.), *Pieter Bruegel the Elder. Drawings and Prints*, exh. cat. Rotterdam, Museum Boijmans Van Beuningen and New York, The Metropolitan Museum of Art (New York and New Haven: Yale University Press, 2001).
Orrock, Amy. "Homo Ludens: Pieter Bruegel's Children's Games and the Humanist Educators," *Journal of the Historians of Netherlandish Art*, 4.2 (2012).
Ortelius, Abraham. *Album Amicorum*, ed. and transl. Jean Puraye, and Marie Delcourt (Amsterdam, Van Gendt, 1969).
Paredes, Cécilia; Sabine van Sprang and Jean-Philippe Huys, "La magnificence du prince," in Heymans/Cnockaert/ Honoré, *Le palais du Coudenberg*, 151-190.
Parker, Geoffrey. *The Dutch Revolt* (London: Penguin Classic History, 1977).
Parshall, Peter. "Imago Contrafacta: Images and Facts in the Renaissance," *Art History*, 16, 4 (1993), 554-579.
Parry, Glyn. *The Arch-Conjuror of England. John Dee* (New Haven: Yale University Press, 2011).
Pawlak, Anna. *Trilogie der Gottessuche. Pieter Bruegels d. Ä. Sturz der gefallenen Engel, Triumph des Todes und Dulle Griet* (Berlin: Gebr. Mann Verlag, 2008).
Perez de Tudela, Almudena and Annemarie Jordan Gschwend. "Luxury Goods for Royal Collectors: Exotica, Princely Gifts and Rare Animals Exchanged Between the Iberian Courts and Central Europe in the Renaissance (1560-1612), in *Exotica. Portugals Entdeckungen im Spiegel fürstlichen Kunst-und Wunderkammer der Renaissance.* Die Beiträge des am 19. und 20. Mai 2000 vom Kunsthistorischen Museum Wien veranstalteten Symposiums. Herausgegeben von Helmut Trnek und Sabine Haag, *Jahrbuch des Kunsthistorischen Museums Wien*, Band 3 (Mainz: Verlag Philipp von Zabern, 2001), 1-127.
---. "Renaissance menageries," in *Early Modern Zoology*, eds. Karel A.E. Enenkel and Paul. J. Smith, *Intersections*, 7 (2007), 419-445.
Petit, Jean-Luc. *Sint Michiel. De Brusselaar* (Brussels, Historia Bruxellae, 12, 2008).
Picquart, Maurice. "Le cardinal de Granvelle, amateur de tapisseries," *Revue belge d'archéologie et d'histoire de l'art*, 19, 3-4 (1950), 111-126.
---. "Le cardinal de Granvelle, les artistes et les écrivains," *Revue belge d'archéologie et d'histoire de l'art*, 17, 3-4 (1947/48), 133-147.
---. "Les livres du cardinal de Granvelle à la bibliothèque de Besançon. Les Reliures Italiennes," *Libri*, 1 (1951), 301-323.
Pigman III, G.W. "Versions of Imitation in the Renaissance,"*Renaissance Quarterly*, 33 (1980), 1-35.
Pignon, Laurent. "Conrad Gessner and the Historical Depth of Renaissance Natural History," in *Historia. Empiricism and Erudition in Early Modern Europe*, eds. Gianna Pomata and Nancy G. Siraisi, (Cambridge, MA and London: MIT Press, 2005), 241-267.
Pinson, Yona. "Fall of the Angels and Creation in Bosch' Eden: Meaning and Iconographical Sources," in *Flanders in a European Perspective. Manuscript illumination around 1400 in Flanders and abroad*, eds. Maurice Smeyers and Bert Cardon, Proceedings of the International Colloquium Leuven, 7-10 september 1993 (Corpus of Illuminated Manuscripts, VIII, Low Countries, 5) (Leuven, 1995), 693-701.
---. "Folly and Vanity in Bruegels Dulle Griet. Proverbial Metaphors and their relationship to Bosch' Imagery," *Studies in Iconography*, 20 (1999), 185-213.
Piot, Charles and Poullet, E. *Correspondence du Cardinal Granvelle* (1565-1586), I-XIII (Brussels, 1877-1896).
Pleij, Herman. *Het gilde van de Blauwe Schuit. Literatuur, volksfeest en burgermoraal in de late middeleeuwen* (Amsterdam: Meulenhoff, 1979).
---. *Anna Bijns van Antwerpen* (Amsterdam: Bert Bakker, 2011).
Popelier, Françoise. "Image des luttes religieuses dans la peintures des Anciens Pays-Bas," *Bulletin des Museés Royaux des Beaux-Arts de Belgique/Bulletin van de Koninklijke Musea voor Schone Kunsten van België* (1969), 3/4, 121-139.
Popham, Arthur Ewart. "Pieter Bruegel and Abraham Ortelius," *Burlington Magazine*, 59 (1931), 184-188.
Porras, Stephanie. "Producing the Vernacular: Antwerp, Cultural Archaeology and the Bruegelian Peasant," *Journal of the Historians of Netherlandish Art* 3.1 (2011).
---. "Rural Memory, Pagan Idolatry: Pieter Bruegel's Peasant Shrines," *Art History*, 34.3 (June 2011), 486-509.
Postma, Folkert. "Granvelle, Viglius en de Adel (1555-1567)," in De Jonge/Janssens, *Les Granvelles et les Anciens Pays-Bas*, 157-176.
Quiccheberg, Samuel. *Inscriptiones vel tituli theatri amplissimi, complectentis rerum universitatis singulas materias et imagines eximias* (Munich: Adam Berg, 1565).
Quiviger, François. "Honey from Heaven," in *Visuelle Topoi, Erfindung und tradiertes Wissen in den Künsten der italienischen Renaissance*, eds. Ulrich Pfisterer, Max

Seidel (Munich and Berlin: Deutscher Kunstverlag, 2003), 317-322.

Rabelais, François. *Gargantua. Pantagruel. Mis en français moderne et présenté par Claude Pinganaud* (Paris: Arléa, 2010).

Ramakers, Bart. "Bruegel en de rederijkers," in Meadow e.a. *Pieter Bruegel*, Nederlands Kunsthistorisch Jaarboek, 47 (1996), 81-105.

---. "Art and Artistry in Lucas de Heere," in *Envisioning the Artist in the Early Modern Netherlands*, ed. Perry Chapman and Joanna Woodall, Nederlands Kunsthistorisch Jaarboek, 59 (2009), 165-192.

*Refereynen ende liedekens van diverschen rhetoricien uut Brabant, Vlaenderen, Hollant, en [de] Zeelant: ghelesen en ghesonghen op de Corenbloeme camere binnen Bruessele, op haer jaerlijcxse Prinsfeeste* (Brussels: Michel Van Hampont, 1563).

Renger, Konrad. "Bettler und Bauern bei Pieter Bruegel d. Ä." *Sitzungsberichte; Kunstgeschichtlichen Gesellschaft zu Berlin*,(1970), 9-16.

---. *Peter Paul Rubens: Altäre für Bayern*, exh. cat. Munich, Alte Pinakothek (Munich: Bayerische Staatsgemäldesammlungen, 1990)-.

Richardson, Todd M. *Pieter Bruegel the Elder: Art Discourse in the Sixteenth Century Netherlands* (Farnham, Burlington: Ashgate Publishing LTD, 2011).

Rikken, Marrigje. "Abraham Ortelius as intermediary for the Antwerp animal trailblazers," *Jahrbuch für europaeische Wissenschaftskultur*, 6 (2011), 95-128.

---. "Conrad Gessners motieven in Antwerpen," *De Boekenwereld*, 29.1 (2012), 21-32.

---. "A Spanish Album of Drawings of Animals in a South-Netherlandish Context: a Reattribution to Lambert Lombard," *The Rijksmuseum Bulletin*, 2 (2014), 106-123.

Roberts-Jones, Philippe and Roberts-Jones-Popelier, et Françoise. *Pierre Bruegel l'Ancien* (Paris: Flammarion, 1997).

Robertson, Claire. *Il 'Gran Cardinale' Alessandro Farnese* (New Haven: Yale University Press 1992).

Rodríguez-Salgado, Maria Jose. "King, Bishop, Pawn? Philips II and Granvelle in the 1550's and 1560's, " in De Jonge/Janssens, *Les Granvelle et les Anciens Pays-Bas*, 105-134.

Rondelet, Guillaume. *De piscibus marinis* (Lyon: Matthias Bonhomme, 1554).

Roobaert, Edmont. "'Prince van den Onwijzen': Jan Walraevens, schilder en rederijker te Brussel," *Jaarboek van de Koninklijke Souvereine Hoofdkamer van Retorica "De Fonteine" te Gent*, 53/54 (2003-2004), 31-111.

Sellink, Manfred. *Bruegel. The Complete Paintings, Drawings and Prints* (Ghent: Ludion 2007).

Sellink, Manfred and Martens Maximiliaan P.J. (eds.), *Bruegel ongezien. De verborgen Antwerpse collecties*, exh. cat. Antwerpen Museum Maeyer van den Bergh (Leuven: Davidsfonds, 2012).

Serebrennikov, Nina. E. "On the Surface of Dulle Griet: Pieter Bruegel in the context of Rabelais," in *Rabelais in Context*, ed. B.C. Bowen, Proceedings of the 1991 Vanderbilt Conference, Birmingham (Alabama: Summa Publications, 1993), 157-179.

---."Imitating Nature/Imitating Bruegel," in Meadow e.a., *Pieter Bruegel*, Nederlands Kunsthistorisch Jaarboek, 47 (1996), 223-46.

Silva Maroto, Pilar and Manfred Sellink. "The rediscovery of Pieter Bruegel the Elder's 'Wine of St Martin's Day', acquired for the Museo Nacional del Prado," *Burlington Magazine*, 153 (December 2011), 784-793.

Silver, Larry. "Pieter Bruegel in the Capital of Capitalism," in Meadow e.a. *Pieter Bruegel*, Nederlands Kunsthistorisch Jaarboek, 47, 126-154.

---. *Bosch* (Paris: Citadelles et Mazenod, 2006).

---. *Peasant Scenes and Landscapes. The Rise of the Pictorial Genres in the Antwerp Art Market* (Philadelphia: University of Pennsylvania Press, 2006).

---. *Bruegel* (Paris: Citadelles et Mazenod, 2011).

Simili, Raffaella (ed.). *Il teatro della natura di Ulisse Aldrovandi* (Bologna: Editrice Compositori, 2004).

Sloane, Kim. *A New World. England's first view of America* (London: British Museum, 2007).

Smith, Pamela H. *The Body of the Artisan. Art and Experience in the Scientific Revolution* (Chicago: Chicago University Press, 2004).

---. "Collecting Nature and Art. Artisans and Knowledge in the Kunstkammer," in *Engaging with Nature. Essays on the natural World in Medieval and Early Modern Europe*, eds. Barbara A. Hanawalt and Lisa J. Kiser (Notre-Dame, Indiana: University of Notre Dame Press, 2008), 115-131.

Smith, Pamela H. and Findlen, Paula. *Merchants & Marvels. Commerce, Science and Art in Early Modern Europe* (New York and London: Routledge, 2002).

Smith, Paul J. "Sympathy in Eden. On Paradise with the Fall of Man by Rubens and Brueghel," in *Spirits Unseen: The Representation of Subtle Bodies in Early Modern European Culture*, eds. Christine Göttler and Wolfgang Neuber, Intersections, vol. 9 (Leiden: Brill, 2007), 211-244.

Smolderen, Luc. "Jonghelinck en Italie," *Revue belge de numismatique et de sigillographie/Belgisch tijdschrift voor numismatiek en zegelkunde*, 130 (1984), 119-139.

Snow, Edward A. *Inside Bruegel. The Play of Images in Children's Games* (New York: North Point Press, 1997).

Spezzaferro, Luigi. "I Carracci e i Fava: alcune ipotesi," in *Bologna 1584; Gli esordi dei Carracci e gli affreschi di Palazzo Fava*, exh. cat. Bologna, Pinacoteca Nazionale, (Bologna: Nuova Alfa, 1984), 275-291.

Speth-Holterhoff, S. *Les peintres flamands de cabinets d'amateurs au XVII^e siècle* (Brussels: Elsevier, 1957).

Staden, Hans. *Een warachtige historie ende beschrijvinge eens lants in America ghelegen, wiens inwoonders wilt, naeckt, seer godloos, ende wreede menschen eeters sijn* (Antwerp: Plantin, 1558).

Staudinger, Manfred e.a. (ed.). *Le Bestiaire de Rudolphe II*. Cod. Min. 129 et 130 de la Bibliothèque nationale d'Autriche (Paris: Éditions Citadelles, 1990).

---."Arcimboldo et Ulisse Aldrovandi," in *Arcimboldo 1526-1593*, ed. Ferino-Pagden, Sylvia, exh. cat. Vienna, Kunsthistorisches Museum and Paris, Musée du Luxembourg (Milan: Skira, 2007), 113-118.

Steppe, Jan Karel. "Spaans tapijtwerk van de 16de eeuw in Spaans koninklijk bezit," *Miscellanea Jozef Duverger. Bijdragen tot de kunstgeschiedenis der Nederlanden* (Ghent: Uitg. Vereniging voor de Geschiedenis der Textielkunsten, 1968), 719-765.

Sullivan, Margaret A, "Madness and Folly: Peter Bruegel the Elder's Dulle Griet," *The Art Bulletin*, 59, 1 (1977), 55-66.

---."Pieter Bruegel the Elder's Two Monkeys: A New

Interpretation', *The Art Bulletin*, 63,1 (1981), 114-126.

---. *Bruegel and the Creative Process 1559-1563* (Farnham and Burlington, VT: Ashgate, 2010).

Swan, Claudia. "Ad vivum, naer het leven, from the life: Defining a Mode of Representation," *Word and Image*, 11, 4 (1995), 353-372.

---. "From Blowfish to Flower Still Life Paintings. Classification and Its Images, circa 1600," in: Smith/ Findlen, *Merchants and Marvels*, 109-136.

---. *Art, Science and Witchcraft in Early Modern Holland. Jacques de Gheyn II (1565-1629)* (Cambridge: Cambridge University Press, 2005).

Sweertius, Franciscus. *Insignium haius aevi Poëtarum Lacrymae in obitum clar. viri Abrah. Ortelii Antverpiani Philippi II indefessi Antiquitatum scrutatoris* (Antwerp, 1601).

Thevet, André. *Les singularités de la France Antarctique, autremment nommée Amerique: et de plusieurs Terres et isles decouvertes de nostres temps* (Antwerp: Plantin, 1558.

Tourneur, Victor. "Le Médailleur Jacques Jongheling et Cardinal Granvelle 1564-1576," *Revue belge de numismatique et de sigillographie/Belgisch tijdschrift voor numismatiek en zegelkunde*, 79 (1927), 79-93.

Valerius, Cornelius. *De Sphaera, et primis astronomiae rudimentis libellus ultilissimus* (Antwerp: Plantin, 1561).

Van Aelst, Pieter Coecke. *Ces moeurs et fachons de faire des Turcz* (Antwerp: Mayken Verhulst, 1553).

Van Bruaene, Anne-Laure. "A wonderfull tryumfe, for the wynnyng of a pryse": Guilds, Ritual, Theater, and the Urban Network in the Southern Low Countries, ca. 1450-1650," *Renaissance Quarterly* 59 (2006), 374-405.

---. *Om beters wille. Rederijkerskamers en de stedelijke cultuur in de Zuidelijke Nederlanden (1400-1650)* (Amsterdam: Amsterdam University Press, 2008).

Van Cleempoel, Koenraad. "De Leuvense school van instrumentenmakers in de 16[de] eeuw," in *Geschiedenis van de wetenschappen in België van de Oudheid tot 1815*, eds. Robert Halleux, Carmélia Opsomer and Jan Vandersmissen (Brussels: Gemeentekrediet/Dexia, 1998), 217-228.

Van den Brink, Peter (ed.). *De Firma Bruegel*, exh. cat. Bonnenfantenmuseum, Maastricht and Koninklijke Musea voor Schone Kunsten van België, Brussels (Ghent and Amsterdam: Ludion, 2001).

Vandenbroeck, Paul. "Rudolf II als verzamelaar van werk van en naar Jheronimus Bosch," *Jaarboek van het Koninklijk Museum voor Schone Kunsten te Antwerpen* (1981), 119-133.

---. "Zur Herkunft und Verwurzelung der 'Grillen.' Vom Volksmythos zum kunst-und literaturtheoretischen Begriff, 15-17 Jahrhundert," *De zeventiende eeuw*, 3 (1987), 52-84.

---. *Beeld van de andere, vertoog over het zelf. Over wilden, narren, boeren en bedelaars*, exh. cat. Antwerp, Museum voor Schone Kunsten (Ministerie van de Vlaamse Gemeenschap, 1987).

---. *Jheronimus Bosch. De verlossing van de wereld* (Ghent: Ludion, 2002).

---. "High Stakes in Brussels, 1567. The Garden of Earthly Delights as the Crux of the Conflict between William the Silent and the Duke of Alva," in *Hieronymus Bosch. New Insights into His Life and Work*, eds. Jos Koldeweij; Bernard Vermet with B. van Kooij, (Rotterdam: Nai Uitgevers and Ghent, Ludion, 2001), 87-90.

Vandenbroeck, Paul, with Cathy de Zegher (eds.). *Amerika, Bruid van de Zon: 500 jaar Latijns-Amerika en de Lage Landen*, exh. cat. Antwerp, Koninklijke Musea voor Schone Kunsten (Ghent: Imschoot Books, 1992).

Vander Auwera, Joost. *Kunst en Financieën in Europa. 16[de]-eeuwse meesterwerken in een nieuw licht*, Koninklijke Musea voor Schone Kunsten van België/Musées Royaux des Beaux-Arts de Belgique, Brussels, 2009 (Brussels, 2009).

Van der Stock, Jan (ed.). *Antwerp, Story of a Metropolis, 16[th]-17[th] century*, exh. cat., Hessenshuis, Antwerp (Ghent: Snoeck-Ducajou & Zoon, 1993).

Van der Wee, Herman, and Jan Materné. "Antwerp as a World Market in the Sixteenth and Seventeenth Centuries," in Van der Stock, *Antwerp*, 19-31.

Van de Velde, Carl. *Frans Floris (1519/20-1570): leven en werken* (Brussels: Paleis der Academieën, 1975).

Van Dijck, G.C.M. *Op zoek naar Jheronimus van Aken alias Bosch. De feiten. Familie, vrienden en opdrachtgevers* (Zaltbommel: De Europese bibliotheek, 2001).

Vandommele, Jeroen. "Mirroring God, Reflecting Man. Shaping Identity through Knowledge in the Antwerp Plays of 1561," in *Understanding Art in Antwerp. Classicing the Popular, Popularising the Classic (1540-1580)*, ed. Bert Ramakers, Groningen Studies in Cultural Change, XLV (Leuven, Paris, Walpole, MA: Peeters, 2011), 173-196.

Van Durme, Maurice. "Antoon Perrenot van Granvelle. Beschermheer van Christoffel Plantijn," *Katholieke Vlaamse Hogeschool Uitbreiding*, XVII, 4, 399 (Antwerp: Standaard Boekhandel, 1948).

---. *Antoon Perrenot, bisschop van Atrecht, kardinaal van Granvelle, minister van Karel V en Filips II (1517-1586)* (Brussels: Paleis der Academieën 1953).

---."Les Granvelles au service des Habsburg, in De Jonge/ Janssens, *Les Granvelle et les anciens Pays-Bas*, 11-81.

Van Eck, Xander. "Margaret of Parma's gift of a window to St John's in Gouda and the art of the early Counter-Reformation in the Low Countries," *Simiolus*, 36, 1/2, (2012), 66-84.

Van Eeghem, Willem. "Het Brussels Rederijkersfeest (1565)," *Jaarboek van De Fonteyne* (1944), 57-82.

Van Elslander, A. *Het Refrein in de Nederlanden tot 1600* (Ghent: Erasmus, 1953).

Van Grieken, Joris; Ger Luijten, and Jan Van der Stock (eds.). *Hieronymus Cock. The Renaissance in Print*, exh. cat. Museum M, Leuven, 2013 (Antwerp: Mercatorfonds, 2013).

Van Mander, Karel. *Het Schilder-Boeck* (Haarlem: Passier van Wesbusch, 1604).

Van Mander, Karel. *The Lives of the Illustrious Netherlandish and German Painters, from the first edition of the Schilder-boeck (1603-1604).* Preceeded by The Lineage, Circumstances and Place of Birth, Life and Works of Karel van Mander, Painter and Poet and likewise his Death and Burial, from the second edition of the *Schilder-boeck* (1616-1618). With an Introduction and Translation, edited by Hessel Miedema (Hilversum: Davaco, 1994-1999).

Van Roosbroeck, Rob. *Willem de Zwijger. Graaf van Nassau, Prins van Oranje. Een kroniek en een epiloog* (Antwerp: Mercatorfonds, 1974).

Van Schoutte, Roger; Hélène Veroughstraete and Carmen

Garrido. "La *Dulle Griet* et le *Triomphe de la mort* de Pierre Bruegel: observations d'ordre technologique," in *Le dessin sous-jacent dans la peinture, colloque X, 5-7 Septembre 1993*, ed. Hélène Veroughstraete and Roger Van Schoute (Louvain-la-Neuve: Laboratoire d'Etude des Œuvres d'Art par Méthodes Scientifiques, 1993), 7-12.

Van Suchtelen, Ariane, and Ben van Beneden. *Kamers vol kunst in zeventiende-eeuws Antwerpen*, exh. cat., Antwerp, Rubenshuis and Den Haag: Mauritshuis (Zwolle: Waanders, 2009).

Vasari, Giorgio. *Le Vite de' più eccellenti pittori scultori e architettori nelle redazioni del 1550 e 1568*, eds. Rosanna Bettarini and Paola Barocchi, 9 vols. (Florence: Sanzoni, 1966-1987).

Vervoort, Renilde. "Bomen en heksen, duivelse bomen of toverbomen?," in *Aan de vruchten kent men de boom. De boom in tekst en beeld in de middeleeuwse Nederlanden*, eds. Barbara Baert and Veerle Fraeters (Leuven, Universitaire Pers, 2001), 259-280.

---. "The Pestilent Toad. The Significance of the Toad in the Works of Bosch," in *Hieronymus Bosch. New Insights into His Life and Work*, eds. Jos Koldeweij; Bernard Vermet with B. van Kooij (Rotterdam: Nai Uitgevers and Ghent: Ludion, 2001), 145-152.

---. "De heilige, de heks en de tovenaar; verklaring van de Bruegel-prent 'De legendarische ontmoeting tussen Sint Jacob en de tovenaar Hermogenes' (1565)," *Millennium*, 16 (2002), 99-113.

Vignau-Wilberg, Thea. "Joris Hoefnagels Tätigkeit in München," *Jahrbuch der Kunsthistorischen Sammlungen in Wien*, 1985 (81; Neue Folge Band XLV), 103-167.

---. *In Europa zu Hause. Niederländer in München um 1600* (Munich: Hirmer Verlag, 2005).

Vitali, Christoph (ed.). *Der Glanz der Farnese. Kunst und Sammelleidenschaft in der Renaissance*, exh. cat. Munichen/Parma/Napels (Munich: Prestel-Verlag, 1995).

Voet, Leon. *The Golden Compasses. The History of the House of Plantin-Moretus*, 2 vols. (Amsterdam/London/New York: Vangendt & C°/ Routledge & Kegan Paul/Abner Schram, 1969-1972).

Wallerstein, Immanuel. "Karel V en de ontluikende kapitalistische wereldeconomie", in *Karel V 1500-1558. De keizer en zijn tijd*, ed. Hugo Soly (Antwerp: Mercatorfonds, 1999).

Wauters, ALphonse-Jules. *Catalogue abrégé des tableaux anciens. Musées royaux de peinture et de sculpture de Belgique* (Brussels: Imprimerie et Lithographie Ad. Mertens, 1900).

Weemans, Michel. *Herri met de Bles. Les Ruses du Paysage au Temps de Bruegel et D'Erasme* (Paris: Éditions Hazan, 2013).

*Wonderlycke dieren op papier in de tijd van Plantin* (Antwerp: Museum Plantin-Moretus/Prentencabinet, 2007).

Woodall, Joanna. *"Patronage and Portrayal: Antoine Perrenot de Granvelle's relationshop with Anthonis More,"* in De Jonge/Janssens, *Les Granvelle et les Anciens Pays-Bas*, 245-277.

---. *Anthonis Mor. Art and Authority* (Zwolle: Waanders, 2007).

Woollett, Anne Tayloe. *The Altarpiece in Antwerp, 1554-1615: Painting and the Militia Guilds* (PhD Dissertation, Columbia University, 2004).

Wouk, Edward H. *Frans Floris*. The New Hollstein Dutch & Flemish Etchings, Engravings and Woodcuts 1450-1700, 2 vols. (Ouderkerk and Ijssel: Sound and Vision Publishers, 2011).

---. "Reclaiming the Antiquities of Gaul: Lambert Lombard and the History of Northern Art," *Simiolus*, 36 (2012), 35-65.

Wouters, Alphonse. *Catalogue abrégé des tableaux anciens. Musées Royaux de peinture et de sculpture de Belgique* (Brussels: Imprimerie et Lithographie Ad. Mertens, 1900).

Yaya, Isabel. "Wonders of America: The Curiosity Cabinet as a Site of Representation and Knowledge," *Journal of the History of Collections*, 20, 2 (2008 ), 173-188.

Zweite, Armin. *Marten de Vos als Maler: ein Beitrag zur Geschichte der Antwerpener Malerei in der zweiten Hälfte des 16. Jahrhunderts* (Berlin: Begr. Mann Verlag 1980).

# List of Figures

watercolor on paper,
32 × 22.4 cm.
Bologna, Bibliotheca Universitaria
© Courtesy of the Biblioteca Universitaria di Bologna. Interdiction of further reproduction of duplication by any means

**Fig. 39**
Museum of Ferrante Imperato, in Ferrante Imperato, *Dell' historia naturale libri XXVIII* (Naples: nella stamperia a Porta Reale, 1599).
Brussels, Royal Library of Belgium
© KBR, Bruxelles

**Fig. 40**
Dried blowfish, early $17^{th}$ century, possibly from the Tradescant collection.
Oxford, History of Science Museum
© History of Science Museum, Oxford University

**Fig. 41**
*Armadillo*, in: Conrad Gessner, *Icones Animalium Quadrupedum Viviparorum et Oviparorum, quae in historiae animalium Canradi Gesneri libro I et II describuntur, editio secunda auctior* (Zurich: Christopher Froben, 1560), 103.
Ghent University Library
© Ghent University Library

**Fig. 42**
Adriaen Collaert after Maerten de Vos, *America*, 1589, engraving, 21.4 × 25.9 cm.
Brussels, Royal Library of Belgium, Print Cabinet
© KBR, Bruxelles

**Fig. 43**
Basilius Besler, *Fasciculus rariorum et aspectu dignorum varii generis quae collegit et suis impensis ad vivum incidi* (Nurnberg, 161), title page.
Paris, Bibliothèque nationale de France, département Estampes et photographie
© BnF

**Fig. 44**
Sloth, in: André Thevet, *Les Singularitez de la France Antarctique, autrement nommé Amérique & de plusieurs terres & isles decouverts de nostre temps* (Antwerp: Christoffer Plantin, 1558), fol. 99 verso.
Antwerp, Plantijn Moretus Museum
© Plantijn Moretus, Antwerp

**Fig. 45**
Sloth, in: Conrad Gessner, *Icones Animalium Quadrupedum et Vivoparorum Oviparorum, quae in historiae animalium Canradi Gesneri libro I et II describuntur, editio secunda auctior* (Zurich: Christopher Froben, 1560), fol. 96.
Ghent University Library
© Ghent University Library

**Fig. 46**
South-American sloth (bradypus tridactylus)
© Photo author

**Fig. 47**
*Ivory Diptych Sundial*, probably made in Flanders, 1586, ivory and brass.
Oxford, History of Science Museum, inv. 64228
© History of Science Museum, Oxford University

**Fig. 48**
Pieter Bruegel the Elder, *Descent of Christ into Limbo*, (c. 1561?), drawing with pen and brown ink, 22.3 × 29.4 cm.
Vienna, Graphische Sammlung Albertina
© Albertina, Vienna

**Fig. 49**
Pieter Bruegel the Elder, *The Fight over Money* (printed after 1570), engraving, 24 × 31 cm.
Brussels, Royal Library of Belgium, Print Cabinet
© KBR, Bruxelles

**Fig. 50**
Ottoman saber or scimitar, $16^{th}$ century.
New York, The Metropolitan Museum of Art. Bequest of George C. Stone, 1935
© 2019. Photo Scala, Florence

**Fig. 51**
Ottoman pointed helmet, possibly early $17^{th}$ century.
New York, The Metropolitan Museum of Art. From the collection of Nina and Gordon Bunshaft, Bequest of Nona Bunshaft, 1994
© 2019. Photo Scala, Florence

**Fig. 52**
Hans Staden, *Warachtige historie* (Antwerp: Christopher Plantin, 1558), book II: *Een warachtig cort bericht vanden handel ende zeden der Tuppin Imbas, diens ghevangen ick gheweest ben [...]*, illustration to chapter XVI: *Wat des mans cieraet is, ende hoe sij haer schilderen [...]*.
Ghent University Library
© Ghent University Library

**Fig. 53**
Cornelius Valerius, *De Sphaera, et primis astronomiae rudimentis libellus utilissimus* (Antwerp: Christoffer Plantin, 1561), fol. 38.
Antwerp, Plantin Moretus Museum
© Plantin Moretus Museum, Antwerp

**Fig. 54**
Jan Brueghel the Elder, *The Element of Fire*, 1608, oil on panel, 46 × 66 cm.
Milan, Biblioteca Ambrosiana
© Biblioteca Ambrosiana

**Fig. 55**
*Seven-headed hydra with crowned heads*, in: Conrad Gessner, *Nomenclator aquatilium animantium.* (Zurich: Christopher Froben, 1560), fol. 363.
Ghent University Library
© Ghent University Library

**Fig. 56**
Maerten de Vos, *Unicorn*, 1572, oil on panel, 137 × 136 cm.
Schwerin, Staatliche Museum
© bpk / Bildagentur für Kunst, Kultur und Gesichte, Berlin / Schwerin, Staatlisches Museum

**Fig. 57**
Maerten de Vos, *Elephant*, 1572, oil on panel, 137 × 136 cm.
Schwerin, Staatliche Museum
© bpk / Bildagentur für Kunst, Kultur und Gesichte, Berlin / Schwerin, Staatlisches Museum

**Fig. 58**
Anonymous painter, *Siamese twins and other misshapen births as well as imaginary 'monsters,'* in Aldrovandi Ms, volume 006.2, fol. 68, between 1550-1605, watercolor on paper, 41.5 × 27.5 cm.
Bologna, Biblioteca Universitaria
© Courtesy of the Biblioteca Universitaria di Bologna. Interdiction of further reproduction of duplication by any means

**Fig. 59**
Joris Hoefnagel, *The hirsute children of Petrus Gonsalus*, in: *Ignis/Fire*,

aus Schloß Sonderhausen
© Klassik Stiftung, Weimar

**Fig.81**
Anthonis Mor, and studio, *William of Orange*, 1555, oil on panel, 105 × 82 cm.
Kassel, Staatliche Museen
© bpk

**Fig. 82**
*Bruxella, urbs aulicorum frequentia[m], fontium copia[m], magnificentia principalis aulae, civicae domus, ac plurium aliaru[m] splendore, nobilissima...*, in: Georg Braun and Frans Hogenberg, *Civitates Orbis Terrarum* (Cologne, 1572-1612)
Brussels, Royal Library of Belgium, Map division
© KBR, Bruxelles

**Fig. 83**
Willem van Schoor, with figures by Gillis van Tilborgh, *The Hotel of Nassau in Brussels*, oil on canvas, 123.5 × 203 cm.
Brussels, Royal Museums of Fine Arts of Belgium
© KMSKB/MRBAB, Brussels / photo : J. Geleyns / Roscan

**Fig. 84**
View on the Spire of the Brussels City Hall viewed from the Coudenberg, site of present Royal Museums of Fine Art of Belgium.
© Photo author

**Fig. 85**
Pieter Bruegel the Elder, *Rest on the Flight into Egypt*, 1563, oil on panel, 37.1 × 55.6 cm.
London, Courtauld Institute of Art, Seilern Collection
© London, Courtauld Institute of Art / The Bridgeman Art Library

**Fig. 86**
Antonis Mor, *Granvelle's Dwarf and Dog*, c. 1558-1559, oil on panel, 126 × 92 cm.
Paris, Musée du Louvre
© Collection Dagli Orti / Musée du Louvre Paris / Gianni Dagli Orti

**Fig. 87**
Clement Kicklinger, *Tazza*, c. 1570-1575
Ostrich egg, emerald, gilded silver and coral, 56.8 cm.
Vienna, Kunsthistorisches Museum, Kunstkammer
© Kunsthistorisches Museum Vienna

**Fig. 88**
Garden with herms and with exotic animals, with coat of arms of Cardinal Granvelle, tapestry woven in the Brussels workshop of Willem de Pannemaker, 1564, 1564, 363 × 520 cm.
Vienna, Kunsthistorisches Museum, Tapisseriensammlung
© Kunsthistorisches Museum Vienna

**Fig. 89**
After Bosch, *Garden of Earthly Delights*, tapestry woven in Brussels c. 1560, gold, silver, silk and wool, 288 × 490 cm.
Madrid, Patrimonio Nacional, Palacio Real Madrid
© Patrimonio Nacional

**Fig. 90**
*Headfooter*, detail of figure. 20 (Hieronymus Bosch, *Garden of Earthly Delights*)
Madrid, Museo Nacional del Prado
© Museo del Prado

**Fig. 91**
*Saint Michael Overcoming Satan*, from an eight-piece set of the Apocalypse. Woven in the Dermoyen workshop, c. 1553-56, wool, silk and silver- and gild-metal-wrapped thread, 525 × 850 cm.
Madrid, Patrimonio Nacional, Palacio Real de la Granja de San Ildefonso
© Patrimonio Nacional

**Fig. 92**
Pieter Bruegel the Elder, *Census at Bethlehem*, 1566, oil on panel, 115.3 × 164.5 cm.
Brussels, Royal Museums of Fine Arts of Belgium
© KMSKB/MRBAB, Brussels / photo : J. Geleyns / Roscan

**Fig. 93**
Marcus Gheeraerts, *William of Orange as Saint George killing the Dragon*, c. 1576, copper etching with washes, 33.5 × 26.8 cm.
London, British Library
© The Trustees of the British Museum

**Fig. 94**
Anonymous, *The Duke of Alba assisted by an Apocalyptic Monster with heads of Granvelle, de Guise and Lorraine*, c. 1572, engraving, 18.5 × 13.5 cm
Brussels, Royal Library of Belgium, Print Cabinet
© KBR, Bruxelles

**Fig. 95**
Caspar Ulich, *So-called "Handstein" with the Resurrection of Christ*, c. 1556/68, gilded silver and ore, 31.7 cm.
Vienna, Kunsthistorisches Museum, Kunstkammer
© Kunsthistorisches Museum Vienna

**Fig. 96**
Pieter Bruegel the Elder, *The Somber Day (February/March)*, 1565, from the *Series of the Months*, oil on panel, 118 × 163 cm.
Vienna, Kunsthistorisches Museum
© AKG-images

# Index of names, places, subjects, and works

*Page reference to illustrations are in italics*

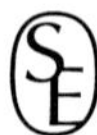

Silvana Editoriale

*Direction*
Dario Cimorelli

*Art Director*
Giacomo Merli

*Editorial Coordinator*
Sergio Di Stefano

*Copy Editor*
Clelia Valentina Palmese

*Layout*
Giuseppe Molinari

*Production Coordinator*
Antonio Micelli

*Editorial Assistant*
*Ondina Granato*

*Photo Editor*
Alessandra Olivari, Silvia Sala

*Press Office*
Lidia Masolini, press@silvanaeditoriale.it



ISBN 9788836629206

Silvana Editoriale S.p.A.
via dei Lavoratori, 78
20092 Cinisello Balsamo, Milano
tél. +39 02 61 83 63 37
fax + 3902 61 72 464
www.silvanaeditoriale.it

Reproductions,
printing et binding in Italy
Printed in October 2019

Royal Museums of Fine Arts of Belgium
Rue du Musée, 9
B-1000 Bruxelles
tel. +32 2 508 32 11
www.fine-arts-museum.be

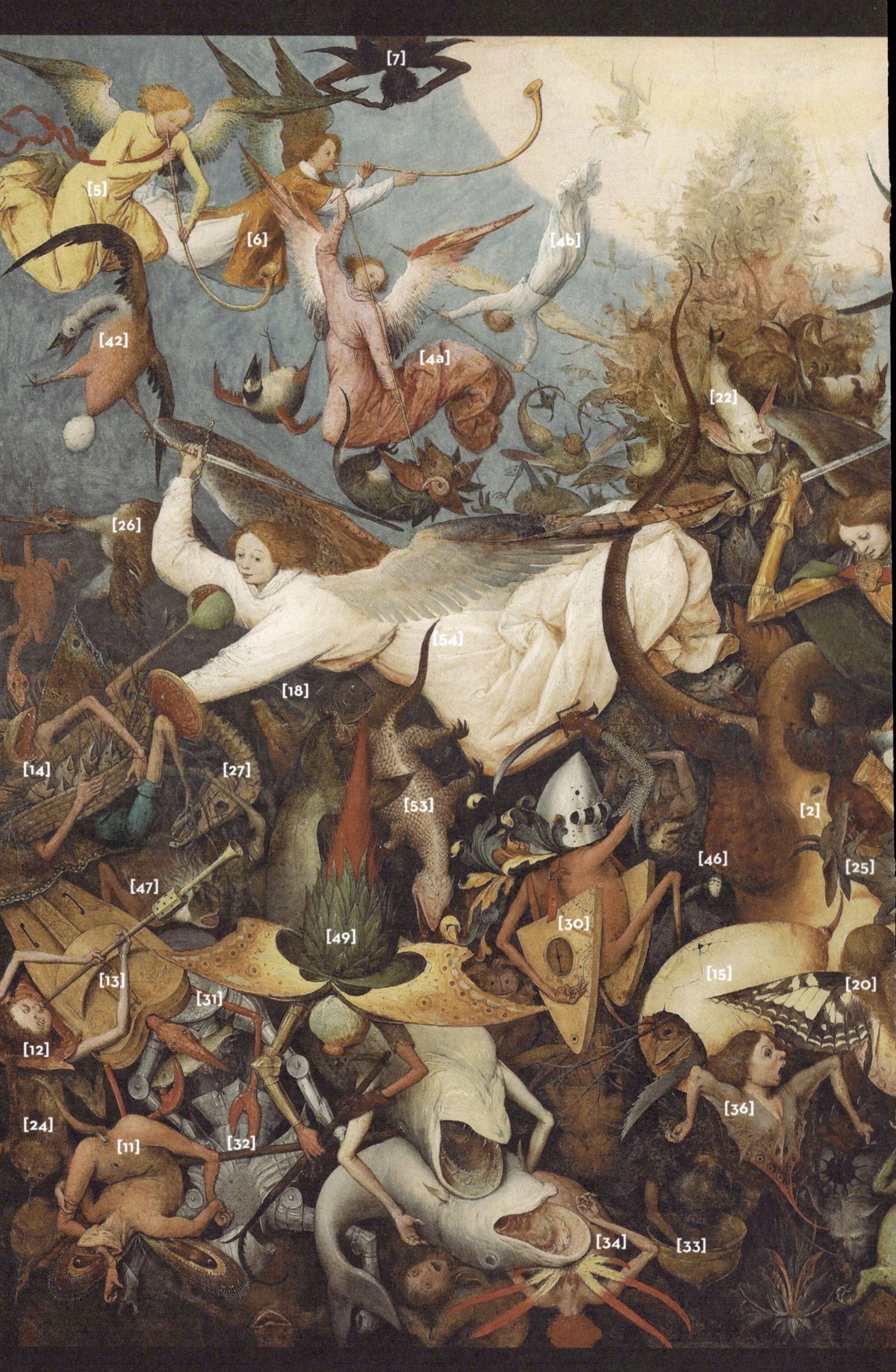
[7]
[5]
[6]
[4b]
[42]
[4a]
[22]
[26]
[54]
[18]
[14]
[27]
[53]
[2]
[46]
[25]
[47]
[30]
[49]
[15]
[20]
[13]
[31]
[12]
[36]
[24]
[11]
[32]
[34]
[33]